The Crowell Book of

Arts and Crafts
for Children

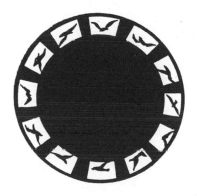

The Crowell Book of

Arts and Crafts
for Children

Arnold Arnold

Thomas Y. Crowell Company
ESTABLISHED 1834   NEW YORK

With grateful acknowledgment to the staff of the Donnell branch of The New York Public Library, The American Crafts Council, the Reading Rooms of the British Museum, the Victoria and Albert Museum, and the Science Museum in London, for cooperation that has made this book possible.

Designed by Abigail Moseley

Manufactured in the United States of America

Library of Congress Cataloging in Publication Data
Arnold, Arnold.
   The Crowell book of arts and crafts for children.

   Bibliography: p.
   1. Handicraft. I. Title.
TT157.A76   745.5'02'4054   75-2333
ISBN 0-690-00567-9

1 2 3 4 5 6 7 8 9 10

Books by the author

The World Book of Children's Games
Teaching Your Child to Learn from Birth to School Age
Career Choices for the Seventies
Violence and Your Child
Your Child's Play
Your Child and You
Pictures and Stories from Forgotten Children's Books
The Yes and No Book
Toy Soldiers
Tongue Twisters and Double Talk

To all children and especially to my own:
  Geoffrey, Marguerite, and Francis;
To the child within me;
To Gail;
And to the future

Contents

The Crowell Book of

Arts and Crafts
for Children

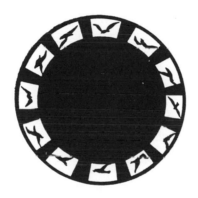

Introduction

"Evidence of noninvolvement and the disinclination to exert effort are appearing in homes and classrooms. . . . What does this behavior mean? . . . What is today's environment feeding back to children? All around, children see adults place greater reliance on mechanical aids than on their own capacities and resources." [1] Written by an astute teacher and observer of children, this is a terrible indictment of our times and attitudes. But what can we expect? We plunk children before the TV set at earliest ages for from three to seven hours each day. Here processes, skills, and achievements are necessarily telescoped. Anything portrayed on TV looks as if it could be done by anyone without experience and with a very small expenditure of time, effort, and devotion. Small wonder that children's endurance and respect for excellence are eroded.

This book offers concerned parents, teachers, recreation workers, and therapists the means to counteract these trends. More than the detailed activities, the suggested attitudes and methods required for introducing them to children and young people can lead to involved and purposeful, though spontaneous, exercises of intelligence, senses, and limbs. The relationship between playful, manual, and other physical exercise in

childhood and the development of intelligence is not yet fully appreciated, despite ample evidence. Certainly the play stimulated by genuine
arts and crafts generates self-discipline. It lays the foundation for a life-
time of engagement and curiosity.

Children need values and ethics. Our society fails them in these respects
more than in any other. Art and craft provide opportunities for awakening practical senses of right and wrong, what works and what doesn't,
what is permissible and possible and what isn't, and an ability to savor
success and cope with momentary failure and frustration. They foster
making judgments. Every stroke of hammer or brush is a decision. The
child learns in art and craft activities to consider each such decision in
advance and to live with the result.

It's a little too easy to blame our children's failures on the educational
system, on teachers, and on parents. They are as much the products of
our time as the children they rear and teach. Every parent and teacher
must now make a conscious effort to reappraise what is right and wrong
with our culture and to resist its blandishments and misdirection. They
can intervene positively at home and in school. This may be difficult at
times but it pays rich dividends. Instead of caving in to promotional
pressures and momentary convenience, we must become concerned with
the character of future generations. The very nature of what it means to
be human is at stake.

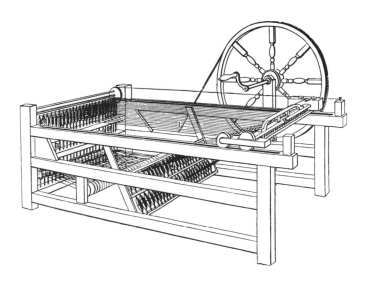

We can't afford to allow our children's creative abilities and endowments to atrophy in expectation that they won't need these in an expected technological future. This anticipated, glowing millennium is now very much in doubt. Its promised benefits have proven elusive. Our fuel and raw materials resources are threatened with depletion. The earth

cannot support ever expanding population growth. The technologies have polluted the environment, concentrated non-absorbable wastes on land and in the sea and air, and are making life hazardous and unhealthy. "Only madmen and economists believe growth can go on forever in a finite world." [2]

Nature inevitably redresses such imbalances if it can. And so the choice is a return to a labor intensive husbandry of resources or disaster. Implicit in either course is the exercise of craft by those who wish to prosper and survive—the change in life style or a possible ecological debacle. It is with hope for the former rather than fear of calamity that this book has been written. Genuine craft attitudes are a vital necessity if our children are to have the means to thrive during the difficult decades ahead. Art can endow them with beauty and purpose. The practice of both will assure that essential human qualities will be preserved and enhanced, come what may.

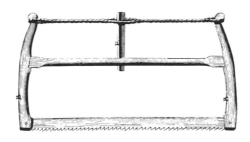

I
Approaches and Attitudes

. . . They have no pleasure in the work by which they make their bread . . . for they feel that the kind of labour to which they are condemned is verily a degrading one, and makes them less than men.—*John Ruskin*

This is a companion volume to my *World Book of Children's Games.* Both are part of an effort "to restore childhood to children, whose rightful property it is." [4] Both books address themselves to social and esthetic experiences from pre-school through junior high school ages. These experiences tend to be crowded out of our children's lives by adult preoccupations with academic achievement and by a crippling urbanized, TV saturated, and technological environment. With these books I hope to encourage the rekindling of human qualities in children and young people: play; laughter; sensory, manual, and creative expression; spontaneity; and exuberance. All are in danger of at least partial extinction.

The background material that precedes each of the following chapters suggests attitudes for introducing art and craft techniques to children and young people. One without the other has no value. I therefore hope that these introductions are read with as much care and attention as the recipes.

Art and craft education has assumed a new significance. Teachers, recreation and rehabilitation workers, and especially parents must become aware of changed conditions of life that demand new attitudes. A redirection of emphasis, style, and form in education is required, based on an astute appraisal of conditions with which children must cope by the time they reach adulthood.

Art and craft education has special value for today's children. Widespread alienation caused by the technologies make such education a virtual necessity. Children develop values and skills that, whether or not required for employment, are essential for emotional and physical well-being. Formerly, craft was a survival necessity for all. Art was a symbol of wealth and leisure, but it was also a spiritual and political necessity. Today craft is practiced only by the few, and art has been debased as a tool for promotion and propaganda and as a lever for consumption. Even our folk art is manufactured and disseminated by machine—the TV set, radio, tape recorder, and printing press.

Before the explosion of the technologies and up to the end of World War II most work, including production, involved highly developed manual skills. Since then, and as a result of automation, labor intensive work has become largely obsolete. But our society now pays an exorbitant price in terms of lost work satisfaction and skills for its seeming

gains in leisure. We must therefore ask when and whether labor intensive work, wherever it is not degrading or injurious to health, may not
indeed be more productive and profitable. There is ample evidence that,
in addition to polluting the environment, an excessive and unrestricted
technology can damage or ruin the cultural and educational ecology as
well, as it already has in many respects.

There are two reasons for educating children. The first is, or should be,
to elicit and develop their humanity. The second is to make them eco-
nomically independent and useful. In automating production, and training young people for work in such an economy, we tend to lose sight of
the first, essential object of learning: the exercise of human species specific skills, irrespective of their economic usefulness.

The definitions that apply to our species could be expanded indefinitely.
Two suffice for the purposes of this book: *Homo sapiens*—thinking and
reflective man, and *Homo faber*—man the tool maker and user. The
abilities to use our hands, to invent tools, to communicate, and to laugh,
are among the most important qualities that distinguish us from all other
species. But in economic life, as in education, there has been a steep
decline in all of these. Man is no longer *Homo faber*. At best he is
"man the programmer." At worst he is "man the consumer." There is
evidence that this latter is the quality fostered by much of contemporary
education.[22]

Obviously, even in an automated society, some people are required to
maintain and improve the technologies. But the actual percentage of tool
makers and users keeps shrinking as the technologies become more
complex, as the required investment in plant and machinery rises astro-
nomically, and as ownership is concentrated in fewer hands. Many of
our schools seem to have concluded that it is no longer important to
teach certain skills for the reasons given. They neglect manual education
at primary and secondary levels as the demand for genuine craft de-
clines. This has caused a deterioration in general competence and also in
the consumer's judgment. It creates "a mechanization of responsibility
as well, taking judgment farther and farther away from the minds, and
therefore the ethics of men." [16]

The creative person, the master craftsman, the skilled artificer, and the
artist have always been something of a nuisance to management. It
deems them to be erratic, unpredictable, temperamental, and likely to be

unpunctual. They sometimes have dirty fingernails and may lead unorthodox lives. These are not necessarily the attributes of creation, but the hygienic computer suffers none of them. The computer may soon displace the human creator, to the satisfaction at least of management. Future generations of computers now on the drawing board will have the capacity to "create" original houses, furniture, appliances, accessories, and tools, and even what may pass for works of art, music, and literature. Once programmed with a wide variety of symbols, styles, and plots, they can spew forth endless variations. Managers will then be unhampered by dependence on seemingly erratic human creation. Education in essential human skills will decline further as it has already in fields in which automation has taken command—in printing and tool and die making trades, for example. Humanness may die piecemeal. And unless this trend is reversed at least insofar as the education of young people is concerned, we may need a redefinition of what it means to be human.

Significantly, there has been a strong revival of arts and crafts, especially among the disaffected young. "How-to" books are flooding from the printing presses. High school and college dropouts are turning to leather, woodworking, ceramics, spinning, weaving, and other handicrafts in large numbers. They are driven by an unconscious need to preserve their species specific skills, even at the risk of ruling themselves out of the mainstream of economic life. Some of these will be among the few able to furnish themselves with tools, artifacts, and comforts denied to most in the coming decades. The world's standard of living is bound to decline due to population pressures, food, fuel, and raw materials shortages, and the misallocation of priorities.

Unfortunately, many who engage in craft occupations as young adults or who practice them for the first time as hobbies in middle or old age suffer a distorted creative sense imposed by miseducation and misinformation. Even when they use tools, they don't exercise craft. ". . . The housewife who bakes her own bread according to a recipe, sews a dress from a pattern [that she did not design] . . . is doing useful, satisfying, but contrary to the women's magazines, uncreative work. . . . To do by hand what a machine ordinarily does is not a creative act." [14]

Most art and craft manuals, instruction books, periodicals, kits, and even teachers stress production, following or tracing patterns, plans, and recipes. This is a denial of the very essence of creative tool use. It is es-

manual skill development, confused production with process, as did most of the educators who followed him. He set the style for an art and craft education of children that relied to a large extent on tracing and copying and that predominates to this day. Inadvertently he showed publishers and manufacturers how to package activities for children and how to merchandise them in the name of education.

Maria Montessori followed Froebel with a new approach during the first decades of the twentieth century. She considered manual education solely a preparation for writing and employment skills. Montessori was unable to recognize any value or purpose in art, craft, or even play unless it served the ends of production, economic autonomy, and practical usefulness. Drawing in Montessori schools was limited to tracing "insets" and templates, as it still is in those that stick to her original curriculum. In Montessori's own words: "Much is said today about free drawing, and many people are surprised that I have set up rigid restrictions on children's drawings. [In my schools] they compose geometric figures, which they then fill out holding the pencil in a certain way, or they fill in with colored pencils those that have already been outlined. . . . The so-called 'free-drawing' has no place in my system. I avoid these useless, immature, weary efforts and those frightful drawings that are so popular in 'advanced' schools today." [21]

Proponents of these "advanced" schools permitted and sometimes encouraged children to break all restraints, due to their misunderstanding of the writings of John Dewey. They allowed children to paint beyond their paper onto tables, walls, and each other, mistakenly assuming that disorder and creativity are synonymous and that the former leads to the latter. This school of education, erroneously labeled "permissive" and "progressive," confused freedom of expression with an undisciplined misuse of materials and tools.

Almost during this same period, and in reaction to the fussy vulgarity of Victorian industry and production, William Morris and John Ruskin, among others, urged a return to handicrafts in England during the last third of the nineteeth century.[28] They found ready disciples on the Continent, in Scandinavia, and in the United States. Despite a certain "artsy-craftsiness," this movement revived and advanced crafts that were driven to the verge of extinction already then as a result of mindless mechanization. It had a profound effect on many architects, designers, artists, craftsmen, and teachers, and on the burgeoning youth

sential that children be sheltered from such production in early as much as in later years. They need exposure to the creative processes of art and craft. Parents, teachers, recreation and camp counselors, and rehabilitation therapists must not only be familiar with tools and materials and their uses, but also with the role played by art and craft in the development of general intelligence, ethics, and competence.

a. Craft and Art Education

Until World War I, American children destined for art and craft occupations were usually apprenticed to master craftsmen at earliest ages, as many still are in European and other countries. Until the end of the nineteenth century, children of the well-to-do dabbled in the arts, sometimes as soon as they could walk. Their daughters were expected to exercise manual skills seriously—spinning, weaving, embroidery, music, and art—presumably because these activities prepared them for domesticity and kept them out of mischief until they became marriageable.

Art and craft as vehicles for developmental education did not come into vogue until Johann Heinrich Pestalozzi's and Friedrich Wilhelm Froebel's ideas seeped into the curriculum early in the nineteenth century. Froebel especially, while enthusiastic and unique in his concern for

movement. It generated a re-examination of manual art and craft education. Frank Lloyd Wright and Walter Gropius became disciples. The Bauhaus in Germany and a few process oriented progressive schools in Europe and in the United States began to demonstrate that art and craft education along these lines affected and benefited the development of character, intellect, and skills in children and young people. This movement found a spokesman in the late Viktor Lowenfeld.[17,18] It flowered in only a few places, as in the now disbanded Young People's Art Center at New York's Museum of Modern Art, under the inspired direction of Victor D'Amico.[9,10,11] Despite their proven success, these efforts did not affect attitudes beyond the spheres of their direct influence. But for the first time art and craft education was correctly identified and stimulated as a process essential to child development and general education.

The majority of U.S. elementary schools still offer no opportunities, facilities, or even teachers for art and craft education. These subjects are usually woven into "social" and other cognitive studies. Ill-equipped teachers urge children in these classes to trace, copy, and color or to assemble prefabricated parts of objects related to academic subjects.

If these were the only activities of this kind that children occasionally encountered, offset by more creatively demanding tasks, they might not be especially harmful, deplorable though they are. But most of today's children are exposed to hardly any other art and craft experiences. Pernicious coloring workbooks, projects, and tests like the Frostig Perception Kit among many others, add to the existing glut and to the disorientation of teachers and students. Visiting and itinerant art teachers inadequately serve a small number of other primary schools. Only a small minority employ fulltime, qualified art and craft instructors.

Some of the better nursery schools and kindergartens introduce art and craft materials to young children in imaginative ways. But even there these subjects are once again pushed into the background by a current preoccupation with "cognition" and "doing things right." Product more than process is stressed by teachers who have received only a smattering of art education themselves and who regard craft as "busy work."

Art and craft classes are "elective" in virtually all junior high schools and high schools. They aren't taken seriously and, for the most part, they offer young people an escape, like home economics, from academic subjects. Even the American Crafts Council, the sole adult organization in this field in the U.S., offers no program or plan in these areas of learning and experience. Canada and European countries have long recognized this as an important aspect of general education. Its need and value have been reaffirmed in recent years by the reformation of the British infant and primary schools.[24]

The excuse given for the downgrading of art and manual education in U.S. schools is that academic subjects have first claim on the schools' and students' attention. Hence little money, space, or time is spared for these supposed frills. This is especially ironic in view of the renewed emphasis placed on vocational education.

Side by side with the devaluation of craft skills, vocational education is stressed once again as an alternative to a higher education.[19] But it is futile and cruel to favor "cognition" and academic achievement as the sole virtues in the primary curriculum, to neglect art and craft education, and then at teenage tell those who don't fit the mold: "You are intellectually inferior. You don't deserve the higher education for which we tried to prepare you. You have failed. We'll now shunt you off to a vocational school. Here's a hammer and a wrench." These young people have usually never held either in hand. They have not seen them used by competent craftsmen or craftswomen. They have no foundation of skills on which to build. They lack the motivation and coordination required for a successful use of tools. Whatever creativity they possess is stifled. They are made to feel second-rate, and the schools to which they are sent are usually inferior and inadequate.

Where schools, museums, and other institutions fail children, it is up to parents to make up the deficit. Proper introduction to the arts and crafts affect a child's personality, outlook, achievement, and future, regardless of his individual bent or eventual career. It refines abilities, no matter which stream of higher education, vocation, or avocation he or she enters later. A young man or woman who enjoys a background and interest in any of the arts or crafts will be more sensitive to people, ideas, and the material world. He or she will be able to choose, care for, value, and use the tools of his or her calling and those required for daily existence with discretion and imagination. And he or she will certainly be more likely to survive successfully in a declining world economy than those who cannot use their hands.

Manual, as much as cerebral, work is not just a way of making a living. It is, or it should be, a way of life. To enjoy both requires more than performance. An aviation mechanic can earn a satisfactory living even if he has never heard of Daedalus and Icarus. But he'll get far greater satisfaction out of his life and work if he enjoys historic and other insights related to his craft beyond the rote skills required for his job. The creative artisan sees himself as a link in a chain that stretches from the distant past into the future. This gives him hope and a kind of immortality. It endows his craft with deserved dignity. These qualities are lacking in our society and they are sorely needed for survival.

Margaret Mead has pointed out that the kind and quality of art and craft stressed in a culture influence children's character development.[20] They can foster a conservative, stable, and docile personality, satisfied to copy traditional forms. Imitation and slight variations on established themes are the hallmark of creativity in such societies, but they cannot cope with sudden change. Unsettling circumstances can cause their disintegration. Or a culture can stress invention and the discovery of a kaleidoscope of new forms. The members of such a society tend to be practical and adaptable individuals, able to survive under drastically changed conditions. It would be futile to make value judgments about which kind of human being or society is preferable. Each has its virtues and faults. But our own ecological and cultural conditions dictate which kind of personality we must foster if we are to survive.

Quite aside from these considerations, the increase in leisure and the nature of employment today make art and craft education a necessity. For the moment at least a large part of the population in technologically developed countries spends more time in leisure than on life supporting labor. Yet most jobs are deadly dull. Many people are retired from work at ages at which they are still vigorous and in full possession of their faculties. For these reasons, in addition to those mentioned earlier, our children need skills that will sustain their interests in adulthood during their hours and years away from work. Those lacking avocational interests tend to become passive; their abilities atrophy; they lack luster and curiosity; they are frustrated and dissatisfied; and their life expectancy is shortened. Genuine craft—and not do-it-yourself projects—could engage and satisfy them. But this requires an education in childhood and youth that stresses creative development.

Misuse of leisure and its commercialization have eroded traditional judgments. Formerly, when a family sought out the woods, fields, and beaches, its members deliberately limited themselves to labor intensive crafts in imitation of their forebears. They took along a minimum of essentials. They lived off the land to whatever extent they could. They enjoyed the loneliness and majesty of open spaces, challenges, discomforts, and dangers. These exercises in survival became perverted. Between that period and the recent gasoline shortage the technological environment was carried to the country in the family camper, including electric toothbrushes and TV set. Without craft or curiosity, motorized man cannot play. Uncommunicative, largely unconscious and unreflective and divorced from his past, he offers his children no future. He lacks awe, wonder, and ethic. He is a spectator and the perfect consumer.

The depletion of organic fuel and raw material, and the decline in the standard of living, will force a reorientation. A return to art, craft, and manual skills cannot solve all these problems. Neither playing, painting, nor weaving can, in and of itself, undo the damage done to our cultural ecology. But a renewal of craft interest will foster healthy, intelligent, and adaptable future generations.

The art and craft education of children requires more than exposure to tools and materials. Children need direct contacts with active artists and craftsmen. They need to see them work in the flesh and be able to touch their work. They need a familiarity with different styles and forms created in former times and in different cultures, as well as in their own. They should not imitate them, but they can be inspired by them.

b. Ages and Stages

The projects described in this book are addressed to children from preschool through junior high school years, though no ages are given at which particular activities should be introduced. No two children develop at the same rate or share the same predispositions. Some activities suggested at the beginning of different chapters and sections can be presented at ages as early as two or three. But a child who has not enjoyed art and craft in early years cannot be expected to practice more advanced skills merely because he is older. He must first explore and play with materials, as might a younger child, until he achieves a level of insight, control, and confidence that prepares him for more mature activities. For this reason the projects in every section are presented in a chronology starting with very simple skills and progressing gradually to more complex ones. Only trial and error can disclose for which level any one child is prepared and to what he or she is inclined. And so this book is adaptable to any child, depending on his or her level of maturity, experience, ability, or disability, regardless of age.

Young children can be introduced to a great variety of tools and materials, provided elementary safety precautions and what the child can and cannot yet do are kept in mind. For example, any five-year-old, who has built with blocks, drawn, painted, and finger-painted, can handle a coping saw or jigsaw into which a spiral safety blade has been inserted. He can draw onto and cut small and ragged pieces off a thin sheet of balsa wood or cardboard. But he cannot as yet follow a pencil line with such a saw. By cutting the balsa apart at random he'll make a jigsaw puzzle of sorts. While doing so he increases his control over the tool and the material, and gains experience, confidence, and skill.

But first the child needs direction. He must be provided with a proper workspace, with tools and materials. He needs incentives and to have the nature of the work pointed out to him. ''. . . No matter how attractive a material may be, it cannot, per se, insure a creative experience. Left without guidance, a child is apt to imitate his neighbors [in the classroom] or fall back on clichés.'' [10] This is true at all stages of development, and it is therefore especially important to shelter today's child from the temptation to imitate TV, comic book, cartoon, and other pervasive stereotypes. They can overwhelm him or her.

The danger of such impositions was illustrated some years ago by a citywide study in the United States that received little publicity. All elementary school teachers asked every child to watch the then popular TV cartoon ''Crusader Rabbit'' show over the weekend. On the following Monday morning, without any reference to the program they had been asked to view and that most children would have seen in any case, all primary grade children in that city were asked to draw a rabbit. With hardly any exception every child drew the same cartoon ''Crusader Rabbit'' character. This simple experiment demonstrates the disastrous influence of TV stereotypes on children's perceptions. Without it these children would have drawn rabbits with a diversity. No two might have been alike. Each child would have given expression to his or her own thoughts and experiences. They were and are overwhelmed by the dictates of the TV set. It is not unreasonable to suppose that all the thoughts, actions, and modes of expression of modern children are similarly affected. A very few manage to shake off such conditioning as they mature. But the rest tend to submit to imitation of media imposed clichés for the rest of their lives unless a special effort is made at home and in school. Only then can they be steered into avenues of individual and imaginative expression.

c. Individual Differences

Not every child is equally inventive or inclined to identical interests. Some prefer to draw, others to sculpt; still others enjoy work with wood, leather, fibers, fabric, or film. A child can learn identical skills from any art and equal satisfaction in craft. All provide opportunities for expression and development of self, provided they are introduced in a proper manner.

Every child enjoys working with his or her hands. His or her inclinations are most readily observable at early ages before they are overlain by outside influences. But you can only discover and nurture them by exposure to direct experience with tools and materials. A child's interest in any art or craft can also serve as a focal point for other learning, including academic skills. One who doesn't read with interest or skill may suddenly become passionately immersed in books dealing with a craft subject that engages him or her. Another, who may be uninterested in numbers, will discover that mathematics has practical uses in making plans, or measuring or weighing the materials with which he enjoys working.

d. Special Children

Conventional definitions of intelligence are extremely limited and inexact. Children are quite often classified as mentally retarded, hyperactive, autistic, slow learners, or even brain damaged when their abilities lie outside of what is usually taught and tested. Art and craft education offers parents, teachers, and therapists alternate opportunities for reaching many children and young people who are otherwise neglected or left behind in the classroom. Some can be returned to the mainstream of education; others can learn adequately or even brilliantly; and the rest can be made more or less autonomous when art and craft experiences are used as keys to unlock previously closed doors to learning.

These children pose special problems at home and in schools. Some are indeed physically, mentally, emotionally, or environmentally damaged. Others are merely misdiagnosed. The value of art and craft as therapy for psychologically disturbed patients has long been understood in more enlightened clinics and hospitals. Manual craft, unfortunately often at rote performance levels, is used in many institutions for the retarded and handicapped. This book, and the approach to education it suggests, can be useful to all who care for children and young people who are disabled, disturbed, retarded, ill, or difficult to educate by conventional means, at home and in institutions.

e. Process versus Production

A misunderstanding of the difference between learning and performance has created confusion in the art and craft education of children as in most other aspects of education. *Production* is not, and should not be, the object of manual skill development and self-expression. Instead, it can and should lead to the discovery of *processes*. The potholder a child produces by following a predrawn pattern may please his relatives and accrue to the esteem in which they hold his teacher. But it has no educational, craft, or creative value. The child must have invented, discovered, designed, added, or contributed something unique before such a potholder can become the product of his creativity.

Creative work involves a progressive discovery of tools, materials, processes, and self, and how they can be transformed imaginatively. Such creation may be frustrating or exhilarating or both. It may lead to messes or masterpieces. None of this is important to the child, except insofar as it leads to exercise, experience, new insights, competence, independence, coordination, wonder, curiosity, intuition, spontaneity, whimsy, discovery, self-discipline, and endurance. Most of these qualities are not measured or measurable. They don't show up on the Stanford-Binet I.Q. test, the Wechsler Intelligence Scale, the Goodenough-Harris Drawing Test, or any of the other barometers of intelligence or achievement. They are especially important because few schools stimulate and none can test them.

Parents and teachers should be delighted when children bang away at something experimentally or scribble to discover the characteristics of crayons. But most are far happier when their children make something in imitation of slick, commercial products. Many insist on it. If the child fails, he is likely to be made to feel inferior or incompetent. When he succeeds and when his product looks as if it might have been bought in a store or manufactured by machine, his work is appreciated and he is praised and rewarded.

The more of such work children produce and the more materials they consume, the more highly they are rated by their adult critics. These activities lend themselves to commercial exploitation. A child given coloring books and "paint-by-number" kits can turn out Mona Lisas or Last Suppers on an assembly line. One who is reared on "hobby kits" can produce a stream of miniature ballistic missiles and detailed facsimile space capsules merely by gluing bits of prefabricated plastic together. This kind of mass production is mesmerizing and habit forming. It fosters an illusion of craft and creativity, and that anyone can be Leonardo da Vinci or Werner Von Braun with relatively little effort. These do-it-yourself kits stimulate only the repeat sales of millions of dollars' worth of similar merchandise deceptively labeled as art or craft activities. Children who are entrapped by them merely do unskilled, menial, and soul destroying labor.

But a child who slowly builds competence by daubing clumsily with a paint brush, another who experimentally squeezes a formless lump of clay, or a third who hammers nails into a board without feeling compelled to produce a product, is deeply involved in the process of creation. These children discover how they can bend materials to their wills. Later they may transform these efforts into expressions of their imagination or vision. They can eventually learn how to give voice to their inner lives. They discover how to use raw materials effectively and how to improvise. They find out how to control and restrain the sense of urgency that is the by-product of creation. They develop self-discipline. They learn to curb their understandable haste or carelessness and how to avoid the disorder that impedes success. Creative work demonstrates the need for self-imposed rules, for methodical care of tools and materials, and for judgment.

A child who is experienced in such craft becomes progressively critical of his own efforts. Not all results will seem equally successful or valuable. He'll want to discard those that don't live up to what he expects of himself. Those that are worth keeping are his very own unique creations. He thought of them and carved them out of his inner self. Production and economic value are incidental to the learning of these processes. They may lead to both eventually, but foremost they develop a child's resources and resourcefulness. These are the most fruitful products of a sound art and craft education. They may seem intangible but they are applicable in every walk of life.

Ultimately the child's creation does turn into a product of some sort. "What shall I make?" is not an unreasonable question for a child to ask once he has mastered new tools and skills. Or he may be inspired to learn because he wants to make or invent something, draw, paint, or sculpt what he experiences or feels, or build an object he wants to use in play or give as a present. Or he may simply wish to make his surroundings more beautiful. Especially then his work should not evade the creative processes of art and craft. It should be self-generated and not depend on prefabricated parts, patterns, or plans.

Only one brief chapter (XIII: Applications) deals with production and ideas for things a child might wish to make. It offers suggestions in the most general terms, leaving it up to the child who asks for them to choose his own media. He can then invent, design, adapt, or improvise according to his perceptions and experience. This approach harmonizes with what is now known about child development and learning. It is not to be confused with the chaotic misdirection favored by the misinterpreters of John Dewey or with the mythology of the "unstructured curriculum." Lack of required guidance is a structure imposed on children as rigidly as that which the most pedantic martinet rams down their throats.

f. Play, Self-Expression, and Creativity

Play, self-expression, creativity, craft, and art are usually inexactly and loosely defined. The following describes what is meant by these terms for the purposes of this book.

Child's play differs from that of most adults because personality, abilities, and intellect are in formative stages during childhood. The child literally "forms" himself through play.[27] It is his work and means to growth. The adult "re-forms" himself by the same process. For most it is recreation. But the quality of *playfulness* is common to both adult and child. It is identical in a baby's trial flexing of muscles, reaching, and exploration and in adult occupations in the arts, in science, and in some aspects of all work and leisure. Such playfulness is the essence of *self-*

expression and *creativity* and it serves as the most useful definition of these hackneyed terms.

Craft describes the exercise of skills. It is the hallmark of competence. An artist practices craft when he paints or sculpts. A scientist practices craft when he prepares a slide for his microscope. A mechanic practices craft when he repairs a car. None of these acts are creative unless an element of inventive playfulness enters into the manipulation of tools and materials. The degree to which a child may depart from prescribed paths in his self-expressive play, within the limits of safety and those imposed by the material, decides the extent to which he can create himself or herself. It determines the level to which he or she may aspire in adulthood in our Western culture, if given the opportunity.

The TV repairman who fixes a broken set by following the wiring diagram does useful, though noncreative, work. He is only creative if he is able to improvise and deviate from given instructions to improve reception without increasing voltages in color TV sets that generate harmful radiation. The main difference then between rote performance and creativity is that the latter demands playfulness, education, experience, spontaneity, insight, and responsible courage. Together they can be the moving spirit for any activity that involves the exercise of skills. A worker can produce profitably by following instructions to the letter. But the quality of his work, life, and mind can only improve if he is able and enjoys opportunities to exercise the playfulness that characterizes creativity.

Self-disciplined performance, enhanced by playfulness, turns craft into art. The use of the word "play" in our language offers clues to these relationships. We speak of a wheel having "play" if it does not ride in a totally fixed position on its axle. Musicians "play" instruments; actors "play" on the stage; and artists, writers, and scientists "play" with symbols, images, words, and ideas.[15] Playfulness is the uninhibited exercise of mental and physical abilities within certain limitations.

Art then involves the playful use of self. This is why children are creative by definition. But by definition they also lack experience, competence, and craft. These qualities cannot be acquired by rote. Children need tools and materials presented to them in a way that allows them to discover their disciplined uses. Craft can accomplish this only if it is introduced as a process rather than as a means of production. Without playfulness the child turns into a mindless producer. Without craft he lacks the means to achieve mature playfulness. And he can only acquire the former through the exercise of the latter. This is why the following or tracing of plans and patterns and the assembly of prefabricated parts is so pernicious. They may seem the shortest routes to success and production, but they stifle playfulness.

A total absence of playfulness can only be seen in individuals suffering from the most severe forms of mental illness. But in our society an autistic apathy is also forced onto many by the mass-production technologies and by an education that stresses consumption rather than playful exploration of materials and ideas. Many of the supportive "experts" of the technologies distrust playfulness, reduce it to behavioral manipulation,[26] or a hip form of anarchy.[6] The drug culture substitutes chaotic, chemically induced spontaneity for active playfulness. The cults of "sensitivity" and "awareness" turn play into a serious, exploitative business. All these may share some of the characteristics of play [7] but they damage the capacity for self-generated creation. Such synthetic and mind-blowing creativity can be bought, swallowed, and consumed as mindlessly as the "how-to" hobby kits of the supermarket.

Hysteria, consumption, passivity, and pseudoscientific seriousness characterize our technological culture. They debase the human spirit and atrophy species specific abilities. They have brought about a deterioration in the quality of our culture and life-styles. Play, art, and craft are essential nourishment. Next to physical care, well-being, and love, they are every child's birthright.

g. What to Teach and When

The judgment of what to teach—and when not to teach—emerges when art and craft are viewed as educational processes. The decision of what to do, make, or express must be left to the child once he sets to work. First, however, work space, tools, and materials must be provided. "At the same time, some materials have to be understood before they can be used fully, and to leave expensive materials out to be played with until their properties are discovered is both unrealistic and foolhardy." [23] The desirable balance between direction and freedom can be achieved only "if the teacher [or parent] is one who inspires rather than dictates, where the discoveries about the nature of materials are discussed so that children learn through [their own and] each other's experience as well as from the teacher. A group of ten-year-olds, for example, might discover that wax crayons resist water-based ink. From this starting point [simple wax resist] the gifted teacher will try to create situations in which the process of using wax to repel water is examined in as many contrasting ways as possible.'' [23]

A child can learn the limits of safety and behavior in art and craft as in all other activities. He needs to discover how to arrange, control, and care for his tools. He must understand that he may not paint on the wall or decorate baby brother's hair with clay. He needs to be shown the disciplines of craft, while the playful and experimental aspects of art must be left in his hands.

Every beginner in art and craft—adult, teenager, or child—tends to lose control over his medium. The materials spread as if they had a will of their own, from the center of the table to its edges and beyond. They seem to behave as if in opposition to the inexperienced tool user. His own lack of disciplined work habits and foresight, and not the tools, fights his efforts. Small parts scatter. A paintbrush, heedlessly dipped into one color after another without rinsing, soon turns all colors a muddy brown. In the scramble to find misplaced materials the work is endangered. Things are spilled, surfaces marred, and an object that is the product of hours of thoughtful labor is shattered in the confusion.

You can show the child that things work better if he keeps materials in bins and boxes, hangs up his tools in prearranged places when they aren't in use, and keeps them in good working order. He needs clothing, table, and floor spaces that are washable. How hammer or coping saw must be held and how to nail or drill to best effect and in safety must be demonstrated. The child needs properly organized material and tool storage places. He needs help with cleaning up messes until he can be expected to do this unaided. But don't expect too much, too soon, from a child. Ceaseless demand for self-discipline and neatness can be as discouraging as constant disorder.

The visual, auditory, and tactile qualities of materials must be pointed out to the child and brought to his attention. He needs to learn how to recognize and identify them and how to express them verbally and in his creative work. Experience and familiarity with the origins of materials will increase his interest in them. Eventually he will want to know how to weigh and measure, plan, and design when projects demand precision. But even these skills evolve from spontaneous experiences that lead from nonnumerical to geometric and eventually to numerical judgments.

Parents and teachers should work with craft materials themselves and become familiar with the opportunities they offer. But in presenting the same materials to children, parents and teachers must remain mindful of the developmental level of each child and of his or her previous experiences. In any event don't show the child tricks—how to draw in perspective, in proportion, or a "stick" man. "Children tend to draw the idea of the thing rather than the thing as one might see it. . . . To a child people come in such different sizes anyway that the actual size of a man is much less part of the idea of a man than what he can do." [12] Further, children can only see and express things one-dimensionally until they reach quite advanced stages of development.[3] But this can never be accelerated. Interference can short-circuit it. "How-to" instructions are meaningless at these ages. A child might mimic you successfully but he has no idea what he is doing. Such mimicry is deceptive. It may seem like precocious competence but it actually discourages the development of genuine skill.

A child's competence expands in stages as does all learning and development. At first he or she is simply intrigued with effects. He is delighted that he can make dots, lines, and scribbles with crayons or felt markers. To insist that he learn to draw formally or realistically at any stage in childhood and early adolescence diverts a needed self-paced exploration of materials and self. The same principles are true for all arts and crafts. A child will be satisfied snipping away at a sheet of paper with his scissors. He neither wants nor does he need to "make something." It can only occur to him that he can give his cuttings shape after he has acquired control and coordination. Each new material poses identical challenges and he will respond to them in an identical manner. He cannot become interested in purpose or production until the tools obey his will. Only then can he begin to think of expressing something; earlier he'll pretend that what he draws or forms "looks like" a person, animal, or object.

Learning is a circular process.[3] Self-rewarding practice increases competence and it, in turn, leads to self-expression that requires more exercise, and so on. The circle is broken and learning interrupted when adult perceptions that are foreign to a child's way of looking at things are forced onto him or her. Similarly, the format of this book should not become a straitjacket that is imposed on any child. He should not be "made" to learn every craft, or any in the order in which projects are presented. His interests should be your guide. You may have to elicit them, but you should never dictate them. Older children, teenagers, and young adults may need to unlearn much of what they were taught before they can discover the creatively rewarding aspects of art and craft.

h. Tools, Materials, and Judgment

Many of our children will inevitably use power tools as adults. But in order to use the technologies, rather than being used by them, they first need a hand-felt knowledge of simple tools and of raw materials. Children must experience how tools affect materials. But it is not possible to take every child back to basic processes and materials in every instance—not in glass and paper making, for example. Still, principles that are hidden from view by the complexity of modern technologies must be made visible for them.

A few years ago I took my then three-year-old daughter to a dairy farm so that she might see cows being milked. It was a frustrating experi-

ence. I had not realized how far the technologies had advanced since I worked on a farm as a young man not too many years before. Though milking machines were used even then, each cow needed to be "stripped" by hand and, at least during that part of the operation, the milk could be seen streaming into the pail. This is no longer true today. All my daughter could see was the farmer attaching the suction cups of the milking machine to the cow's teats. The milk flowed invisibly from udder to storage tank through a maze of rubber, glass, and steel tubes. I had to show my daughter pictures of how it used to be done to make the process comprehensible to her.

A child familiar only with mechanized farming is not likely to be sensitive to the consequences of an unrestricted use of chemical fertilizers or pesticides, or of increasing yields beyond a certain point. As a result he may acquiesce in or contribute to the destruction of the sensitive balance of nature. He lacks insights into processes that can only be understood through a familiarity with labor intensive farming. Even if such a child works on a modern farm as an adolescent he is likely to view it from the high above ground perspective provided by tractor or combine cab. His main concern is for the machine that seems to produce for him; but he is out of touch with the soil—the true raw material.

Children and young people can only discover the allowable limits of the technologies through an education in manual arts and crafts. None of this suggests a return to hand labor for the sake of misplaced nostalgia. Production should be based on whatever ecologically sound technologies we can invent. Yet we must learn to distinguish between these and others that impoverish our lives and threaten our well-being and that of future generations.

Preindustrial societies were unconsciously aware of these limiting factors. They prescribed ritually how tools and materials were to be used. In Japan, up to a few decades ago, the loading and opening of pottery kilns involved formal Shinto ceremonies. These not only assured successful, traditional products, but also provided an ethic that had evolved from the experience of generations of craftsmen. Creation in all its forms was a holy act, governed by sanctified rules that applied to every craftsman, tool, and material, and ultimately also to the user of the product. This, among other such examples, suggests that the very origin of ethics may reside in tool use. The rule "Thou shalt not kill" may have sprung from an awakening of a consciousness that weapons in the hands of one member of the prehistoric tribe threatened the tranquility and equilibrium of equality among the rest. Their possession by one man at a time when the rest were unskilled in their manufacture and use created an intolerable imbalance of power, endangering the survival of the species, as it does once again in our own time.

Since the advent of industrialization and with the explosion of the technologies, tools have proliferated to an extent that most have escaped ethical governance. As a result, we lack principles required to guide us in their use, from steam to internal combustion engine, from chemicals, drugs, and plastics to nuclear energy. Among the rules that might be inferred from all tool use could be that "whoever cannot repair or maintain a tool does not really own it." [5] In our daily lives and households most of the tools we use but cannot keep in working order actually own us. In many instances we labor to pay for them out of all proportion to the benefits we derive from them.

It is of course unrealistic to expect every owner of the usual assortment of appliances to be expert in the different technologies from which they spring. But every reasonably well-educated twentieth century man and woman should be familiar with the production principles on which the manufacture of common objects is based. It should also be within the owner's competence to judge the relative value, efficiency, and usefulness of objects, and the ease or difficulty with which they can be maintained, before they are acquired. Every owner should be able to diagnose simple malfunctions and make minor repairs. But to be able to do so he or she needs an education in craft, in basic processes, and in the use of hand tools. The same skills are required for creative crafts as in elementary maintenance and repair.

An accelerated rate of breakdown, obsolescence, power and equipment failure, and deterioration in facilities is visible all around us. This is due to a misapplication of the technologies; an unethical use of raw materials, energy, and tools; and a lack of education in craft. There are no indications of a reversal of this trend. It has become chronic within and even outside the cities. It may eventually prove disastrous except to those able to use their hands as well as their brains, without total dependency on the technologies and their specialists.

All these are persuasive reasons for educating children and young people in handicrafts. A wooden plank cut up with a handsaw teaches a child more than the gift of a factory-made box, ready for decoration. A fabric remnant that the child cuts, glues, staples, or sews to form an abstract design or an ill-fitting doll's apron provides more valuable experiences than a gift of patterns that assure a perfect result, or a whole wardrobe of Barbie doll dresses. It is infinitely more productive if a child improvises a paper, cardboard, or twig loom than if he weaves on a miniature, prefabricated, and prestrung one. These suggestions are not made for the sake of economy but for the sake of the child. Both boys and girls need these experiences to develop the judgments required for ethical life in a technological society.

i. Mixed Media, Skills, and Found Materials

Once a child has learned how to handle a hand drill and how to choose the right bit for making a hole in a particular material, he can apply the same skill and knowledge to wood, metal, brick, or seashells for that matter. He should be encouraged to look for and find a variety of materials on which to exercise his skills, tools, and imagination, rather than limiting himself (or herself) to one application.

A raft of specialized kits and books are now merchandised as craft. Beadcraft, shellcraft, foamcraft and flowercraft, among others, pretend to lend respectability to mass production and to be what they are not. These non- or anti-crafts profit only their manufacturers. They sell waste or by-products that can generally be found or assembled without cost. They debase rather than hone skills.

For example, jewelry-making need not involve only metal and stone, but can include the use of clay, wood, metal, glass, leather, paper, fibers, and even ice cream sticks. The threading of wool through holes in a card should inspire the child to do the same thing with perforated metal and leather thong. Experience with and especially the discovery of a variety of raw, manufactured, and found materials enable the young craftsman to draw on and choose from a large reservoir of different media. He will make these judgments based not only on what is at hand or what comes prepackaged in a box, but on what he knows exists and can be improvised or found. He'll use the proper tool required for each different material because he is sensitive to their differences in texture, density, and weight. He can shape any material to achieve a desired effect. These abilities are necessary for life in a world rich with diverse materials and experiences.

The search for diversity in effect and for possible combinations of different materials is a creative act in itself. It brings harmony to what, on the surface, may seem like clashing or divergent characteristics. A large part of the art consists of discovering how each can support, complement, or counteract all others. This is why collages and assemblages are stressed in many of the following chapters. They are not "modern" art; they are essential experiences. Abstraction underlies the work of even traditional and realistic artists and craftsmen. It is also the structure that underlies a child's later outlook, as in creation. He learns to see, recognize, and create structure, instead of being confused by surface detail. These are equally important prerequisites for painting, carpentry, photography—as in film making, for example. And so the assemblage the child makes out of scraps of paper and wood enables him eventually to get greater satisfaction out of his still or movie camera than if he lacked this experience.

j. Work Spaces, Lighting, and Clothing

(See also III.A.d, IV.A.b and c, and VI.A.b.)

A child does not need a carpenter's bench for work with wood any more than he needs an easel for painting. He does need a solid worktable for either, large and low enough so that he can work in comfort, sitting or standing. A well-built trestle table can serve the purpose (see diag. I). It should consist of a ¾" plywood top, with all surfaces carefully sanded and coated with several light applications of varnish or shellac. Saw-

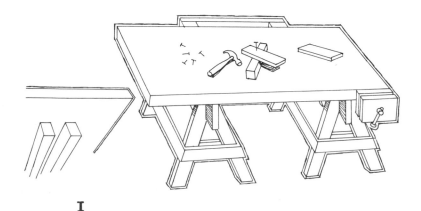

I

horses make practical legs provided the table top is attached to them firmly. A child outgrows other worktables rapidly. Metal sawhorse angle brackets can be bought inexpensively in any hardware store. $1'' \times 2''$ lumber legs can be inserted into these and replaced with longer ones as the child grows taller. $1'' \times 2''$ strips should be glued and screwed also to the underside of the table top so that it cannot slide off the sawhorses as the child works (see diag. I). See III.A.d for designs for a table-top carpenter's bench.

Either trestle table or table-top carpenter's workbench can be accessorized for any kind of art or craft work. A woodworking vise (see 113) or one for metalwork (see 147) can be attached. Wooden rails can be nailed or screwed in place to secure small parts, bins, tools, and paint jars. A pegboard, hung within reach, can become a tool storage center.

Shelves and receptacles are required for materials storage. The floor under and around the worktable should be covered with linoleum or vinyl tile or, if you wish to protect a wooden floor, with heavy wrapping paper taped down firmly with strapping tape so that a working child does not slip or slide.

The worktable or bench should be placed next to a window so that the light falls on the work from the side opposite the child's handedness (from the left for a right-handed child, and from the right for a left-handed child). He should not face, nor should his back be turned to, the window while he works. An overhead light is needed for work after dark or on overcast days. It should be hung, or the worktable moved, so that work spaces are relatively shadow-free. Keep extension cords out of the way, out from underfoot, and out of the child's reach.

A smock or old clothing will protect the child from spills that are bound to occur. Sleeves should be buttoned at the wrist or rolled up above the elbows. Shirts should be tucked into belts or skirts and buttoned. When heat producing or power tools are used, smocks should be belted. These suggestions allow for safe, unhampered limb and manual movements.

k. Safety

Only you can tell whether your child can use a tool safely at his or her stage of development. Can he or she understand and follow your instructions? Have you explained yourself simply and repeatedly? Can he remember and heed your warnings? Can he be depended on to use his hammer only on pegs, tacks, or nails and the pieces of lumber you have furnished? (Or is he likely to wander away and try it out on your favorite knick-knacks?) Will he keep his hand *behind* the linoleum cutting tool? Can he be trusted with knife or chisel? Or does he still get carried away while he works so that he becomes careless and invariably hurts himself?

A child needs experience before he can appreciate and remember the logic of caution. A totally protected and inexperienced child is far more likely to injure himself and others than one who is gradually exposed to experiences, including those that pose minor hazards, provided he receives guidance and supervision. Children usually confine themselves to working with tools on appropriate materials *if these are furnished*. A hammer given without tacks or wood invariably invites inappropriate use. Insisting that a child follow given patterns and plans also leads to potentially damaging experimentation when no one is looking. The gift of new tools must coincide with a time at which the child understands what he may and may not do with them. You must become aware of hazards, and foresee and point them out as often and as patiently as necessary. Do not expect a child, even at ages when he or she can read, to study and heed the cautions on labels or packages. You must do this yourself and then make appropriate judgments about the possible dangers.

Any materials, including totally safe ones, are likely to be misused by some children. A spiral coping saw blade is perfectly harmless once the blade is inserted into the saw; even pre-school children could not possibly hurt themselves while using it. A loose blade poked into a live electric socket can cause serious injury. But then a paper clip in the hands of a child too young to use it for its intended purposes can be similarly dangerous.

Proper arrangement of the child's work spaces (see I.j), when and how materials are introduced, and foresight will prevent accidents. All tools and materials suggested in this book are safe if given as and when recommended, with some exceptions for which special cautions are listed in every case. Your attention is drawn to those tools and materials that are sharp, pointed, or potentially toxic in the hands of children too immature to use them with caution.

Two materials—plastics and glass—are largely excluded from this book for safety reasons. Plate glass is suggested for monoprints (see 215) and as a painting surface (see 247 and 248). But glass blowing, forming, and molding, despite the creative opportunities these processes afford, require too much heat and special equipment to be considered safe for young people unless they work under close professional supervision. Glass cutting is also too dangerous.

Much the same is true for plastics. To be worked, most require high heat and poisonous or carcinogenic catalysts, and when sawed or drilled sharp slivers can fly off the material. Plastic scrap, like vinyl, can be glued to collages and assemblages without danger, provided organic glues are used, but such scraps will not adhere permanently.

Virtually all synthetic paints and glues, except acrylics, and all aerosol spray paints and adhesives are highly toxic and potentially carcinogenic. Some synthetic glues bond so effectively that any of the material that dries on the skin, or a part accidentally glued to a finger, may require surgery for removal. Many tar and cellulose derived finishes and glues, as well as paints, dyes, and ceramic glazes that contain lead, are dangerous and inappropriate for use by young people. (See also 227.)

I. Organization of Contents

Each of this book's chapters deals with one major craft, art, or materials subject, designated by a Roman numeral (I, II, III, etc.). Every chapter is divided by capital letter subheadings (A, B, C, etc.) in an ascending order of skill and difficulty. General background or cautionary information given under these subheadings is identified with small letters (a, b, c, etc.). The art and craft projects themselves, irrespective of chapter or subheading, are numbered consecutively from the beginning of this book to its end (1, 2, 3, etc.). The number of projects and the amount of subject matter included are possible only because duplication is avoided through cross-references. For example, pre-school cutting with scissors requires the same instructions and cautions whether the material is paper, foil, cloth, or thin, split leather. Beveled tools require the same methods of sharpening and honing, whether they are used for cutting or carving linoleum, wood, leather, or cardboard. These overlapping skills are described only once, in appropriate places, and cross-referred whenever the same technique applies elsewhere.

Examples:

"(See III.A.e)" refers to Chapter III: Carpentry; subheading A: Background; item e: Safety.

"(See II.G)" refers to Chapter II: Paper and Foil Craft; subheading G: Winding and Weaving.

"(See 305)" refers to the project of that number: Linoleum Block Cutting.

The page number for each cross-reference can be found quickly by consulting the table of contents at the beginning of the book.

Chapter XIII: Applications is a general idea file, designed to help children think, invent, and create on their own when they wish to make something useful, or decorative, or as a gift. Every idea is related to a representative variety of projects, arts, crafts, tools, and materials from which the child can choose a medium or a combination of media in which he or she may decide to execute the work.

For example, a child who has decided to make a puppet is referred to paper constructing and jointing, papier maché, wood carving, clay and plaster forming and molding, and cloth cutting and sewing, among others. He or she can choose which method of construction and which medium or combination of media to employ. His or her maturity, prior experience, available tools and materials, inventiveness, and willingness to learn new skills and find new materials will decide the final form of the product. This is what is meant by creativity.

The audiovisual idea file at the end of that same chapter is intended as a similar idea stimulator. Like the first section, it is far from exhaustive. All these are only points of departure for a child's independent search for ideas and forms of expression.

Much the same applies to Chapter XIV: Found Materials. A basic list of common household and locally available scrap, waste, found, and inexpensive materials is related to likely sources of supply. Once a child begins to look on everything he can lay his hands on as potential art and craft materials, many possibilities will occur to him that are not listed here. For example, empty match boxes are wonderfully versatile. In the hands of an imaginative child they can become components of a large number of projects, designs, and activities.

m. Recommended Further Reading

Parents, teachers, recreational and therapy workers, and young people may wish to delve into some of the subjects covered in this book beyond the skill levels to which it is limited. More advanced techniques that harmonize with the approach of this book and additional background material can be found in the books, periodicals, catalogues, and other materials listed in the bibliography and notes. As stated earlier, many books about art and craft concentrate on "how-to" production instead of on processes that stimulate creative development. Most include patterns, plans, and designs to follow that in some cases are very poorly designed, but even when in good taste are undesirable from teaching and learning points of view (see I.e and VI.A.a). But a few even of these offer excellent descriptions of techniques, tools, and materials. Wherever no other book exists that combines truly creative approaches with craftsman-like descriptions of processes, I have selected those that detail the latter ably at least. But the reader is urged not to suggest to a child that he or she follow any of the plans or designs offered in such books. For details on how to select and distinguish between the different categories of further reading material, see the introduction to the bibliography and notes on page 429.

II

Paper and Foil Craft

We need craftsmanship in education, in a machine age as much, if not more than any other, because it is a fundamental *mode of education,* through which the child explores, discovers the qualities of, and comes to terms with the world in which he lives.—*Mairi Seonaid Robertson*

A. BACKGROUND

Paper was first invented in China by Ts'ai Lun in the year 105 A.D. It was made of the bark of the mulberry bush, similar to tapa cloth still used by Pacific islanders. By the time of Marco Polo paper was made in the Far East by pressing vegetable fibers into sheets in a manner not very different from modern techniques. Paper objects and miniatures were also used in religious ceremonies. Foil covered paper money was a part of Chinese funerary rites as early as 739 A.D.

The ancient Egyptians used the leaves of the papyrus tree—hence our word "paper"—pasted into sheets for record keeping. They also made lightweight skiffs out of this material for fishing on the river Nile. The

Romans discovered how to make parchment—sheepskin sliced very thin. This remained the sole writing surface throughout Europe for many centuries, used primarily by scribes who copied books by hand in monasteries. England's first paper making factory was established in 1495 but failed almost immediately due to a lack of demand. A second, similar venture was started in 1586. It thrived as a result of Gutenberg's invention of moveable type some fifty years earlier (see VIII.A). Paper making remained a laborious process until the nineteenth century and the invention of power driven machinery. The basic raw materials and processes—vegetable and cloth fibers; wood pulp; clay and chemicals added for different weights, textures, and colors, laid onto a variety of screens and then dried and pressed, washed, and bleached—remained virtually the same. More recently plastics have been introduced to paper and paperboard making. Yet a few craftsmen still produce handmade papers for special purposes.

In China, Japan, Korea, and India children have enjoyed a profusion of paper and papier maché toys and paper folding, pasting, and related craft for centuries. Many, like origami, are traditional by now and children develop skill, patience, and a quality of mind peculiar to the culture of childhood in the Orient. Until the late eighteenth century paper did not fall into the hands of European children, save for occasional waste scraps. But from about 1800 onward it became an impor-

tant raw material of play and for the production of kites, balloons, toy soldiers, and doll and structural cutouts, among other playthings. Poland and Czechoslovakia are the only two European countries where paper, used sparingly and ingeniously, turned into a distinctive folk art during the past one hundred and fifty years.

Paper and cardboard are among the most versatile art and craft materials. Today's artists, designers, architects, inventors, model makers, stage designers, dressmakers, and other craftsmen and craftswomen work out their ideas structurally on paper before translating them into more permanent materials. Mathematicians use paper to demonstrate topological principles. Experienced children and young people can use paper similarly for mock-ups, preliminary models, and templates before executing their designs in wood, metal, leather, or cloth. But paper and cardboard are perfectly satisfactory and durable materials for art and crafts in themselves. Paper is malleable, easily cut, scored, bent, formed, adhered, combined with other materials, painted, and decorated, even in the hands of relatively inexperienced children. It can help them convert many of the processes of the arts and crafts into the products of their imagination.

Modern packaging, design, and model making techniques, added to the traditional ones described earlier, have inspired new and creative uses of paper. These forms are useful to parents and teachers in stimulating craft and expression in children. I have drawn on this sum of interdisciplinary and intercultural experience for a selection of processes that enable children to discover themselves and their abilities.

B. FIRST PROJECTS

1. Crumpling, Twisting, and Tearing

Tools and materials
Colored tissue paper; bond paper; newsprint

Crumpling paper, rolling it into balls, twisting it into sausages, or simply tearing it to shreds can be extremely satisfying to a young child. It calls different sensations and muscles into play. The child discovers textures and other properties of the material as he experiments and exercises his fingers. Tissue and other paper balls can be strung, taped, or pasted together; or, tied to twine, can be dragged by a toddler behind him.

Place the child before a table at which he can work in comfort (see I.j) or in his highchair. Give him an assortment of paper and a large, empty box. Then show him how to crumple, twist, and tear and put the pieces into the box. (See also 295.)

2. Sorting

Tools and materials
Same as 1
Empty egg carton or assortment of small boxes

Once a child enjoys crumpling, twisting, and tearing paper, he can be shown how to sort the different pieces. Set him up with an empty egg carton or a number of small boxes or containers. Demonstrate how he can distribute the shapes he creates, sorting them by relative size, shape, or color. Aside from sheer play value, this sets the stage for size, shape, and color recognition, and sorting and labeling skills and controls that are necessary for other learning.

3. Wrapping

Tools and materials
Tissue paper; newsprint; small paper bags
Small empty boxes; toys and other objects
½" masking tape cut into 1" strips, each taped to the edge of the table top by one corner

Unwrapping presents is one of the joys of childhood. Wrapping things up can give a child similar pleasure. Wrapping a box and making it "disappear" is a kind of magic. Quite incidentally the child discovers how to fold paper and tape down corners, edges, and folds.

Note: Do not give young children plastic bags or cellophane tape. The first can be hazardous and the second frustrating.

C. LACING

4. Making a Threader

Tools and materials
Drinking straws cut into 1" lengths
White paste (see 9 and 11–15)
Strands of colored-wool yarn

Before a child learns to lace he can be shown how to make his own threader. Choose lengths of yarn long enough for whatever is to be laced or strung.

It takes nearly 50″ of yarn to lace around the edges of a perforated piece of 8½″ × 11″ bond paper. Dip about ½″ of one end of the yarn into the paste and twirl it between thumb and forefinger to point the tip. Insert this end into one of the straw cutoffs while the paste is still wet and let it dry thoroughly. Tie a thick knot into the other end of the yarn, and the child is ready to string beads and macaroni shapes, or lace punched paper (see 5). A blunt lacing needle, used in leather craft (see 179), is also a good, safe tool for young children. Plastic or metal tipped shoe laces are usually too short and not nearly as colorful.

5. Punching Holes

Tools and materials

Paper hole punch (see 178 for revolving punch)

Assorted white and colored construction and bond papers; foil; paper cups and plates

Threader (see 4)

A child old enough to thread and lace may not have the strength to use a hole punch. This may have to be done for him at first. Punch holes at regular or irregular intervals around the edges of the paper. Holes can be punched into inside areas by folding the paper one or more times (see diag. 5.a). Show the child how to insert his threader at whichever hole he chooses, pulling the yarn all the way through to the knotted end. Demonstrate how he can lace over and under (see diag. 5.b) or bind the

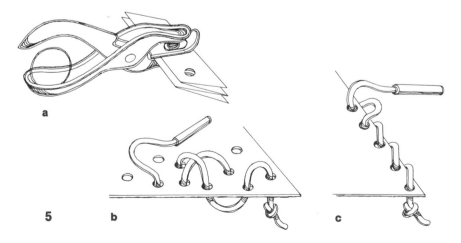

a

5   b   c

edges (see diag. 5.c), always pulling the spare yarn all the way through each hole at every turn. He'll discover the variety of patterns he can create going from one hole to the next, skipping some and criss-crossing in every direction. Prepare several straw-tipped threaders in advance so that he can work with concentration until he tires.

Eventually the child will be able to punch his or her own holes. Save the punched-out paper discs for use in pasting (see 9), collages (see 27), and paper mosaics (see 29). Commercially available, prepunched sewing cards do not develop nearly as many insights and skills.

6. Grommet Lacing

Tools and materials
> Grommet and die set (available in notion stores and counters) (see also 185)
> Child-size hammer (see 106)
> 12″ × 12″ × ¾″ well-sanded pine board, plywood, or scrap lumber, or a sheet of heavy cardboard
> Paper hole punch (see 5)
> Threader (see 4)
> Paper products (see 5)

After the holes have been punched as in 5 above, tape one edge of the paper to the wooden board and show the child how to push one grommet up through one of the holes. Use the grommet die and hammer to demonstrate how to bend the rim of the grommet so that it is securely fastened to the paper (see diag. 6). Make sure that the threader fits through the grommet. When the child has finished attaching all the grommets, he can lace and unlace his designs since the grommets strengthen the paper holes so that they won't tear.

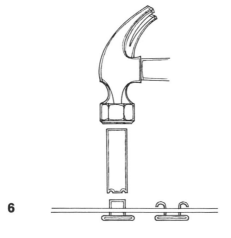

6

7. Lacing Cut Paper Shapes Together

Tools and materials
Same as 6
Scissors (see 37)

Small paper shapes—circles, squares, triangles, rectangles, and irregularly shaped pieces—can be laced, one to all others, if holes have been punched into each. They can be grommeted (see 6) for durability and repeated use. Once a child is able to handle child-size scissors (see 37–39), he can cut out his own paper shapes for lacing.

8. Lacing and Braiding Patterns

Tools and materials
Same as 6

Paper lacing and braiding involve many of the same basic forms that apply to leather craft (see 179 and 180) and reed and fiber craft (see X.A, B, and C) and can be an introduction to paper (see 42–47) and other weaving (see X.D). Once the child has explored and improvised on the methods suggested in 5 above, he can be introduced to some of the elementary skills detailed in these various sections.

D. PASTING AND GLUING

9. Early Years Pasting

Ordinary white school paste, casein based glues, mucilage, and acrylics are water soluble and harmless if swallowed. Do not give pre-school and early grade children other adhesives, rubber cement, or epoxy (see I.k and 227). (See 11–18 for homemade paste and glue recipes.)

10. Adhesives for Older Children

Use organic and acrylic adhesives only, until the child is sufficiently mature and reliable to heed and follow cautions and instructions (see I.k and 227). Children have accidents, even at older ages. They are not likely to wash their hands as often or as well as they should after handling glues that might be toxic. Rubber cement, like airplane dope and other adhesives commonly used by young people, is toxic and flammable.

11. Making Your Own Adhesives

The following glues can be made easily and require only materials that are found in any home or available at neighborhood stores. They keep well in the refrigerator or other cool place in closed, screw-cap jars. If glue becomes too stiff to use or dries out, it can be restored by addition of a little water. All except one of the recipes (see 16) are entirely non-toxic, and many are useful for paper as well as for bonding other materials, as detailed in each instance.

12. Flour Paste (Short-Term Adhesion)

Tools and materials
    Flour
    Water
    Mixing bowl

Mixed to a consistency of heavy cream, this is a useful adhesive for paper, cloth, and other materials. It is not permanent but the adhesion will last long enough for most pre-schoolers' purposes.

13. Flour Paste (Long-Term Adhesion)

Tools and materials
    Flour
    Water
    Muslin or cheesecloth
    Glass dish

Wrap a handful of flour in the muslin. Wash and knead the flour inside the muslin bag under cold, running water until the water is no longer milky as it runs off and most of the starch is removed. The remainder is almost pure glutin. Allow to dry in a glass dish. The dry glutin will store indefinitely without refrigeration.

To use, chip flakes off the glutin cake, add a few drops of cold water, and allow to stand for a few minutes. Then knead the flakes until they become soft and pliant. Add more cold water to thin out to the required consistency.

14. Common Paste

Tools and materials
    Gum arabic (available in art supply or drug store)
    Boric acid (available in drug store)

Sugar
Cornstarch
Water
Cooking pot

Dissolve one part gum arabic in eights parts warm water. Add four parts sugar and one part starch and boil the mixture until it thickens to the consistency of light cream. Add a pinch of boric acid to keep the paste from mildewing.

15. Library Paste

Tools and materials
2 oz. Cornstarch
¼ oz. White gelatin
16 oz. Water
Oil of cloves
Double boiler

Mix cornstarch in warm water and then add gelatin. Stir until the mixture turns into a thin, smooth paste. Pour into double boiler and heat. Allow to boil until the paste thickens to the consistency of heavy cream, stirring continuously. Add a few drops of oil of cloves to preserve.

16. Transparent Glue

Tools and materials
2 oz. White gelatin
5 oz. Acetic acid (available in drug store)
6 oz. Water
Cooking pot

Soak gelatin in water for twelve hours. Then heat the softened gelatin in the same water until it dissolves. Stir in acetic acid and add cold water until the mixture comes to about one pint.

This glue is slightly toxic, but it is strong enough to cement glass. It can be made stronger or weaker by using more or less gelatin. An older child can use it to mount photographs, pictures cut from magazines, or his own drawings on paper, wood, or glass. By brushing the adhesive on top of the pictures as well as coating them on the reverse side, they will adhere and be protected at the same time. Wipe off any excess before the glue sets with a cloth soaked in warm water.

17. Wallpaper Paste

Tools and materials
  4lb. Rye flour
  2 oz. Pulverized rosin (available in drug or chemical supply store)
  1½ gal. Water
  2½-gal. cooking pot

Work the flour and some of the water into a smooth batter. Boil and add the rest of the water. Keep the mixture boiling and add a little rosin at a time. Allow to cool, adding a little more hot water to thin out the mixture if it is too stiff. This paste is extremely strong. It will bond paper, cardboard, fabric, wood, and thin leather.

18. Rye Flour Paste

Tools and materials
  2 tablespoons Rye flour
  ¼ teaspoon Alum
  1 cup Water
  Oil of cloves
  Cooking pot

Mix flour, alum, and part of the water to form a smooth cream. Add the balance of the water, stir, and cook over low heat until the mixture becomes translucent. The longer it cooks, the greater the adhesive power. Add a few drops of oil of cloves after the mixture is taken off the stove. Keep in closed jar in the refrigerator and stir thoroughly before using. This is a useful adhesive for paper, cloth, wood, and thin leather especially.

19. Rubber Cement

Rubber cement is an adhesive for use by older and mature young people, provided they are cautioned to work in a well-ventilated room, not to inhale fumes from open containers, and never to use the cement near an open flame or heat source, as it is highly flammable. When stored, containers should always be tightly closed and kept far from heat. Dilute the cement in its container periodically or it will tend to solidify. (Rubber cement thinner is available in art and stationery supply stores.) Rubber cement is a useful bonding material for drawing and photographic paper, cardboard, film, acetate, and leather. Things can be glued down lightly for easy removal or more permanently, depending on the method used. The various applications are described below (see 20–25).

20. Making a Rubber Cement Eraser

Tools and materials
Rubber cement
Small sheet of tracing or wax paper

A small lump of thoroughly dry rubber cement must be used to clean excess cement that may dry around the edges of adhered surfaces or spills on any material other than cloth. Fabric can be cleaned only with thinner (see 19). Spread a small amount of the cement onto the paper. Let it dry out completely. Then roll the dried cement into a small ball. It will grow as the picked-up cement adheres to the eraser. Rubber cement "pick-up" erasers can also be bought in art supply stores.

21. Wet-Mounting with Rubber Cement

Rubber cement should be applied with a brush or, if a large surface is to be covered evenly, with a plastic or rubber squeegee or a small square of cardboard (see diag. 21). Cover one of the two surfaces to be bonded with rubber cement. Paste one to the other before the cement dries. This is the least permanent method for pasting with rubber cement. It has the advantage that the pasted surfaces can be separated easily, if necessary. But wet rubber cement tends to bleed through thin and porous materials, staining them permanently.

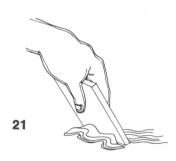

21

22. Dry-Mounting One Side with Rubber Cement

Coat the underside of the thinner, more porous of the two surfaces to be bonded with one coat of rubber cement. Let it dry thoroughly. Then coat the surface to which it is to adhere and glue both together before the coating on the second surface has a chance to dry.

This is a more usual method of using rubber cement. The child can slide one surface into position on top of the other and still get a fair bond.

23. Dry-Mounting Both Sides

Coat each of the two surfaces to be bonded with one or more thin coats of rubber cement, letting each dry thoroughly before applying the next. When the final coating on both surfaces has dried completely, paste them together, pressing down firmly after they are joined.

This method is favored for permanent bonds, especially for leather. Pound the cemented leather surfaces with a hide mallet to assure good adhesion. (See also 24.)

24. Slip-Sheeting

Before mounting two large surfaces dry-coated with rubber cement, it's a good idea to "slip-sheet" them. Insert a plain sheet of wax or tracing paper, larger by about one inch all around, between them before laying the top surface on the bottom one. Pull this slip-sheet down, exposing about $^1/_{16}$" to ¼" of one edge of the dried rubber cement on the bottom surface (see diag. 24). Paste the top edge of the sheet to be mounted on top along this exposed strip of rubber cement. Then work the slip sheet down an inch or so at a time between the two coated surfaces, pressing them together as the cemented coatings come into contact before withdrawing the slip-sheet further. This procedure allows precision gluing and removal of wrinkles and air bubbles.

24

25. Lifting Glued Surfaces

All except wet-mounted rubber cement surfaces (see 21) are difficult to separate unless the dried cement is dissolved with thinner. Flood the glued-down surface with thinner. When it has discolored and penetrated the material, lift one corner gently and add more thinner under the lifted paper edge or corner. Continue lifting and flooding on more thinner until the surfaces are separated. Let both separated surfaces dry thoroughly. Remove the dry rubber cement with a pick-up eraser (see 20) if the same surfaces are not to be glued together again. For remounting them, coat each with another layer of rubber cement and let them dry, or follow any of the various methods for gluing with rubber cement described in 21 through 24 above.

26. Acrylic Adhesives

Acrylic media are a relatively recent development. They are available from art supply stores and school material suppliers. The painting medium itself is water soluble and nontoxic and can be used as an adhesive and, at the same time, as an opaque or transparent varnish and protective coating. When totally dry, it waterproofs whatever it covers. Acrylics are therefore ideal adhesives for collages (see 27) and assemblages (see 28), and as varnish for papier maché (see II.H), painting (see VI.C and D), and sculpting (see VII.D).

27. Collages

Tools and materials
> Paste or glue (see 9–26)
> Empty egg cartons or small boxes
> Found materials (see XIV)
> 8½" x 11" or larger sheets of white construction, drawing, or other paper; brown wrapping paper; shirt board or other cardboard
> Bowl with wide base, filled with water
> Sponge or rags

Keep glue, water, and other materials to one side of a newspaper covered table, depending on the child's "handedness" (see I.j). Let the child sort the different found materials by kind, shape, or color in the egg cartons or other small containers. Then suggest that he or she arrange and paste the materials down on the paper or cardboard. Once started, a child will think of ingenious and original ways of combining the materials, pasting them next to and over each other to achieve a variety of effects.

Demonstrate working methods—how to apply a little glue at a time; how to brush it on; and how to keep the jar closed to prevent the glue's drying out. Point out the contrasting qualities and textures of the materials. Name colors and shapes and assist—but don't do all the work—in cleaning up. Don't show the child how to make pictures or designs. Let him paste as he pleases.

Praise inventiveness, good work habits, and endurance. Don't compare his creations with those produced by other children or by adults, or with reality. Display the child's work. Comment on unique features of his conceptions. Restrict your suggestions to those that will help him achieve what he wants to make in an effective, organized manner.

One of the benefits of arranging and pasting collages is that this accustoms the child to use a variety of materials in unorthodox, inventive combinations. Nothing needs to be what it seems. Anything can be imagined and transformed. His work will become increasingly deliberate as what and how he pastes turn into an act of decision and expression.

Ordinary newsprint can be similarly cut apart and pasted together again so that different patterns of type and portions of photographs are reformed into unique designs. A child can draw or paint into his collage, cut up and use his own drawings, and combine them with found and other materials in decorative ways.

28. Assemblages

Tools and materials
    Found materials (see XIV)
    Paste or glue (see 9–26)
    Wire (see IV.B and C)
    Wood, plywood, or heavy cardboard base

Assemblages are three-dimensional collages. They can be constructed on or around a wood or cardboard base or free-standing wood, wire, or cardboard forms or frames to which other materials are adhered. These can be pasted, nailed, screwed, bolted, or worked on, depending on the availability of materials and tools and the child's level of skill development. Portions can be painted, shellacked, or varnished, and the finished assemblage may stand free, or hang on a wall or from an overhead fixture.

The gradual development of skills and a recognition of the different qualities and possibilities offered by the variety of available materials should be part of a sequence of connected experiences, from tearing pieces of paper to collage and assemblage. Various tools are called into play with a purpose. Those not directly related to paper and foil are discussed elsewhere in this book. But foremost, in order to exercise skills, the child needs encouragement, guidance, opportunities for experience, and appreciation.

29. Paper Mosaics

Tools and materials
> Shallow jewelry or shoebox lid; or picture frame or molding nailed or glued to a
> wood or cardboard base
> Paste (see 9–26)
> Seeds; beans; peas; macaroni shapes; seashells; snippets of white or colored
> paper; punched-out paper (see 5) and other small or cut-apart scrap mate-
> rials (see XIV)

A mosaic can be a kind of collage of small, more or less uniform or dis-
similar, varicolored or monochromatic snippets of material, pasted or
glued within a given area. The box lid or frame helps the child confine
his work area. Within it he can arrange and paste the materials. The area
to be covered should be small. Show the child how to start pasting on
one side or corner of the frame, adhering one small fragment to the tray,
placing another next to it, and working toward opposite sides until the
whole is covered.

Point out to the child that he can design forms, shadings, and shapes
through contrast of color and material as he pastes. Different textures
can be created by juxtaposition of various snippets and fragments. The
object, in this as in all other such activities, is to allow the child to
create his or her own raw materials. This is far preferable to giving him
prepared ones. Here the importance of sequence is demonstrably important. The child can tear paper into small, irregular shapes and use them
to make mosaics before he can cut with scissors. Later he can cut geometric and other shapes out of colored paper for similar assembly. In
turn, this prepares him for more advanced craft, like making and designing with his own ceramic mosaic tiles (see VII.E).

E. FOLDING AND SHAPING PAPER

30. Paper Folding

Tools and materials
> Sheets of bond writing or typing paper; or colored construction paper
> Burnisher; or letter opener with a rounded point; or spoon handle

Paper folding is an art form as old as paper making and, significantly, it
originated in the Orient. Almost every Japanese child still learns
origami—the art of paper folding—on his or her parent's knee. As
pointed out earlier, exclusive exposure to traditional craft forms tends to
create personalities that are the very opposite of those favored in techno-

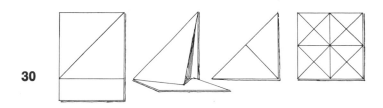

30

logical societies. Yet traditional crafts do preserve essential human qualities. In combination with others that demand greater inventiveness and individuality, they can help foster skills that are in danger of extinction in the modern world. Thus traditional art forms are useful even to children of industrialized cultures, East or West. They need not be followed slavishly, but can be adapted and modified.

The ability to fold a square of paper neatly, corner to corner and edge to edge, should be second nature by the time a child enters school. But how many young people today who are well past this age know how to execute this simple operation? Show your child how to line up one paper edge with another, corner to corner, folding the paper in half neatly and running a finger along the fold once edges and corners meet exactly. The crease should then be burnished with the tool. Unfold the paper to show the crease. Refold and halve the paper a second time, quartering it. Unfold it again.

Most paper folding, like origami (see 32 and 33) or Polish paper cuts (see 41), requires a square piece of paper for a start. With writing and other square-cut papers no measurement is required to turn a rectangle into a square. Take one corner of the paper and bend it over without creasing until one of the two short sides lies directly on top of and parallel to one of the long sides (see diag. 30). Holding the parallel edges in position, make a sharp crease first with a finger and then with the burnisher. A section of the paper will extend beyond the folded triangle. Bend this up and over the side of the triangle so that this new crease is parallel to the paper edge. Burnish the crease, open this flap, and tear or cut it off carefully along the crease. When the triangle is opened it will form a perfect square (see diag. 30).

Suggest that the child make several such squares. Let him then fold and refold the square and subsequent triangles corner to corner, burnishing each crease, until the bulk of the paper prevents further folding. Unfold and point out the diagonal and triangular patterns of creases (see diag. 30).

A child who acquires these simple skills will have first-hand experience with a number of basic geometric principles, even before he can count and measure. This is far more important than the ability to name or construct triangles, squares, and circles with drafting instruments (see XII), precocious counting to one hundred, or tracing templates. Understanding does not follow imitation, rote performance, or memorization, but naming and labeling, as well as understanding, are the by-products of activity. Children learn best by doing what they can do and enjoy.

31. Accordion Folds and Pleats

Tools and materials
Same as 30

Once a child's arm, hand, and finger coordination becomes more refined as a result of simple paper folding, he'll be more adept and deliberate in everything he touches and does. He is now ready for pleating.

Start by folding the paper in half—the long way if it is rectangular. Fold one half of this rectangle in half again and again, each crease parallel to the last (see diag. 31.a) until the first strip is about ½" wide. Unfold. Now, using the first two folded strips as a guide, refold the paper, alternately in one direction and then in the other, to make an accordion pleat (see diag. 31.b).

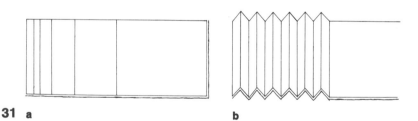

31 a   **b**

By using paper clips and rubber bands to hold different portions in place, the pleated paper can be formed and pasted into various shapes (see diag. 31.c). Several of these can be combined to form more complicated constructions.

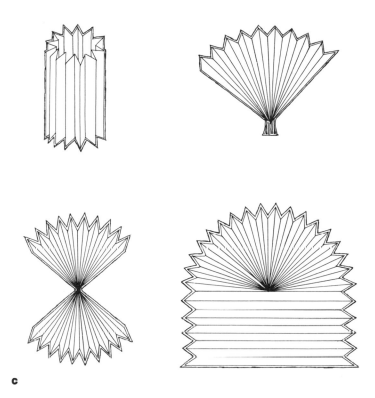

c

Lightweight colored papers offer many design possibilities. Foils can also be used by older children who are sufficiently mature and cautious so as not to cut themselves on sharp corners and edges. Once the principle of accordion pleating is understood, it can be combined with other forms of paper craft and construction (see 38, 39, 42–47, 60–68).

32. Origami for Beginners

Tools and materials
    Square, colored, lightweight paper (see 30)
    Burnisher (see 30)

No one, regardless of age, can tackle origami with any degree of success until he has perfected the skills described in 30 and 31 above. The following examples are not intended to be copied. Encourage the child to invent his own folds and combinations of folds, and to improvise. He

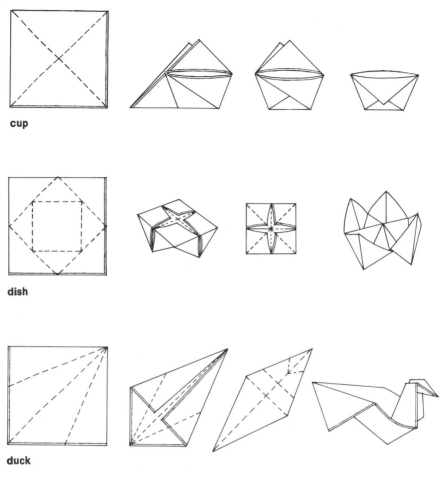

cup

dish

duck

32

will find delight in the shapes he creates. He'll "see" things, animals, and people. Like Ludwig Bemelmans' *Madeline,* he'll discover "that the crack in the ceiling had the habit of sometimes looking like a rabbit."

33. Advanced Origami

Tools and materials
Same as 32

The following are additional and more complex origami folds and constructions that demonstrate some of the possibilities:

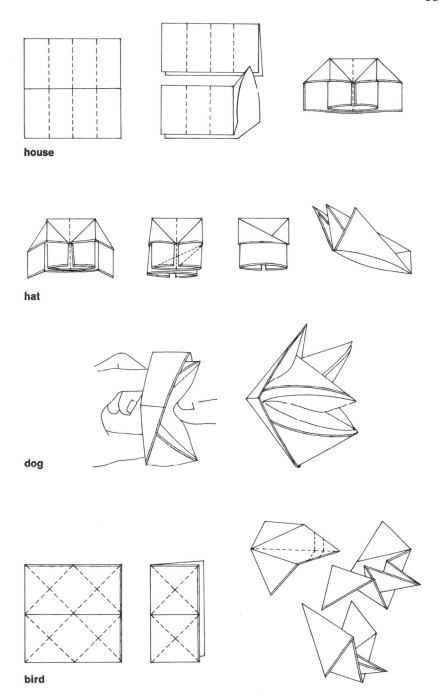

house

hat

dog

bird

33

34. Paper Curling and Curving

Tools and materials
Construction or writing paper
Dowel; unsharpened pencil; rolling pin; or burnisher

A child can curve sheets and strips of paper by winding each around a dowel, pencil, bottle, or rolling pin (see diag. 34.a). He can achieve a similar effect by pulling a paper strip with one hand out from under his other hand or thumb, over a table edge (see diag. 34.b). To make curled paper strips or shapes, pull the paper over one edge of the burnishing tool, wedging the strip between the tool's edge and thumb while pulling.

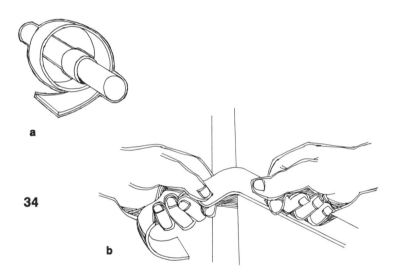

a

34

b

F. EMBOSSING AND CUTTING

35. Embossing on Paper and Foil

Tools and materials
Any pointed, dull instrument; a used-up ballpoint pen; a scriber; or the end of a
    pointed paint brush handle
Several sheets of blotting paper
Masking tape
Writing or any other soft paper; or foil

A pre-schooler can run a scriber across paper or foil taped to blotting paper. Show him how to make impressions deep enough to be visible, but sufficiently light so that the paper does not tear. He can make scribbles, designs, patterns, dots, and dashes. When he turns paper or foil over, he'll discover his designs raised on the other side. He can deepen the impressions by scribing along all edges of the raised designs on the "wrong" side of the paper. Wooden blocks or letters, the ends of short dowels, wire or plastic netting, and other raised designs like cookie cutters can also be pressed into foil placed on top of several sheets of blotting paper or a rubber pad. The aim should be to make embossed designs with a combination of found and created effects, rather than copying or reproducing existing shapes. (See also VI.A.a.)

36. Cutting Paper

Tools and materials
   School scissors (with rounded points)
   Newspaper; construction or bond paper

Don't give your child battery or house-current operated scissors. They may intrigue him but they stand in the way of his developing coordination. Watch a young child's first efforts with a pair of scissors. Notice how many different motor responses are required to guide the tool and cut paper while the two blades are moved in opposite directions. Buy good, school-grade scissors with rounded points. Once he matures the child can be trusted with small, pointed scissors. Make sure that the scissor grip loops are twisted at an angle so that they fit flat against the skin of thumb and forefinger. Inexpensive scissors do not have twisted grips and they cut into the flesh during extended use. Attach the scissors to your child's worktable or workbench with a long ribbon or string— long enough so that he can work without difficulty, but short enough so that it does not quite reach the floor should he drop them while working.

37. First Scissor Cuts

Tools and materials
   Same as 36

Encourage pre-schoolers to cut sheets of newspaper and other paper into snippets at random. Holes can be punched into the cut paper shapes (see 5). They can be laced together (see 7), or used for pasting (see 9–26), collages (see 27), and assemblages (see 28). Later, similar strips can be cut for acetate stained glass (see 40) and for paper weaving (see II.G).

Do not give the child patterns, preprinted or drawn shapes, pictures, or lines to follow in his cutting. He must experiment freely to get the "hang" of the tool. Cutting out printed paper dolls can be fun once in a great while—when he is sick in bed and restricted in activities—but this is not how children develop creatively.

The child's cutting will be ragged at first but it will improve in time. He'll acquire greater control faster if he is left without patterns to follow than when these are imposed on him. The strips and fringes he cuts can be used in a variety of projects (see 42–47 and 52).

38. Folded-Paper Cutting

Tools and materials
Same as 36

A child can cut along the burnished lines of paper he has learned to fold (see 30–33). Folded and accordion-pleated papers allow the child to make "interior" cuts in the paper with scissors (see diag. 38).

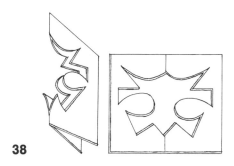

38

39. Cutting Out Paper Shapes

Tools and materials
Scissors
Colored construction paper; drawings and paintings made by the child; photographs and pictures cut from magazines; semi-stiff, starched fabric and felt; ribbons

At this stage of proficiency a child can begin to cut out shapes that interest him from some of the above-listed materials, among others. He can use these cuttings in his collages (see 27) or mount them on bulletin board or wall. Do not show the child how to cut paper flowers, dolls, and other clichés. Let him discover and invent his own forms as he acquires the required skills and feels a need to make them for play and other projects. This may seem like asking each generation of children to reinvent the wheel. But these are precisely the experiences they need to become skilled. Limit what you show the child to basic principles, working method, tool and material use, neat work habits, and safety measures appropriate to his or her maturity.

40. Paper and Acetate Stained Glass

Tools and materials

Lightweight, colored, transparent sheets of acetate or plastic (art supply stores sell this with and without "pressure adhesive" backing); or theatrical lighting gelatin
One sheet of heavier clear acetate or plastic
Clear cellophane adhesive tape
Scissors
Paste or rubber cement (see 9–25)
Black construction paper or insulating tape

Let the child cut long strips of black construction paper or tape, each about ⅛″ to ¼″ wide. The colored transparent acetate or gelatin can then be cut into a variety of shapes and adhered to the clear plastic sheet. The acetate can be overlapped so that different colors are mixed. Then show the child how to paste the strips of black paper or tape all around each separate colored acetate area, as in a stained glass window. The black borders enhance the brilliance of the colors when the completed design is hung against or pasted to a window pane.

Another way of achieving a similar effect is to show the child how to fold the paper to make interior cuts (see 38) or to cut shapes out of the black paper with a knife (see 86), leaving a lace effect. Different-colored pieces of acetate can then be pasted to each opening of the paper lattice.

41. Polish Paper Cuts

Tools and materials

Same as 36

Poland has produced its own unique paper folk art. Some of the classical paper cuts have infinitely variable applications. A child can learn to adapt these to his collages and assemblages and to make decorations and paper objects (see XIII). He will need all or most of the skills described previously in this chapter before he can be expected to manip-

ulate paper in the required manner. These principles are widely used in commercial paper decorations that, after cutting, can be stretched into three-dimensional shapes.

The following diagram shows two of the standard folds and cuts that can be varied, adapted, and combined.

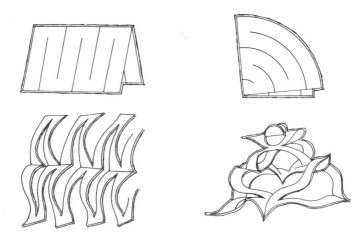

41

G. WINDING AND WEAVING

42. Paper Winding

Tools and materials

Rolls of colored-paper party streamers; or ½″ strips of paper pasted together to
form long ribbons

Transparent glue (see 16); or paste; or water glass (sodium silicate), available in
drug or chemical supply store

Coil the end of the streamer or ribbon to form a solid core (see 34).
Keep winding, pasting the beginning of the next strip to the end of the
last until a firm and solid round, square, or triangular disc of the desired
dimension has been wound (see diag. 42.a). Paste down the end of the
last strip and soak the whole coil thoroughly in transparent glue, paste,
or water glass. Gently press into the center of the saturated coil to form
a hollow shape (see diag. 42.b), or leave the coil in its original state.
Such coils can be combined with others to make mosaics (see 29 and
289), wall hangings, and decorations (see XIII).

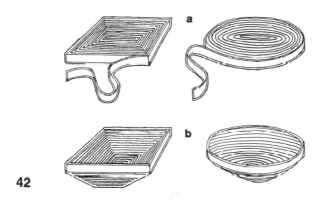

42

43. Paper Strips and Streamers

Tools and materials

Same as 42

Small cardboard cigar boxes; empty, washed glass or plastic bottles

Paper streamers and strips can be wound and pasted around containers,
bins, boxes, and cans. Coat one side or part of the object to be decorated with glue, paste, or water glass. Wind paper strips or ribbons
onto the glued portion. Coat the next section a small area at a time so
that it does not dry before it is covered with paper. The child can paste
snippets, strips, or ribbons of paper side by side, overlapping or criss-

crossing one another in any pattern of his or her choice. When the container has been totally covered, paste down all loose paper ends and coat the whole with transparent glue, paste, or water glass.

44. Rolled and Pasted Paper Beads

Tools and materials
  Sheets of colored construction paper, newspaper, or wallpaper
  Scissors
  Paste or glue (see 9–26); or water glass (see 42)
  Clothespins; or rubber bands
  Wire or string; or toothpicks

Cut 14″ × 2″ strips of paper. Cover one side of each strip with paste, glue, or water glass and roll it up tightly over wire, string, or toothpicks while the glue is wet. Heavier papers must first be curled (see 34) and then pasted or strung onto a dowel or pencil (see diag. 44). Secure the rolled beads with rubber bands or clothespins until dry. Move the beads back and forth along the wire from time to time so that they don't adhere to it. They can be used for jewelry and other ornaments (see XIII), and as modules for mosaics (see 29 and 289), collages (see 27) and assemblages (see 28).

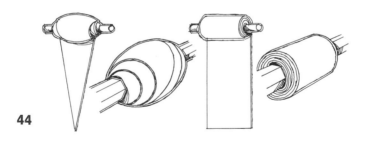

44

45. Paper Weaving

The principles of paper weaving are similar to those required for caning and weaving with fibers, yarn, and thread (see X). A child can discover the basic processes by first experimenting in paper. They are more understandable when first tried on a loom that the child makes himself (see 46 and 47), weaving with strips that are less flexible than spun fibers and more manageable than reeds.

Weaving cloth can be a natural development following weaving with paper. The child then possesses skills on which to build. He will have insights into characteristics of a craft that, once a part of him, is never forgotten. A child who has never woven with paper will find a fabric loom puzzling. He can learn to use it by rote, but he may never fully understand what he is doing.

46. Constructing the Loom

Tools and materials
　　Sheets of 8½″ × 11″ bond or colored construction paper
　　Scissors
　　Sheet of 9″ × 12″ shirt board or other cardboard
　　Masking tape

Fold one sheet of paper in half and cut slots into it at the fold at more or less regular intervals without cutting all the way to the ends of the paper (see diag. 46). Later, when able to use ruler and triangle, the child can lay out the slots with a pencil, each about ¼″ to ½″ apart. Once the principle is understood, various paper shapes—round, triangular, square, and those used in Polish paper cuts (see 41) or scrolls (cut from adding machine tape)—can be used to make looms for different paper weaves.

Tape one end of this "loom" to a sheet of cardboard and it is ready for use.

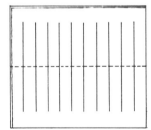

46

47. Paper Weaves

Tools and materials
　　Paper loom (see 46)
　　Colored construction or other papers
　　Scissors
　　Paste (see 9–26)

Cut the paper into strips, each ¼″ to ½″ wide and longer than the loom is wide by at least one inch. Show the child how to start the weave by feeding the first strip over and under successive strips of the loom, and the second over and under alternate strips, and so on (see diag. 47.a).

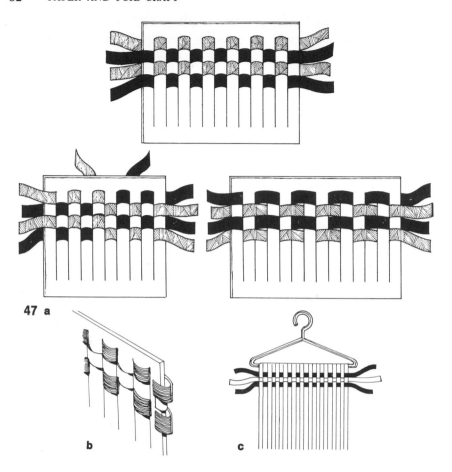

47 a

b   **c**

Different-colored strips can be used in a variety of ways, or different-colored strips can be pasted together to achieve different patterns.

When the loom is filled, cut off all but about ¼″ from each end of the protruding horizontal paper strips that extend beyond both sides, and bend and paste them under the outside vertical strips (see diag. 47.b).

Longer and larger weaves are possible by cutting or pasting long strips of paper together, hanging them, side by side, from a wire clothes hanger to which they are fastened with tape or clothespins (see diag. 47.c). Twist the hook of the clothes hanger so that it can be hung from the back of a chair. Start the paper weave as before. When the loom is filled, bend back the ends of the vertical strips at the bottom of the loom and paste them down on the back side; then bend and paste the protruding horizontal ends on each side; and finally, after carefully removing the tops of the vertical strips from the clothes hanger, bend and paste these ends as well. Then the weave cannot separate.

H. PAPIER MACHÉ

48. The Process

Modeling, building, and forming with papier maché are a favored craft in Japan, China, India, and Mexico. Papier maché consists of shredded paper soaked in a flour paste or glue, formed as a mash or laid in strips over an armature (see 51–54). The objects that can be formed range from abstract and decorative sculpture, landscapes, and panoramas, to play figures, toys, masks, jewelry, pottery, and household articles and utensils.

The two basic papier maché techniques can be used singly or in combination. The mash is useful for forming and molding small objects, or for sculpting or adding detail to larger constructions. The paper strip technique works best when used in combination with armatures (see 52–54). Other materials—string, twine, tinsel, cloth scraps, ribbon, mesh, or netting—can be embedded in or adhered to the papier maché surface or pressed against it to add textures. When thoroughly dry, papier maché can be painted (see 58) or waterproofed (see 59).

Papier maché compounds can be bought commercially. But it is much more useful if the child learns to prepare his own (see 49 and 50).

49. Mash

Tools and materials
> Newspaper; egg cartons; construction and tissue paper, shredded and torn into small pieces
> Large mixing bowl
> Flour
> Water
> Common or library paste (see 14 and 15)
> Oil of cloves

Soak the torn and shredded paper for a day and a half in warm water until it turns to pulp. Drain off excess water and squeeze whatever surplus water you can out of the remainder. Mix flour and water to the consistency of heavy cream. Add paste (see 14 and 15) for extra stickiness. Stir and knead in the pulped paper. The mash should be the consistency of clay for use as a modeling compound. It must be thinned with water until it can be poured if it is to be used as a molding compound or for adding detail to or decorating papier maché strip constructions (see 50). The proportions of the ingredients can be varied for different uses. Finally, add a few drops of oil of cloves as a preservative.

Instead of the above mixture, prepared wheat paste can be added to the pulp.

50. Papier Maché Strip Construction

Tools and materials
Same as 49, except that the paper is torn into strips of different widths

Prepare the same paste mixture detailed in 49. Add a small handful of paper strips to the mixture, letting them soak for from ten to fifteen minutes before use. Run each strip through between the second and third finger of one hand to remove excess moisture and paste, before laying it over the armature (see 51–54).

Papier maché strip construction requires ample working space, arranged so that the child can reach and use all the required materials without confusion (see I.j). Cover all work surfaces and the floor with several layers of taped-down newsprint and provide boxes to hold the different widths of torn paper strips. A wide-based bowl filled with paste is less likely to spill than one that has a narrow base.

51. Armatures

Armatures are essential for working with papier maché strips and for large modeling and sculpting projects involving mash. An armature is a three-dimensional skeleton of the object to be formed, over which the papier maché strips (or other modeling compounds) are laid. Armatures can be made out of a large variety of materials (see 52–54).

52. Armatures Made out of Paper

Tools and materials
Newspaper
Masking tape
String or twine
Scissors

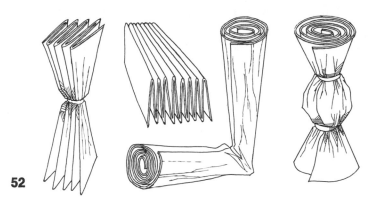

52

Show the child how to fold, twist, and bundle newspaper into skeleton shapes of whatever he wishes to make out of papier maché. Each individual bundle should be taped or tied and then attached to others until the shape of the wanted figure is roughly constructed (see diag. 52). The armature need only be solid enough so that it can be worked with while the papier maché strips are laid over it. Once dry, the papier maché will add strength to the armature and it will become rigid. When the child is satisfied that the armature approximates the contours of the intended object, show him how to cover it with individual strips of paper soaked in paste (see 50), fleshing out shapes and adding detail with wadded, soaked strips or mash (see 49), adhered with other strips to the main body of the work.

The paste-soaked strips should overlap. Several layers are required until the wall thickness is built up, to withstand usage. When the armature has been covered with one layer, the next should be applied at right angles to the first wherever possible. The width and length of the strips depend on which fit the contours of the object being formed: $2'' \times 12''$ strips can be used for gently curved or relatively flat surfaces, $\frac{3}{4}'' \times 6''$ strips are required for more acute curves.

53. Armatures Made out of Cardboard

Tools and materials

    Shirt board; shoe or jewelry boxes; corrugated board and boxes
    Coping saw, jigsaw, or keyhole saw (see 114 and 120); sharp mounting or craft
       knife for more experienced young people (see 86 and 87)
    Masking or packaging tape

The age, maturity, experience, and strength of the child determine which materials and tools he can use. Shirt board can be cut with a large scissors, but heavier cardboard and corrugated board must be cut with a coping saw, jigsaw, keyhole saw, or sharp knife. Young children can bend, twist, and tape shirt board into desired shapes and, in combination with bundles of newspaper (see 52) and lumber scraps, form armatures for papier maché. Suggest that, wherever possible, existing shapes be used and combined with others. For example, a small cardboard box or box lid can, with a few additions, form a satisfactory armature for a papier maché toy house, tray, or container.

54. Armature Made out of Other Materials

Tools and materials
> Toy balloons; sand filled plastic bags; empty plastic bottles; wire; pipe cleaners; wood scraps; pebbles; clay; modeling compounds, among other materials

Virtually any expendable, easily worked material can be used by itself or in combination with others to form papier maché armatures. A blown-up toy balloon, approximately the same size as a child's head, can be a useful armature for a papier maché mask, bowl, or other container. Puncture or deflate the balloon and remove it when the papier maché has dried completely. Paper or sand filled plastic bags can be used similarly as armatures for different shapes that need to be hollow when completed. Coat any material that must be separated from the dried papier maché with a thin layer of Vaseline or vegetable oil before covering it with strips or mash, or the papier maché may adhere to it.

Pipe cleaners (see 142), plastic covered wire (see 145 and 146), and coat hanger wire (see 149–152) are useful for armatures that will be totally enclosed with papier maché. Wire or plastic mesh or netting fastened to the wire armature will cut down on weight and the amount of papier maché required to cover these armatures.

Wood scraps and waste lumber can be taped or nailed together (see 107–111) and combined with other materials to make larger and more substantial armatures when required.

55. Papier Maché Pottery

Tools and materials
> Same as 49–54

Most Oriental lacquered bowls and dishes are made out of papier maché painted with several coats of lacquer. Similar vessels can be constructed using either mash (see 49) or strip (see 50) techniques, or a combination of both. The papier maché can be pressed into various Vaseline-coated molds (see 57) or laid over similarly greased armatures that are removable, like paper boxes, inflated balloons, or sand-filled plastic bags (see 54). (See also 262–267 for clay and other pottery techniques, many of which are applicable to papier maché; and 282–284 for additional molding information.)

56. Adding Detail to Sculptures and Objects

Tools and materials

Twigs; dowels; paper clips; string; twine; buttons; ribbon; discarded Ping Pong, tennis, and other balls; whole and cut-apart egg boxes; bottle tops; and other found or discarded parts and materials (see XIV)

Any of these can be embedded in or covered with papier maché, and added and adhered to armatures or partially completed papier maché constructions to add detail and texture. Make the child conscious of the possibility of such improvisation whenever possible. Help him discover the diversity and nature of found and improvised materials. Provide him with some and suggest that he discover others for himself.

57. Molding with Papier Maché

Do not give the child prepared toy molds to fill with papier maché mash, or objects to copy. This, like every other art and craft, should foster invention. However, molding is a process with which the child should be familiar. The molds should consist of found materials or they can be improvised or made by the child from materials he has combined, invented, or constructed. A child may wish to duplicate his own work or make multiples—like wheels for a toy he builds.

Show the child how to make the original object. In the case of a wheel, for instance, he will only need to press a dowel end or some other circular object into modeling compound, clay, or plaster of Paris (see 282–285). When the mold has dried thoroughly, it must be coated with Vaseline or vegetable oil. Papier maché mash or strips (see 49 and 50) can then be laid into the open mold. Remove the molded object after it has dried completely, coat the mold with more Vaseline, and repeat the process for additional identical castings.

Papier maché shrinks considerably as it dries. Hence there is likely to be some variation between successively cast papier maché shapes. Do not apply heat or place papier maché into an oven. It is flammable, and the slower it dries, the less shrinkage and distortion there will be.

Plastic ice cube trays and other existing shapes and cavities can be used to mold components for child originated constructions. They differ from commercially produced toy molds insofar as they make a demand on the child to discover them, their possibilities, and the uses to which they can be put as a part of his own creations.

58. Painting Papier Maché

(See below for required materials.)

When thoroughly dry, papier maché formed, sculpted, or molded objects can be painted with any medium. Poster paints (see 206) and acrylics (see 237) are recommended. More mature children who can be relied on to wash hands and brushes with the required solvents and with soap and water after they have completed their work, can use oil paints, japan colors, lacquers, and enamels applied in thin, successive layers (see 227–247). Water glass (see 42) or wood sealer (see 137), which closes the pores of the material, is a useful undercoating for these finishes. Or several coats of white poster paint or gesso (see 232–235) when overpainted with other poster colors or acrylics will bring out their brilliance.

59. Preserving Papier Maché Objects

Several thin coats of shellac, clear varnish (see 139), water glass (see 42) or transparent glue (see 16) brushed on lightly over fully dry, unpainted or painted papier maché objects, will strengthen, protect, waterproof, and preserve them indefinitely. Wait until each coat is completely dry before applying the next. Never allow a child to use spray cans and, preferably, do not use them yourself (see I.k and 227). Read carefully the labels on cans of commercially available coatings and follow given directions and cautions.

I. PAPER CONSTRUCTION

60. Building with Paper

In the Orient, especially in Japan, paper has been used extensively for hundreds of years as a building and construction material for houses and furniture. In the West even paper bags as we know them were not in use until about one hundred years ago. Before then, back to the late seventeen hundreds, dry foods like sugar and cereal were sold at retail packaged in folded paper cones. Traditionally, similar cones were filled with candy, a slate, and chalk, and given to children by their parents when they first entered school.

Paper construction as a craft for children became popular in Europe around the end of the eighteenth century. At about that time large sheets of paper imprinted with cutout designs appeared in France, Germany, Holland, and England. They included toy houses; dress-up dolls; toy soldiers; theaters and puppets; and panoramas of towns, farms, castles, and battlefields, some printed in black and white, others hand or stencil colored. They involved very complicated scissor cuts, gluing, and assembly. Later such paper cutout sheets included mechanical toys and scenes, operated by string or by sand running out of a funnel over a paper wheel.

Many of these same cutouts were still available in France twenty years ago, by which time they included three-dimensional railway train, ship, early dirigible, balloon, and airplane models, similar to those now only available in plastics. The publishers of these prints were descended from fourteenth and fifteenth century woodblock engravers and printers of religious pictures, playing cards, game sheets, and, later, ballad sheets bought by adults. During the late eighteenth and early nineteenth centuries these same publishers turned to creating children's cutouts. One of them, the Imprimerie D'Epinal, founded in 1748, is still functioning at its original location in Alsace-Lorraine. Unfortunately, this printer doesn't publish children's cutouts any more. The original woodblocks, the stencils by which these early cutouts were colored, and the paper constructions of the past can now be seen only in museums. More recent published paper constructions include a working model of a pendulum clock, every gear and part made out of paper, that can still be bought in France today.

During the past seventy-five years paper and cardboard construction graduated from the toy store. It became a craft employed by architects, engineers, artists, and designers. Around 1900, textbooks for engineering students included complicated paper-constructed exploded views and sometimes partially operating models of inventions, including steam engines, airplanes, and submarines, designed as teaching and learning aids. These examples demonstrate just what is possible with paper construction. As a craft medium for children it requires experience in some of the more fundamental skills detailed in earlier portions of this chapter. When these are mastered to some degree, and after young people have become familiar with the basic characteristics of the material from direct experience, the way is open for more advanced paper construction.

61. Slot Construction

Tools and materials
> A deck of old playing cards; or 3″ × 5″ rectangular file cards; or similar size shirt board or heavy construction paper
> Scissors

Demonstrate how cuts can be made into the sides of cards so that each can be slotted to the next, slot to slot (see diag. 61.a). Cards with cuts made at right angles to their sides up to and slightly beyond the center can be slotted together so that they will stand on a more or less level surface. Four square or rectangular cards with two such slots cut into one side each will form a free-standing box that needs only top and bottom pasted or taped to it to enclose it fully. Show the child the dividers in corrugated food and beverage cartons that are joined in just such a manner. A child can use this principle for a great variety of paper and cardboard construction. Paper plates, cups, and lightweight cardboard tubes can be jointed in the same way (see diags. 61.b and 92).

To stimulate the use of this principle in children's paper and cardboard craft, I originated a toy, The Builder, first shown in New York's Museum of Modern Art in 1953. That year Charles Eames, the furniture designer, created his House of Cards, coincidentally employing the same principle although in a slightly varied form. Both toys, enjoyed by several generations of children, have since been copied widely. Regrettably such playthings are given children as substitutes rather than as inspirations for craft activities. These and similar experiences should be used to encourage them to explore principles and materials in related craft.

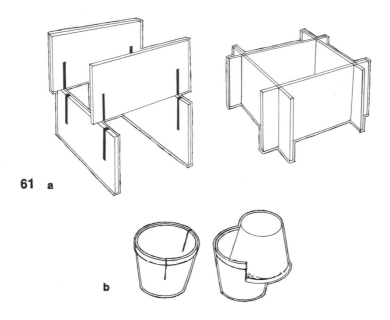

61 **a**

b

When slotting material thicker than playing card or construction paper stock, and especially when using cardboard (see 83), the slots should be cut a shade wider than the thickness of the material or else it will bind at the joints when pieces are slotted together.

62. Paper Joints and Levers

Tools and materials
> Shirt board; old playing cards; file cards; heavy construction paper
> Scissors
> Hole punch (see 5)
> Paper clasps; or grommet set (see 6) and hammer
> String or twine
> Heavy sheet of cardboard, plywood, or scrap lumber for working surface

Jointed paper dolls and jumping jacks were among the first European paper toys produced during the late seventeen hundreds. They were children's favorites, then as now. Similar jointed, lever operated puppets, made out of parchment and used for shadow plays, were known in Indonesia, Burma, and Turkey for many centuries. In Europe jointed paper dolls were printed on lightweight paper and sold as penny sheets. They needed to be mounted on stiffer paper or cardboard, cut out, and

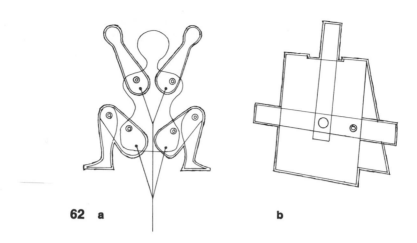

62 a   **b**

assembled with string. Any child can use these principles of paper joint-ing to create a great variety of playthings, mobile constructions, and lever operated toys.

Cut the paper or card stock into strips 1″ × 5″ or longer, punch a hole at both ends of each (see 5), insert grommets, and join one to the next with string or paper clasps (see diag. 62.a). The same principle, using paper strips as levers, can be employed to make mobile and animated toys, mechanisms, and designs (see diag. 62.b).

63. Scoring Paper with a Scriber

Tools and materials
  Soft pencil (see 203)
  Ruler
  Construction paper
  Scriber; used-up ballpoint pen, or other dull, pointed instrument

Paper construction often requires sharp folds (see 30–33 and 41) and creases. Sometimes the texture and weight of the paper cause ordinary folds to be uneven or wavy, or to crack. Heavy or textured papers should always be crease scored with a scriber before they are folded.

Draw a line with pencil and ruler from one side of the paper to the other, or wherever the paper is to be folded. Then place the ruler so that the line is just visible. Next, run the scriber along the ruler's edge, pressing on the point sufficiently hard to emboss the paper without breaking its surface. It will then fold easily along the scored line.

Wavy, round, and semicircular scores can be made free-hand or along templates (see 68). Such scores are especially effective in paper sculpture (see 98). When combined with straight scores and cuts, curved scores lend dimension and texture to paper design (see diag. 63).

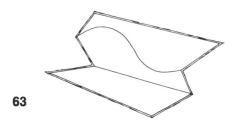

63

64. Scoring with a Knife

Tools and materials
Same as 63
Metal-edge ruler
Mounting or craft knife; X-acto blade; surgical scalpel

Heavy paper and cardboard require cut-scores before they can be folded. Obviously this is not to be done by young children. Instead of using the scriber (see 63), run the knife blade along the marked line and the metal edge of the ruler, cutting no deeper than halfway through the material. It will then bend without cracking. Needless to say, the material is substantially weakened at such a fold and may require tape or other interior support in some constructions. (Observe the safety cautions suggested in 86 and 87 when making such cuts.)

65. Making a Scoring Board

Professional package designers and paper sculptors use a scoring board to emboss sharp creases into paper. If a child or class plans to do a great deal of paper folding or constructing, it pays to make such a board.

Tools and materials
12″ metal-edge wooden ruler
Two pieces of sanded, seasoned pine, 14″ × 3″ × 1″ each
One dowel, ¾″ × 6″
Three dowels, ½″ × 4″ each
Brace and ½″ drill bit (or hand drill)

Mallet
Two woodworking clamps with at least 7″ jaw openings (see 112)
Woodworking vise (see 113)
Plane
Sandpaper
White paste (see 15–18)
Soft pencil

Mark and drill three ½″ holes into the wooden ruler at indicated points. Drill three matching holes, as indicated, into one edge of each pine board, each at least 1⅞″ deep (see diag. 65.a). Lock one of the boards into the vise, the edge with holes drilled into it facing up. Cover that edge and the three ½″ dowels with paste, and glue the ruler to it, using the pegs as fasteners. Cover the edge of the second board into which holes were drilled with paste and glue it to pegs and ruler. Tap the uppermost edge of the second board with the mallet until ruler and boards are closely joined. Then remove the construction from the vise and clamp it lightly until the glue has dried thoroughly (see diag. 65.b). Wipe off any excess glue that seeps out of the joints.

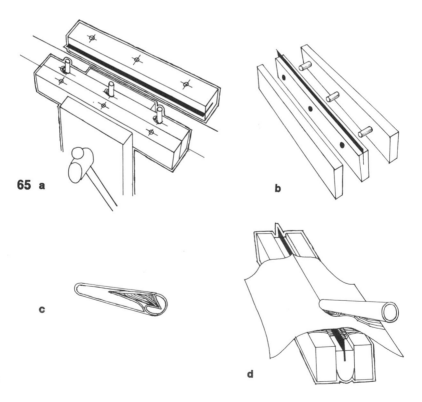

65 a

b

c

d

Use the plane and sandpaper to even the bottom of the unit, if required, so that the board lies flat and firm on the table when placed right side up. Now shape the ¾″ dowel end and notch as shown (see diag. 65.c). Sand the notch until it is well rounded.

Show the child how to draw a line on paper where it is to be creased or folded. Be sure to extend the pencil line to the very edges of the paper. Then place the paper on top of the scoring board and line up the ends of the pencil line with the protruding metal edge of the ruler. Holding the paper firmly down with one hand, run the notched dowel along the pencil line so that the notch engages the metal edge under the paper (see diag. 65.d). Press sufficiently hard to emboss the line into the paper, but not so hard as to crack the paper surface. When removed from the scoring board, the paper will fold easily along the score. If an even, clean score is not achieved at first, the notch carved in the dowel may need further sanding or shaping.

66. Planning and Layout

At early stages all paper construction should be spontaneous and improvised. Parts can be cut, formed, scored, and pasted to one another as the work progresses. There is no need to measure or to construct along geometric lines. Even professional model makers often make such spontaneous constructions to develop new forms. Parts are added with tape or stapled to previously constructed ones. Others are cut off or moved to a different position. When the design has reached its ultimate pleasing shape, it may be a mass of small pieces joined to one another. Component forms can then be disassembled, laid out flat, and used as templates (see 68) for more finished work. Reconstruction from these templates requires some use of drafting instruments in many cases. Even before he can count, add, and subtract, a child can learn to use a compass, triangles, and a ruler for simple geometric designing (see XII). Such planning can also be learned from paper folding (see 30 and 31).

The following details some of the designing skills that are useful in paper construction. Be sure to encourage the child to develop a form spontaneously as a paper mock-up (see 67) before he details his design and works it out more precisely. Placement of folds, scores, glue laps, and locks and other tabs must first be established by trial and error and by improvisation before they can be placed with precision.

67. Paper Mock-Ups

Tools and materials
Construction or heavy bond paper
Scissors
Scriber (see 63) or scoring board (see 65)
Masking tape, paper clips, stapler, and paste

There are many ways of constructing an ordinary paper cube or box. Teaching a child one or all of the various methods is futile. He must experiment spontaneously before he can understand construction principles. Let him cut out pieces of paper and join them with tape, paper clips, or a stapler to form solid shapes. They may not be neat and square, but he'll discover methods of construction—what works and what doesn't work.

This technique is useful for discovering and inventing geometric as well as nongeometric organic forms. It is used by professionals for working out folds, creases, angles, curves, and shapes, and for fitting one surface to the next while taking advantage of the tension and malleability of the material. In working in this manner, it soon becomes obvious that different weights of paper and other supplementary materials can be useful or are essential in various portions of a complex structure.

A young child will be perfectly satisfied with such a relatively crude mock-up. Rough construction details can be covered with colored paper or poster paints. At later stages young people may wish to execute more-finished versions after working out construction details on their paper mock-ups. Show them how to cut through some of the taped or stapled sides and folds so that the whole design, or major portions, can be separated and unfolded to lie flat on the table. The whole design, or significant portions, is then seen as one continuous surface with the required scores, folds, and joints clearly indicated. Be sure to mark on this layout which side must be glued or jointed to which edge. Then such a layout can serve as a rough template or plan for more precise construction.

68. Paper Templates

A paper or any other template is simply a shape worked out so that it can be reproduced or traced onto another piece of material. For example, it is easier to design a single equilateral triangle (see XII) and, having made a template of it, to repeat it as often as necessary, than to construct a whole figure, such as shown in diag. 76, for example, geometrically throughout.

The paper mock-up (see 67), cut apart and unfolded, can become a rough model for a more-finished and precise template made with ruler, compass, triangle, and other drafting instruments (see XII). A final template can then be constructed to be copied, reproduced, or repeated as many times as required.

69. Geometric Reconstruction of Mock-Ups

Tools and materials
Tracing paper or lightweight bond paper
Pencil and drafting instruments (see XII)

The unfolded mock-up (see 67) allows the child to study structure prior to making a final template (see 68) and adding required construction and closure details (see 70–72). Suggest that he make such a drawing on tracing or bond paper for later transfer to a clean sheet of construction paper (see 291). The addition of glue laps and joints where edges of the construction meet is essential (see 70–72).

70. Glue Laps

Tools and materials
Same as 67 and 68

The flattened-out mock-up template will contain one or more sides that, when reassembled, need to be fastened to other edges. One method of making such joints neatly requires the addition of a glue lap to one of each set of two sides that are to be fastened (see diag. 70.a). Each such

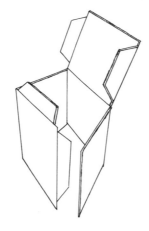

70 a

glue lap should be slightly shorter than the length of the side to which it is to be attached so that the corners don't bulk and buckle when the two matching edges are pasted together. Each glue lap should be pasted to the underside of the paper edge to which it is to be attached.

When making geometric constructions like a cube or a box, the side to which a glue lap is attached should be shorter by the thickness of the material used than the other sides (see diag. 70.b). Add each required glue lap to the template or layout, score the line where glue lap and side are joined, bend the glue lap down, and paste it to the underside of the matching edge.

b

71. Slot and Tab Joints

Tools and materials
> Same as 67 and 68
> Mounting knife (see 64)

If you have taken folding cartons apart, you may have noticed that many are not glued together. Some are held firmly with slot and tab joints (or with lock joints; see 72). A child can learn to make these also. He can then build paper constructions that can be set up, taken apart, folded and stored flat, and set up again repeatedly.

Each of two edges to be joined in this manner requires the addition of a tab, identical to the glue lap (see 70). One of each set of two tabs should be shorter than the other (see diag. 71.a). If the sides to be joined are longer than two or three inches, two such short tabs should be added to one of the two sides instead of one (see diag. 71.b). The longer tab must then be cut at the score so that the short tab or tabs can be pushed into and through a matching slot or slots.

To assure that tab and slot line up precisely, center the shorter of the two tabs on top of the score at which the longer tab is attached to its

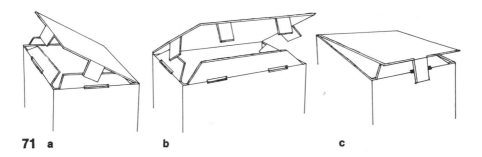

71 a   b   c

side and mark the width of the short tab onto the score (see diag. 71.c).
With a sharp blade, cut the slot a shade wider than the marked space.
Bend both tabs down and, after all have been added in required places,
fold the construction and push the short tabs into matching slots.

72. Lock Joints

Tools and materials
Same as 67 and 68

Slot and tab joints can be constructed so that they lock and cannot be
separated, once joined, without tearing the paper. Design tabs and
matching laps as before (see 71). Cut the sides of the short tab or tabs at
acute angles and trace their widest dimension onto the laps. Make a
small incision—less than $^1/_{16}''$ deep—on each side of the tab where it
joins the side to which it is attached (see diag. 72.a). Cut the matching
slot on the lap a shade shorter than the greatest width of the tab. Then,
when the construction is assembled, force the tab into the cut made in
the lap (see diag. 72.b). Such a joint will not open or separate.

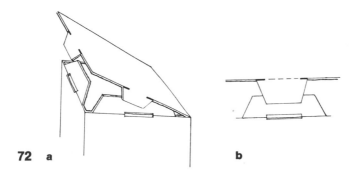

72 a   b

73. Basic Geometric Forms

Tools and materials
    White bond or construction paper
    Drafting instruments (see XII)
    Scissors and sharp knife blade (see 64, 86, 87, 134, and 135)

The basic forms illustrated in following sections can be adapted, changed, and combined with others a young paper craftsman may improvise on his or her own. Proportions, rather than measurements, are given. These can be converted easily into inches or centimeters. All closures are glue lap joints (see 70) but they can be altered to be slot and tab or lock joints without difficulty (see 71 and 72). All cuts, except internal slots, are designed to be made with a pair of scissors. Once the young craftsman can be trusted with a sharp knife blade, he or she can make these constructions with precision. (See also III.D and XII for geometric construction instructions.)

74. Designing a Tube and Cylinder

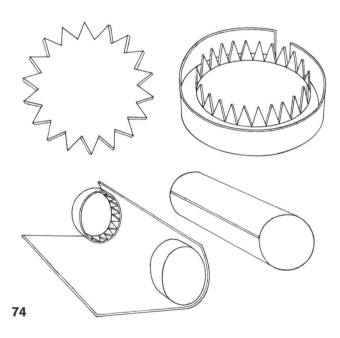

74

75. Designing a Cube and Rectangular Box

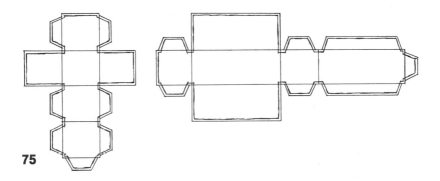

75

76. Designing a Pyramid

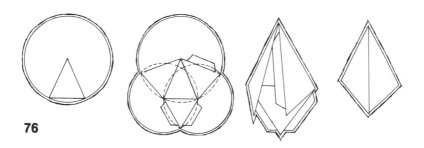

76

77. Designing a Cone

77

78. Designing a Sphere

78

79. Designing a Hexagon and Octagon

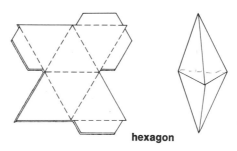

hexagon

79

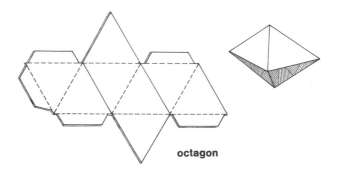

octagon

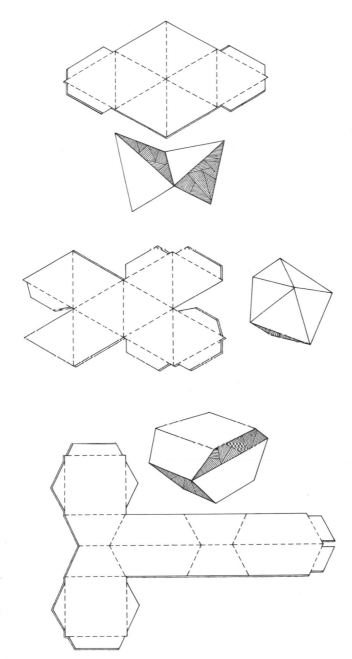

80. Other Geometric Shapes

81. Designing Nongeometric Shapes

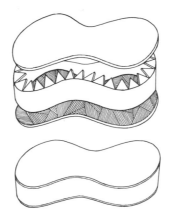

81

82. Combining Shapes

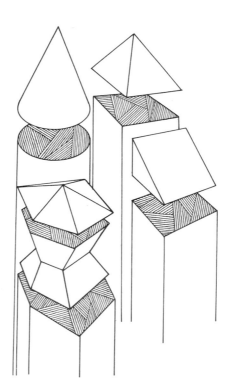

82

J. CARDBOARD CONSTRUCTION

83. Building With Cardboard

Collages, assemblages, designs, models, toys, usable child- and adult-size furniture and storage spaces can be made entirely out of cardboard or corrugated board or with these materials in combination with others. Cardboard "carpentry" has become something of a separate craft. It is a useful preparation for working in wood. Most of the methods employed can be used for both wood and paper. Most of the tools required for paper construction apply, as well as some used in woodwork. Young people as yet too inexperienced to use a sharp knife blade can work safely with a coping saw or jigsaw (see 114) or a keyhole or back saw (see 120) to cut cardboard and corrugated board.

Cardboard is a mixture of raw wood pulp, scrap paper, and cloth fibers, cooked and pressed, like paper (see II.A), into unbleached sheets of varying thickness. These different plies are then glued together and laminated depending on the required thickness. First used as a packaging material in the nineteenth century, cardboard has become increasingly important as construction material as well. Because it is largely composed of recycled fibers, it also has value in conserving the diminishing reservoir of natural raw materials.

Cardboard is available in a large variety of grades, ranging from soft, pulpy board used for egg cartons and shirt board, to heavier boards lined on one or both sides with paper. The latter are used for folding and set-up boxes and posters. Still better grades include railroad board, illustration board, backing board for pads of drawing and writing paper, and binder's board used for library bindings of books. Fluted, corrugated cardboard is now available in several plies also. In addition, there exists a range of composition boards consisting of paper or cardboard laminated to thin sheets of plywood, foam-core plastics, and asbestos, used mostly for packaging and building insulation. Finally, there are cardboard tubes that are available in a range of wall thicknesses, diameters, lengths, and strengths. All of them, with the exception of asbestos board, make excellent craft materials for young people. Asbestos board tends to crumble, and the dust, if inhaled, is a health hazard.

Raw or lined cardboard and corrugated board can be used as is or painted (see 206 and 227–240). Raw cardboard can be primed before painting with other than poster paints (see 137). It can also be lined with white or colored paper or foil (see 10–26 and 84).

84. Laminating Paper and Foil to Cardboard

Tools and materials
  Cardboard or corrugated board
  White or colored papers and foils
  Paste or glue (see 10–26)

It is easier and quicker to laminate large sheets of paper to cardboard before cutting it up into smaller pieces. Slip-sheeting (see 24) is necessary if rubber cement and the dry-mounting method are used. When covering large areas of paper and cardboard with paste or cement, use a square of cardboard as a spreader instead of a brush. Faster, better, and more even coverage is then obtained (see 21).

85. Cardboard Cutting and Drilling

Professional model makers use mounting knives, surgical scalpels, and X-acto blades to cut and score cardboard (see 86–88). If sufficiently experienced and mature, the young craftsman should learn to use these tools. At younger ages children can cut flat cardboard and tubes using a coping saw or jigsaw (see 114) or a keyhole or back saw (see 120). Holes can be drilled with a hand drill and bit (see 116) or punched with an awl (see 132). Older children can cut lightweight cardboard, like shirt board, with scissors. The size, strength, maturity, and reliability of the child determine which of these tools he can use safely.

86. Using Sharp Tools and Knives

(See also I.k and III.A.e.)

Until he is sufficiently experienced and reliable, even an older child should not work with sharp tools except under close adult supervision. Anyone is bound to cut himself at some time while using them. The relative severity or harmlessness of such cuts depends on observance of simple but imperative safety rules. To deprive children of developing the necessary self-discipline and caution means to invite possibly serious injury later. My five-year-old daughter, practiced in craft since earliest ages, has learned to cut linoleum blocks with sharp gouges, under supervision, without harming herself. My four-year-old son can do the

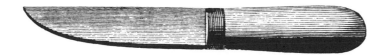

same. They know how to handle tools with respect and they recognize that the privilege of working with tools depends on their willingness to stick to the rules. They have learned that even momentary inattention, carelessness, taking a short cut, or nonobservance of the rules can lead to painful and possibly bloody results, to say nothing of the possible loss of privilege to work with these materials.

Set the stage for eventual careful use of potentially dangerous tools by introducing children to simple and safe ones at early ages and by insisting on the same precautions and disciplines in their use as for those they will need later. With such preparation sharp and pointed tools can be introduced eventually. The following precautions are worth observing:

a. Never walk about holding a pair of scissors or a knife, unless absolutely necessary. Then carry the tool by the handle, blade pointing ahead and toward the ground.

b. Provide only finely sharpened and honed, rust-free tools inserted into an appropriate holder. The handle should be long enough to fit the child's hand, allowing him to hold the tool without touching the blade itself. Dull, ragged, or rusty tools cause serious and infectious injuries.

c. Check before use the locking device that holds a knife blade in its holder and assure that there is no "play" in the blade.

d. When not in use store the tool, metal parts lightly coated with oil or Vaseline, wrapped in wax paper, in a cloth or leather sheath or in a tool rack, out of reach of young children.

e. To cut paper foil or cardboard with a knife blade: Draw the line along which the cut is to be made with a pencil and a ruler or T-square. Cut only along the edge of a metal T-square (see diag. 86); never use a straightedge (it can slip), or a plastic or wooden edge, along which to

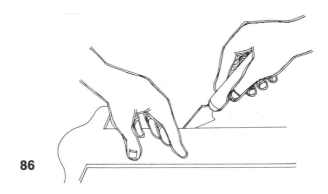

86

run a knife. Hold the knife in one hand and the T-square down onto the paper or board with the fingers of the other hand spread apart. Check the position of the fingers on the T-square before cutting, to make sure that no finger tip projects beyond the metal edge along which the cut is to be made. Make several passes with the knife blade along the pencil line using the metal edge as the guide. Never attempt to cut through heavy paper or even lightweight cardboard with a single pass of the blade.

f. Teach young people to keep their eyes on the blade while cutting: never to look away, even for a moment, and to stop cutting if their attention is required elsewhere.

g. Demonstrate how to keep the hand holding the T-square or the material *behind* the knife blade and never ahead of it. This is especially important when whittling or carving wood, cutting wood and linoleum blocks, and using chisels and gouges. Always make cuts or gouge material in a direction away from the hand holding the material.

h. Sharp knives and tools momentarily laid aside on the work table should be embedded in a kneaded eraser.

i. Teach young people how to hold sharp and pointed tools.

j. Keep a first aid kit near work areas. The kit should include Band-Aids, bandage, surgical tape, mild disinfectant, a rubber band to use as a temporary tourniquet, and a tube of Vaseline or other protective salve for burns.

87. First Aid Hints

Accidents need not happen but sometimes they do. It's good to know what to do when they occur. A slight cut in finger or hand made with a sharp tool may be deep, but it is seldom dangerous if attended to at once. Let the cut bleed for a few seconds unless the blood gushes. Wash a slightly bleeding wound with soap and warm water and then run cold water over it for a second or two. Dry the wound with sterile gauze and pour a small amount of mild disinfectant over it before applying Band-Aid or bandage. If the wound does not close by itself when the finger or hand is held normally, seek a physician's or clinic's advice at once; it may need a stitch or two. Further, unless the child has received a tetanus shot or booster within the past year, he should be taken to a clinic and injected at once, especially if the tool used was dirty or rusty.

If the bleeding does not stop within a few minutes or if the blood gushes, hold the child's hand overhead to give the blood a chance to clot. If it continues to gush or spurt or refuses to clot, prior to taking the child to clinic or physician apply a rubber band or tightly bound bandage to the base of the finger or to the wrist (or at the nearest pressure point) for a minute at a time (but no longer), until the child reaches medical care. Release this tourniquet periodically and apply again as needed. Keep an eye on the finger or limb continually. Remove the tourniquet at once if the limb changes color or turns pale due to lack of circulation.

In the event that the tip of a finger is cut off, replace it at once and hold it firmly in place with Band-Aid or taped-down surgical gauze. If this is done promptly, the tip can be sewn back by a physician or it will grow back in place by itself.

All this may sound frightening. None of it is likely to happen if safety precautions are heeded. Still, it pays to be prepared for all contingencies. (See also I.k.)

88. Scoring Cardboard

Cardboard, unlike paper, cannot be scored with a scriber or with a scoring board. It requires knife scores (see 64 and 86).

89. Jointing Cardboard

Rigid cardboard can be glued (see 10–26) surface to surface, surface to edge, or edge to edge (see diag. 89.a). It can be taped together with paper packaging tape or plastic strapping tape, or scored (see 88). It can also be slot jointed (see 61).

Layers of cardboard can be laminated and built up to be jointed like wood. For example, two layers of cardboard, one smaller all around and centered on the larger of the two, form lap joints all around (see diag. 89.b). These can be glued or taped to other lap jointed shapes and, if necessary, supported by braces glued into corners for additional strength. Many of the standard wood joints (see III.E) can be built up and used in cardboard constructions.

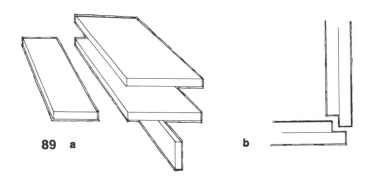

89   a   b

90. Flexible, Fluted Cardboard Strips

Flexible, fluted cardboard, more malleable than the corrugated kind, can be bought in rolls or found, used as protective wadding and as buffers in containers for large appliances. It can be cut into strips with scissors or a knife, bent parallel with the fluting (cut-scored for folds at right angles to the fluting), rolled, curved and coiled, glued, taped, or stapled to itself and to other materials. It is especially useful for making armatures (see 51–54 and 277) and as a base for papier maché, clay, or plaster panoramas or landscapes.

91. Corrugated Cardboard

Cut-apart grocery cartons or sheets of corrugated board available from stationery stores, storage warehouses, and movers can be cut into various shapes with a sharp knife blade or with a coping saw, jigsaw, keyhole saw, or back saw (see 85). It can be bent parallel to the fluting without scoring. Bends at right angles to the fluting require cut scores (see 64). Several layers of corrugated board, laminated to each other, are sufficiently strong for large collages, assemblages, and life-size, usable tables, chairs, storage shelves, and other furniture, as well as play material, building blocks, and toy vehicles on which the child can ride, and life-size doll houses and play stores.

Slot construction (see 61) provides greatest strength and flexibility. Tape the edges of finished corrugated board constructions with packaging tape to prevent fraying and separation of the cover papers from the fluting. Corrugated board can be painted like any other paper or cardboard (see 83).

92. Cardboard Tubes

Cardboard tubes, cut into different lengths with a sharp knife blade, coping saw, jigsaw, keyhole saw, or back saw (see 85), are useful in three-dimensional design, in assemblages, or as components like table and chair legs in combination with other materials. They can be pasted, tied, taped, or jointed.

Semicircular cross-laps can be cut into the ends of cardboard tubes with a saw. Use one such cutoff as a template for marking identical joints into other tube ends. Several tubes, notched in this manner, will fit together like logs used to build a cabin (see diag. 92.a). Slot jointed tube ends can fit to slot jointed flat cardboard shapes (see diag. 92.b).

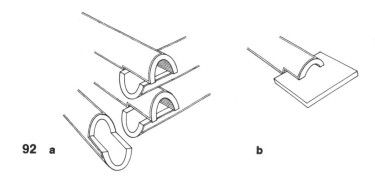

92 a   b

93. Construction Details

Cardboard in all its different forms lends itself to bold, abstract design as well as to fine detail, depending on the young craftsman's purpose, conception, and skill level. Three-dimensional shapes can be built up out of successive layers of smaller shapes, each following a desired contour and glued to the last (see diag. 93.a). Solid geometric constructions can be built with cardboard, following the principles for paper construction (see 73–82). The cardboard must be cut-scored (see 64) or else the individual shapes taped together with packaging or strapping tape.

Lighterweight cardboard can be moistened or steamed and then bent, glued, or nailed in position to hold its shape. To make more complex, convolute, or undulating cardboard constructions—for a model landscape or bridge, for example—build up a skeleton framework out of cardboard. When this frame is complete (see diag. 93.b) cover it with flexible, fluted cardboard, heavy paper, papier maché, or cloth (see 48–59 and 90). Similar cardboard constructions can be used as armatures for clay (see VII).

b

93   a

Accordion-folded paper and corners of paper constructions can be rein-forced with cardboard to give them rigidity (see 95). Finally, cardboard templates (see 68 and 123) are useful for preparatory work with other materials.

94. Designing for Cardboard Construction

Cardboard is useful and satisfying for both spontaneous and planned design. When making utilitarian objects and others requiring close-fit-ting parts, it is best to make a paper mock-up first to avoid unnecessary mistakes and cutting. (See 73–82 and XII for simple layout and design suggestions.)

95. Reinforcing Cardboard Construction

Cardboard constructions can be strengthened by fitting and fastening wood, lath, balsa, leather, or cloth to joints and other places that require support (see diag. 95).

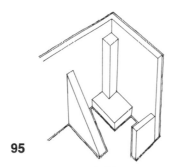

95

96. Cardboard Colleges

Cardboard, fluted board, and corrugated board are versatile materials for collages, used by themselves or in combination with other materials (see 27, 111, 177, and 300).

97. Cardboard Assemblages

The relative ease and speed with which constructions can be built out of various kinds of cardboard make them ideal for framework and detail in combination with other found and natural materials (see 28).

K. PAPER SCULPTURE

98. Formed Paper Relief

Tools and materials
> White and colored construction paper; fluted cardboard
> Scissors; sharp knife blade (see 64, 86, and 87)
> Scriber; scoring board (see 63 and 65)
> Cellophane tape; masking tape; stapler
> Paste (see 10–26)
> Heavy cardboard base

Paper can be sculpted in relief by cutting, scoring, and folding (see 30–35, 41–43, and 60–82), using the same techniques as those required to form fully three-dimensional paper objects and shapes. Such sculpture should not be attempted until the different methods of paper folding, cutting, and scoring have been explored.

For spontaneous paper sculpture a wood or heavy cardboard base is essential. Paper shapes can be curved and curled and attached to it with tape, paste, or staples. These shapes can be given three-dimensional detail and texture (see 63).

L. MAKING DECORATIVE PAPERS

99. Techniques and Methods

Paper making is beyond the scope of this book (see II.A). But a child can create interesting and decorative papers by pasting (see 9–27), printing (see VIII), drawing, and the techniques described below (see 100–102). Such decorative papers can be used in paper constructions, collages, assemblages, sculpting, and making useful objects, and for bookbinding (see II.M).

100. Spatter and Stippling

Tools and materials
> White drawing or bond paper
> Sponge; toothbrush or stippling brush
> Bowl of clean water
> Poster paints (see 206)
> Muffin tin or clean, empty baby food jars
> Tongue depressors or ice cream sticks

Prepare thick poster paint mixtures, each color in its own muffin cup. Show the child how to dip sponge or brush into the paint and then dab it lightly onto the paper. The lighter the touch, the more interesting and varied the effects will be. After stippling one sheet with a single color, wash out the sponge or brush, squeeze it dry, and use a second color, as before. A third color and more can be added in turn, either while previous coatings are still wet or after they have dried. A great many different effects and color mixtures can be achieved in this way. (See also 216 and 319 for additional spatter effects.)

101. Ink Patterned Paper

Tools and materials
>White drawing or bond paper
>India ink in various colors
>Eyedropper, one for each color
>Sponge
>Bowl of clear water
>Sheets of newspaper or blotting paper
>Colored felt markers (optional)

Place the drawing paper on top of several layers of newspaper or onto heavy blotting paper. Moisten the drawing paper with water and sponge. Drop blots of colored ink onto the moistened paper, using the eyedropper. The inks will crawl and bleed, creating a variety of patterns and designs. Several different colors can be used in succession. Additional variation can be achieved by dropping small amounts of soapy water into the design, again using an eyedropper. Do not disturb or move the paper until the water and inks have dried thoroughly.

Such moistened paper can also be flooded with watercolor applied with a brush, which is then drawn into with colored felt markers and drawing pens dipped into India ink. These and other ''resist'' methods (see 219 and 229–231) can be combined with each other.

102. Marbled Paper

Tools and materials
>White drawing or bond paper
>Two enamel, plastic, or rubber trays, each larger than the paper and about 2″ or
>   more deep (e.g., photographic developing trays)
>Tubes of oil paint in different colors
>Turpentine (see 227)
>Muffin tin or empty baby food jars, one for each color
>Tongue depressors or ice cream sticks, one for each color
>Eyedroppers, one for each color
>Bowl of clear water

Oxgall (optional)
Newspaper or blotting paper
Wallpaper paste (see 17)

Dilute the wallpaper paste with water to the consistency of smooth light cream. Make sure no lumps remain. Pour enough of this mixture into one of the trays so that it covers the bottom to a depth of about ¼" to ½". Dilute with turpentine as many of the oil colors as are to be used, one color to each muffin tin cup, using a different tongue depressor to stir each. Using a different eyedropper for each color, drop a little blob of the oil paints into the paste mixture in the tray. Each droplet will spread and form a pattern on top of the surface of the paste, since oil and water do not mix. To achieve swirls of color, stir the paint with a clean tongue depressor.

When the oil paint pattern is satisfactory, gently place a sheet of drawing paper on top of the oil-paint-design-covered paste in the tray. Do not submerge the paper, but let it float on top. Tap the top of the paper surface gently with finger or clean tongue depressor to force out air bubbles that might be trapped between paper and paste surface. Finally, lift the paper off the oil paint and paste surface, keeping it as level as possible. Turn the sheet over quickly and place it, face up, into the second, water filled tray. Agitate the water slightly to help remove any paste that may cling to the paper. Then remove the paper from its bath and let it dry, design side up, on a sheet of blotting paper or a stack of newsprint.

Other substances, like oxgall or India ink, dropped into the first, paste-and-oil-paint-droplet tray, will permit an even greater variety of design effects and marbling.

M. BOOKBINDING

103. Gathering a Signature

Books are printed on individual sheets, each containing several pages. Before the type is set the printer lays out a large imposition sheet the same size as the sheet to be printed, on which each separate page is indicated. When printed, the pages on each side of the sheet seem out of order, and many upside down. But each falls into its proper, consecutive place and can be read right side up once the sheet is folded. Each set of pages that fit onto such a sheet is called a signature. Most signatures contain multiples of sixteen pages—32, 48, 64, or more—depending on

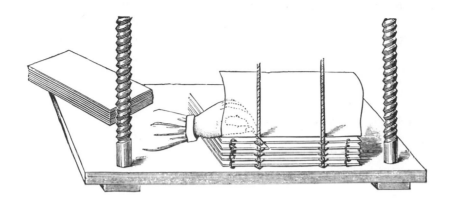

the size of the book, paper, and printing press. Large books may contain several signatures.

To make a scrapbook, sketchbook, or other book, fold large sheets of paper into individual signatures of the required page size, using the suggested folds (see diag. 103.a). Professional bookbinding requires special equipment and considerable strength. To avoid the need for both, young people can punch holes into the fold of each gathered signature, using a hole punch (see 5 and 178) or a grommet die and hammer (see 6 and 185), or a stapler, and fasten the folded signature with grommets or paper clasps (see diag. 103.b). If more than one signature is required, paste the last page of each to the first page of the next. Professional bookbinders glue, sew, and staple signatures to one another and to the spine of the binding.

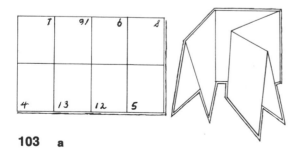

103 a

b

Once the signature is folded, gathered, and fastened, slit the remaining folds on the three sides other than the spine with a letter opener or dull knife. The paper edges may be slightly ragged but this can be decorative, like the deckle edge of handmade papers. Trimming a signature with a knife is difficult; don't try it. In the bindery this is done on a guillotine.

104. Portfolio Binding

Tools and materials
> Sheets of cardboard
> Sharp mounting knife (see I.k, 86, and 87)
> Decorative papers (see II.L)
> Paste (see 10–26)
> Lightweight canvas or other cloth
> Scissors

Lay out each of two covers for the book or portfolio about ¼″ larger all around than any signature that is to be bound into it. Check all corners of the cardboard covers with a right-angle triangle to assure that they are perfectly square. Cut a strip of canvas as long as the covers are high and 2″ wider than the thickness of the signature or signatures. Paste this strip neatly to the two facing edges of the cardboard covers, leaving a space between them equal to the thickness of the signature plus twice the thickness of a cardboard cover (see diag. 104.a). Fold over the ends of the canvas that extend beyond the spine, double them over, and paste them down.

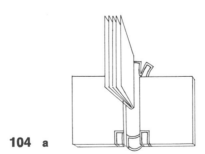

104 a

Now open the cardboard covers and canvas spine and place them, spine side down, onto the "wrong" (undecorated) side of one of the decorative papers. Cut V-shaped notches at all corners of the boards and spine (see diag. 104.b). Cover the spine with paste and glue it to the paper, making sure to line up the V-shaped notches with the corners of the spine. Next close the covers, and cover the topmost side of one of the boards with paste. Glue the paper flap that extends beyond the spine on that side down to the board. Turn the binding over and repeat this operation on the other side. The reason for pasting the paper to the boards while the cover is closed is that, were they pasted while the cover lay open, the paper might crack at the folds when the book was folded. Now open the portfolio and paste all the flaps down over the various edges (see diag. 104.c).

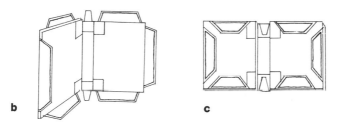

b   c

Cut a second sheet of decorative paper, about ⅛" smaller on all sides than the outside dimension of the book cover, including the spine, when it is laid out flat. Cover the inside, as yet uncovered boards and spine with paste, and glue the decorative paper to boards and spine. Wipe any excess paste off the paper with a damp cloth.

If these are to be covers for a scrapbook, sketchbook, or other book or one that is to be re-bound, glue the first and last pages and the spine side of the gathered signatures to the inside covers and spine (see diag. 104.d).

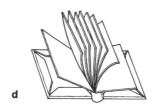

d

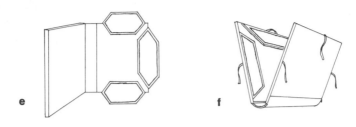

If such a binding is to be a portfolio for loose sheets, prints or photographs, cut flaps out of black linen or construction paper for each of the three sides of one cover (see diag. 104.e), and paste them in place before gluing the second, inside decorative paper to the binding. Holes drilled or punched under these flaps, with leather thong or lacing tied or glued in place, allow such a portfolio to be securely tied (see diag. 104.f).

Carpentry

Life without industry is guilt, industry without art is brutality.
—*John Ruskin*

A. BACKGROUND

Carpentry invokes the smell, feel, and texture of wood and wood shavings and of hand-held tools. Wood is a vanishing resource despite remaining forests of hardwood trees in South America and Australia and softwood "tree farms" in the northern hemisphere. With the Transcontinental Highway being bulldozed through the tropical jungle of the Amazon basin, those last, untapped virgin stands in the world are in danger of destruction as they become accessible. It will be impossible for a second growth to keep up with the demand.

Today's farming, printing, building, packaging, plastics, and chemical industries eat into the surviving and replanted reservoir of forests at a rate faster than they can regenerate. But trees are not only a source of prime raw materials. They are the major converters of carbon dioxide into breathable oxygen. For all these reasons wood will certainly become a treasured commodity once again, used discreetly as a craft material. This will also stimulate a revival of interest in its unique properties, care in its use, and preservation.

As recently as one hundred years ago much of Europe, North America, Asia, and Africa was covered with dense forests. They were decimated by a wasteful burning of wood to clear land for agriculture, for fuel, and for conversion into charcoal for iron smelting and other industrial processes, and by pulping to supply the paper making (see II.A) and chemical industries. Wood was also the prime raw material used for furniture and common household articles. But since the American Civil War, "anything which hitherto had been made of wood was quickly duplicated and mass-produced in iron." [46] And with this decline of wood as a precious raw material, the craftsmen who were skilled in transforming it for utilitarian and esthetic purposes became scarce.

As a first introduction to carpentry, cardboard—corrugated and chip— and the various wall and composition boards are as useful as wood and sometimes more so. They are softer and easier to saw, joint, and work and they are usually less expensive. Therefore many of the projects described in this chapter apply equally to materials other than wood on which carpentry tools can be used (see II. I and J).

a. Carpentry Tools

Today's production and hobby carpentry involves the use of a profusion of power tools. But the judgment demanded for working in wood requires training in and use of simple hand tools, not only as a learning process for young people but also as preparation for an eventual use of machinery. Sawing, hammering, drilling, jointing, and other operations in woodworking require a familiarity with the characteristics of the raw material that can only be gained from working with hand tools. The miniature power tools often given to children as toys make it impossible for them to acquire a hand-felt knowledge of the material or the coordination and inventiveness that lead to a creative exploration of the unique properties of wood. "For, like the nails on a beast's paw, the old tools were so much an extension of a man's hand or an added appendage to his arm, that the resulting workmanship seemed to flow directly from the body of the maker and to carry something of himself into the work." [45]

There's a knack to driving a nail with a hammer that, if it becomes second nature, frees a child or young person so that he or she can concentrate on the creative aspects of crafts. There are efficient ways of using a screwdriver, a hand drill, or a saw, setting up work, preparing jigs, or making a mortise, so that the process of creation can take precedence over production (see I.e). These operations require experience that, cumulatively, lays the foundation on which more advanced skills can be built.

But it's not enough to give a child a hand tool kit or a workbench. He needs experiences and an outlook that make it possible for him to use carpentry tools imaginatively and with a purpose. He needs to be given raw materials on which to exercise tools, skills, and his own ideas. He needs guidance to enable him to understand that the purpose of the exercise of his skills is expression and not mere production.

Most children's tool kits are shoddily made. They are intended for make-believe rather than craft. They foster the delusion that ownership of a profusion of tools makes the craftsman. Hardly any of these kits include materials on which the tools can be used. None offer a program of developmental craft education that encourages the expansion of the child's abilities. Many include sharp and dangerous tools, like an awl, that are inappropriate and useless for the age groups to which they are given.

It is important to give a child only one or two tools at a time, together with materials on which they can be used. They should be presented so that he or she is encouraged to explore them and be inventive. The child needs a properly illuminated table at which he can work comfortably and safely. He also needs to be shown basic craft disciplines and have some of the possible effects of violating them explained to him.

Some parents and teachers are afraid to give carpentry tools to young children. They worry that a child might hurt himself, misuse the tools, or create havoc among siblings or furniture. Yet children to whom tools and materials are properly introduced, who are fired with enthusiasm for creating self-originated ideas and objects, and who are given guidance, are not likely to misuse tools. Only those who are ill equipped and unprepared and have no satisfying craft goals in view tend to scratch away destructively at table legs with toy saws. Besides, as pointed out earlier, anything is dangerous in the hands of an undisciplined or inexperienced child. Even an infant's mallet can do great damage if it is given to a child who has no pounding bench on which to use it. Such a

child is naturally inclined to try out his tool on mother's crockery to see what happens.

Tools for children are best bought from educational, jeweler's, or art supply stores and hardware shops, rather than in toy shops. Most professional tools come in a variety of sizes and weights, some sufficiently small and light that they fit the hands of children mature enough to use them. An upholsterer's tack hammer, of which the handle has been shortened, makes an excellent child's carpentry hammer. Model makers' and jewelers' coping saws and jigsaws fit the hands of any five-year-old. A regular compass, keyhole, wallboard, or dovetail saw or a back saw is far more useful and workable than the miniature cross-cut saws usually found in children's toy tool chests. And they are much less dangerous. The least expensive, lightweight carpenter's hand drill is preferable to its shoddy toy counterpart and is no more expensive. Real tools inspire a respect for craft and a sense of purpose and responsibility in children.

If tools are presented to children one at a time, the child will eventually posess a complete tool kit that is permanently valuable. He'll know how and when to use each tool and how to care for it. The next tool can be provided when the child is ready for it and when he knows how to use all other previously supplied ones effectively.

A clear division is made in this chapter between "sharp" and "first" tools. The latter are safe even for pre-school children unless they are grossly misused. "Sharp" tools require considerable experience, coordination, and self-discipline. Few children below the age of eleven or

twelve are sufficiently mature to use such sharp tools safely unless they have had ample experience with first tools in carpentry and other craft since early childhood, and unless they work under close supervision.

b. When to Provide Tools

Give the child a new tool only when he can hold it properly. If the smallest or lightest weight professional tool is too heavy or difficult to hold and guide, then the child should not be expected to work with it. The same principle applies to the material. A child mature enough to handle a coping saw may not have the strength and endurance to saw through ⅛″ plywood. Give him balsa, wallboard, or soft carboard instead. The chronology in which tools are given is important. Before a child can learn how to use a hand drill, he must know how to clamp the wood to the table so that it does not slip when drilled, and how to place scrap lumber under it so that the bottom edges of the holes don't fray and splinter and the table surface is not damaged. The forethought, planning, and care the child learns will become second nature, not only in the operations detailed in this chapter but also in everyday life and work at home and in school.

c. Spontaneity and Planning

The more advanced forms of carpentry, like all other craft, require planning, measurement, marking, and transfer of designs for parts that are to be sawed, drilled, or jointed. Before a child can be ready for such work he needs ample time and experience with tools and materials that permit spontaneous experimentation. Don't teach a child how to mark or saw along a straight line, or how to joint or make objects that require numerical or geometric measurement, until he has experienced spontaneous craft. The meaning and purpose of numbers, measures, weights, and proportions can become clear only when the child has the maturity, skills, and desire to apply them to creative ends. Carpentry creates the need for an application of measuring and other mathematical skills, and it demonstrates their practical uses.

d. Work Spaces

Carpentry involves work that can ruin household or school furniture. It is therefore important to provide proper and safe working spaces and surfaces. Most commercially made children's worktables and benches (other than those made for school use) are inadequate, expensive, and last for only a short time. They also take up an excessive amount of space. As an alternative to the trestle worktable (see I.j) that is adjustable as the child grows, the table top workbench shown here can be made in any home or school workshop. It can be stored in a closet or on a shelf or stacked in the classroom when not in use. It can be clamped to any child- or adult-size table top to serve wood, metal, leather, and other craft activities.

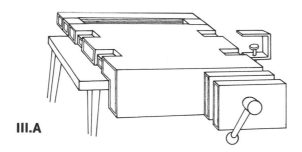

III.A

e. Safety

Carpentry requires some special precautions, which are detailed for each tool and project to which they apply. (See also I.k, 86, and 87.) Teach the child to be especially conscious of the hand and fingers that hold the material while wood is sawed, drilled, gouged, or chiseled, or a nail driven. Insist that a vise or clamp hold the material to the table whenever possible, instead of holding it in hand. Whenever the child uses sharp tools, chisels, knives, gouges, or even a screwdriver, the hand resting on or holding the material should always be well away from, behind, and out of the way of the stroke of the tool (see 131).

B. FIRST PROJECTS

105. Play Preparation

Tools and materials
Large wooden building blocks
Peg and hole toys
Wooden or plastic nuts, bolts, and slats; wrench
Pounding bench; wooden mallet and screwdriver

These toys are essential preparation for later craft skills and interests. Piling building blocks on top of one another and fitting pegs to matching holes are not only exercises in coordination; they stimulate understanding of which shapes fit and which don't, and of relative sizes. I have detailed elsewhere the most effective methods for introducing wooden blocks to young children: which to give and when to provide them.[3] Large plastic or wooden nuts and bolts and sanded wooden slats with holes drilled through them so that they can be bolted together, with a large wooden or small metal wrench to tighten the bolts, and similar toys prepare the child for insights and skills he will need for carpentry as for other craft and learning.

A pounding bench is the most useful first tool kit for children one and a half to three years old. Remove all tools but the mallet at the start. Teach the child to hold it near the end of the handle and not near the head, as young children are wont to do. Suggest that he or she keep eyes fixed on the peg to be hammered and the other hand well out of harm's way.

106. Tack Hammering

Tools and materials
    Splinter-free, well-sanded, short lengths of 2″ × 2″ lumber
    Several boxes of long-stemmed thumb or carpet tacks
    Tack or upholsterer's hammer with shortened handle
    C-clamp (see 112)

At nursery school or kindergarten age a child who has enjoyed the preparatory experiences detailed above (see 105) should possess sufficient coordination to use a small hammer to drive tacks into planks. Show him how to start the tack by holding and tapping it gently into wood clamped to the work table. He can hammer designs with colored tacks.

107. Nailing

Tools and materials
    Splinter-free, well-sanded 2″ thick lumber scraps; lath; tongue depressors
    Carpet tacks or roofing nails
    Tack or upholsterer's hammer with shortened handle
    10″ × 10″ × ¾″ plywood as a work surface

Do not give young children small-headed brads or common or finishing nails to hammer. They are difficult to strike. Roofing nails have extra-large heads and are therefore especially useful at early ages.

Set the child up at his or her worktable or workbench (see I.j and III. A.d) or, if the work is to be done at a regular table, make sure that a wooden workboard is provided. Then show the child how to nail lath and tongue depressors to scrap lumber shapes. Demonstrate how a single nail only hinges the lath to the wood; a second and third nail will hold it firmly. Teach the child to check the length of the nail against the depth of the layers of wood he plans to join before nailing them together so that the nail ends do not protrude beyond the material (see diag. 107.a.).

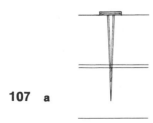

107   a

You may have to show the child repeatedly how the nail must be started at a slight angle away from the carpenter, and held between fingers only until the point has penetrated the wood and the nail can stand up by itself; and how the hammer should be held (see diag. 107.b). Point out that the hammer's head will strike the nail squarely if he keeps his eyes fixed on the nail's head. Teach him how to tap the nail rather than hit it hard. Then let him work on his own and discover the different ways of nailing pieces of wood to each other.

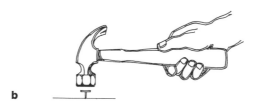

b

108. The Nail Set

Tools and materials
Same as 107
Common nails
Nail set

Once the child is adept at nailing with large-headed roofing nails and tacks, he can be given common nails of various lengths. A nail set can now be added to his tool kit. It will enable him to drive common nailheads slightly below the surface of the wood for a better and safer finish.

109. Sanding

Tools and materials
Bag of lumber scraps and cutoffs, obtainable from lumber yard or woodworking shop
Two blocks of wood, each 2″ × 3″ × 1″ (more or less)
Two sheets of medium sandpaper
Two sheets of fine sandpaper

Cut the sheets of sandpaper with scissors so that they fit round the wooden blocks. Tape or staple one sheet of each grade of sandpaper to

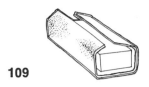

109

the blocks, sandpaper side facing out (see diag. 109). Then let the child sand scrap lumber until it is splinter-free and smooth, using the coarser paper first and then the finer one to obtain a good finish. The child must be shown how to sand with the grain of the wood.

This is a good opportunity to point out the different grains of various woods and the difference between the texture and appearance of end grain and that running lengthwise on the board. Show the child how the wood is marred when sanded against the grain.

Carpenters generally do not sand wood until the work is finished. However, it is important to safeguard young children from splinters and rough edges and surfaces. An inventory of sanded scrap lumber is useful for a great number of future carpentry projects.

110. Gluing

(See 9–26 for tools and materials.)

Professional carpenters prefer hot glues, resins, and synthetics for permanently bonding wood. But for use by children and young people most of the recommended pastes and adhesives serve wood as well as paper, with only a few exceptions. Wallpaper and flour pastes and rubber cement do not bond wood effectively.

Commercially available casein glues, mucilage, and acrylics are recommended for children's carpentry projects. Show the child how to apply a minimum of adhesive and yet cover one or both surfaces with an even coating of glue. Have him wipe away excess glue around joints with a damp cloth before the glue begins to set. Later he can use clamps to hold pieces of wood together while the glue dries (see 112). The child must learn to be patient and not to disturb glued joints and surfaces until the adhesive has cured completely.

111. Collages and Assemblages

Tools and materials
> Sanded scrap lumber (see 109); lath; tongue depressors; found and waste wood turnings and molding
> Tack or upholsterer's hammer (see 107)
> Assortment of common nails, each size kept in its own screw-top glass jar or in separate compartments of an egg carton
> Paste (see 9–26)
> 12″ × 12″ × ¾″ pine or plywood board, to be used as a base or working surface

The child can nail different shapes of wood on top of and next to one another onto the board, or make an open or partially enclosed hollow framework (see diag. 111), or combine both techniques. Such constructions can be accessorized with natural and processed found materials (see XIV). When completed, they can be painted (see III.G and VI). (See also 27, 28, 96, and 97.)

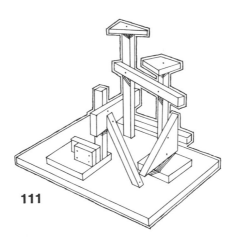

111

C. EARLY YEARS CARPENTRY

112. Clamping

Tools and materials
> Two C-clamps
> Two corner clamps
> Two model maker's or wood hand-screw clamps

Once a child enjoys woodworking, clamping will expedite gluing and other operations. He can then attempt more ambitious projects. The model maker's or wood hand-screw clamps are optional, but they are essential for advanced carpentry.

It doesn't matter if the wood is marred or scratched during a child's early carpentry efforts. Nevertheless it is important to instill care and good work habits as early as possible. Teach the child to keep a scrap of wood or lath between the jaws of any metal clamp he may use and the outside surfaces of the wood that is held. When the wood is protected in this manner, C-clamps can be useful for nailing and gluing. The corner clamps enable the child to join wooden pieces at perfect right angles (see 120). The model maker's and wood hand-screw clamps are designed for more delicate work.

113. The Vise

Tools and materials
Carpenter's vise

Once a child understands the purpose of clamps, he'll benefit from being given a carpenter's vise. It is available at any hardware store and can be attached to a trestle table (see I.j), table top workbench (see III.A.d), or any other worktable. A combination of clamps and vise is the equivalent of several extra pairs of hands.

A light duty, clamp-on metal vise is less desirable for carpentry, though it is less expensive than a carpenter's vise. If such a metal jaw vise is used for woodworking, be sure to instruct the child in the cautions detailed earlier (see 112) so as not to damage wood surfaces.

114. The Coping Saw or Jigsaw

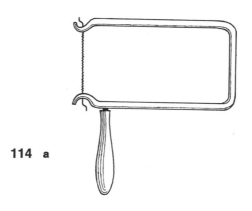

114 a

Tools and materials

Jeweler's or other coping saw
Coping saw workbench attachment (see diag. 114.b)
Package of spiral coping saw blades
Cigar box lids; or 4″ × 6″ × ⅛″ cardboard; or ¹/₁₆″-to-⅛″-thick balsa
Gummed white paper sheets, each about ¼″ larger all around than the cardboard or balsa (if no pregummed paper is available, white drawing paper or bond paper and paste will serve the same ends)
Box of wax crayons
Scissors
6″ × 9″ manila envelopes

The diagram shows how the coping saw workbench attachment can be made if none is available in local hardware or craft shops. Without it a child will find it difficult to use a coping saw effectively.

The project detailed below demonstrates how a young child can use a new tool inventively if the materials are presented properly. Let him or her draw a picture or design onto the paper. Make sure that the whole paper surface is covered with color. Paste the drawing to the cardboard and trim off any excess paper. Clamp the workbench attachment to the table. Insert a spiral saw blade into the jaws of the coping saw. A child

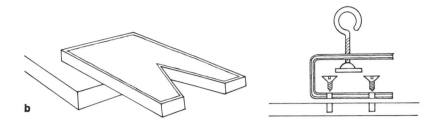

b

cannot cut himself with such a blade while working with it. Show him how to hold the saw by the handle after he is seated before the table. Saw cuts should be made inside the V-shaped notch of the workbench attachment. Then suggest that the child cut the picture into as many small pieces as he chooses. He'll make his own jigsaw puzzle.

Demonstrate how to start the first cut (and all future cuts) by moving the saw blade up and down gently against the edge of the material, keeping the blade as perpendicular as possible. Any five- or six-year-old can make such a puzzle without difficulty at one or more work sessions. He can put the cut-apart pieces of his puzzle into an envelope as a gift. Once he becomes proficient in the use of the coping saw, he can be shown how to cut interlocking puzzle pieces (see diag. 114.c) and other shapes.

c

Note: For other work with a coping saw involving interior cuts, it is necessary to drill a hole inside the area to be cut away (see 116), large enough so that the coping saw blade can be inserted through it before it is fitted to the saw itself. Then attach the blade to the saw handle and cut away the interior portion. If any blade other than a spiral blade is used, be sure that the teeth of the blade face *down* when inserted into the coping saw.

115. Inlay

Tools and materials
>Two 6" × 9" × $^1/_{16}$" pieces of cardboard; shirt board or balsa
>Two sheets of different-colored glazed, glossy, or flint paper, each about ¼"
>   larger all around than the cardboard
>Paste and rubber cement (see 9–26)
>Coping saw, blades, and workbench attachment (see 114)

Paste different-colored flint paper onto each cardboard and trim off the excess around the edges. Then, using rubber cement, spot-glue the paper side of one board to the bottom side of the other so that they fit perfectly. Apply the rubber cement wet (see 21) so that the boards can be separated easily later.

Now let the child cut into the glued-together boards with his saw as before (see 114). Make sure that he keeps all cutoff pieces of both colors. When both boards have been sawed into as many pieces as desired, separate the two layers wherever they remain glued together and clean off the rubber cement with a pick-up eraser (see 20). Two identical shapes, each of a different color, are now available for each cutoff. The child can use them to make two different inlay puzzles, each a different combination of snug-fitting shapes of the two colors (see diag. 115).

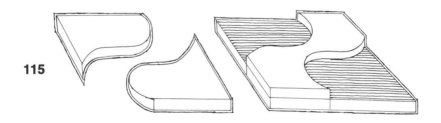

115

More complex and interesting inlays can be made, using more than two sheets of different-colored paper mounted to cardboard. After rubber cementing them together and cutting them apart as before, each inlay can be reconstructed and pasted permanently to balsa, shirt board, or other cardboard.

116. Drilling

Tools and materials
>Hand drill with ¼" chuck
>Assorted drill bits (including ¼" bit)

Coping saw (see 114)
Mallet
¼" dowel
Sandpaper (see 109)
Carpenter's vise or C-clamps (see 112 and 113)
Sheets of 6" × 6" × ¾" pine or plywood (to be drilled)
One sheet of 8" × 8" × ¾" pine or plywood (to be placed under the wood to be drilled)
Try square (see 121)
Pencil

Let the child sand the wood to be drilled until it is splinter-free and smooth. Then show him or her how to clamp it into the vise for horizontal drilling of the surface (see diag. 116.a) or vertical drilling of the edge (see diag. 116.b), or flat to the table with C-clamps for vertical drilling. Place the larger piece of scrap wood behind or underneath the wood to be drilled. It will assure a clean hole and it protects the table or other surface from being penetrated by the drill bit. Insert the ¼" bit into the chuck of the drill and tighten it firmly. Then show the child how to mark a small cross on the wood, using try square and pencil, wherever he wishes to drill a hole. Demonstrate how the point of the bit must be placed against the center of this cross, and how to turn the handle of the drill to keep it at a right angle to the wood and assure a clean, perpendicular hole.

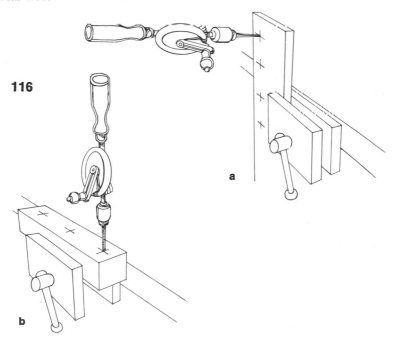

116

a

b

After the drill has penetrated all the way through the first layer of wood, give it a couple of extra turns to assure total penetration and a clean hole. Remove the wood from vise or clamp and let the child inspect it. Then allow him to drill as many holes as he wishes.

When he has finished, place the length of dowel into the vise or secure it to the edge of the table with a clamp (see diag. 116.c). Let the child saw off several short lengths with his coping saw. He can then drive these dowels into the holes he drilled into the wood, using his mallet.

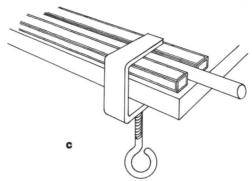

c

Due to variations in diameter and possible swelling of the wood, he may have to sand the dowels before they fit the holes. Once the child has learned these operations, he can drill different scraps of wood and lath and peg them together to build, form, and construct.

117. The Wrench

Tools and materials
Same as 116
Nuts and ¼" bolts in different lengths
Small adjustable wrench

Once the child has learned to drill holes into the wood and lath, he can join them with nuts and bolts. Strips of lath, drilled and bolted to others and to pieces of scrap lumber, will familiarize him with levers. Empty thread spools bolted to drilled lumber enable him to invent moving designs, mechanisms, and toys.

118. The Screwdriver

Tools and materials
Small screwdriver
$^3/_{32}$" × ¾" (more or less) flathead screws

Hand drill and bits (see 116)
¾" soft pine scrap lumber; lath; tongue depressors
8" × 8" × ¾" pine board or plywood (to be placed under the wood as it is drilled
   and screwed together)

There is no point in giving a child a screwdriver until he has learned how to use a drill. Unless holes are predrilled slightly smaller than the diameter of the shank of the screws, a screwdriver is extremely hazardous—far more so than many sharp tools—and difficult to use. Unlike nails, screws should never be held in hand while a screwdriver is used; the tool can slip and inflict a deep and painful wound. It is therefore important to teach the child to drill the required hole with an appropriate bit, almost as deep as the screw is long. Insert the pointed end of the screw into the hole and turn it hand-tight before using the screwdriver.

Clamp two pieces of lumber, one quarter again as thick, when clamped, as the screws are long, to the table or into the vise, together with the ¾"-thick backing board. Select a bit slightly smaller in diameter than the screw to be used. Insert it into the chuck of the drill and drill a hole through the two pieces of wood that are to be joined, no deeper than three quarteers of the way through the second piece. Show the child how to check the screw length against the thickness of the two pieces of wood to assure that the sharp point of the screw will not penetrate the far side after it is screwed into the wood (see diag. 118). Then screw the two pieces of wood together. Once the child has observed and understood these various operations, he needs ample opportunity to practice on his own.

118

119. Countersink

Tools and materials
   Same as 118
   Countersink

The top of the shank of any screw is slightly larger than the threaded part. Hence the head is likely to protrude above the surface of the wood unless it is forced into it. Show the child how to insert the countersink into the chuck of the hand drill to enlarge the hole he first drilled into the wood, so that the screw, once fully driven into the wood with the screwdriver, lies flush with the surface of the wood or slightly below it.

120. Miter Box and Back Saw

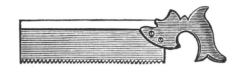

Tools and materials
Back saw (for younger children provide a keyhole, wallboard, or compass saw)
Miter box
Try square (see 121)
Pencil
Two C-clamps and two corner clamps (see 112)
2″ × 10″ × ½″ pine board

Clamp the miter box to the table edge firmly. Place the pine board inside it (see diag. 120). Demonstrate the different cuts that can be made by placing the saw into the different slots cut into the miter box. Show the child how 90° and 45° cut pieces can be joined for gluing, nailing, and screwing. Corner clamps are useful for demonstrating some of the possible joints, (see III.E), as well as for holding the cut lumber in place for jointing.

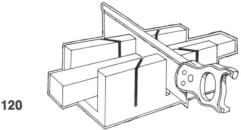

120

It is important that the child learn how to hold the saw properly from the very start, using the "pistol grip" with index finger extended as a guide (see 129). This assures the most effective control of any hand saw. The miter box is the best introduction to sawing since it teaches the importance of maintaining the proper angle of the saw to achieve the desired cut. Once the child understands these operations and requirements, he is ready to saw. Later he can learn to mark the lines, using try square and triangle, along which he decides to cut (see III.D). He must then line up the marked line with the appropriate miter box slot.

Starting the cut without fraying the wood is a matter of practice and experience. Start at one edge of the wood with short, quick strokes of the saw blade until the teeth make a small notch within which they remain. Then, using longer, even strokes of the saw, the wood can be cut all the way through. When the child nears the end of his cut, he must shorten the strokes of the saw once more so that the further edges of the board do not splinter at the finish.

If the saw blade binds, either the saw is not held perpendicular to the cut already made, or it may require a little soap applied to the teeth. If the ease of sawing does not improve, the teeth of the saw may require setting and sharpening. Any hardware store will have this done at nominal cost. Keep the saw blade covered with a thin film of oil while it is not in use.

D. PLANNING AND MEASUREMENT WITHOUT NUMBERS

Identical rudiments apply to all crafts in making plans, drawings, and measurements (see XII). Some of the tools used in carpentry make it possible for young people to plan and duplicate parts without using numerical measurements.

Tools
> Try square
> Right angle triangle
> Compass
> Dividers
> Marking gauge
> Pencil
> Miter box

Making a simple six-sided box usually requires measurements to achieve duplicate identical sides and matching top and bottom, even if all the boards are square. An allowance must be made for the thickness of the wood in calculating the dimensions, and simple fractions are required for some of these measurements. But such a box can also be made by a child who is not yet familiar with these mathematical operations.

Materials
> 24″ × 3″ × ¾″ lumber
> 12″ × 12″ × ¼″ plywood

The child marks off a short length of the 3″-wide lumber. He then places it inside his miter box and cuts along this mark (see 120). He places the short, sawed-off piece on top of another, longer piece of 3″ lumber, with ends lined up, and runs a sharp pencil point along the other end of the top piece, marking another of the same size onto the bottom one (see diag. III.D). After this second piece is cut, he will have two identical pieces for opposite sides of the box. When the same operation is repeated a second time, the four pieces required for the frame of the box will be complete. He can glue, nail, or screw these sides together, using corner clamps (see 112). This frame can then be traced onto the 12″ plywood to form the bottom and lid of the box. After being cut with a saw, they can be glued, nailed, screwed, or hinged to the frame. Use the marking gauge to indicate the line on the top and bottom pieces along which nails or screws are to be driven (see 122). The box will be reasonably square and a satisfying piece of work.

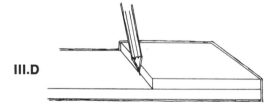

III.D

121. The Try Square

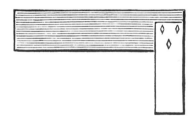

This tool is of value only if at least one side of the wood is perfectly straight. For younger children all sides of the lumber should be trimmed square before it is given to them.

122. The Marking Gauge

This tool is especially useful at a stage at which the child cannot as yet make numerical measurements with precision. He can set it to any desired width and duplicate this measurement elsewhere. For example, he can set the gauge to approximately half the width of the edge of a piece of lumber and mark this distance on the top side of any other wood to which it is to be nailed or screwed. Nails or screws driven along such a line, unless they are driven crooked, are unlikely to protrude through the outside surface of the wood beneath.

123. Templates

Templates are useful in any craft, especially at an age when the child cannot measure with accuracy or where organic shapes defy measurement (see 68). Once a child knows how to make templates, he can

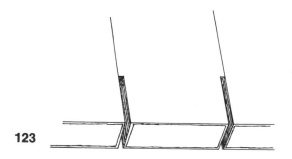

123

duplicate or transfer any shape he wishes. Insist that the child invent his own templates. Don't furnish him or her with readymade plans or printed and die-cut templates that he merely copies. Be sure to point out that when a template is used, a pencil line drawn around the outside produces a slightly larger (and one drawn around an interior shape a slightly smaller) duplicate of the original. In sawing or otherwise cutting out such a shape an allowance must be made for the difference by cutting either slightly inside or outside the marked line, as appropriate, or redrawing it beforehand (see diag. 123).

124. Using Tools to Make Tools

Braces, struts, temporary supports for pieces that are to be jointed, strips of wood fastened to the workbench to hold a board that is being worked on, and other temporary aids devised by the young craftsman are a sign of mature craftsmanship. Encourage the invention of tools that aid or speed the work. For example, a strip of ½″ × 1″ × 12″ wood into which holes, small enough to hold a pencil snugly, are drilled at intervals, and a nail driven through one end, can be turned into a useful beam compass (see diag. 124).

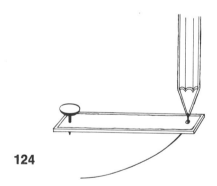

124

E. JOINTING

Use of the miter box (see 120) and corner clamps (see 112) gives the young craftsman ideas about jointing wood. Other, more complex and durable joints will enable him to use his craft with greater versatility. The following are six useful jointing methods (see 125–127) that do not require the use of chisels.

125. Bracing

Wooden strips and right angle and other braces can be glued, nailed, or screwed to a wooden base to provide temporary or permanent support for other pieces that are attached to them and each other (see 93 and 95).

126. Peg Jointing

Carpenters and shipwrights of former times preferred to peg wood instead of nailing, screwing, or bolting, long after the invention of metal fasteners. Wood tends to dry away from nails, screws, and bolts; and the metal rusts. But wooden pegs swell and shrink at the same rate as the wood they hold together. Hence pegged wood lasts longer. Boards can be pegged edge to edge (see diag. 126.a.), edge to side (see diag. 126.b), or side to side (see diag. 126.c). The first two joints require finding the center line of the edges of both pieces or of one of the pieces to be jointed, and marking it on the two edges or on one edge and one side (see 403). Then both pieces must be clamped together as shown so that the crossed lines that indicate where holes are to be drilled match precisely (see 65).

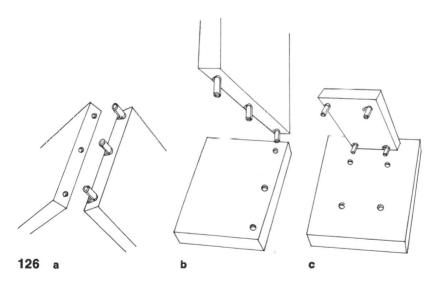

126 a   b   c

Drill a hole at each mark (see 116). Drill no deeper than to three quarters of the thickness of the board (see diag. 126.d). Using a dowel of the same diameter as the drill bit, saw pegs a shade shorter than the

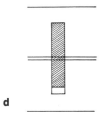

d

combined depth of each matching set of holes in both boards. Tap together both boards, with pegs inserted, before gluing to assure a proper fit. Take the boards apart again and glue all the pegs into the holes drilled in one of the boards. Then cover the protruding pegs and the spaces between them with paste or glue. Insert the pegs glued to one board in the matching holes in the other. Tap the boards gently together with the mallet and with a damp rag wipe away any excess glue that seeps out of the joints. Clamp the boards firmly until the glue has set (see 65).

127. Rabbet, Half Lap, End Lap and Butt Joints

The flush rabbet joint requires careful measuring and marking of half the thickness and width of the lumber on one end of one of the pieces of wood to be jointed (see diag. 127.a). Half lap (see diag. 127.b.) and end lap (see diag. 127.c) joints must be marked on both boards, as

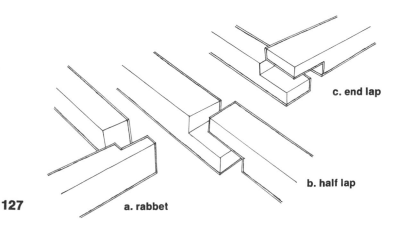

c. end lap

b. half lap

127   a. rabbet

d. butt

shown, before sawing. For butt jointing, saw and sand joints and fit them carefully square before securing them with glue, nails, or screws (see diag. 127.d.).

128. Other Joints

The following are some other common wood joints; these do, however, require the use of a chisel (see diags. 128 and 131). Some can be built up out of wood or cardboard, but this should be done primarily as an exercise. Such built-up joints do not have much strength (see 89).

128

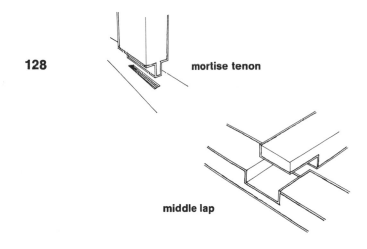

mortise tenon

middle lap

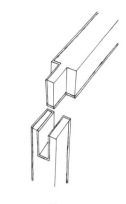

open mortise tenon

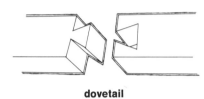

dovetail

miter

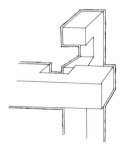

cross lap

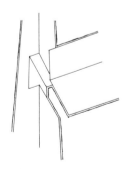

dado

F. SHARP TOOLS

The tools described in this section are very sharp. They require careful use under supervision and periodic honing (see 135). These tools are not recommended for younger age groups or inexperienced young people. A child above the age of eleven or twelve may be able to use them under supervision, provided he is given ample preparatory experience.

129. Crosscut Saw and Ripsaw

Tools and materials
    Crosscut saw
    Ripsaw
    Carpenter's vise or C-clamps (see 112 and 113)
    Miter box (see 120)
    3" × 10" × ½" lumber

The crosscut saw is designed to cut across the grain of the wood; the ripsaw, with the grain (see diag. 129.a). Each has a different number, set, and shape of sawteeth, suited to the job for which they are intended. These are large and heavy carpenter's tools that are more difficult to guide than those described earlier for use by younger and less experi-

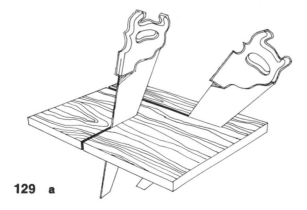

129 a

enced young people. For this reason a miter box, though not usually used by carpenters with these saws, is especially recommended for novices. If a miter box is not used, because none is available or the wood is too large, make sure that the boards to be sawed are firmly clamped down or held in a vise before sawing starts. The pistol grip (see diag. 129.b) is the proper way to guide these saws.

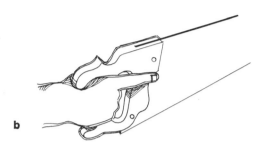

b

130. The Plane

Tools and materials
> Block or trimming plane
> Workbench (see III.A.d)
> 2″ × 6″ × 14″ pine
> 1″ × 2″ × 10″ pine

A block or trimming plane is best to teach young carpenters how to shave warped, uneven lumber; to trim wood too thick to fit; or to round edges. Nail a strip of 1″ × 2″ lumber to the worktable against which to brace the wood for planing (see diag. 130). Demonstrate how and why the wood *must always be planed with the grain,* and how to adjust the blade setting at the knurled knob attached to the handle of the plane.

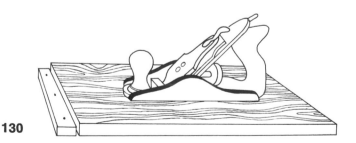

130

Check the depth of the cut by inspecting the knife edge on the bottom of the plane and try it out on scrap lumber. A thin, level, even sliver, and no more, should be removed with each pass of the plane. Too deep a bite or a blade set crooked will nick and crease the surface so that it requires endless planing and sanding before it is smooth and level again.

131. The Chisel

Tools and materials
    Butt chisel (¾″ to 1″)
    Mallet
    2″ × 4″ × 14″ pine
    Workbench and vise (see III.A.d and 113)

Chisels are dangerous. They require great care and concentration. Show the young carpenter how easily a chisel can slip or jump if the bite is too shallow or too deep. Insist that the chisel always be worked away from the user (see diag. 131.a) and that the wood be firmly clamped before the work begins. The suggested 2″ × 4″ block is useful for practice. Working with the grain is essential except when mortising a joint (see 128). To do the latter, the chisel must be held with the flat side facing away from the edge of the mortise (see diag. 131.b). Then tap the top of the chisel handle gently with the mallet and carve away slivers until the knife edge reaches the saw cut and the wedge can be severed. Once a young carpenter is sufficiently experienced to use a chisel safely, he will need a small assortment of different sizes.

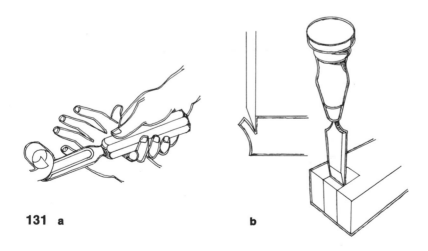

131 a   **b**

132. The Awl

Of all the carpenter's tools, this is the most hazardous, and yet it is one that is included in most toy tool kits. It is also relatively useless except to start a nail hole or one for a drill bit, though it is not essential for either operation. Keep the point of the awl firmly embedded in a wood block or a kneaded eraser except when in use. Keep it out of reach of young children.

133. Wood Burning

This is not recommended for any age group. It is hazardous and offers few opportunities for creative work.

134. Whittling and Wood Carving

Tools and materials
    Sharp knife blade (see 86, 87, and 135)
    Gouges (see 135)
    Chisels (see 113 and 135)
    Mallet
    2″ × 4″ × 10″ pine
    Vise (see 113)
    Rasps and files
    Sandpaper

These are hazardous activities that require extreme care and constant adult supervision. Make sure that all tools are finely sharpened and honed, rust-free, and firmly implanted in their handles. The wood block should always be held in a vise or, if this cannot be done, clamped to the worktable or held in hand behind the tool, away from the direction in which it is worked.

Wood carving requires gouges, chisels, and mallet. It is best for beginners to design the shape to be carved in advance and draw it onto the wood, rather than carving spontaneously. Draw a silhouette of the top view onto both the top and the bottom surface of the wood block; draw side view silhouettes onto each side surface (see diag. 134.a). Then, with the wood firmly held in the vise, carve the contours in top and bottom with gouges and mallet. Tap the end of the gouge handle with the mallet and remove slivers rather than chunks of wood.

When the top and bottom silhouettes are carved roughly, cover them with thick layers of cloth so as not to mar the wood when these sides are locked into the vise or clamped to the table. Carve the other sides; then add detail all around. Additional shaping can be done with rasps, files, and sandpaper (see diag. 134.b).

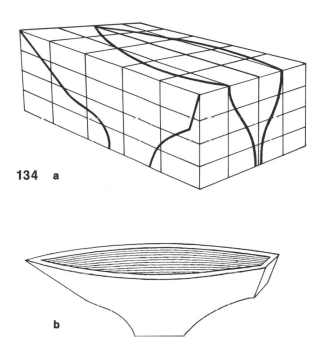

134 a

b

135. Care and Sharpening of Tools

Tools and materials
Oilstone
Light oil
Leather strop

Young and relatively inexperienced tool users cannot be expected to grind their own tools on a wheel. If the edges of tools become too dull to be restored through honing, they should be taken to a knife sharpener. But any young person old enough to use knife, plane, chisel, and gouge should be able to hone them.

To sharpen a plane or chisel, place a few drops of oil on the stone and hold the beveled edge of the tool against the stone, at a steeper angle than the bevel (see diag. 135.a). Move the blade back and forth steadily, making sure that the same angle is maintained between blade and

135 a

stone. Do not hold the blade against the stone so that the whole beveled area touches it. The bevel itself can only be restored on a grinding wheel.

When a sharp cutting edge has been obtained, turn the blade over and place it flat on the stone (see diag. 135.b) to remove burrs, moving it back and forth on its side. Finally, pass both sides of the blade back and forth over a leather strop. Apply a thin film of oil to the tool (keep it oiled at all times).

b

The same technique applies to knife blades, though these have no ''flat'' sides. Keep the dull edge of the blade raised slightly off the stone (see diag. 135.c) and hone each side in turn. Gouges that have round cutting edges require a flat stone for honing, but the burrs are removed on a rounded stone after honing (see diag. 135.d).

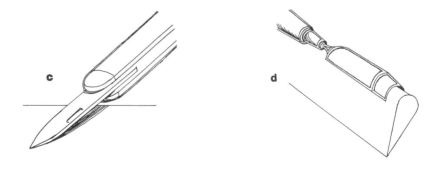

c

d

G. WOOD FINISHING

After a construction or an object has been made, the young carpenter may choose to preserve the wood—paint, varnish, shellac, or stain it. Younger age groups will find it sufficiently satisfying to paint wood with poster colors (see 206). If they wish, they can protect the painted surfaces with water glass (see 42), transparent glue (see 16), or a light coat of varnish or shellac. Bear in mind that the last two are volatile and toxic, and constitute a serious fire hazard. They also ruin paint brushes unless these are thoroughly rinsed in a proper solvent after use and then washed in warm water and soap (see 141 and 227).

136. Wood Filler

Tools and materials
>Sawdust (of the same wood as that used)
>Clear varnish
>Paste or casein glue
>Plastic wood

Any indentation, crack, or scar on the surface of the wood should be filled with wood filler before painting, staining, or varnishing. Plastic wood is commercially available. It can be sanded smooth like the wood, but when stained or given a natural finish it will not match the wood around it. For a matching filler it is necessary to make a mixture using sawdust collected from the same wood being repaired. Add a few drops of clear varnish and paste. Fill the indentation in the wood, let it dry thoroughly, and then sand.

137. Sanding and Sealing Wood

Tools and materials
>Sandpaper (in two or three different grades, ranging from medium-coarse to fine)
>Steel wool
>Sealer
>Flat 1″ paint brush (or wider if the work is large)
>Rags

Wood should be sanded and sealed before it is painted, or most of the paint will sink in, giving it an uneven coating. Sealing compounds for wood are best bought in hardware and paint stores. The wood should be thoroughly sanded, first using a coarse paper and then finer grades, always with the grain, until it is perfectly smooth to the touch. For a high finish it should then be polished with fine steel wool. Two light coats of sealer, each evenly applied with a brush, will close the pores of the wood. The second coat is applied only after the first has dried completely. Wipe away any excess with a cloth or rag after each application. After the final coat has dried, rub it down gently with steel wool once more.

138. Painting the Wood

The variety of oil-base and synthetic paints, enamels, and other finishes is so great that it would be futile to try to list and describe them. Dress the child in old and protective clothing. (See I.k and 227 for essential general safety precautions.) Cover table and floor space around the work area with several layers of newspaper to protect them from spills. Be sure to have an ample supply of the appropriate thinner for cleaning hands and brushes (see 141), for thinning the paint or other finishing material, and to remove stains from clothing or other fabric.

If the construction or object is to be painted in a single color, it is best to do so after final assembly of all parts. However, if small sections or parts are to be painted in several different colors or shades, it is best to paint them before assembly, provided no edges that are to be glued are covered with paint. Painted surfaces give poor adhesion.

139. Natural Wood Finish

Tools and materials
    Linseed oil
    White (clear) vinegar
    Turpentine
    Rags

Mix all three liquid ingredients in equal proportion. Keep in a closed jar and shake well before using. After the wood has been filled and sanded (see 136 and 137) but not sealed, apply this mixture to the surface with a cloth; wipe off any excess. Repeat this process two or three times, rubbing with steel wool after each application has dried, until the wood is thoroughly penetrated and the pores are sealed. This provides a matte finish that is resistant to water, alcohol, and other stains.

140. Staining

Tools and materials
    Linseed oil

Turpentine
Stain
Cloth

Fill in blemishes and sand as before (see 136 and 137) but do not seal the wood. Coat it with a mixture of linseed oil and turpentine in equal proportions. Wipe off any excess with the cloth. When this coating has dried completely, apply the desired stain, which can be bought in any hardware or paint store. Wipe off any excess with a cloth before the stain dries. Repeat the staining after each successive coating until the desired color emerges.

141. Brushes

Use bristle brushes, ½″ wide or wider, for painting wood, depending on the size of the object or the delicacy of the design. Use long-haired, narrow brushes for stripes, and round ones for painting detail. Instruct the young craftsman never to leave paint-filled brushes lying about but to rinse them at once after use, in the appropriate solvent.

Brushes on which paint has dried are difficult to restore, and may be totally ruined. Wipe the brush on newspaper or rags and rinse it in thinner poured into a jar. Then wash it in mild soap and warm water. Brushes should never be stored standing on their hair. Keep them lying flat or standing on the wood handle in a jar, or, preferably, hang them by the handle so that none of the hair touches any surface. If paint has dried on a brush, it should be hung in solvent. Make a brush holder out of wire that allows the brush to soak without its hair touching the bottom or sides of the jar (see diag. 141).

141

H. Power Tools

Well-experienced and mature craftsmen may find the following power tools of value:

Wood-turning lathe and chisels
Grinding wheel
¼" electric drill
Electric jigsaw

Any of these, but not necessarily all, are useful to those young people who have mastered all the foregoing hand-tool skills, and who are capable, trustworthy, and deeply involved in work that requires specialized tools. They should have good reasons and creative uses for these tools before acquiring them. Since this book has a scope covering primarily hand tools and younger age groups, I suggest manufacturers' handbooks and manuals as the best sources for instructions on how to operate, use, and care for these power tools.

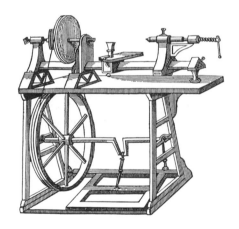

Wire and Metal Craft

> . . . This is an art
> Which does mend nature—change it rather: but
> The art itself is nature.—*William Shakespeare*

A. BACKGROUND

The ability to mine, smelt, and work metal is a sign of civilization. It is
one of the divisions, arbitrary though it may seem, between primitive and advanced societies. In early cultures that discovered the material and the means to refine and work it, the tribal smith or metal craftsman was a man set apart from the rest. His secrets were sanctified by
ritual and custom. His strength was legendary. Magic powers were at-
tributed to him, supposedly transmitted by a god, like Vulcan. Methods
of refining metals, hardening them, combining them to make alloys, and
casting and forging them were passed from father to son, as were the
paths to the secret places where they could be found. The metal smiths
of Benin in Africa, who wrought magnificent bronzes, the artisans of
ancient China, Mesopotamia, Greece, Rome, and South America, were

versed in metal craft even while the people of central and northern Europe and those east and west of the Ural Mountains had barely become aware of the existence and possibilities of these materials. North American Indians were still in the Stone Age at the time of the arrival of Europeans, despite rich mineral deposits close to the surface on their continent. Yet today there is hardly any tribe or group of human beings, no matter how isolated, that does not possess some idea of how to work and use metals—if only those obtained from discarded tin cans or crashed airplane fuselages.

Some of the common metals we take for granted, like aluminum, were discovered less than two hundred years ago. The French emperor Napoleon treasured aluminum more than gold and ordered a special set of tableware to be cast from this metal for his court. But like all limited resources of this planet, many metals will soon become scarce once again at the present rate of wasteful consumption. Even scrap metals, many of them essential in the smelting of alloys, are now in short supply. Huge quantities of discarded metal are heaped daily onto rubbish dumps to rust and be irretrievably dissipated.

a. Tools and Materials

A raft of metalworking tools have evolved as a result of the experience of generations of craftsmen. Hardly any are required for early age children's metalwork. Even more advanced students need only a few tools and materials that are inexpensive or free. As in carpentry, only one or two tools should be given at one time, as required for specific skills and projects. They are described below in a chronology that eventually provides young people with skills, incentives for invention, and the required basic equipment. Four metal products are of special interest and value to the young craftsman:

Wire
Sheet metal
Metal rods, tubes, pipes, nuts, bolts, and other hardware components
Scrap instrument, machine, and engine parts and components

Most principles of workmanship, processes, tools, and skills apply to all metals, whether tin, copper, brass, or iron. Precious metals like silver and gold are usually out of reach of young craftsmen, but they are worked very much like the rest. Aluminum does require special handling as it cannot be soldered or otherwise jointed except by riveting.

Further, it can't be painted, but must be anodized. Galvanized sheet metal is not recommended for early years craft since it cannot be painted unless it is first dipped into an acid bath.

Fabric and plastic covered wire allows even pre-schoolers to enjoy an introduction to this craft. Ample scrap and waste metals are available in and outside the home to provide older boys and girls with an inexhaustible supply without cost—wire coat hangers and clean, empty tin cans, among others. Whole or cut-apart scrap and junked metal rods, tubes, nuts and bolts, discarded hardware, cog wheels, and broken watch, instrument, and other machine casings and parts are valuable for metal collages and assemblages, as well as for working parts of useful objects invented and made by young people.

b. Work Spaces

(See I.j and III.A.d.)

c. Safety and Developmental Education

The development of metal craft skills should begin at early ages. It may at first glance seem dangerous to introduce young children to metal craft. Working with metal is actually less so than many other crafts that are regarded as safe. At earliest ages a child needs no tools other than his or her fingers to bend and twist pipe cleaners or plastic covered wire. The sharp ends of such wire are easily covered with friction tape.

Metal foil has edges that are not much sharper than those of paper. The young child must learn that they should be treated with care and that the foil can be folded or rolled to be perfectly safe. Metal and the required tools can't be worked by a child in whose hands they are unsafe—he just doesn't have the strength. Coat hanger wire, for example, is very difficult to form. Ordinary pliers require relatively large hands and a firm grip. Considerable muscle is needed to cut even through tin can sheet metal with metal shears.

Any misused, abused, or forced tool or material is hazardous. Even a crayon can be a weapon if poked into a child's eye. But a reasonably well-disciplined and cautious child can be taught to approach every tool and material with the required respect and foresight that will keep him safe. Only inexperienced children lack inner control and tend to get into serious trouble.

Soldering metal involves safety problems. Soldering should never be attempted except by young people who have considerable experience in the craft, who can be depended on to be careful, and even then only under supervision. Any tool or material that is sharp or pointed or that requires or generates heat should never be used by any child, save with these provisions.

B. FIRST PROJECTS

142. Pipe Cleaners

Tools and materials
    Pipe cleaners
    Modeling clay or modeling dough (see 54, 146, 252, and 277)

As in all early age craft, the child needs ample opportunities to play with the materials. He also must have some of the possibilities demonstrated that might not occur to him unaided. Initial stress must be on spontaneous exploration—never on "making something." It is sufficiently difficult and intriguing to discover how to bend pipe cleaners

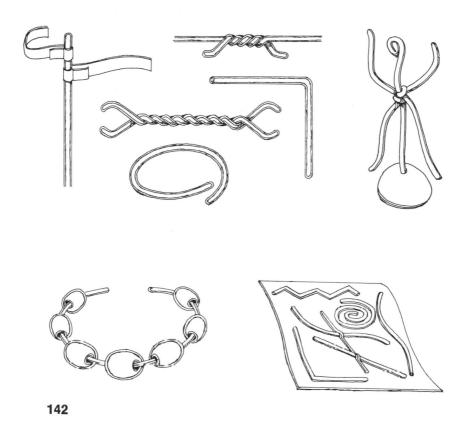

142

into curves and angles; how to twist two or more strands together; how to splice several lengths; or how to insert one end of a pipe cleaner into a lump of clay to make it stand up.

Other possibilities include gluing paper or ribbon to a pipe cleaner; using pipe cleaners as armatures for clay or modeling-compound objects, figures, and shapes; stringing wood or clay beads onto pipe cleaners; and pasting formed pipe cleaners to construction paper (see diag. 142).

Any one or any combination of these activities affords the young child satisfying play exploration of the material. Don't insist on realism or finished production. Admire the result no matter how clumsy it may seem.

143. Foil Projects

(See II.D–G, 160, and 163.)

144. Tin Can Craft

Tools and materials
> Washed used tin cans with labels soaked off
> Small metal vise (see 147), anvil, or wood block
> Ball peen hammer
> Cold chisel
> Metal file (round or half round; see 152)
> White paste and brush (see 9–26)
> White and colored construction paper; bond paper
> Scissors

Show the child how to hammer the edges of the clean, empty tin cans until all ragged, sharp metal edges where the tops were opened lie flat against the inside wall of the can. Demonstrate how to place the edge of the can against vise or anvil to tap it smooth, using the cold chisel where needed (see diag. 144). Then let the child decorate the outsides of the cans by gluing on colored paper strips, and streamers (see 42 and 43).

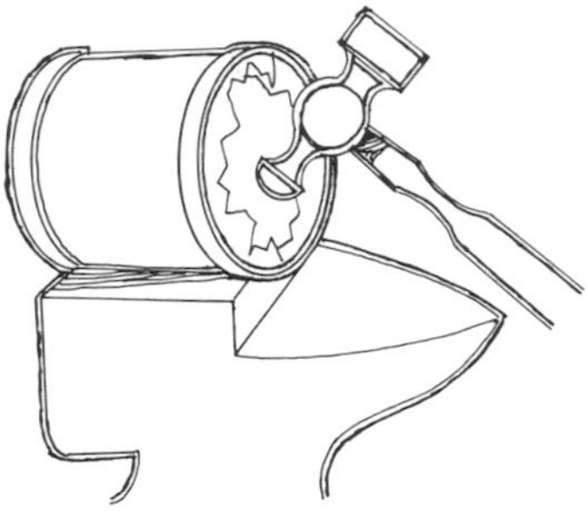

144

C. EARLY YEARS METAL CRAFT

145. Covered Wire Construction

Tools and materials
> Diagonal cutting pliers
> Combination nose pliers
> Single-strand plastic covered wire
> Roll of friction insulating tape
> Scissors

Use the same techniques as those described in 142. Show the child how to snip off required lengths of wire with the cutting pliers; how to bend, form, and twist the strands by hand and with pliers. Dowels, cardboard tubes, and other preformed shapes can be used as jigs (see diag. 145). As a precaution suggest that the child cover any wire that protrudes beyond the plastic covered ends with small pieces of friction tape.

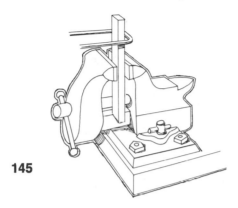

145

146. Making Armatures

(See 54, 142, 145, and 277 for tools and materials.)

Any available wire that the child can work will do. For younger children pipe cleaners are best as armatures for modeling with clay and dough. Older and stronger children can use coat hanger wire (see 149–152). Sculptor's armature wire is available from art supply stores. It is fairly large in diameter but is made of soft, flexible, lightweight alloy that is easily cut with pliers, hacksaw (see 155), or jigsaw (see 156).

Provide a ½″ to ¾″ plywood base in which holes have been drilled (see 116), into which the armature wire ends can be inserted and secured. Or nail, screw, and brace a dowel on the base to which the wire can be attached (see diag. 146). Once the wire armature is made, the child can cover it with clay or other modeling compound (see VII).

146

147. The Metalworking Vise

There are substantial differences between a woodworking vise and one used for metalwork. For young people's craft purposes a metal vise can be adapted to woodwork (see 113), but not vice versa. For early years wire forming, a lightweight vise that can be clamped to any table is sufficient. For later, heavier work a vise, preferably one that swivels at least 180°, that can be bolted to a worktable is needed.

The vise is a practical, essential tool for safety. Materials held in hand can slip and cause injury as they are worked. Sheet metal and wire can be bent safely by hand or with a mallet when they are firmly locked into the jaws of a vise. Besides, most vises include a small anvil on the side away from the jaws that can serve as a sheet metal and wire forming surface. Wire forming jigs (see 151) and sheet metal forming stakes and forms (see 162 and 163) can be locked into a heavy-duty vise.

148. Pipe Jointing

Tools and materials
> Small adjustable wrench
> Metalworking vise (see 147)
> Short lengths of straight and bent copper pipe, threaded at both ends; pipe joints

Demonstrate how to lock the pipe into the vise. Some metalworking vises have special jaws for pipe jointing. But even without this feature any small, light-duty, clamp-on vise will suffice, provided the pipe is not squeezed between the jaws. Show the child how to thread a pipe joint to the end of the pipe and attach the next length. Different constructions can be designed (see diag. 148). Once all the joints are hand-tight, they can be tightened further with the wrench.

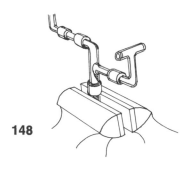

148

Jointed pipe can be used for assemblages in combination with other materials, as armatures, and, attached to a garden hose, as sprinklers and fountains.

D. WIREWORK

Once the first metalworking skills, tools, and experiences have been acquired, a child is ready for more advanced work. Wire forming, aside from being an art form in itself, has many practical applications, from electric circuit wiring and repair to jewelry making. No matter what the future holds, every contemporary young man or woman needs these skills in daily life—in vocational employment and for home maintenance and repair, as well as in self-expressive art and craft.

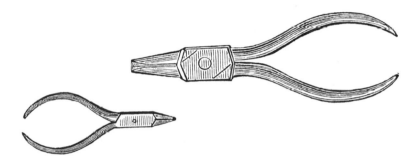

149. Wire Cutting

Tools and materials
    Ordinary pliers
    Diagonal cutting pliers (for cutting up to 22-gauge wire)
    Combination nose pliers
    Hacksaw or jigsaw (for cutting 20-gauge or heavier wire) (see 155 and 156)
    Metalworking vise (see 147)

Copper, steel, and brass wire is available in different thicknesses, varying from 26-gauge (fine) to 12-gauge (heavy). It can be bought round, half round, and square.

Ordinary pliers can be used to cut wire, but they are not very efficient, especially in the hands of young people. Even diagonal cutting pliers will not cut heavy wire, like a coat hanger. Wire that cannot be cut easily with pliers must be locked into the vise so that the place where the cut is to be made protrudes slightly from the jaws. A hacksaw (see 155), a jigsaw, or coping saw (see 156) or a half round or triangular file (see 152) should be used to cut heavy wire.

150. Twisting and Jointing

Tools and materials
Same as 149
Copper, brass, or other soft alloy wire

The same basic twists, bends, and joints apply as in 142. Wire that is too difficult to form in hand should be locked into a vise and bent with a mallet or a ball peen hammer. To make a sharp angle, lock the wire into the vise just below the place where the bend is to be made and tap it with the hammer until the required angle is formed (see diag. 150.a). Curve the wire around pipe or dowel for round and oval shapes. To twist two heavy wires into a double strand, bend each at the center into a 45° angle and lock both pieces into the vise side by side (see diag. 150.b). Twist the protruding ends with ordinary pliers, starting near the jaws of the vise (see diag. 150.c), or use a wrench if the wire is very heavy.

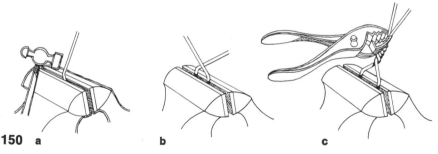

150 a   **b**   **c**

With these techniques, by themselves or in conjunction with a wire forming jig (see 151), wire can be bent and twisted into interesting shapes. Start with copper wire that can be easily formed in hand, twisted around itself or paper, cardboard, or wood armatures (see 52–54 and 146). At later ages such wire sculpture can also be soldered (see 166–173).

151. Wire Forming Jig

Tools and materials
Same as 149 and 150
Wire forming jig

Several different jigs are available. Most can be locked into a vise. The wire is then bent around one or a combination of the protruding shapes molded into the jig. Instructions furnished with the tool show how different forms are shaped. Wire hinges (see 165), chain links (see 173), shaped wire for jewelry, collages, assemblages, armatures, sculptures, and other objects can be fashioned with such a jig, using wire alone or in combination with metal pipe (see 150) or other found metal shapes.

152. Filing and Finishing

Tools and materials
  Round metal file
  Half round metal file
  Triangular file
  Needle file
  Steel wool
  Emery cloth or paper
  Buffing compound and cloth
  Metalworking vise (see 147)

Hacksaws (see 155), coping saws (see 156), pliers (see 149), or files (see diag. 152) leave sharp, ragged ends on wire and sheet metal when used for cutting. Ends and edges must be blunted and rounded before the metal is worked. Heavy wire can be locked into the vise to file ends smooth and finish them with emery cloth or paper. Wire or sheet metal can be cleaned, polished, or given texture or a high finish by rubbing with steel wool, emery paper, or buffing compound and cloth.

152

E. SHEET METAL

Sheet metalwork requires considerable strength, planning, caution, self-discipline, and endurance. Provide empty, washed tin cans, opened at both ends, slit down one side, and with the rolled edges at both ends cut off (see diag. IV. E). Children below the ages of ten or eleven usually lack the strength to cut tin with shears (see 154). And so they must either cut it with a hacksaw (see 155) or a jigsaw (see 156), or this must be done for them. Young people should work out in paper (see 67, 68, and 153) the shapes they wish to cut before cutting the metal "blank."

The required techniques are detailed below.

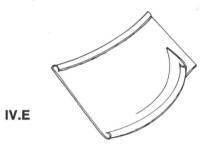

IV.E

153. Planning the Work

Sheet metal takes time to form. A spoiled part can cause tedious extra work that can be avoided with planning. Make a paper or cardboard model (see 66–68). After construction the model can be flattened and the shape transferred onto metal (see 291). Then the blank can be cut (see 154–156), ready to be formed by bending or hammering.

Tape the sheet metal to the workbench and tape the paper template on top. Trace the outline of the template onto the metal, using a nail, divider point, or engraving needle (see diag. 153). To make a circle,

153

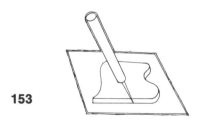

mark the place where its center is to be with a cross, and punch a small indentation into the metal at that point with a nail, deep enough to hold the point of a pair of dividers but not so deep as to dent the metal. Then inscribe the required circumference. If the design has been traced onto the metal with pencil and carbon paper, it is best to retrace the lines with a pointed instrument or etching needle (see 313 and 314) since pencil or carbon rubs off metal.

154. Cutting with Shears

Tools and materials
    Sheet metal (see IV.E)
    Metal shears

Metal shears are available in different sizes. All are difficult to work and hold by children and young people. If the young craftsman is strong enough to cut metal with shears, suggest that he clamp the metal sheet to the edge of the workbench so that the portion to be cut extends beyond it for easier cutting. Instruct him to file and emery-paper the edges of the shapes that he cuts out (see 152) since they are likely to be sharp and ragged.

155. Cutting with a Hacksaw

Tools and materials
    Sheet metal (see 154)
    Hacksaw and blade

Sheet metal, from tin can gauges to heavier ones, can be cut with a hacksaw, though it is impossible to cut any save the most gradual curves. Pipe, rod, and heavy wire similarly can be cut with this tool. Make sure that the blade is inserted in the saw so that the teeth *face away from the handle*. File and emery-paper edges after cutting (see 152).

156. Cutting with a Coping Saw or Jigsaw

Tools and materials
    Sheet metal (see 154)
    Coping saw and metal-cutting blades

This is the most effective metal-cutting tool for young craftsmen. It requires special metal-cutting blades, available in jeweler's supply stores. Make sure that the blade is fitted so that the teeth *face the handle*. The procedure (including the need for a special V-shaped table extension) is the same as for using this tool on wood (see 114). Cutting metal, however, requires shorter strokes. Simple or intricate shapes can be cut into tin, copper, and brass. (See 153 for suggestions concerning the transfer of designs from model or template to metal.) File and emery-paper edges after cutting (see 152).

157. Bending

Tools and materials
Sheet metal (see 153)
Vise
Rawhide or wooden mallet

Scratch a line or lines into the metal where the blank is to be bent, using a nail, divider point, or engraving needle. Secure the blank in the vise so that the inscribed line appears just above the jaw and is parallel to it (see diag. 157.a). Using the mallet, hammer the metal as close as possible to the line, gently and all along it, until the metal bends to the required angle. A bend in a long strip requires that it be moved back and forth in the vise, a little at a time, as the metal is hammered. Or such a strip can be clamped to the edge of the worktable top and then slowly hammered into shape (see diag. 157.b).

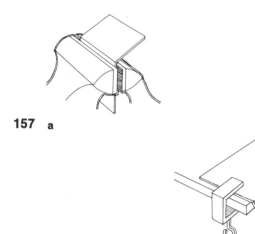

157 a

b

Bends should be hammered gradually so that the metal does not split or crack. To make a small metal box or cube, bend each side partially in the vise until all surfaces are slightly angled. Finish the bends by hammering each side over a flat anvil with the mallet, or bending them by hand if the gauge of the metal allows, until they are at right angles to each other (see diag. 157.c).

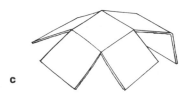

c

158. Strip Metal Coiling and Forming

Tools and materials
   Same as 149 and 152
   Sheet metal cut into strips 1″ to 2″ wide

Strips of sheet metal can be formed like wire (see IV.D), riveted (see 164), hinged (see 165), soldered (see 166–170), or chain linked (see 173) to make armatures; sculptures; jewelry; toys and other objects; molds and dies for clay or modeling compounds; and cookie cutters (see diag. 158). Bend the strips around found materials, metal forming dies, jigs, vise, or anvil (see 150, 151, 157, and 162). Roll one edge for dies, molds, and cutters; both edges for decorative uses (see 159).

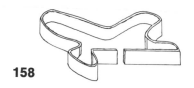

158

159. Rolling the Edges

When making metal designs and objects with thin gauge sheet metal or strips, it is safest to roll the edges of the blank. Bend or hammer ⅛″ to ¼″ of the metal edge until it lies flush with the flat metal surface. (See also 157 and 158.) The metal edge should be filed and emeried before rolling.

160. Embossing

Tools and materials
Sheet metal blanks (tin, copper, or foil)
Ball peen hammer
Rawhide mallet
Assortment of small and large nails, screws, cold chisels, punches, and dies
10″ × 12″ × ¾″ plywood work surface
Masking tape

Tape the blank to the plywood. The child can then hammer dots, lines, and shapes into the metal. If the blank warps during embossing, it can be straightened by hammering it gently with a rawhide mallet. The embossed design will appear raised on the other side of the blank. The indentations can be made more pronounced by embossing along the raised edges of the design on the ''wrong'' side. (See also 35.)

161. Drilling

Tools and materials
See 116
Metal drill bits

Save for the special bits, the same techniques apply to metal as to wood. Scratch a small cross with nail or divider point where the hole is to be drilled. It is easier to start a drill if a small indentation is hammered with a nail at the center of the cross. Make sure that the indentation is no larger than the size of the hole that is to be drilled. It may take several turns of the drill before the bit bites into the metal. Drill slowly and without exerting great pressure on the bit.

162. Hammering and Forming

Tools and materials
Rawhide or wooden mallet
Cross peen hammer
Sheet metal (see 153–156)
Forming stake and anvil; or tree trunk section hollowed to receive stake; or vise
Drill; jigsaw

A circular, oval, or other flat blank can be formed by hammering it into a shaped wooden form (see diag. 162.a), or over a metal stake fitted into the stake hole of an anvil, or over the anvil itself. Precast stakes can be ordered from art and craft supply shops. If no anvil is available, the stake can be locked into a large vise or sunk into a section of tree trunk. Forming stakes can also be carved out of blocks of wood (see 134).

If the hollow vessel or shape is to stand on a flat base, inscribe its cir-cumference into the blank with a nail or divider point (see diag. 162.b, and 153). Then, whether or not a base is required, place the edge of the flat blank against the stake and tap it gently all around with the mallet.

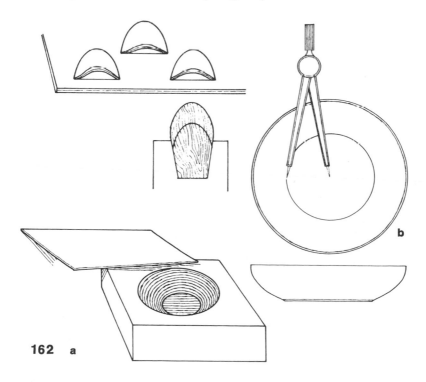

162   a

b

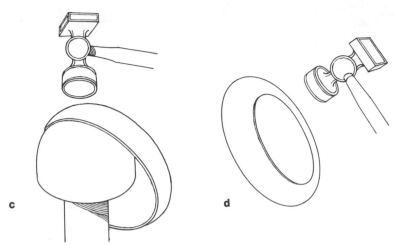

Keep tapping in concentric circles, working toward the inscribed base line or center until the desired shape is reached (see diag. 162.c).

More or less intricate hollow shapes can be formed in this manner. Deliver gentle, even blows with the mallet, each placed next to the last, all around, working from the outer edge to the center as many times as required. Use the cross peen hammer to make a sharp ridge where the shaped side and the flat base of the vessel meet (see diag. 162.d). Or, if no base has been inscribed, solder a curved strip of metal to the bottom to form the base (see 166, 169, and 170).

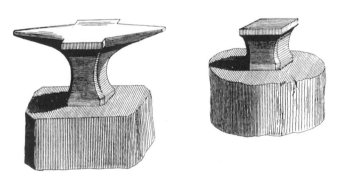

Other shaped sheet metal forms can be made by working blanks placed into hollowed-out and carved wooden forms (see diag. 162.a, and 134). Interior cuts made with drill and jigsaw (see 114 and 156) permit dimensional, textured, or relief shapes to be raised in the metal. Hammer the cut portion over an anvil with mallet or hammer until the desired shape is raised. (See also 98.)

163. Planishing and Chasing

Tools and materials
Same as 162
Planishing hammer

Formed hollow shapes can be planished to give them texture and to refine contours. Place one hammer mark next to the last, starting from the base line or bottom center of the formed shape (see 162), and work toward the outer edge. Repeat this procedure until the desired shape and texture are achieved.

Due to the fact that the metal is thinned out by the hammering, the finished edges will change in contour and require trimming. Place the shape or vessel on its base and press it against a needle point fixed to a dowel or stand. Then slowly turn it to inscribe an even line around the top or outside edge (see diag. 163.a). Use a metal shears or file to restore an even edge along the inscribed line and rub it with emery cloth. The completed work should be finished as in 152.

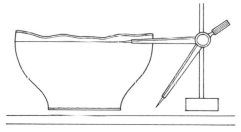

163 a

The texture of the hammer marks can be varied by spacing them closer or farther apart. Irregular shapes can be planished by using portions of ready-made forming anvils, found scrap metal shapes, pipes, or carved wooden forms (see diag. 163.b, and 134).

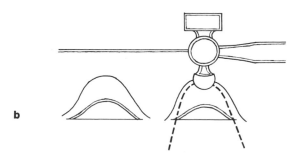

b

Designs can also be chased into formed sheet metal with chasing tools and hammer. The technique requires great control—beyond that possible for the age groups to which this book is addressed.

F. JOINING AND JOINTING METAL

164. Riveting

Tools and materials
    Rivet die set and rivets
    Hand drill and metal drill bit, a shade larger than the rivet size
    Ball peen hammer
    Mallet
    2″ ×4″ × 4″ pine board
    Sheet metal blanks

Mark the metal pieces to be joined where the rivets are to fit and drill holes at the appropriate places (see diag. 164.a, and 161). Tap a rivet head into the wood block to make an indentation that fits the rivet head (see diag. 164.b). Insert the head of a rivet into this indentation and fit the shank of the rivet through both holes drilled in the metal (see diag. 164.c). Tap the metal so that all pieces are snugly joined. Then, using the ball peen hammer and rivet die, shape the protruding end of the rivet (see diag. 164.d). For a tight fit, tap the rivet until there is no play between it and the metal pieces.

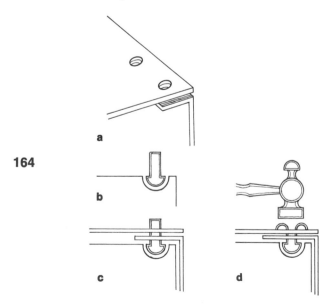

164

165. Hinging

Tools and materials
Metal blanks
Vise
Ball peen hammer
Metal rod
Wire
Combination nose pliers

To form hinges out of the metal blanks to be joined, lay out the blanks as shown (see diag. 165.a). Bend and curve the tabs around a metal rod held in the vise, using the ball peen hammer to form the hinge tubes (see diag. 165.b). Then fit the blanks together and join them with wire inserted through the tubes (see diag. 165.c). Bend the wire at each end of the hinge so that it cannot work itself loose. Sheet metal blanks can also be hinged with chain links soldered to their edges or attached through holes drilled into the edges (see 173).

165

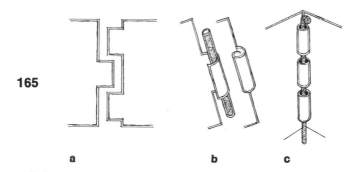

a   b   c

166. Soldering

Tools and materials
Electric soldering iron
Solder, in wire form (either with or without flux core)—available in three grades, #1 #2, and #3, each with a progressively higher melting point (#2 solder is best for beginners); color of the solder should match the color of the metal
Flux
Files (see 152)
Emery paper or cloth
Asbestos pad; or wire stand; or ceramic charcoal or sand filled table-top brazier

Soldering is both hazardous and tricky. It is hazardous because it involves sufficient heat so that a careless or inexperienced user of the soldering iron can burn himself or herself or burn holes into clothing or furniture. It is tricky because solder is hard to control. The metal surfaces to be joined must be perfectly clean and properly covered with flux. The soldering iron must be tinned. The less solder used and the more evenly it is applied, the more durable the adhesion.

Before soldering wire or sheet metal, all ends, edges, or surfaces to be joined must be entirely free of grease, dust, rust, or fingerprints. Clean these surfaces and the soldering iron tip with emery paper, holding the metal at places that will not be soldered. Then give the surfaces to be soldered and the soldering iron tip a thin, even coating of flux. Heat the soldering iron and "tin" it by covering the tip with a film of solder. Rest the iron on an asbestos pad, wire stand, or brazier edge, and away from any flammable surface. Hold the material to be soldered in the vise or place it on asbestos pad or brazier. Never solder on a wooden surface.

167. Drip Soldering

Solder, dripped with a heated iron onto a metal plate, forms interesting shapes and patterns. This sculpture or jewelry-making technique is a useful first exercise in soldering. It acquaints the young craftsman with the characteristics of the tools and materials and allows him to acquire control (see diag. 167, and 166).

167

168. Wire Soldering

Tools and materials
Same as 166
Single- or multiple-strand wire (without insulation or with insulation stripped from the ends to be soldered)

This skill is essential for metal collages, assemblages, jewelry making, and electric circuit wiring. Two wire ends to be soldered can be twisted together (see diag. 168) or, if the wire is heavy, soldered end to end. Clean the wire with emery paper, and hold it in place in the vise or on the brazier (see 166). Apply flux to the joint and soldering iron. Tin the iron and heat it and the solder until the solder starts to melt, at the same time applying the iron to the wire ends to be joined. Use a minimum of solder—no more than required to coat the joint thinly.

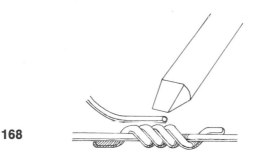

168

If the solder does not flow evenly across the joint or if it forms into small beads, the chances are that the joint is not clean or is improperly fluxed, or that the soldering iron is too hot. In that event, heat the joint with the iron until the solder drips off and start again as at first, cleaning, fluxing the metal, and tinning the iron. When the metal has cooled, test the joint and remove any excess solder with a file and emery paper or cloth.

169. Sweat Soldering

Tools and materials
>Same as 166
>Solder, in sheet or flat strip form
>Scissors
>Sheet metal blanks and shapes

Sweat soldering is the preferred method when soldering surfaces other than wire or edges of metal. Cut the sheet or strips of solder into small squares. Place these at more or less regular intervals onto the cleaned and fluxed surface of the blank to which other metal shapes are to be soldered (see diag. 169). Then position the cleaned and fluxed metal shapes to be adhered on top of the solder squares. Using the soldering iron, heat the tops of the metal shapes until they transmit the heat to the solder and it begins to flow and create a bond.

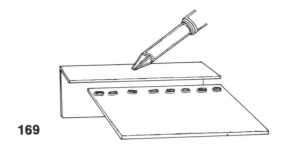

169

Test the adhesion after the metal cools. If the joint is not firm, remove the metal parts, clean and flux all surfaces, and begin as before. When the metal has cooled remove any solder that has bled out from under edges with files and emery paper or cloth (see 152).

170. Soldering Edge to Surface

Tools and materials
Same as 166

Parts to be soldered that cannot be twisted like wire or held in a vise, and that do not remain in place, must be held together with wire and positioned on an asbestos pad or brazier. Place small portions of solder wire against the cleaned and fluxed joint and heat with the tinned iron (see diag. 170); the solder will flow into the joint. (See 168 if the solder beads and does not flow.)

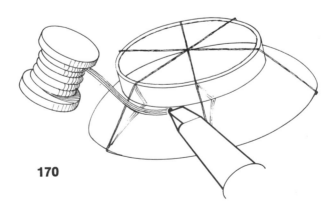

170

171. Collage Soldering

Tools and materials
    Same as 166
    Metal plate
    Wire; found metal parts and objects (see XIV)

Use any of the various soldering techniques described in 166–170, depending on the nature of the individual metal pieces to be adhered.

172. Assemblage Soldering

Tools and materials
    Same as 166 and 171

Clamp or wire parts into position before soldering, whenever the assemblage cannot be laid on its side or parts placed flat on top of surfaces to which they are to be adhered. Use whatever soldering techniques are appropriate (see 166–171).

173. Chain Links

Tools and materials
    Wire (see 149)
    Pliers (see 150)
    Wire forming jig (see 151)
    Vise (see 147)
    Soldering tools and materials (see 166)

Form individual wire chain links, using the wire forming jig or a metal tube or rod locked into the vise (see diag. 173.a). Cut each formed link off the wire. Links can be joined to one another as a chain (see diag. 173.b), or can serve as hinges attached to metal blanks into which holes have been drilled (see diag. 173.c), or can be soldered to them (see diag. 173.d). After attaching the links in one or another of the methods de-

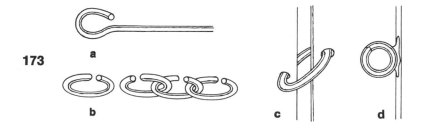

173   a
     b   c   d

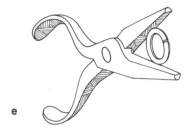

e

scribed, squeeze each one closed with the pliers and solder the closures in turn (see diag. 173.e, and 166 and 168).

G. DECORATING METAL

174. Painting

Most metals, other than untreated galvanized iron, can be enameled. But this process involves extremely high temperatures and is unsuitable for young craftsmen. However, any metal (except galvanized) can be painted with enamel paints or with japan and oil colors (see 227 and 244). Be sure to remove all dirt, grease, or rust from the metal surface with emery cloth before painting. Do not allow children and young people to use spray cans, and observe the cautions on the container label for every kind of paint (see I.k).

175. Combining Metals and Other Materials

Interesting decorative effects are obtained in metal by working in relief (see 162) and by gluing or soldering different metals to one another (see 166–172). Other materials—wood, leather, or fibers—also can be combined with metals. For example, leather thong or wool can be laced around metal edges; wood and metal can be inlaid or combined for collages and assemblages; tin or copper can be used to cover a wooden shape and so achieve substance and dimension without weight.

V

Leather Craft

Never forget the material you are working with, and always try to use it for what it can do best.—William Morris

A. BACKGROUND

American Indian tribes cured animal skins by salting and burying them in wood-chip-and-water filled holes dug into the ground, and then drying and working them until they became pliable. Eskimo women still scrape and chew reindeer skins with their teeth to make them durable and soft enough for wearing. Tanning and tooling of leather were known among the Egyptians more than 1,300 years before Christ; in China this craft was perfected even earlier. The ancient Jews discovered how to preserve hides with oak bark, and they used leather for making ritual articles, sandals, leggings, and shields and armor, as did the Greeks and Romans.

Some of the first craft guilds were formed by British and European leatherworkers in the fourteenth century. Two different guilds became responsible for the preparation of animal skins—the tanners and the skinners. The tanners preserved fur-free skins for makers of shoes, belts, gloves, purses, saddles, carriages, harnesses, and sword sheaths, and for armorers and clothiers. The skinners prepared hides on which the animal's fur remained. for furriers who made coats, cloaks, jackets, stoles, hats, trim, and other articles of fashion.

The tanners soaked the animal skins in lime water for twelve hours to loosen flesh and hair before stretching them over smooth, bark-free logs to scrape them clean. The cleaned skins were then placed into three different vats in turn, each containing a progressively stronger "liquor" made of chipped oak bark and water. The hides stayed in the first vat for up to thirty days; in the second for up to three months; and in the final one for from four to seven months. The tanned leather was scraped and shaved once more, rubbed with a mixture of tallow and neat's-foot oil, washed with a soda and lime solution, dried, dyed, and finally polished with a smooth stone. Thick leather was split with sharp knives into thin layers for finer apparel like gloves. In the nineteenth century most of these processes were mechanized.

Cutting, working, and tooling leather take time and patience even when they are done by machine. But the ancient ways of working are still practiced in Morocco, India, and Mexico, and to a lesser extent by a few remaining European and American craftsmen.

Leather from various animal species has different thickness, texture, and other characteristics. With the threatened extinction of many species of wildlife due to their merciless destruction for the sake of their skins, no leather made from other than domestic breeds should ever be used for craft.

Cowhide is used most commonly for shoe leather and soles. It is difficult to work unless split, especially in inexperienced and weaker than adult hands. Split cowhide can be cut easily with scissors and worked by young children. Calfskin, steerhide, sheepskin, pigskin, and goatskin in various grades are obtainable from tanneries and craft supply houses. Suede is the flesh side of the leather regardless of its source.

Leather can be bought in whole and half skins, in sides, and as findings. The back side of the skin is the most valuable, fault-free grade. Findings are small cutoff remnants left over after the better portions of the skins have been used in manufacture and by craftsmen. The best material for work by children and beginning young craftsmen, they are available from tanneries, shoemakers, leatherworkers, and craft supply houses. Like all leather, they should be stored flat, grain side up, on an open shelf. Leather thong—thin strips of leather used for lacing and binding—is expensive. Vinyl lacing, while lacking the quality of the organic material, is a useful substitute, available from craft material suppliers.

The first efforts in leatherwork by children should be spontaneous. Earliest projects involve activities that familiarize children with the characteristics of the material and with the techniques and tools required to work it successfully. More mature young people should be encouraged to make paper templates and mock-ups (see 67 and 68) before working with the leather itself. Many of the paper and foil craft techniques—punching (see 5), lacing (see 7), weaving (see II.G), scoring, scribing, and cutting (see II.F)—are essential preparations for leather craft. They involve similar, and in many cases identical, procedures, in less expensive, more easily worked, and expendable materials.

B. BEGINNING LEATHER CRAFT

176. Scissors Cutting and Gluing

Tools and materials
> Split leather (see V.A)
> Scissors
> Sheets of heavy cardboard
> Leather glue
> Wax or tracing paper
> Mallet

Leather is usually cut with a sharp knife. However, young children can cut split leather with ordinary scissors. Split leather scraps can often be obtained free or inexpensively from manufacturers of wallets, purses, and gloves.

Scissors-cut split leather can be glued to itself or to cardboard, wood, metal, felt, and other materials. Rubber cement, both sides mounted dry (see 23), is the most commonly used and effective adhesive. Slip-sheet the material (see 24) and, once the leather is positioned and glued, tap it with a mallet and then clean off excess cement with a rubber cement eraser (see 20).

White vegetable, casein, and acrylic glues are also used. Rye flour paste, which can be made at home (see 18), adheres leather especially well. Suggest that a minimum of glue be used for such pasting so that it does not stain the leather. Brush two or three light coats of the rye flour glue on both surfaces. Press the leather together before the glue dries.

Wipe off any excess with a damp cloth, then place the leather between two pieces of wood larger than the glued surfaces and hold them together with C-clamps (see 112) for half an hour or more, until the glue is complely dry.

177. Collage and Appliqué

Tools and materials
    Same as 176
    Leather findings
    Found material (see XIV)

Split leather from different hides, or dyed in a variety of stains, can be used for collages and assemblages (see 27, 28, 96, and 111). Cut into very small pieces, leather can be used as mosaic modules (see 29 and 289); use the adhesives suggested in 176. Appliqué consists of pasting smaller pieces of leather to a larger piece.

178. Stamping and Punching

Tools and materials
    Round drive punch
    Revolving punch
    One-pronged chisel
    Multiple-pronged chisel
    Dividers
    Rawhide mallet
    10" × 12" × ¾" wooden workboard
    Leather findings

The listed punches and chisels are required for basic leatherwork, though one of each suffices for beginners. Punching holes into leather is the first step for all lacing (see 179), sewing (see 186), and studding and grommeting (see 185). Demonstrate how a line is marked with a ruler and soft pencil wherever the leather is to be laced, sewn, or grommeted. After marking with a pair of dividers the places on the line where the holes are to be made (see diag. 178.a), use a punch or chisel of a size that matches the lace, thread, or grommet to perforate the leather (see diag. 178.b). All punching dies, including the revolving punch, can be hammered with a mallet.

Two different hole patterns are generally used for lacing around the edges of leather. The first consists of holes punched in a straight line (see diag. 178.c, and 179). The second consists of alternate, staggered holes for a different lacing effect (see diag. 178.d, and 179). The

178

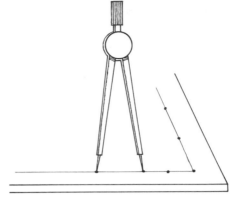

a

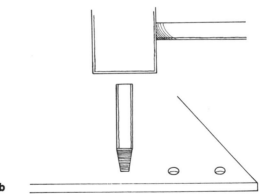

b

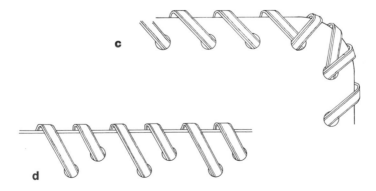

c

d

punched-out circles of leather can be saved and used for collages and mosaics (see 29 and 176).

The punches can also be used to create hole designs anywhere in the flat leather for lacing with thong or fibers. Be sure to keep the leather on a wooden workboard when driving punches and chisels with the mallet so as not to mar furniture surfaces.

179. Lacing

Tools and materials
Leather or vinyl thong
Lacing needle
Hole or die punched leather shapes

Old leather belts can be cut into thin strips to provide thong. After holes have been punched into the leather (see 178), secure one end of the thong in the lacing needle (see diag. 179.a). Push the needle into the first hole and pull the thong through, leaving about 1″ protruding from it. This end can be knotted and trimmed with scissors and then pulled up close to the first hole, or it can be tucked under the first few stitches. Then show the child how to lace around the edge of the leather, from hole to hole, using the whipstitch (see diag. 179.b). If the holes are

179

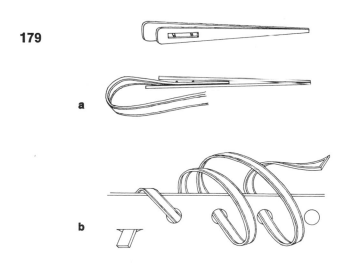

a

b

staggered, a more decorative version of the whipstitch can be laced (see diag. 178.d). Diagrams 179.c and d show additional simple, common lacing methods that can be adapted and varied.

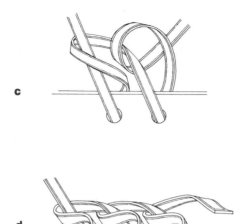

180. Braiding and Plaiting

Tools and materials
Leather or vinyl thong

Thong can be braided and plaited like fibers (see X.c); the same techniques apply and can be adapted. Leather or vinyl is especially useful for this since it does not break easily and can be unraveled again and again.

C. SHAPING AND FASTENING

181. Making Templates

Before making a useful, rather than a decorative, object out of leather, or during various stages of completion, it's wisest to make a paper mock-up or template (see 66–68, and XII). Then expensive or hard-to-replace leather is not ruined, parts can be fitted and altered, and problems of construction can be worked out in advance.

182. Cutting and Skiving

Tools and materials
    Sharp knife blade (skiving or head knife optional)
    Metal T-square
    Leather
    10″ × 12″ × ¾″ wooden cutting board

Heavy leather must be cut with a knife. Leatherworkers use head and
skiving knives (see diag. 182.a), but these require skill and experience.
They are not recommended for young people below high school age. A
sharp mounting knife is best for younger ages, provided all cautions are
exercised to prevent accidents (see 86 and 87).

182

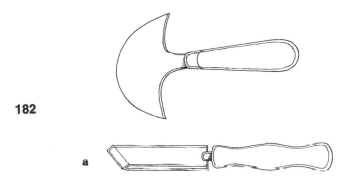

a

When cutting a corner with blade and T-square, do not complete the
first cut. End it about ½″ short of the corner and then make another cut
in reverse from the corner to the end of the first cut (see diag. 182.b).

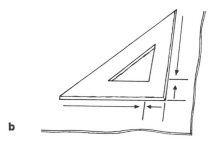

b

Skiving—cutting a bevel into the edge of the leather—is necessary to prepare edges that are to be glued together (see diag. 182.c), or for edges of heavy leather that are to be folded (see 183) or sewn (see 186). The safest method is to clamp the leather to the edge of the cutting board and draw a spokeshave (see 130) along the leather edge that lies parallel to the edge of the board (see diag. 182.d).

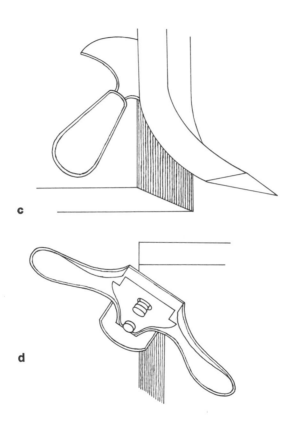

c

d

183. Moistening and Folding

Tools and materials
    Leather
    Rags or sponge
    Bowl of clear water and soap; towel
    Straight edge

Leather can be creased or folded without cracking the surface, provided it is first moistened slowly until it becomes pliable. It can then be folded over a wooden or metal straight edge. Moisten the flesh side until the water begins to darken the finished side of the leather.

Very heavy leather, especially if it is to be carved or folded, should always be cased. This means scrubbing it clean with mild soap and water. Rinse off all soap and then let the leather soak in water for about five minutes. Wrap the wet leather in a towel and leave it overnight. Next day it will be soft enough to be worked. (See also 190.)

Leather can also be folded if it is first scored, like cardboard (see 86–88). This method tends to weaken the leather considerably.

184. Stretching and Forming

Leather is sufficiently pliable, especially after it has been moistened, so that it can be molded in relatively shallow cavities and then pressed into a forming die. For example, to form a cup shape, the desired circumference of the shape is cut out of a 1″-thick pine board, using a coping saw (see 114). First drill a hole to insert the blade and then cut a beveled edge all around the shape (see diag. 184.a, and 182). Be sure to hold the coping saw at the required angle.

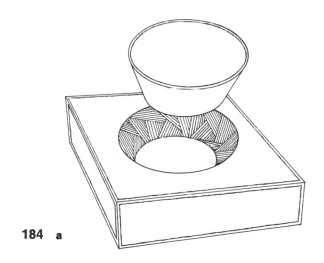

184 a

After the leather has been cased (see 183) nail it to the side of the forming die that has the larger opening, without driving the nails all the way into the wood, so that they can be pulled easily later. Then line up the cut-out wooden disc, narrow side down, with the larger opening in the wooden die and clamp it onto the leather with a C-clamp (see diag.

184.b, and 112). Force the wood and leather into the die opening with the C-clamp until they will go no further without cracking. After the leather has dried completely, it can be removed and will retain its new shape. The edges of the piece can then be trimmed with a knife and laced, finished, or adhered to other shapes or materials.

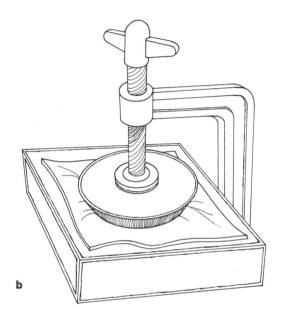

b

185. Studding and Grommeting

Tools and materials
Same as 178
Grommets and grommet die
Eyelets and eyelet die
Rivets and rivet set
Snap fasteners and die
Rawhide mallet
10″ × 12″ × ¾″ wooden workboard

Holes must be prepunched for all of the above-listed fasteners and attachments (see 178), each the exact same size as or a shade larger than the diameter of the shank of the attachment. A variety of each kind is available, together with the required die or set, in craft supply shops. The metal piece is inserted into the hole and spread with the die and mallet (see 6).

186. Sewing

Tools and materials

Leather

Space marker wheel; or dividers

Harness needle (for younger age groups or for heavy thread); "sharps" (for older age groups or for finer thread)

Revolving leather punch

Rawhide mallet

Spool of saddler's or bookbinder's linen thread; or coarse nylon thread or twine

The harness needle is ideal for young children since it is blunt. "Sharps" are available in various sizes. The line where the leather is to be sewn must first be marked (see 179), and spaces for stitch holes marked with the space marker wheel (see diag. 186.a) and then punched (see 178), before it can be sewn. Heavy leather to be sewn at the edges should be skived and if possible glued before marking, punching, and sewing. If no marker wheel is available, the places where holes for the stitches are to be punched can be marked with dividers (see 178 and 179). The following stitches are those most commonly used in sewing leather:

Running stitch (diag. 186.b)

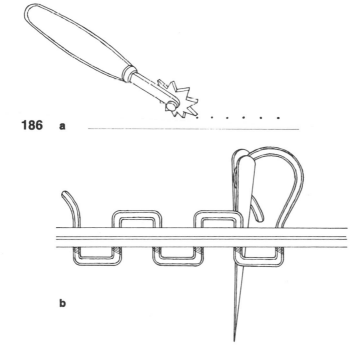

186 a

b

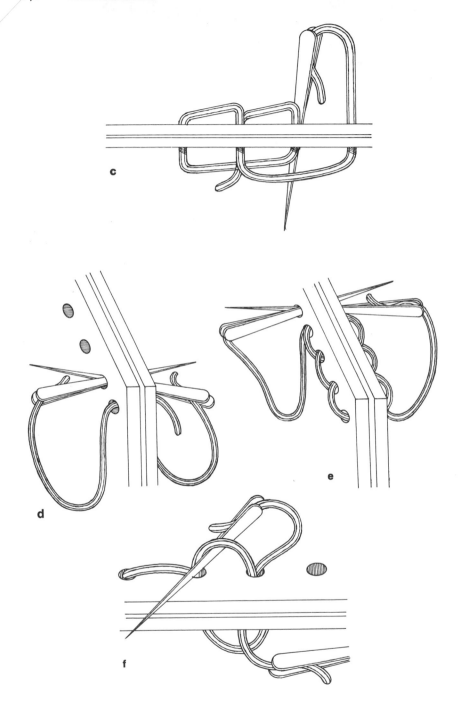

Back stitch (diag. 186.c)
Saddler's stitch (diags. 186.d and e)
Locked saddler's stitch (diag. 186.f)

Awls for leather sewing are also available from craft supply shops. Such awls are useful in more-advanced sewing projects. Instructions are furnished with each different model.

187. Care of Tools

Leatherworking tools, like all sharp tools, require frequent honing and occasional sharpening. They need to be kept rust-free and covered with a thin film of light oil, especially when not in use. (See 135 for detailed instructions.)

D. FINISHING AND DECORATING

188. Dyeing and Coloring

(See also 245.)

Do not let young children use leather dyes; they are highly corrosive and toxic. Young people can dye leather successfully with ordinary waterproof or India inks. These should be applied with a sable or camel's-hair brush or, if large areas are to be tinted, with a sponge. The leather will take the ink only if it has not been polished or waxed and if it has been sanded with fine sandpaper. First wash the leather with mild soap and water and let dry before it is tinted. Dilute the inks if subtle tints are required.

Wax-free, unpolished, and sanded leather can be painted with oil and acrylic paints (see 237 and 238). All dyeing, tinting, or painting should be done after the leather has been cut, embossed, or carved, but before it is glued, laced, plaited, studded, grommeted, or sewn.

Exposed leather edges that are not laced can be sanded and stained with ink or burnished with a bone burnisher. Rub the burnishers back and forth over the leather edge until it develops a glossy patina.

Saddle soap provides a good finish for stained leather. Apply it with a damp sponge and rub it well into the leather with a circular motion. Do not rub too hard over ink stained portions. Polish with a soft, dry cloth after the saddle soap has dried.

189. Stamping and Embossing

Tools and materials
Leather
Stamping dies
Embossing ball end modeler
Rawhide mallet
10″ × 12″ × ¾″ wooden workboard

Stamping, punching, and embossing dies for leather are available in a great variety of designs. Provide only those that make simple geometric shapes—a circle, square, triangle, bar, or the like. A child can combine these to make his or her own designs. Do not give children dies engraved with flower, star, and other prepared decorative effects.

Tape a scrap of leather to the wooden workboard, polished side facing up. Demonstrate how to hold the die in one hand and the mallet in the other, striking the flat, solid end of the punch to stamp the shape into the leather. Show how the different-shaped dies can be punched into the leather next to one another to form various designs.

Embossing—engraving by pressing into the leather with a rounded modeler—is usually done on the flesh side of the leather. This raises designs on the other side that can be made more prominent by modeling along the edges of the raised portions on that side of the leather (see 35).

190. Tooling and Carving

Young people sufficiently mature to work with sharp blades can use an incising knife or swivel knife. Younger and less mature children can carve and tool into leather with well-sharpened linoleum cutting gouges (see 305).

The leather must be moistened before tooling or carving (see 183). Cuts should be no deeper than half the thickness of the leather. Read and follow the descriptions of techniques and the cautions detailed in 86, 87, and 305.

Use of the swivel knife requires considerable practice. Provide ample scrap leather on which to try out different methods of holding and working these leather carving tools.

191. Combining Leather with Other Materials

The different leatherworking methods can be combined and used for work in other materials. For example, metal or wooden shapes can be covered with leather; leather shapes can be embedded into wood; and leather, fibers, and fabrics can be combined in a number of ways (see 175). The inventive combination of different media is in itself a creative act, providing a variety of sensory and esthetic experiences. When media are mixed, the differing working disciplines and methods that apply to each are brought into sharp focus.

192. Burning

Leather burning, like wood burning, is not recommended for young people. Aside from the potential dangers of working with hot and flammable materials, very similar effects can be achieved by embossing (see 189) and tooling or carving (see 190).

193. Preserving the Leather

Apply several light coats of leather preservative to all leather goods about twice each year. Use a clean cloth as an applicator. Be sure first to dust and clean the leather with a damp cloth and saddle soap and let it dry completely.

Warm neat's-foot oil is the best preservative for boots, including the soles. Clean first as detailed above, then rub castor oil into the leather and let dry before applying the neat's-foot oil. Patent leather should be treated with castor oil once each month to keep it from cracking.

To waterproof leather, mix neat's-foot oil and tallow in equal proportions. Heat this mixture over a low flame while stirring. Apply it to the leather with the palm of the hand after the mixture has cooled to skin temperature. Pour whatever remains into a pan and let the soles of the shoes or boots stand in it for about ten minutes to waterproof them and the seams.

VI

Drawing and Painting

Art is a natural discipline.—*Sir Herbert Edward Read*

A. BACKGROUND

Drawing, painting, and forming are developmental necessities for children. A child learns to speak, not to become a TV announcer, but to be human. He learns to sing, dance, and play music, not to become a virtuoso, but to recognize and make meaningful sounds, to listen, respond, and move ably and gracefully. He learns to read and write, not to become an author, but to understand and become understandable. Similarly, a child needs art experiences, not to become an artist, but to exercise essential human qualities—coordination, vision, craft, imagination, thought, and expression.

All learning requires a foundation of sensory experience. A child who lacks exposure to seeing, hearing, smelling, and touching experiences, and one who has not played with materials, is unlikely to enjoy drawing and painting, or working with clay. He must first have the opportunity to feel different textures, sizes, and weights of materials; smell their odors; learn the sounds they produce when they are touched gently, struck, scratched, or plucked; and judge and compare the appearance of their different shapes, colors, and textures.

The development of a baby's speech depends on his hearing sounds and associating them with comfort and pleasure. If he receives encouragement he'll create his own noises and eventually have his say. If never allowed to babble spontaneously he is likely to become more or less autistic. If never permitted to finish a sentence in childhood he may become a stutterer. Similarly, a child who is given no free rein in the use of art materials, who is restricted to coloring books that speak for him or clay molds that are preformed, who is told what to draw, paint, sculpt, or mold, may never realize his graphic and plastic self-expressive faculties.

These are self-evident truths recognized in every branch of education—save in the art education of children or young people. Here they are violated at every turn. When the child uses art materials at home or in the classroom, he is usually given little opportunity to play with them or discover their properties. Instead he is often shown how to draw cliché clouds, ocean waves, or people, smiling moons and suns, or the stereotype houses, trees, flowers, and animals found in comic strips and TV cartoons. Or the child is given molds to fill with modeling dough, or predrawn pictures to color and trace. Once he can count, numbered outline pictures are provided that he is required to fill in with matching numbered pencils or paints.

When such an art education predominates, children learn early to stay within restrictive boundaries, not just in their art but in all their thoughts and activities. And when they break out of such confinement in adolescence they are not likely to know or recognize the legitimate bounds to their actions. They are prepared only for rote learning and mindless production. They lack endurance. They fail to learn how to make rules for themselves. They are likely to remain incurious and unimaginative in their adult personal and economic lives. Parents and teachers who favor the "busy work" of the coloring book sacrifice children's development for an instantly gratifying and pacifying, but worthless, activity. The damage done to children by these bromides is incalculable. But the benefits of a considerate art education, while subtle and less apparent on the surface, do become evident in the child's later life.

". . . [It is] not advisable to engage a child under the age of twelve or fourteen in any but the most voluntary practice of art . . . and it should be allowed to scrawl at its own free will, due praise being given for every appearance of care, of truth, and of its effort." [64] John Ruskin knew this close to one hundred years ago, and Pestalozzi expressed similar ideas more than a century before him. There are quite evident reasons why children draw, paint, and sculpt as they do at different stages of maturation. Yet very little study has been devoted to the developmental aspects of art, craft, and the creative urge. This lack is illustrated in a 1,365-page review of college level tests in the United States, which discloses that only one percent of those tests currently available to be given concern aptitude or achievement in art or music.[59] Whether or not such abilities can or even should be tested, this illustrates how thoroughly the arts are slighted in the curriculum by those who design and direct it.

Yet there is convincing neurological evidence that about one third of all children are primarily visually-aurally, rather than verbally, oriented and intelligent.[66] No accommodation is made for this substantial proportion of the child population in education or in intelligence testing. "A system of education which aims at the creation of a uniform standard of intelligence and, more indirectly, at the creation of a uniform culture, only ends by producing a widespread neurosis within the structure of society." [63] This may or may not be true for primitive or relatively isolated and self-sufficient societies, but it is certainly true for our industrial and interdependent one.

Jean Piaget, the noted Swiss child psychologist, has paid attention only to the verbal expression of the children he has studied. He has failed entirely to notice the similarity in the unfolding of the child's graphic and plastic expressive abilities, which parallels that of his objective judgment and reasoning powers. Yet Piaget is explicit in his finding that early sensory-motor activation—coordination of multisensory experiences with active, manipulative play, art, and craft—is essential for the full emotional and intellectual development of the child. Educational researchers rediscover this theme periodically, test and verify these conclusions, and publish their findings—which then gather dust in Ph.D. thesis depositories and computer banks. Such studies fail to affect what art education takes place in the home or in the classroom, with some notable exceptions.[24]

Cognitive and creative development run parallel in the child, and each affects and is affected by the other. ". . . A child's development of quantitative concepts is influenced by the one-dimensional view to which he is limited in early years. But this one-dimensional judgment and his lack of concern with qualities that escape his notice give children's art its special quality. Each individual child concentrates on and expresses that feature which is most significant to him. The child's elimination of all but the most significant features enables the astute observer to tell a great deal about his [or her] inner thoughts, feelings and development. Perceptual immaturity produces insights that the mature artist must often struggle to achieve. Self expression consists of the choice of features and their arrangement in a context of significance. It should be encouraged in all creative activities. What the child first does out of necessity and because of the limitations imposed on him by his lack of perceptual development can later turn into a deliberate act.'' [3]

Every child and every adult possesses a sense that is not generally recognized—a *sense of esthetic necessity*. It dictates a preference, shared by our whole species, for a particular balance and order, symmetry and asymmetry, that, when experienced or created, evoke a deep sense of satisfaction. The sense of esthetic necessity is undoubtedly innate in each of us, although certainly in varying degrees of acuity, as are all other senses. With education, we can be similarly gratified by a Neolithic mural, an African sculpture, a Chinese vase, an Egyptian frieze, a Gothic cathedral, a Cubist painting, and a photograph. Each in its own way and for identical reasons satisfies our need for particular forms and patterns that, in a master's work, could not be otherwise. This same sense of esthetic necessity imbues human thought, language, music, science, mythology, and art with a universality. At its highest cultivation it allows people from any culture to understand and appreciate all others. It embraces faith, belief, and religious experience. In children this commonality lies closest to the surface of consciousness; it is not yet overlain with cultural prejudice.

It is the dual responsibility of parent and teacher to introduce the child to his own culture and, at the same time, to nurture his universal sense of esthetic necessity to protect him from cultural parochialism. The arts are one of the avenues by which these goals can be reached. Art education integrates the child's need to be active with his sense of esthetic necessity and the drive to leave his or her private mark on the world. It gives every child a chance to become immortal in some measure and to share in the immortality of the human spirit. It can arouse a dissatisfaction with disorder and confusion, sufficient to inspire active intervention to create a new and greater harmony. It stimulates the desire to improve the environment and the human condition. It develops an appreci... ...ou... e motivation to preserve what is most valuable and satisfying in the legacy of the past.

One cause of confusion in art education stems from a misunderstanding of the processes involved in learning how to write. Here the child must eventually draw symbols with accuracy. Yet early free drawing is an essential preparation for writing skills. The child can only learn to control his writing instrument by scribbling at random until his coordination increases to a point at which the pencil follows his dictates.

Once that is mastered he is ready to learn to write. And so, free scribbling is an essential prerequisite even for academic skills. Thereafter the child still needs freedom in his art, though for different reasons. The real purpose of writing is expression; but this exercise is denied the child while he learns his letters. Especially then, he needs free rein in his artistic activities so that he does not lose the faculty of expression in the process of acquiring rote skills.

Art should be a creative challenge, providing great satisfaction when it is met with whatever skill, ability, imagination, and capacity for involvement the child possesses. Art activities create values. They educate the emotions and foster an ethical viewpoint. Forms and feelings can be tried out and their ethical implications explored without consequence. Art education provides a beneficial release of physical and psychological energy.

Inevitably, there is an implied ethic in the execution of art. Here readily apparent differences exist between the adult's and the child's work. As stated, the child's art is a trial; the adult's art on the other hand influences the environment profoundly. In mature art there is no separating the esthetic from the social awareness. For example, New York City's Avenue of the Americas from Forty-second Street to Fifty-ninth may be esthetically moving in some respects. But the ice cube beehives, with their curtain walls of glass behind which hundreds of thousands of people are trapped during their working hours, are monuments to the repression of the human spirit. The same can be said of London's Centre Point. These massive corporate tombs are ecologically and psychologically disastrous, no matter how profitable or architecturally impressive they may be. The architects who cater to such clients lack all social and ecological foresight or consciousness. The child, however, when he piles his building blocks too high, learns soon and harmlessly that his structure must collapse—as may our urban centers if current architectural trends prevail.[61]

Art education familiarizes the child with the origins of materials, processes, tools, and fabricated objects. It stimulates a curiosity to know and understand. "Children of earlier generations were reared on farms or in small or self contained communities. They absorbed essential information informally and on their own. The woodsman who felled the tree, the saw mill operator who cut up the logs, and the carpenter who converted the boards into furniture and tools were their neighbors." [3] Today's child seldom sees the artisan at close proximity. At best he watches him on TV, where, due to the limitations of the medium, laborious crafts turn into instant production. Art activities give children much-needed incentives to explore their own environment. The firehouse around the corner or the neighbor's cat can be the inspiration for their art; the local stone, wood, clay, or pavement their art materials.

a. Chronology of Development

No child should ever be made or expected to draw, paint, or sculpt. Some children prefer other arts and crafts. But the materials should be made available and attractive to all children. The particulars suggested in this chapter match materials and techniques children can handle to a chronology of skill and perceptual development. Art interests and skills require encouragement. But even more than that, they require opportunity. Given these, and with a climate of freedom and appreciation and some guidance, most children will draw, paint, and sculpt eagerly and with invention.

The suggested order is not intended as a curriculum. It can be changed—projects left out or related to other crafts—depending on the availability of materials and the child's inclination. Yet some basics are worth observing. For example, crayons are easier to control than chalks; yet chalks are a more satisfactory medium. A compass is fun, but it should not be given to young children until they have enjoyed several years of free-hand drawing, or else the use of mechanical drawing instruments may become so attractive that they may preclude the development of other, more important skills.

As with all materials of play, the child's first efforts center around an exploration of what the materials can be made to do and how he can affect and transform them. He must *play* with them. He increases his control through play. His abilities unfold in the act of discovery. The crayon scribbles turn bolder, into long, sweeping, involute lines, and then are converted into random dots and dashes. (By all means show the child that he can also lay the crayon on its side and, after peeling off the paper, make broad strokes and textured masses of color.) The same principles hold true for chalk or paint, for squeezing, pressing, and rolling clay into beads, sausages, and flat sheets, or for scratching into dried slabs of modeling compound or plaster (see VII). While the child experiments with the materials, he cannot be concerned with "making something." He is too busy doing something that has value to his development as an able human being. The awakening to the idea that illustrative or representational creation is possible comes much later, and only after the child has gained considerable mastery over himself, his tools, and his medium.

When he has exhausted the possibilities of spontaneous exploration, he may discover by accident that what he has drawn, painted, or formed reminds him of a figure, animal, object, or plant he has seen. The similarity between what he sees in his art and reality may be remote or nonexistent. "Look! I've made a fire engine," means no more than seeing a man in the moon. The child merely imagines or wishes that his creation is what he wants it to be. It is quite enough. His picture probably looks like a mess, or the clay shape may be a formless lump—it doesn't matter. What matters is that the child has reached a stage at which he recognizes that what he draws, paints, or sculpts *could* represent something he has experienced or imagined. It's a big step forward, but it's one that cannot be forced or accelerated.

At this stage many adults feel compelled to ease the child's development by showing him or her how to make a drawing or sculpture look "real." Such short cuts to adult reality (or pop symbology) short-circuit the process of self-discovery. The child needs to invent his own forms of expression. The wonder and enthusiasm inspired by such private invention is miraculous. But adult guidance is needed to teach him orderly and safe methods that facilitate work. Help the child acquire disciplined habits like keeping tools, paints, and brushes clean and to one side while he works. Awaken the child to processes and experiences he might never discover on his own. But the unfolding of his or her inventive faculties must be left undisturbed.

Teach control of the material: "Let's arrange all the paints over here, each jar with its own tongue depressor to spoon out the paint into the muffin tin. Dip out a little of each as you need it. But keep the paint jar lids closed so that the paint doesn't dry out. Also don't dip a tongue depressor or brush loaded with blue paint into the yellow by accident. It'll turn all the yellow paint green." Suggest free experimentation: "Make whatever you like. Try some big, long lines and then some very little ones." Appreciate the result: "That looks very good" (or happy, or sad, or rough, or smooth). Encourage discovery of the different effects possible with different materials: "Try drawing the comb through the wet paint" (or clay) "and see what happens." Suggest to the child that he try out what happens when he rubs the paint with his fingers, or other tools that he chooses. Some techniques, like those for smoked paper, gesso painting, and batik, must first be demonstrated before a child can experiment with them on his own.

Ultimately the child begins to be able to predict what he is going to do with increasing certainty and sureness. The results may still seem unreal or abstract to adults, but they are very real to him. His main satisfaction stems from his ability to make tools and materials obey him. This is most gratifying to a child, who is told at every turn what he can and must not do. He now has a private domain in which he is in total command. He is master of his tools, materials, and wishes—he can bend them to his will: "I've made it myself. My crayons did what I wanted them to do."

Even if he succeeds only partially, the rewards of invention are far greater than those of production. The latter only teaches that quantity, slickness, and consumption are more prized than creation, endurance, self-discipline, and discreet use of materials. The child's character development suffers when he evades the laborious processes of invention.

Art teaches the child how to cope with failure. If something is messed up, it's easy enough to start over again, and improve with practice. Fear of failure (and refusal to try repeatedly once they have failed) is one of the major learning handicaps suffered by children in our success-driven time.

The main functions of the adult in the art education of children is to provide opportunities and experiences in the world around them; to make the child aware of the characteristics of his materials and of his ability to affect and transform these materials; and to teach him control and good work habits. The adult should encourage the child to play with materials, sensations, and forms of expression, and give him incentives to combine and convert these into unique and personal, though not necessarily representational, creations. The child may suffer occasional frustration, especially at times when his understanding is ahead of his ability to express himself—as it usually is at all stages of development. But coming to grips with these frustrations and coping with them, instead of being frozen into passivity, is an essential lesson for every art and craft and for all of life. "It is only fear that prevents the child from becoming an artist—fear that his private world of fantasy will seem ridiculous to the adult. . . . Cast out fear from the child, and you have then released all its potentialities for emotional growth and maturation." [63]

As stated earlier, the child needs exposure to working artists and to the art of his own and other cultures and times. He can then become aware of the variety of forms and styles that is available. Reality and fantasy, filtered through his perceptions and limited only by the discipline imposed by physical circumstances, allow the child to create a *new* reality. This is what art is all about. Through his art the child participates in the real world—and at the same time he can invent his own, in which anything is possible, anything can be invoked or imagined. The ability to synthesize a personal symbology distinguishes human beings from all other life forms. It is one of the approaches to godliness. In helping a child develop this faculty, parents and teachers enable him or her to reach for the highest level of existence possible to our species.

b. Materials and Work Spaces

Every child needs his own private work space or, at the very least, room at a table low enough so that he can work comfortably, sitting or standing. He needs space to lay out his materials within reach. Preferably the working surface should be spillproof—Formica, linoleum, plastic, glass, or oilcloth; or covered with protective material—a heavy sheet of cardboard, or layers of newspaper firmly taped down.

Children don't need an easel for painting. Most children's easels are too flimsy to be of any use. As an alternative work surface, layers of newspaper, a large sheet of cardboard or corrugated board, or a bulletin board, blackboard, or wallboard can be tacked to, nailed to, or hung on a wall. Or a portion of wall can be sized as a painting surface (see 224). The child then needs a tray hung below the wall work surface to hold paint jars, brushes, crayons, or chalks, or a small table placed to his left or right, depending on his handedness. (See also I.j.)

c. Surfaces

For drawing
Newsprint (available in 17″ × 24″ pads)
Brown or white wrapping paper
Butcher paper
White or colored construction paper
Shirt board and other cardboard
Panels cut from corrugated cartons
For painting
All the above
Sheets of printed newspaper
Wallboard or plasterboard panels

Other surfaces for drawing and painting are detailed below. Drawing and painting papers and surfaces should be large enough so that the child can make bold strokes with crayon or brush. This may seem wasteful, especially at early ages, when children tend to make a few scribbles on a sheet and then claim they have finished. But a preschooler can be encouraged to work all over the paper with some endurance if the paper is large enough and the supply limited.

Impress on the child that he must not draw or paint beyond the paper surface onto wall, table, or floor. Freedom has its limitations. It carries with it the responsibility to confine the work and to exercise essential restraints. Insist that the child help clean up after he has finished, until he or she is old enough to do this unaided. These are the right kind of controls—more beneficial than those imposed by staying within the lines of a coloring book.

B. DRAWING

194. Crayon Scribbling

Tools and materials
School grade crayons
(See VI.A.c for surfaces.)

Children's wax crayons are available in a variety of grades. Provide only "school grade" crayons. They are less brittle, larger, and more easily handled by young children than those usually found in toy, chain, and stationery stores. Let the child experiment. (See VI.A.a and b for additional suggestions on how to introduce him.)

At first, give the child a small assortment of primary colors only—red, yellow, blue, black, white. Add others later. Provide a cigar box into which he can tumble them out of their packages; in the package they are too closely packed to be handled with ease. Keep each drawing session short, ending it as soon as the child tires. Keep paper and crayons on open shelves where he can reach them unaided. Don't set particular hours or days aside as drawing times. Rather suggest, from time to time, that he or she use the materials in between other play activities.

Crayons are not an ideal drawing material. Chalks are much better. But the younger age groups can handle crayons more easily at first, without breaking or crumbling them as they work.

195. Chalk Drawing on Paper

Tools and materials
> Lecturer's colored chalks
> (See VI.A.c for surfaces.)

Large, fat lecturer's chalks are best. Provide the child with a plastic apron or dress him or her in old clothes. Show him how to smudge colors chalked on the paper, with a rag, fingers, or hand. Demonstrate some of the basic color mixtures—blue and yellow, red and yellow, red and blue. Make the child aware of the three basic qualities of form— line, mass, and texture (see 210–212); explain that "texture" means both roughness and smoothness. (See 194 for other suggestions that apply to both the crayon and chalk media.)

196. Chalk Drawing on a Blackboard

Tools and materials
> Same as 195
> Blackboard (see below for making your own)
> Felt blackboard wiper

Large slate blackboards are expensive. A satisfactory blackboard can be made by painting "blackboard paint" onto well-sanded and sealed plywood (see 137). Apply several coats of the paint, each after the last has dried, using brush strokes at right angles to the preceding coating.

The advantage of a blackboard is that it is always in view once it has been hung. The picture can be wiped out and another started, without ever running out of drawing surfaces. But this is also a disadvantage: you cannot keep the result and hang it on a wall permanently. Children need to have their art admired and respected. They thrive on praise—it is an incentive for future work. Yet be discriminating. Once you have hung and admired some of the child's work, let him or her become aware of your critical judgment. Let him know that you prefer some of his drawings to others; that one seems produced without effort or thought, and that this one is not worthy of display. Such criticism can be a spur to his future efforts. It assures that he doesn't mass-produce scribbles only to elicit your admiration.

197. Felt Marker Drawing

Tools and materials
Small assortment of felt markers
(See VI.A.c for surfaces.)

Many felt markers are indelible. They contain dyes that, while nontoxic, discolor fabric and wood surfaces. Provide protective clothing and cover table and floor for beginners. Teach the child to replace the cap of each marker when he has finished using it for the moment, before he picks up another. Otherwise felt markers dry out quickly.

Felt markers are available in a variety of nib sizes. Provide the child not only with a small variety of colors but also with different-size nibs, ranging from fine to broad. Suggest that he or she combine felt marker drawing with chalks and crayons. This increases variety of possible effects. (See 194 for other suggestions that apply to felt markers as well.)

198. Action Drawing

Tools and materials
Same as 194, 195, and 197
Large drawing surfaces (see VI.A.c)

Encourage gross motor movement with crayon, chalk, and felt markers—broad sweeps made more or less at random across the paper. The child will then not get bogged down working in one small area of paper. As the child's arm moves in arcs, he'll become aware of effects that might not otherwise occur to him. Suggest that he cover the whole paper or board with a single line that curves or zig-zags in and out and doubles back on itself, without lifting the drawing instrument off the paper.

199. Crayon Transfer

Tools and materials
> School grade crayons
> Two or more sheets of bond (writing) paper
> Large sheet of heavy cardboard (for working surface)
> Stylus; used-up ball point pen; or short knitting needle

Show the child how to cover one section of a sheet of paper with heavily applied wax crayon of one color. Turn this colored paper over on top of a second sheet. When the child draws onto the back of the heavily colored area with a stylus, crayon lines will be transferred onto the second sheet.

Eventually the child may wish to draw several adjacent areas of color on a new sheet of clean paper. When the paper is turned over and used as before, he will achieve surprising effects wherever one color area changes to another. The position of the top sheet can also be varied so that different colors are superimposed in successive drawings with the stylus.

200. Crayon Engraving

Tools and materials
> Same as 199

Show the child how to make a solid area of a single light-toned crayon color on one sheet of paper taped to the cardboard. Be sure to apply the crayon in a thick coating. Then cover this area with black crayon so that hardly any trace of the first color shows through. Use the stylus to draw into the black area. As the child works, his design will show through the black in the color that was applied first.

Two or more different light colors can be laid on top of one another and then covered with black crayon as before. Multicolored lines will appear, depending on the amount of pressure applied to the stylus.

201. Smoked-Paper Drawing

Tools and materials
> Sheets of heavy bond paper
> Wax candle
> Stylus (see 199)
> Heavy cardboard work surface

The paper must be smoked for younger age groups; more-mature children can do this for themselves. Hold a lit candle to the paper so that the smoke blackens, but does not burn or scorch, the paper. When the paper is thoroughly coated with soot, the child can draw onto it with a stylus.

202. Mural Drawing

Tools and materials
    Large sheet of wrapping paper tacked to a wall
    Crayons; chalks; felt markers

One child or a group of children will enjoy drawing a mural. Don't expect it to be completed in a single day—let this be a continuing project. Suggest that, in addition to drawing onto the paper, the children adhere cut paper (see II.F), fabrics (see XI.B), and other found materials (see XIV). Don't insist that the mural be representational or assume any particular form. Let the result grow out of the child's or children's own efforts and experience.

203. Pencil Drawing

Lead pencils are available in different grades of hardness and softness. Commercial pencils are numbered from 1 on up, with No. 1 the softest. Artists' pencils are designated from B to H, each letter being assigned a number denoting a greater or lesser degree of hardness, in ascending order in both cases. Don't give children any pencil harder than a No. 3 or 6B with which to draw (except for drafting purposes; see XII). A harder lead interferes with a child's freedom—he will become heavy fisted if he has to press down on a hard pencil to produce an effective line.

Colored pencils seem attractive for children because they don't break as easily as crayons or chalks. But they are very poor art material since they suffer the same deficiencies as the harder lead pencils. Children need soft, fat drawing materials, which allow them to develop deftness; they discover that a delicate touch offers greater control than bearing down hard.

204. Compass Drawing

Tools and materials
    Compass with 6B lead; or 4B or No. 3 pencil
    Sheets of bond or drawing paper
    Heavy cardboard work surface

Mechanical drawing instruments should not be given to children until they draw freely and spontaneously with crayons, chalks, and felt markers. A compass introduced to young children may fascinate them, but it will ultimately frustrate them needlessly when they discover that their free-hand drawing is less neat and controllable. However, in due time the compass can be used both as a creative and as a measuring instrument, provided it becomes a supplemental experience and not a substitute for free-hand drawing. Once the child has the need to measure and design, he can mark off distances with compass or dividers and create symmetrical or asymmetrical patterns and constructions, using the compass and a ruler (see 124 and 403–408).

C. FIRST PAINTING

205. Water Painting

Tools and materials
 Large sheet of white or brown paper
 Bowl of clear water
 Long-handled, flat student grade bristle brush (No. 8, 10, or 12)

Young children need and enjoy water play. Painting with clear water, without color, confines the mess and introduces the child to painting materials and techniques. A two- or three-year-old will get great satisfaction out of painting with water. No directions or safety precautions are required, save for a mop and a towel.

206. Poster Paints

Tools and materials
 Red, yellow, blue, and black powdered tempera pigment (available in packages
  from school and art supply stores); or the same assortment of ready-mixed
  poster paints in screw-top jars
 Long-handled, flat student grade bristle brush (No. 6, 8, or 10)
 8-oz. baby food or other glass screw-top jars
 Muffin tin or paper cups
 Bucket, bowl, or pail of clear water
 Tongue depressors or ice cream sticks (to stir the paints)
 Painting paper (see VI.A.c)
 Newspaper or blotting paper
 Rags or sponge (for wiping hands and paint brush handle)

Powdered poster pigments are more economical than ready-mixed paints. Besides, they can be used for making finger paints (see 207) and other purposes. For brush painting, mix the pigments with water to the consistency of heavy cream, a sufficient quantity of each to fill an 8-oz. jar. Keep the lids tightly closed when the paints are not in use or else they'll dry out and cake. Distribute the different colors in the cups of a muffin tin or in paper cups for the child's painting, so that the whole batch is not ruined if he fails to rinse a brush loaded with one color before dipping it into another.

Premixed poster colors are equally useful, though more expensive. Do not buy fluorescent poster colors, even though they may appeal to children. They are toxic, though this fact is not marked on the label.

Dress the child in a plastic or other apron and roll up his or her sleeves before painting begins. Set up the muffin tin and water container within easy reach next to the paper or other work surface. Be sure to change the water when it gets muddy from repeated brush rinsing. Secure the paper firmly to the table or wall surface with masking tape.

Start the child at his first painting session with a single color. When he has some experience in applying it to the paper, a second color, a third, and more can be added to his palette. Once a second color is provided, teach the child to rinse his brush thoroughly in water before dipping it into the different paint, or else he'll mix the colors inadvertently. Suggest that he mix paints on his painting or in unfilled portions of the muffin tin. Show him that, in addition to painting over other colors he has painted, he can paint one color next to another. Insist that the child confine his work to the provided painting surface and not venture beyond it. These are the first and essential disciplines required for painting. Accidents will happen; overlook them. You can guard against them by placing ample newspaper under and around the work.

Teach the child to thin out his paints whenever they get too thick (as they may). If he thins them too much you can always add a little more powder pigment.

Encourage the child to experiment—to try his or her brush in different ways, including the wooden end; to make lines, dots, and solid shapes; even to use his fingers. Suggest large, bold strokes with the brush, as well as small, delicate ones. Then let him paint to his heart's content for as long as he enjoys daubing away.

When the painting is finished, help the child remove it. Let it dry on newspaper or blotting paper, flat on the floor or table, before hanging it for display. Ask the child if he wants to paint another picture. Let him make the necessary preparations to whatever extent he is able and help him with the rest. At the end of a painting session, insist that he help clean up, screw the lids to the jars, wash out his brush and water container, and remove the protective newspaper from table and floor. The paint brush should be rinsed and then washed with mild soap and warm water. (See also 27, 28, 58, 210–214, 218, 219, and 221–226.)

207. Finger Painting

Tools and materials

Red, yellow, blue, and black finger paints (see 209 for recipe to make your own)
Roll or sheets of finger painting paper (see 208 for alternative finger painting surfaces)
Four tongue depressors or ice cream sticks
Two large bowls or buckets of fresh water
Sponge or rags
Masking tape
Newspaper or blotting paper

Finger paints are more difficult to use than poster paints—a fact that is not generally appreciated. Finger painting should follow, rather than precede, a child's introduction to painting with a brush (see 205 and 206). Separate one sheet of finger painting paper and tape it to the table surface. (The table should be washable—preferably plastic, Formica, or glass topped.) Set out the open paint jars, each with its own tongue depressor; the two bowls of water; and rags or sponge to one side and within easy reach, depending on the child's handedness. Spill a small quantity of fresh water onto the paper and distribute it with the palm of the hand or with the sponge until the paper is evenly moistened. Sponge away any excess moisture. Then dip out a small blob of paint from one of the paint jars, using a tongue depressor. Spread the blob of paint on the paper with the palm of a hand. Then draw into the paint with a finger. Let the child work into the paint with his or her hands and fingers.

Provide the child with a single color at first. Later a second, third, and fourth color can be added, each dipped out of its jar and dropped onto the paper as before. Show the child how to spread each color *next to* the others on the paper, before mixing them in portions of the painting. This is important, or else each painting will turn out the same muddy purple or brown.

The disciplines of not mixing paints in their jars and not painting beyond the work surface (see 206) apply here as well, as do the guidelines concerning line, mass, and texture effects (see 210–212). However, in finger painting some application beyond the paper is unavoidable as the child works up to and along the paper edge; this is why a washable table surface is essential.

Encourage experimentation with different effects the child can create, using his or her hands and fingers only. Suggest frequent washing of hands in one of the fresh water buckets or bowls to help keep the colors fresh. One of the advantages of finger painting is that, as long as paper and paints remain moist, a design can be wiped out and started again or changed. A few drops of water added when necessary will keep the paint and paper workable.

Once some of the hand and finger effects that are possible have been thoroughly explored in succeeding sessions, add a comb, dowels, wooden blocks, and other found materials to the child's inventory of work tools. He can draw these through the wet paint or press them into it, creating many different effects.

Let a finished painting dry on several layers of newspaper or sheets of blotting paper. If the painting buckles as it dries, it can be ironed between layers of newspaper or blotting paper. In succeeding painting sessions encourage the child to do as much of the preparatory work, paper wetting, and dipping out of paint as possible.

208. Alternative Finger Painting Surfaces

If finger painting paper is not available, the following materials will take the paint adequately enough to permit the child to work in this medium:

Any slick, glossy paper, including the covers of magazines
A glass or enamel tray
A sheet of metal or foil
Oilcloth

209. Making Your Own Finger Paints

Tools and materials
Powdered poster pigments (see 206)—½ tablespoon each of four colors
1½ cups Laundry starch

1 qt. Boiling water
½ cup Talc (optional)
Four screw-top glass jars
1½ cups Soap flakes
Tongue depressors, one for each color

Mix the laundry starch with cold water to the consistency of a creamy paste. Add the boiling water and cook until the mixture becomes transparent and glassy. Stir constantly. Let the mixture cool somewhat before stirring in the soap flakes. Once these are completely dissolved, add the talc. Let the mixture cool and then pour it equally into the four jars, filling each to about an inch below the lip at most. Stir a half spoonful of each powder color into its respective jar.

Soap flakes, liquid cornstarch, or wheat paste mixed with water to a creamy consistency can also be added to powdered pigments to make finger paints, depending on availability of materials.

210. Dot Painting

Suggest to the child that he paint with brush or finger (see 206 and 207) using dots or short dashes only. They can be placed closely next to one another or farther apart, or they can overlap. The same color or different colors used in this manner will produce a great variety of effects when the finished painting is viewed from a distance. French pointillist painters at the turn of this century explored this technique with great imagination. Show your child black-and-white and color reproductions of photographs, illustrations, and paintings through a magnifying glass. He'll discover that all the different colors and shadings in printing are achieved through the use of small dots of only four colors, each printed next to the others. He can achieve similar effects with his dot paintings. This is a project that will give him insights into the characteristics of materials and processes and what can be done with them.

211. Line Painting

Take your child to your school's or public library's art book section and show him or her examples of "Op" art. This art form, popular in the nineteen-sixties, had its origins in the scientific experiments of the nineteenth century concerning vision and optical illusion (see IX). Op artists use line patterns, sometimes in combination with others, to achieve surprising effects. In nature, animals—zebras and tigers—are camouflaged due to the line patterns on their skins. Encourage the child to work with various line patterns and designs that occur to him or that emerge as he paints with finger or brush.

212. Mass Painting

When different shadings of a color, or different colors, are placed next to each other, each affects and is affected by the other. Sometimes two perfectly pleasing colors "clash," or vibrate, when seen together, especially along a common edge. Others seem to go together without optical disturbance. Every possible combination of colors and tints, regardless of whether they harmonize or clash, can be interesting and useful, depending on the skill, purpose, and imagination of the artist.

Do not provide the child with a color wheel or system that purports to teach which are complementary and which noncomplementary colors. Let the child discover all possible combinations through painting large areas of color, some with directly adjoining edges, others separated by white or black spaces or lines.

213. Line and Blob Blowing

Tools and materials
    Drinking straws
    Liquid watercolors or inks
    Eyedroppers, one for each color
    Sheets of white drawing or bond paper

Many effects in drawing and painting are accidental. Once discovered, an artist can re-create them at will. This quality of art makes it playful and, therefore, of special value to children and young people.

Tape the drawing paper to a newspaper- or cardboard-covered table top. Use one of the eyedroppers to drop a small amount of ink or watercolor onto the paper. Show the child how he can "chase" the color across the paper by blowing at it with a drinking straw. Hold the straw while blowing so that it comes close to, but does not touch, the paint or ink. Different colors when blown in this manner can be used to create delightful effects and designs.

214. Blot Pictures

Tools and materials
  Same as 213, omitting drinking straws

Fold a sheet of bond paper in half and then unfold it. Drop a small amount of ink or watercolor into the crease with an eyedropper. Now refold the paper and rub a finger along the crease without exerting pressure. When the paper is unfolded, a complex blot design will appear. Some control can be exercised, depending on where the ink is placed and how much pressure is exerted after the paper is folded. The variety of designs is as infinite as cloud formations. Such ink blots are used in Rorschach tests by psychologists to discover what a subject or patient "sees" in them. Encourage the child to talk about the shapes he recognizes in the ink blots he makes.

215. Monoprints

(See 290 and 297.)

216. Spatter Painting

Tools and materials
  Old, discarded toothbrush, or stipple brush
  Poster colors (see 206)
  Watercolor paints or India ink in different colors (optional)
  Drawing or bond paper

Poster paints should be diluted to the consistency of light cream; liquid watercolors or India inks can be used undiluted.

Attach the paper to a wall (see VI.A.b). Load the toothbrush or stipple brush with paint. Then, holding the brush as shown (see diag. 216.a), run a thumb over the tops of the bristles so that the paint spatters onto

216 a

the paper. Different colors spattered next to or over one another, or one or more successive colors spattered past a straight or shaped piece of paper or cardboard (see diag. 216.b), will create a variety of effects. The color effects and mixtures will be similar in some respects to those possible with pointillist painting (see 210). The spatter technique, used by itself or in combination with others, can suggest forms, textures, and designs that are limited in their variety only by the child's inventiveness and imagination.

b

217. Comb Painting

Tools and materials
Same as 206 and 207
An old comb

A comb drawn across wet poster or finger paint can create different line patterns. Parallel straight, wavy, and crossed lines, and stipples (dots) made by moving the comb's teeth rapidly up and down on the paint, supply textures and increase the child's arsenal of possible effects. But more than this, such use of materials can stimulate the child to discover and create other, different effects.

218. String Painting

Tools and materials
Poster colors (see 206); transparent watercolors or inks
Different lengths of string, twine, or thread
Sheets of bond paper
Newspaper-covered or washable table surface

Dip one length of string into one of the paint jars or ink bottles. Then lay the wet, colored string onto one of the sheets of paper and pull the string to form colored lines and smeared areas of color. When the first color has dried, or even while it is still wet, draw another, differently colored piece of string across the page, and a third if desired.

Or, the paper can be folded in half as for blot painting (see 214). Place and draw the colored string through the folded paper. With a little experimentation, a variety of effects can be created.

219. Painting on Wet Paper

Tools and materials
    Same as 206
    India inks or watercolors

When paper is thoroughly moistened and the excess water wiped off prior to painting onto it with poster paints, the color, once applied, will run and spread in surprising ways. It will seep across the paper surface and blend into any other color applied subsequently if the paper remains moist. The paper should be placed on a flat, level surface. If the child picks the paper up while the paint is still wet, he can make the paint run in whatever direction he chooses, and exercise some control over its spread and mixture. India ink, black and in colors, or watercolors can also be dropped onto the wet paper and paint (see 213). These don't mix readily with poster paint; hence they will run over and around the poster paint and will dry in interesting patterns.

When completed, let the painting dry flat on top of newspaper or blotting paper. If the child wishes, he can draw with crayons, chalks, or felt markers, or paint with thick poster paint into and over portions of the dry, textured paint.

220. Painting on Window Glass

(Note: Do not allow children to paint on any except ground-floor windows or on plate glass, and never while standing on a chair or ladder.)
Tools and materials
    Soap flakes or detergent
    Poster colors (see 206) and brush
    Muffin tin
    Newspaper
    Rags
    Bucket of fresh water

Mix the soap flakes or detergent and water to the consistency of heavy cream. Pour into screw-top glass jars and mix in the powder colors as in 206. Dispense each different color into one cup of the muffin tin or paper cup. Cover the floor under and around the window to be painted with thick layers of newspaper, and remove the curtains if any are hung.

Place all materials onto a newspaper-covered table next to the window, on whichever side matches the child's handedness. Dress him in a smock, apron, or old clothes and have him roll up his sleeves. Caution him not to lean against the window while painting. Suggest that he paint in large, bold strokes and masses. (See 248 if the painting is done on the inside of a room for viewing on the outside.)

221. Action Painting

Tools and materials
Same as 206 or 207

See 198 for a discussion of purpose. Some caution is required so that the child does not splash paint, helter-skelter, beyond the painting surface. But it is important to encourage sweeping brush strokes, especially at times when a child seems to tighten up or is unable to paint spontaneously with large movements.

222. Found Materials Painting

Tools and materials
Same as 206
Found materials (see XIV)

Found natural and fabricated materials—egg cartons, shirt board, lumber scraps, feathers, pebbles, paper cups and plates, egg shells, boxes—can be painted, decorated, or used as the basis for a variety of art experiences. Suggest that the child design with the materials, rather than just coat them with paint. The shapes and divisions of sundry packaging materials can in themselves suggest patterns and color areas. (See also 27, 28, 58, 82, 96, 97, 171, 172, and 175.)

223. Mixed-Media Painting

After a child has had some experience with different drawing and painting media, he can combine some of these for a variety of effects. As discussed in 219 and in the various sections that deal with "resist" techniques (see 229–231), even and sometimes especially those media that do not mix naturally offer opportunities for creating interesting effects when they are combined. Encourage the child to experiment—to invent techniques and to apply them imaginatively. He will eventually transfer the versatility of approach he learns in art to all his other activities.

224. Painting onto a Washable Wall

Children and young people like to scribble on walls. As stated earlier, this should generally be discouraged (see VI.A.c) unless a specially prepared wall surface is available.

Tools and materials
> White or off-white painted wall
> Sizing, sufficient for two successive coats to cover the available wall area; house painter's brush
> Poster colors and brush (see 206)

Cover the available wall area—no higher than the child can reach—with two coats of sizing, applying the second after the first has dried completely. Thin the sizing, if required, to obtain even coats. Read the directions on the can label. For best results apply the second coat with brush strokes at right angles to the first. Now the wall is prepared so that a child can paint on it with poster colors. The painting can be washed off with soap or detergent and water, and the area reused for painting, as often as desired. Or the finished mural can be protected permanently with yet another coat of sizing.

225. Communal Painting

Tools and materials
> Sized wall (see 224); or large sheet of brown wrapping or white "no-seam" paper taped to the wall
> Poster colors and brushes (see 206), one brush per child
> Muffin tins, one per child
> Buckets of clean water

Several children can be encouraged to paint a communal design or picture. Each child can be assigned his own area in which to paint whatever he or she pleases. Or all children can agree to one common theme, each assuming responsibility for particular portions, shapes, colors, or subjects (see 202, 234, and 236).

226. Painting on Dry Clay, Modeling Dough, or Plaster

Tools and materials
> Same as 251–253, 267, 268, and 271
> Poster colors (see 206)
> Round student grade bristle brush (No. 4, 5, or 6, depending on delicacy of work)
> Shellac and solvent (see 227)

Clay, modeling dough, or plaster, when dry, can be painted with poster colors by pre-school and older children. The painted shapes will not be waterproof and the paint is likely to flake off or stain fingers when handled. Do not bake or fire water-base-painted clay shapes—the paint will blister and discolor. To preserve such shapes after they have been painted, cover them with several light coats of shellac, each applied after the last has dried completely.

Shellac is difficult to apply. It can create severe problems when spilled. It is a skin irritant, and the solvent is highly flammable. The working area should be well ventilated. For these reasons, shellac coatings should be applied only by adults and by mature young people able to observe the required precautions.

D. ADVANCED DRAWING AND PAINTING

227. A Note of Caution

The media and techniques detailed in the following sections are suggested for young people nine years old or older, depending on their experience, maturity, dexterity, and interests. Some of these media require considerable caution (See also I.k, 138, 174, 188, 226, and 274.) Paints, other than water based, casein, and acrylic, and their solvents are often highly toxic and flammable chemicals. Some contain high concentrations of lead that can cause brain damage if inhaled or ingested even in small quantities over a period of time. All the solvents for oil base paints, japan colors, varnish, shellac, and model making and plastic paints—turpentine, alcohol, and acetone—can injure eyes and cause severe lung and skin irritation, especially when they come into contact with broken or sensitive areas. If that should happen by accident, or if any of these paints, or flakes of dried paint, or solvents are swallowed by a baby or child, call your local hospital or poison control center for information about instant antidotes and remedies. As these paints and solvents are flammable, they should only be used in well-ventilated rooms or workshops.

All such volatile, flammable, and toxic substances require great care in handling, protective clothing, gloves, and, if used over long periods of time, inhalator face masks. They should be stored in their proper closed containers well away from other flammable materials—preferably in a paint shed outside and away from living quarters or work areas. Read and heed the instructions and warnings on paint can labels before buying and allowing young people to use them. Some, like fluorescent colors, are toxic even though their manufacturers are not required by law to state this fact on the label.

Never allow children and young people to use aerosal spray paints, fixatives, or, for that matter, any pressurized spray product. All chemicals inhaled as fragmented particles, and especially paints, are damaging since they coat the lungs. The substances in which these paints are suspended are usually volatile, highly flammable, and possibly explosive. Never permit an empty spray can to be tossed into a fire or furnace—it will explode.

Transparent watercolors, though perfectly harmless, and pastel chalks are unsuitable art media for children and young people. Paintboxes, usually sold as children's art materials, that contain small, dried cakes of paint that must be moistened with a brush are especially frustrating and useless, except to professional artists.

228. Scratchboard

Tools and materials
Scratchboard (available from art supply stores)
One curved and one pointed scratch knife and holder
Scratchboard multiliner tools (optional)
Lithographic points (optional)
Black India ink
Inexpensive No. 6 or 8 watercolor brush

Scratchboard consists of fine white clay laid over a sheet of heavy paper or lightweight cardboard. It is therefore extremely brittle and cracks easily. Cut a piece of scratchboard from the sheet with a sharp knife blade—3″ × 4″, perhaps, as a trial. Cover this piece with a solid coating of black India ink, using a brush. Rinse the brush and wash with mild soap and water, or the Indian ink will ruin it. Let the ink dry on the scratchboard for at least a half hour. Then draw by scratching into the inked surface with the pointed tools. Cut deep enough to create a sharp white line, but no deeper. Whole areas of black can be removed with the curved scratch knife or with the side of the pointed blade. Do not try to remove all the ink at once when scraping a large area; scratch away a little at a time until the desired area is pure white.

After practice with a solidly black-covered piece of scratchboard, cut another piece and try painting a bold design onto it, leaving some areas white. Colored India inks can also be used to cover the scratchboard or to create designs before scratching into them. (For similar effects with other materials, see also 201, 223, 268, and 279.)

229. Wax Crayon Resist

Tools and materials
    Colored wax crayons (see 194)
    Poster colors and bristle brush (see 206); or India inks
    Muffin tin (to hold paints)
    White drawing paper

Draw lines, masses, dots, textures, and designs or pictures onto the paper with colored wax crayons. Then, using poster paint thinned so that it flows like watercolor, or India ink, paint over the whole sheet of paper in one or several colors. The water base ink or paint will flow into all the areas that have not been covered with wax crayons and in some places will be separated from the crayon designs by a fine white line. This combination of media that resist one another can be varied. For example, use only white crayon to make the drawings and paint over them with different-colored paints or inks. The white drawings and textures will show up in sharp contrast to the paint. Experiment with different combinations of light-colored crayons and dark paints or inks, and vice versa.

230. Dripped Wax Resist

Tools and materials
    Wax candle
    Poster colors and bristle brush (see 206); India ink or watercolors
    Heavy drawing paper

Light the candle and drip wax onto the paper in different patterns and designs. Then paint onto the paper over the wax with poster paints, inks, or watercolors. The principle is the same as for wax crayon resist (see 229) but the effects differ.

231. Paper Batik

Tools and materials
    Same as 229 and 230
    Sheets of newspaper or brown wrapping paper
    Steam iron and ironing board

Make drawings and designs as in 229 and 230. After the paint has dried, sandwich the work between layers of newspaper or two sheets of heavy brown wrapping paper. Then iron it with the steam iron. The wax (crayon or candle wax) will transfer and adhere to the newspaper or wrapping paper; the water-base-paint design will remain untouched. Make sure that the iron is not so hot as to burn the paper. Areas previously covered with wax will stand out white and clear on the drawing paper in contrast to the paint-covered areas and, depending on how the wax was applied, will reveal interesting textures.

Paraffin can also be used instead of candle wax or wax crayons. It is available in small cakes from grocery stores. Beeswax, available in art supply stores, is used by professional artists. With either, place the wax in a double boiler (see 278) and boil the water until the wax melts. The melted wax can be dripped onto the paper with a spoon or with a Tjanting needle—a special tool used for batik drawing and wax painting. (See also 399.) Paint with poster colors, India inks, or watercolors as before (see 229 and 230) and then iron the work sandwiched between newspaper or wrapping paper.

232. Gesso Painting

Gesso is a prepared white painting surface that brings out the brilliance of colors. It can be used in either opaque painting (paints applied thickly, so that no previously applied color shows through) or transparent painting (thinning so that each successive layer of paint is tinted by the previously applied ones). Another advantage of gesso is that the paint sinks into the ground and dries rapidly, so that it can be painted over within a short time. Many different kinds of gesso can be prepared, some of which are detailed below. Gesso was a common technique among painters of the past, but it lost favor when inexpensive canvas became available as a painting surface. It is still widely preferred as a ground by many modern artists, who use rabbit's-skin glue as a binder. Prepared gesso panels can also be bought in art supply stores.

Tools and materials
　　Wallboard; composition board (Masonite); or well-sanded ⅛″ to ½″ plywood
　　Gesso ground (see below)
　　House painter's brush, 2″ to 3″
　　Poster colors (see 206); acrylic paints (see 237); oil paints or japan colors (see
　　　238); designer's or casein colors (see 239)
　　Long-handled student grade brushes
　　Muffin tin (to hold paints)

Gesso ground mixtures include the following
　　a) Ordinary white water base paint

b) White poster paint
c) White poster paint mixed in equal proportions with white wallpaper paste
d) White poster paint, white wallpaper paste, and fine sand, mixed in equal proportions
e) Fine sand mixed with white wallpaper paste
f) Plaster of Paris, thinned to the consistency of medium cream

Coat the panel of wallboard or other surface with the chosen gesso ground, using the wide brush. Two or more coats should be applied to the panel, each after the last has dried completely, and brushed at right angles to the previous one. The gesso ground can be sanded to a glassy finish or it can be textured by applying the ground thickly and unevenly without sanding.

Gesso will take water base or oil base colors, japan colors, or inks. Try out different methods of applying paint—opaque, transparent, or monochrome (using different shades of a single color) as an underpainting and then tinting with brilliant transparent colors. (See also 233 and 234.)

233. Etching into Gesso Ground

Tools and materials
Same as 232
Stylus; scratch blades (see 228); etching point

It is possible to scratch into and inscribe gesso, either while it is still moist before painting or after the paint has dried. This technique provides texture, or it lets white lines show through the colors.

234. Painting into Wet Gesso

Tools and materials
Same as 232

Prepare the panel with a single thick coating of gesso ground. While it is still wet, paint into it with water base, oil base, or japan colors or inks, or any combination of these. The ground can be kept moist by covering it from time to time with a wet cloth. Possible effects include those described in 219, 229, and 230, depending on the media used. Also, since different media dry at different rates, crackle patterns will emerge as mixed media dry. Either the ground or the painting may be incised (see 233) or overpainted with opaque or transparent colors after it has dried.

235. String Inlay into Gesso

Tools and materials
    Same as 232 and 233
    String or twine
    Scissors

Press string or twine into or lay it on top of the wet gesso ground immediately after it has been applied. The twine may be painted in any color or left natural. Paint into and around the twine design with water base or oil base paints, japan colors, or inks.

236. Painting on Wet Plaster of Paris

Tools and materials
    Same as 271
    Paints (see 232)

The young painter must be prepared to paint at once into the wet plaster, as soon as it is poured and before it begins to set. The paint and plaster combine chemically to create brilliant color effects. Once the plaster has set—about fifteen to thirty minutes after pouring—the painting must cease, whether or not it is complete. Any portion in which the plaster has set before being painted must then be dug out, and more plaster poured in its place before it can be painted. For this reason it is wise to confine the painting to small plaster bats or tiles. This method was employed by old masters for painting on church, cathedral, and palace walls and ceilings; it is called "fresco" painting. Professional artists cover as much of a wall as they can paint within the time it takes the plaster to set, dig out any unpainted areas that have set, and begin again, adding to the fresco section by section.

237. Painting with Acrylics

Acrylics are a relatively recently developed synthetic painting medium. They are nontoxic, water soluble, but they dry as a waterproof film. They can be applied thick, like oil paints; or in flat tones, like oil, tempera, or casein colors; or transparent, like oil tints; or in washes, like watercolors, depending on the degree of dilution. Acrylics are available that give a matte or a glossy finish, which does not yellow with time and requires no varnish or other protective coating. In addition to a standard assortment of colors, colorless acrylic preparations are available that can be mixed with paint pigments to increase or retard drying time, to make them more or less glossy, to give them more body or texture, as waterproofing over any other surface or paint, or as an adhesive (see 26, 59, and 226).

238. Oil Painting

Oil paints are available in great variety, ranging from interior and exterior house paints to artist's oil and japan colors. All require turpentine as a solvent. Each, except japan colors, takes considerable time to dry thoroughly. Overpainting of oil painted surfaces that have not dried completely causes crackle, as each layer dries at a different rate. Oil paints can be thinned and used transparent, as well as thick and opaque. Paint vehicles—linseed oil or varnish—added to the paint in varying proportion change the drying characteristics and the degree of gloss of the paint.

These variables make oil painting relatively slow, difficult to control, and painstaking, especially for younger children. It should not be attempted except by young people who have a great deal of experience in water base media and acrylics, which are much more immediate since they dry within minutes.

239. Water Base Colors

Water base paints include casein paints, designer's colors, poster paints, and watercolors. Casein paints enjoy some of the same characteristics as oil paints and become impervious to water in time, yet they dry within minutes. Designer's colors are identical to poster colors, except that the pigment is more finely ground and the choice of mixed colors far greater. They are expensive and are used primarily by professional artists and designers. (See 206 for details about poster paints, and 227 for those pertaining to watercolors.)

240. Inlay Cardboard Painting

Tools and materials
> Poster colors (see 206)
> Sheets of heavy cardboard; shirt board; backing of drawing or writing pads; or corrugated board
> Cardboard cutting and pasting materials (see 10–28 and 83–97)

Design and build a cardboard collage or assemblage and paint different portions to enhance the design and the three-dimensional effect. Contrast of dark against light tones, such as painting two adjacent sides or edges a light shade and the other or others a darker shade of the same color, will give the construction greater depth and interest.

241. Inlay Plaster of Paris Painting

Tools and materials
>   Plaster bat (see 271)
>   Scrap wood shapes and dowels; found materials
>   Knife or other carving tools (see 279)

Press different wooden shapes into the plaster as soon as it is poured, each to a different depth. Carve into the plaster while it is wet and after it has set. Embed string and other materials into the wet plaster for additional effects. When the plaster has set, it can be painted with poster or japan colors (see 206 and 238) to achieve some of the same three-dimensional effects described in 240.

Alternatively, a wooden collage can be built to be cast in plaster (see 285), and the plaster painted after it has set.

242. Sand Painting

Tools and materials
>   Sifted fine sand
>   Vegetable coloring or poster paints (see 206)
>   Screw-top jars, one for each color
>   Painting cones (see 77), one for each color
>   Scissors
>   Masking tape
>   White paste or glue (see 13–17)
>   1″ house painter's brush
>   Sheet of cardboard or brown wrapping paper
>   Newspaper

Fill each jar about three quarters full of sand. Then add sufficient coloring to stain the grains of sand thoroughly, using a different color for each jar. Close and shake each container to assure even penetration of the color. Then pour the colored sand from each container onto a separate sheet of newspaper; spread the sand and let it dry. Rinse and clean all jars and let them dry. Pour each batch of colored sand back into its jar as soon as it has dried.

One painting cone is required for each separate color. Cut a small hole into the end of each cone, tape it closed, and fill the cone with the sand.

242

(If necessary, enlarge the hole until the sand can flow freely; see diag. 242). Fold over the top of each cone and arrange all on the table, ready for painting.

Now brush the cardboard or wrapping paper with a thick coating of glue. Pick up one of the painting cones loaded with colored sand, being sure to keep the tape adhered to the hole to prevent the sand from running out prematurely. Remove the tape and let the sand run out of the cone onto the paste-covered board or paper, moving the cone to make different shapes, lines, patterns, and designs. Use the different painting cones to achieve a variety of effects, bearing in mind that the sand will adhere only as long as the paste remains moist. For this reason, it is important to use a good deal of very moist paste at the start and to paint rapidly with the sand cones.

To form solid areas of color, outline the area with sand and then move the cone back and forth to cover the area evenly. Keep in mind that the sand will not adhere to itself but only to the exposed glue-covered area. When the design is finished or the glue has dried so that no more sand will adhere, let the painting stand and dry thoroughly for a while. Then, holding the painting over a waste basket or sheet of newspaper, shake off the excess sand that is bound to have accumulated but not adhered in some portions.

243. Painting on Wood

(See III.G, 227, and 237–239.)

244. Painting on Metal

(See IV.G, 227, and 237–239.)

245. Painting on Leather

(See 188, 227, and 237–239.)

246. Painting on Fabrics

(See 312 and XI.E.)

247. Painting on Glass

(See also 40, 220, and 248.)

Tools and materials
> Oil paints, japan colors, enamel paints, acrylics; appropriate solvents and
> brushes (see 227, 237, and 238)
> Muffin tin (to hold paints)
> Pane of glass
> White blotting paper

Great care should be exercised in handling glass to avoid breakage or chipping, or injury by edges and corners. Place the glass on white blotting or construction paper before painting. Glass is an interesting though difficult painting surface. It is hard to get good paint coverage. Paints should be mixed to the consistency of medium cream so that they flow onto the glass, and the brush must be heavily loaded with pigment. For these reasons, shading and blending of colors require experimentation. Start by painting flat, even areas of color and letting them dry before adding detail.

248. Painting on the Reverse Side of Glass

Tools and materials
> Same as 247

The technique is the same as that described in 247 except that all painting must be done in reverse order. Start by painting in detail. Let it dry. Then add the next layer of color, leaving uncovered those areas into which background colors are to be painted later.

An alternative technique consists of painting the outline of a design entirely in black, leaving fine lines, textures, and some areas uncovered.

When the paint has dried, cover the back with silver or gold foil or with colored paper. When turned right side up the design will stand out against the brilliant color of the background. Or a reverse effect can be achieved by painting large areas in color, with unpainted lines or areas between them, and then covering the whole of the back with foil or colored paper.

249. Painting on Acetate or Vinyl Film

Tools and materials
    Acetate, vinyl, or cellophane sheets or rolls
    Acetate ink (available in art supply stores in a wide range of opaque or transparent colors)
    Drawing pens and holders
    Sable watercolor brushes
    Muffin tin
    White construction or drawing paper

The same techniques as those described for glass apply (see 247 and 248). The material is safe to use (except acetate, which is highly flammable). The inks give better coverage than do the paints used on glass. It is possible to draw on the film with pens as well as with brushes. This is an especially useful experience for those who are interested in making transparencies and movie animations (see 328–330, 348, and 352).

250. Painting on Plastics

Water base and oil base paints, enamels, and other conventional paints, inks, and dyes do not adhere well to any of the common varieties except foamed plastics, like Styrofoam. They require special paints and solvents, all of which are toxic. (See I.k and 227 before providing young people with any of these.)

VII

Plastic Arts and Crafts

Art is both a form for communication and a means of expression of feeling which ought to permeate the whole curriculum and the whole life of the school. A society which neglects or despises it is dangerously sick. It affects or should affect, all aspects of our life from the design of commonplace articles of everyday life to the highest form of individual expression.—*The Plowden Report*

A. BACKGROUND

Working with clay and other modeling compounds should, at least at first, involve no tools other than hands. The young child or even the more mature beginner should get the feel of the material and its handling characteristics before using tools or becoming involved in technical detail. Later, as the child's skills and interests expand, supplementary materials can be useful.

Pottery is stressed in the opening sections because the initial forming efforts of the child are closer to the potter's craft than to the art of the sculptor, to which it is historically related. The chronology of how clay and other forming materials came into use is much like that of skill development in the child.

The craft of pottery is more than seven thousand years old. Decorated pot sherds have been unearthed in Iran that date back more than five thousand years. The earliest potters formed clay found next to river banks and in swamps. Using the same methods described in 262 through 266, they worked the material, which, when dried for a period in the shade, provided them with storage vessels for grain and other dry solids. Such thumb pressed, coiled, hollowed-out, or slab built pottery, without the use of a wheel, is still produced in many parts of Africa and South America.

Air dried and unfired natural clay pots are easily broken; they cannot be used for cooking since they crack when heated over an open fire. Liquids can seep through the pores of the clay. Prehistoric craftsmen discovered that slow heating and cooling hardens clay that is free of air bubbles, and makes it impervious. Some of the impurities left in the clay, like fine silicone sand or even soot from the fire, provided accidental, primitive glazes that strengthened and waterproofed the vessels further. African potters still sift and add fine sand to the clay before they form it so that it glazes the finished pottery in the grass and kindling kilns in which it is fired. By about 1500 B.C. the Egyptians and the Chinese had independently produced highly colorful and successful glazes. Those used by the Egyptians were eventually adopted by the Greeks and Romans. A great variety of glazes have been developed since, most of them lead based, that provide durable and decorative finishes for different ceramics. Even brine or borax can be used for impervious glazing of pottery.

In ancient Crete, Egypt, and Greece, as in China and South America, succeeding generations of potters contributed innovative techniques and styles, leaving distinctive marks on their pottery. Classic earthenware forms evolved, based on utility and convenience but also on what was pleasing to eye and hand, and these were eventually sanctified by ritual and custom. Potters invented variations in shape and proportion. Some scratched and etched lines and shapes into moist or dry clay products. Others added bands of color made of tinted ''slip''—watered-down clay—and glazes colored with earth and vegetable dyes. Later artists drew designs and pictures on vessels with these coloring materials. Still others built up designs in relief, using slip as a modeling compound or adhesive. All these techniques are available to the modern craftsman, giving him a great many choices for working the material and for creative expression.

Incising into clay led to the development of the alphabet. At first pictures were drawn on moist slabs of clay. In time these turned into a kind of shorthand that evolved into cuneiform, the early writing of Mesopotamian civilizations. Writing in cuneiform meant pressing wedge shaped tools into moist clay, each wedge or combination of wedges standing for a different word or idea. The inscribed tablets could be sent as dispatches and orders to generals and administrators of outlying provinces. Records could now be kept by scribes and tax collectors and the recorded history of kings and empires preserved for future generations. Early in the first century A.D. the Chinese discovered that incised clay tablets could be inked and the design or picture transferred to paper by rubbing to make multiple copies (see II.A and VIII.A). Thus ceramics played a crucial role in the discovery of printing.

Sculpting and carving in stone are related to forming with clay as well as to the bone and flint chipping of Stone Age civilizations. Prehistoric societies like those of the North American Indians learned how to flake chips off flint, using other stones as tools. These flints were carefully formed into arrowheads, spearheads, and cutting edges for hunting, skinning, and meat cutting. Animal bones, soapstone, soft sandstone, limestone, and alabaster were eventually worked in different cultures for utilitarian, decorative, architectural, and ritual purposes. Once iron was mined and formed (see IV.A), harder and more durable stone like marble could be worked with metal tools. And with the discovery of casting techniques and materials, clay came into wide use in sculpture again since clay-formed objects could be duplicated in plaster of Paris—a form of powdered alabaster—and in bronze and other metals.

This brief overview of the history of forming, modeling, and sculptural arts and crafts should suffice to whet the young craftsman's appetite to try his hands, and may inspire him to seek more detailed information about the cultural heritage that enables him to exercise them. It also demonstrates how one material or craft is related to all the others.

Mosaic craft is included in this chapter, though mosaic tiles are traditionally made of glass. Glass mosaic tiles are too difficult and hazardous for young craftsmen to make and cut. Commercial glass tiles are available, but it seems more productive to encourage young people to make their own tiles out of clay or plaster. (See also 29.)

B. BEGINNING POTTERY AND MODELING

In pottery and modeling more than in other arts and crafts, it is useful for young children and even older ones to gain experience in a particular chronological order. It is futile to place a child before a potter's wheel if he has never made a vessel without one. And even before that he needs developmental experience in forming with clay or modeling compounds spontaneously so that he can discover their qualities and how they respond to handling and forming.

Clay is delicate. Learning to wedge clay as a matter of course (see 255 and 270) will assure the young craftsman that his creations will not crack while drying or being fired. Attaching components of pottery or sculptures with slip (see 256 and 272) assures that they won't drop off as the clay dries. Evading these simple disciplines leads to disappointment. The work becomes increasingly satisfying and productive if these and other operations become second nature.

251. Commercial Modeling Compounds

There are any number of modeling compounds other than natural clay available in art and craft supply stores and in toy shops. Some are claylike or clay derivatives that dry impervious without firing. Many of these can be painted with poster paints (see 206), acrylics (see 237), and other media. Many are useful for children and young people.

Some modeling compounds, like Plasticine, retain their malleability indefinitely and never dry out. They are not recommended for use by children. One satisfaction of working with modeling materials is the production of tangible, dimensional results that can be handled. Plasticine requires considerable muscle until it is worked in hand to a consistency that makes it usable by young children, and the finished work does not harden sufficiently to retain its shape when handled. The child's work is easily destroyed. Other synthetic modeling compounds, like plastic wood and metal, are highly toxic.

Commercially available modeling "dough" is a good working material for young children, though expensive, considering that it can be made at home or in the classroom at practically no expense.

252. Homemade Modeling Compounds

a. *Modeling dough* (I)

Tools and materials
2 cups Nonrising flour
2 tablespoons Olive oil
Small plastic bags and closures
Cold water
1 cup Salt
Vegetable colors

Mix flour, olive oil, and salt until they are uniformly distributed. Add water until the dough is stiff without being sticky. Divide the dough into as many parts as the number of different vegetable colors that are available. Press a thumb into each lump of dough and pour a few drops of vegetable color into the dent made. Then work the color evenly into each lump and place it in its own plastic bag. If the bag is kept closed in the refrigerator, the dough remains usable for three to four days. Periodic moistening and working of the dough will keep it fresh and workable for a longer time.

b. *Modeling dough* (II)

Tools and materials
1 cup Salt
Saucepan
Vegetable colors
½ cup Boiling water
½ cup Cornstarch
Plastic bags and closures

Stir salt, cornstarch, and water over low flame until stiff. When cool, knead until the dough reaches a pliable, even consistency. Add vegetable colors and store as described in 252.a.

c. *Modeling dough* (III)

Tools and materials
Nonrising flour
Vegetable colors
Cold water
Salt
Plastic bags and closures

Mix flour and salt in equal amounts, add cold water, and knead until the dough is uniformly stiff, yet pliable. Add vegetable colors and store as in 252.a.

d. *Wood dough*

Tools and materials
  1 cup Sawdust
  ½ cup Wallpaper paste, common paste, or flour paste (see 13, 14, and 17)
  Cold water
  Plastic bag and closure

Mix ingredients and knead dough until it becomes uniformly pliable. Store as in 252.a.

Any of these can be used successfully by children. They can be rolled into beads, coils, and slabs (see 258), used for hand-formed hollow pottery (see 262–266), and for simple modeling with or without armatures (see 52–54, 142, 145, and 146). If no vegetable colors are added, any of these compounds can be painted after they have dried (see 226).

253. Clay and Clay Storage

Natural clays are available either moist or in powder form. Powdered clay takes a long time and is arduous to work up to a usable consistency; it is therefore not recommended for young children. Moist clay can be kept indefinitely if it is stored properly. Natural clay improves in time. Japanese potters matured clay for their grandchildren, as French families laid wine in their cellars for future generations.

There are three basic types of clay: earthenware clay bodies, stoneware clay bodies, and porcelain clay bodies. All are found in different colors, each containing different minerals. Stoneware clay is best for young craftsmen. It is available in gray and in a reddish-brick color (terra cotta). Other clays vary in color, ranging from black or white to various shades of gray and brown.

Clay is best kept in a metal can with a tight-fitting cover, like a garbage can. Place three bricks in the bottom and cover them with a wooden board. Add clear water up to just below the level of the board. Then place lumps of moist clay on the board and cover them with burlap or other rags, leaving an end hanging in the water to act as a wick, drawing up water as needed to keep cloths and clay moist (see diag. 253). Add another layer of lumps of clay, wrap the cloth over them, and so on until the can is filled to a level where the cover fits snugly. As long as water is kept in the bottom of the can and the cloth is kept moist the clay will remain soft and workable indefinitely.

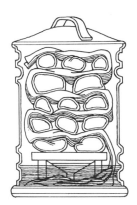

253

Clay that has been permitted to become too dry to be workable can be reconditioned. Don't try to recondition almost dry clay; wait until it is completely dry and hard. Then place large chunks in a burlap bag and break them up with a hammer or mallet. Sift out the powdered clay and keep hammering the large lumps until they are reduced to very small pieces, granules, and powder. Place the dry clay particles in a metal can and cover them with several inches of water. Let stand for a week or longer, until the clay has turned uniformly mushy and no granules remain. Pour off excess water. Let the clay stand for several more days and then pour off whatever water has settled on top. The clay is now reconditioned though still too moist to be workable. Remove portions as needed and set them onto a plaster bat (see 271). The excess moisture will be absorbed by the plaster within one half to one hour; then the clay is ready for wedging (see 255 and 270) and use.

Clay should be soft, yet firm for pottery, and somewhat stiffer for modeling and sculpting.

254. Work Spaces

For work with clay and modeling compounds, a child should be dressed in old clothes, in a smock, or in an apron. Sleeves should be rolled above the elbows.

Provide a table at which the child can work in comfort, standing or sitting (see I.j). He or she also needs a sheet of heavy cardboard or plywood, approximately 14″ × 17″ × ⅛″, as a work surface. Cover the rest of the table with oilcloth or newspaper. A bowl of slip (see 256), a bucket of water, and a towel or rags should be available to wash and dry hands periodically. For special materials relating to particular projects, see the various sections below.

255. Working Up and Drying Clay

Get the child used to wedging clay before using it for pottery or forming. It is unlikely that he or she can do this properly at an early age, since it requires a good deal of strength and perseverance. (For more craftsmanlike wedging, see 270.) Until the child is more mature, encourage him to break the amount of clay needed for a project in half repeatedly and press and beat both portions together again. The purpose is to work out as many air bubbles as possible. Clay that contains air bubbles may crack even while drying in air and especially when fired in a kiln.

Allow the finished work to dry thoroughly at room temperature for at least two to three days. If this ''greenware'' suffers any flaw—air bubbles; walls too thin; clay or dough too dry while it was worked so that it cracks; or added parts fall off because they were improperly adhered to the main body (see 259)—it can be repaired with slip (see 256). Discuss possible reasons for these flaws with the child and encourage him to avoid them in future work. Works that dry more or less properly deserve ample praise and prominent display.

Pinched, coiled, and slab built pottery or sculpture can be bisque-fired in a kiln (see 273) and glazed (see 273 and 274) if the proper clay was used; it was properly wedged; coils and slabs were properly joined with slip; and the pottery or sculpture was thoroughly air dried. It is unlikely that pre-schoolers and early grades children can keep all this in mind, even under supervision. Their work is therefore best left unfired, though it can be painted once it is thoroughly dry (see 226).

Modeling doughs cannot be fired, of course. When dry they can also be painted (see 252), preserved, and waterproofed to some extent with several coats of acrylic medium (see 237), transparent glue (see 16), shellac, clear varnish, or nail polish (see 227). The same is true for self-setting clays.

256. Slip

Slip is required for successful clay or pottery work. It consists of clay thinned with water to the consistency of medium or heavy cream so that it can be applied with a brush. Slip serves many functions: it can be used to smooth out rough or jointed portions of clay, cement coils, and slabs (see 263, 264, 266 and 267), or fill cracks that appear as the clay is worked into shape. (Filling cracks is not recommended for clay that is to be fired.) Slip is also the required adhesive for attaching small parts to the main body of the work—arms to a clay figure, a handle to a cup, or other formed details and decorations.

Fill a small bowl about one quarter full of clay or modeling compound and add and work water into it until the proper consistency is reached. Keep the bowl of slip next to the child and get him or her used to working with it as with the regular clay.

257. Drying Finished Work

Unfinished work can be kept workable as long as required by covering it with a damp cloth. Be sure to keep moistening the cloth periodically. Once the object is completed it must be air dried, whether or not it is to be glazed or fired. It is important that the vessel or shape dry as evenly as possible. Cover small extensions or additions to the main body of the work with dry clothes or rags to retard the rate of drying out of these portions. Due to the usually thinner wall thickness of handles, spouts, and other small added parts, they tend to dry more rapidly than the rest and may crack, especially at slip jointed edges. Once the rest of the vessel or shape has dried partially, the small additions should be uncovered so that they will dry along with the rest.

Keep a drying clay shape on a sheltered shelf, indoors, in the shade. Do not move it while drying and do not try to speed up the drying process. Clay shapes of average wall thickness take at least a week to dry out thoroughly, or longer if they are unusually large or the walls are very thick.

258. Basic Forms

I.a through g and VI.A.a explain why a child should be encouraged to discover his or her own forms and shapes. But children also need some instruction. It's a very poor idea to teach children how to make anything through a combination of stereotype and cliché forms and shapes. Children need to learn some of the basic processes to which the material lends itself and through which they can develop their own forms. In work with clay or modeling compounds these introductions are essential. Then let the child pinch, pull, or pound the material to see what happens. He or she can combine and attach them to each other with slip or toothpicks and develop an endless variety of adaptations.

a. Rolling beads

Break off a small lump of clay, about the size of an adult's fingernail or larger. Show the child how to roll it between thumb and forefinger or between his two palms to shape it into a roughly formed sphere and to continue rolling it with a circular motion of his palm on the table or other work surface until it turns into a ball. Thread finished balls onto toothpicks or a threader (see 4) and let them dry completely. Perfectly round or slightly flattened beads can then be painted, strung, or used for mosaics (see 29 and 289).

b. Rolling coils and strips

Break off as much clay or dough as fits comfortably into a child's hand. Show him how to squeeze and then roll it between his palms to form a sausage. Break off a small section of the sausage and roll it between palm and table or workboard surface until it reaches the desired thickness. Keep breaking off lengths for easier handling. The rest can be rolled into coils later, and the coils can be flattened with a small strip of wood if so desired. Either round or flattened coils have many uses in making pottery (see 263 and 264) and in decorating and adding detail to shapes and objects constructed of clay or modeling dough. Keep the coils covered with a damp cloth so they will stay moist until they are used.

c. Forming a flat slab

Break off as much clay or dough as the child can hold comfortably in his or her hand. Place it on the cardboard or woodworking surface and pound it more or less flat by hand. Place this roughly formed slab between two strips of ¼" or ½" lath, depending on the thickness of clay slab required, and roll out the clay or dough between the pieces of lath with a rolling pin or bottle (see diag. 258). Be sure to keep the rolling pin or bottle on the lath. When the clay is rolled out to a uniform thickness, it can be cut into strips or other shapes with a dull knife edge or

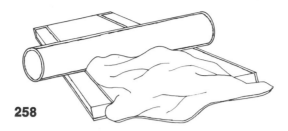

258

with cutters (see 158) made out of strip metal. Such a slab can be used for pottery (see 266 and 267), sculpture, and building. Patterns and textures can be drawn, etched, or pressed into it.

259. Combining Basic Forms

The three basic clay forming techniques can be modified and combined. The spherical beads (see 258.a) can be rolled into ovals or, pinched in the center, turned into barbell shapes, among others. The coil strips can be twisted into spirals or other curves (see diag. 259.a), or the slabs can be folded back and forth to form accordion shapes (see diag. 259.b). These and other variations can be combined, stuck to each other with slip or toothpicks while still moist, or used as decorative devices on pottery and other objects.

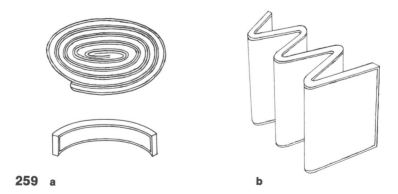

259 a   **b**

260. Textures

The moist clay, whether formed into balls and beads, coil strips, or slabs, can be scratched into with toothpick, wire, or pointed tool. Short lengths of wooden dowel, children's wooden blocks, sanded scrap lumber shapes (see 109), and bottle caps can be pressed into clay slabs to form patterns and designs. Plastic or wire mesh, rope, twine, embossed wallpaper scraps, and any other textured material can be used to make impressions in clay. The materials named and others the child finds or improvises allow him to discover the number of ways in which he can affect, modify, and treat the material. These methods are especially interesting to blind children, but are equally valuable to all. Don't neglect to point out that smoothness is a texture too. Show the child how to make slabs or shapes velvet smooth by brushing over the surface with slip (see 256). When dry, the smooth clay shapes can be polished with wax to heighten the effect. Textured clay slabs can be painted after they have dried (see 206 and 237), or printed (see 261).

261. Clay Printing

(See 296, 303, and 304.)

262. Thumb Pressed Pottery

Give the child a small lump of clay, no more than fits comfortably in his hand. Suggest that he wedge it (see 255) as well as he can. Let him form it into a more or less round or oval shape. Then demonstrate how he can press his thumb into the center of the ball and smooth the inside and outside with slip (see 256). He's made his first thumb pot.

Once he has made several thumb pots, show the child how he can work on his next one with thumb and fingers to extend and thin the wall of the pot. Demonstrate how he must work all around, pressing the clay, a little at a time, so that the pot remains more or less round and the wall thins out evenly. He can smooth the inside and outside of his pot with slip, incise textures or designs on the outside, or add handles made from coil strips (see 258.b) or slabs cut into strips (see 258.c), using slip as an adhesive.

Other variations and refinements consist of squeezing a finished thumb pot into a number of pinched shapes; pressing a pouring lip into the rim;

and adding a slab built rim or base. Don't insist on perfection, and do admire the result of the child's work.

263. Coiled Pottery

Let the child make a number of coil strips and cover them with a damp cloth (see 258.b). The base should be made out of a tightly wound coil (see 259) or it can be formed by cutting it out of a slab with the rim of a glass (see diag. 263.a). Curl up the edge of the base all around and smooth it with slip. This is essential whether or not the coils of the pot are to remain visible, since the slip makes the coil strips adhere to each other and fills in small gaps that may not be visible.

263 a

Place the next coil all around the inside of the curled up base. Pinch off any extra length and pinch both ends of the formed coil so that they fit together to form a joint no thicker than the coil itself (see diag. 263.b). Professional potters cut each end at matching 45° angles and fit them together with slip (see diag. 263.c). Now add coil after coil, adhering each to the last with slip. To make the pot belly outward, attach each

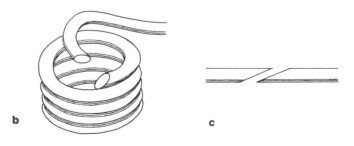

b   **c**

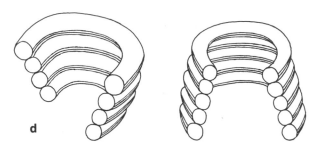

d

succeeding coil layer on top but toward the outside of the last, overlapping it by about one-half the thickness (see diag. 263.d). To make the vessel narrower, attach coils to the inside of the previous strip in the same manner. It is wisest not to make the walls of a coiled vessel perfectly perpendicular. The coils work best when they overlap. After adhesion of three or four strips, go over all of them with slip: either smooth them out by working both clay and slip into an even wall, or, if the coil texture is to remain visible, use slip to provide an additional bond for the coils. In working the coil walls they can be thinned, flattened, and given additional shape; they are then less likely to separate when drying.

Once the child has experience in forming coiled pots, he can decide beforehand precisely what shape he wishes his vessel to assume. Show him how to draw the shape on a piece of heavy construction paper and cut out the interior. Cut the remaining paper in half (see diag. 263.e). He will then have a template that he can use during the coiling process to determine where each coil should be placed so that the vessel assumes the desired shape.

e

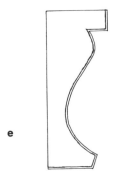

Coiled pots can have wide, narrow, or multiple necks. If dressed with slip and smoothed on the outside, they can be incised and lined, and decorations can be added with beads, coil strips, or slab strips adhered with slip. Handles, lips, and stoppers can be added. There is no limit to the size of pots built with coils. Early Egyptian, Incan, and African pottery was mostly coil built and some of their vessels reached enormous size.

Slip smoothed coil pots, when fully dry, can be decorated with colored slip (see 272).

264. Coiled Sculpture

The technique described in 263 can be applied to sculpture. Simple and complex shapes can be built up with coils of clay. It's like building with logs, except that the clay coils can be bent and formed in any way desired. More experienced young people may need a basic assortment of sculpting tools to enable them to realize the possibilities offered by this method of forming and building with clay.

Tools and materials
> Wedging wire (to cut off large chunks of clay)
> Wedging board (see 270)
> Knife (for cutting clay)
> Sharp-pointed tool (for incising)
> Modeling sticks
> Wire hook tools
> Sponge (for smoothing clay with water)
> Brushes (for applying slip)
> Syringe (for wetting clay surfaces)
> Wet rags (for keeping clay moist)
> Pail or bowl of fresh water

265. Hollowed-Out Pottery and Sculpture

Solid clay forms take a long time to dry completely. It is therefore best to remove as much excess clay as possible from the interior of any formed shape without weakening the structure to the point that it collapses. Large, free-standing objects can be easily hollowed out through their bases, leaving at least a ½" wall. Some solid shapes, an egg for example, must be cut in half with the wedging wire. Scoop out the excess clay, leaving a ½" wall, being careful not to squeeze or distort the outside shape while hollowing it. Fit the halves together and seal with slip. Correct any external distortion with clay and slip and let the hollowed-out egg air dry on the shelf.

Any form of pottery and sculpture can be made out of a solid chunk of clay, formed and then hollowed out, either for air drying or firing in a kiln.

266. Slab Built Pottery and Sculpture

Using the technique described in 258.c have the child form a ¼"-thick slab of clay. Use a knife, wire, or pointed tool to cut as large a square or rectangle of clay as possible out of the slab. Use a file card, paper, or cardboard template (see 68 and XII) or a right-angle triangle to assure that the slab is reasonably square. Now show the child how to lift the clay slab and form it into a cylinder, sealing the joint with slip (see diag. 266.a). Stand this cylinder on another slab that is larger than the circumference of the opening and that has been thoroughly moistened with slip. Trim around the base of the cylinder with a sharp tool. Brush more slip into and around the joint, inside the vessel and out, to make sure of a good bond. A simple slab built vessel has been formed.

Once the principle of slab built pottery is understood, any number of shapes, vessels, and constructions can be designed and modeled. Make a paper mock-up first; cut it apart and use the flattened paper as a template for the clay slab (see 68 and 153). Slab walls can also be set on a slab base and jointed by scooping out a small channel along the joint (see diag. 266.b) and filling it in with slip and coil strips to form a good bond.

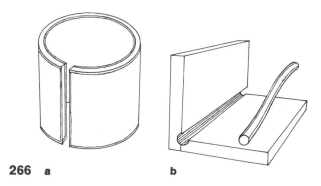

266 a   **b**

Slab built pottery and sculptures can be built and draped around various forms or pressed into molds (see 282). Fill a plastic bag with sand and drape a large slab of clay around it, joining the edges with slip. Use additional slabs to form the bottom and top, leaving a small opening. When the vessel or sculpture is almost a closed figure, puncture the plastic bag, let the sand run out, and pull out the plastic bag slowly through the opening (see diag. 266.c, d, and e). Paper tubes, egg carton bases, a blown-up balloon, a cigar box, a clay shape wrapped in newspaper, or any other found object can be used in the same manner, provided one end of the slab built structure is left open enough so that whatever is used as the form can be withdrawn. If desired, this opening can be sealed partially or entirely with an additional slab and with slip.

These slabs can be given texture (see 260) before they are assembled or draped around a form. While still flat they can have shapes pressed into or cut out of them, or they can be incised or etched.

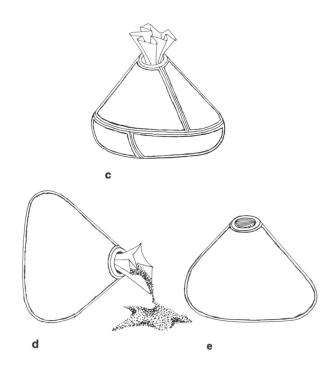

c

d   e

267. Slab Relief

After he has formed clay slabs as described in 258.c and 266, suggest to the child that he make two large slabs. Cut one into a square or a rectangle. Let him use the other slab to cut out small geometric and nongeometric shapes with a pointed or wire tool or with a knife. He can adhere the smaller shapes with slip to the remaining slab to build a dimensional clay relief. The edges of the smaller shapes can be left or they can be rounded with modeling sticks. He can incise the clay or add beads (see 258.a), coil strips (see 258.b), or strips cut from slabs (see 258.c); or he can decorate the relief with slip or press textures into the clay (see 260).

268. Engraving into Dry Clay Slabs

Using the techniques described in 258.c and 266, have the child prepare a number of clay slabs. He can cut them into whatever shapes he chooses and then set them on the shelf to dry for several days. When the slabs are fully air dried, he can etch into them with pointed tools—a scriber, pointed wire, or engraving tool, or the point of a compass or a divider. Lines, shapes, and textures can be scratched into the slabs. Such an engraved slab can also be printed (see 304).

C. ADVANCED POTTERY

269. Digging and Preparing Clay

Once familiar with the basic properties of clay and some of the methods required to form it, more advanced techniques can be introduced to young people, including finding, digging, and processing clay. This is not an essential experience and is impossible to provide in many places. Yet wherever clay can be found, digging and forming it dramatizes the relationship between discovery and use of the material. As stated earlier, this relationship is not self-evident to most of today's children and young people. Clay not only makes it possible to demonstrate it, but also allows children to participate in the whole chain of events from raw materials source to end product.

Clay is found near streams, rivers, and swamps. It can usually be recognized by its smooth, dense texture and the pattern of cracks that appear on the surface when it begins to dry out. Dig up a sample and let it dry in the air. Break it up and crush it, sift it through a sifter to remove grit, sand, and other impurities, and condition it as described in 253. Wedge the conditioned clay (see 255 and 270) and then form it by any of the methods described in 262 through 268. Let the completed object dry on an open shelf and, if a kiln is available, test fire it to see whether the clay is suitable. More should be dug only if, having been properly sifted and conditioned, wedged, worked, formed, and dried, it does not crumble or crack after air drying or develop similar serious flaws in firing.

It is possible to combine fresh, conditioned clay with broken-up fired clay that has been ground to a fine powder. This is called grog. The fired clay can consist of broken, glazed crockery, drainage tile, or brick. Mix the pure clay and the powdered glazed products in equal proportions and work them together with water. Condition the grog as described in 253. The grog is more crumbly than ordinary clay, but it is also more firm and less subject to breakage after air drying and firing.

Let the prepared grog stand overnight before using. Then drain off excess water again and let it stand on a plaster bat (see 271) until it reaches the desired pliability without being tacky. Be sure to hollow out solid sculptures and forms before drying (see 265). After the vessel or sculptured object has been formed and hollowed, let it stand for two days, covered with a dry cloth. This slows the drying process and reduces the probability of flaws developing due to too rapid evaporation of the moisture. Then remove the cloth and let the formed grog dry at room temperature, whether or not it is to be fired.

Cover handles and small protruding parts with a dry cloth for more than two days, to assure that they dry last. If grog pottery or sculpture is to be glazed, it requires more glaze than ordinary clay. But slip decoration on grog (see 256) is relatively easy and usually successful since the slip adheres better to the rough texture of grog than to clay, which is smoother.

270. Wedging Board

Before working with clay, either for pottery or for sculpture, it must be wedged (see 255). For wedging, the clay should be moister than for forming. A wedging board should be built if clay is used regularly in fair amounts.

A wedging board consists of a shallow wooden tray to the rear of which a wooden post is attached; from the post piano wire is strung to one corner of the board. Clay is cut on the wire and wedged in the tray.

Tools and materials
18" × 24" × ⅜" plywood
Two strips of 17¼" × 3" × ⅜" pine
Two strips of 24" × 3" × ⅜" pine
Twenty-two ¾" screws
One strip of 24" × 1" × ½" pine
One 30" length of piano wire
Hand drill and bits; screwdriver; pliers

Assemble as shown in diag. 270.

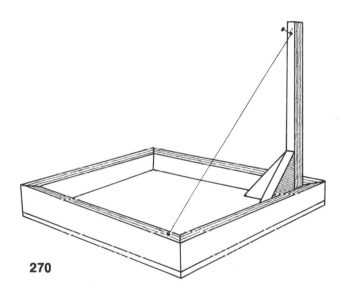

270

Scrape or break clay out of the storage bin (see 253), add water if required, and work it into a solid lump. Then use the wedging board wire to cut the lump of clay in half. Rejoin the halves: turn one at right angles to the other and pound together by beating and squeezing the clay by hand on the wedging board. Repeat several times to be sure that all air bubbles have been worked out of the clay and that it has a uniform, moist, and workable consistency. It will in all likelihood be too moist and sticky for pottery or sculpture. Place the clay on a plaster bat to remove excess moisture quickly (see 271).

271. Making a Plaster Bat

Plaster that has set absorbs moisture. If you place wedged or other clay on a plaster bat—a slab of plaster—it loses moisture within thirty minutes to an hour, by which time it should be ready for pottery or sculpture (see 253). To make a plaster bat:

Tools and materials
    Plaster bat mold (a 6" × 10" × 1½" open box built of wood or a foil metal pie
        plate with about a 1½"-high rim)
    1" × 12" × ¼" sanded board
    2 qts. Plaster of Paris
    1 qt. Water (clear and cold)
    Mixing bowl
    Large metal spoon

Sift the plaster slowly through your fingers into the water-filled bowl. Do not mix the plaster and water until all the plaster has been sifted and has formed a small mound about 1½" above the level of the water. Then stir the plaster slowly with the spoon. Do not remove the spoon while mixing the plaster but keep it immersed until the mixture has turned into a smooth, lump-free, creamy paste, ready for pouring. Pour the plaster into the plaster bat mold at once. Smooth the top surface of the plaster bat with the sanded board, if required. The plaster itself will set and be sufficiently hard to use within fifteen to thirty minutes. After it has set, tap the plaster bat out of its mold. Several bats should be made at one time. Each can be used repeatedly.

Place each lump of well-wedged but too moist clay on a plaster bat until it has lost enough moisture to be workable.

After work with plaster of Paris is completed, do not empty plaster remnants into or wash plaster covered hands in a sink. Plaster clogs drains. Instead, wait until the plaster has set and hardened in the bowl or on hands. Add water to the bowl, then rinse your hands in the bowl. The dried plaster will flake off easily. Drain the excess water through a sieve, collect the flaked plaster, wrap it in a newspaper, and burn.

272. Decorating Clay with Slip

Tools and materials
    Prepared slip (see 256)
    Poster paints (see 206); vegetable colors; acrylic pigments (see 237); India inks
    Pottery or sculpture

Slip can be used to decorate sculpture or pottery that is to be air dried, with or without kiln firing. If the clay is not to be fired in a kiln, colored slip can be made by adding one of the pigments listed above to the slip.

If the clay product is to be fired, it is best to buy colored slip of the same clay that was used to make the object. Such colored slip is available in a variety of tints from art and craft supply shops.

Homemade or purchased slip can be painted on pottery or sculpture with student grade water color brushes. To paint even stripes on a pot or vase, tie a flat lettering brush of the desired width to an upright stake (see diag. 272). Load it with slip, using another brush. The bowl, placed against the brush and turned slowly on the table, will receive an even stripe.

272

273. Firing in a Homemade Kiln

Before clay sculpture or pottery can be considered for firing it must be thoroughly air dried (see 257). This takes a week or longer. Then, if it has not developed any flaws, the "greenware" is ready for its first, "bisque" firing.

Kiln firing is essential for any clay vessel that is expected to be durable and impervious to liquids, unless it is made of self setting clay (see 251). A vessel can be glazed and fired at a first and only firing. Professional potters fire the unglazed clay during the bisque firing and then glaze it with a second "glaze" firing. A single bisque firing, glazed or unglazed, is enough for young people's work.

Commercially available electric kilns, small or large, are expensive. The smallest ones severely limit the size of objects that can be made and fired. But it is possible to build and use a simple homemade kiln for unglazed bisque firing of pottery and hollowed-out sculpture.

Tools and materials

Large metal garbage can with tight-fitting cover
Spike or cold chisel, and hammer
Three burlap sacks filled with sawdust (or enough to fill the garbage can)
Sufficient coal or coke to line the bottom of the garbage can about 2″ deep
Newspaper
Air dried pottery or sculpture

Use the hammer and spike (or cold chisel) to punch holes into the sides and lid of the garbage can, each ¼″ to ⅜″ wide and about 3″ from the next. Line the bottom of the can with coal or coke and place the largest air dried pottery or sculpture on this layer (see diag. 273). Fill all spaces in and around the object and coal with tamped-down sawdust. Add a layer of 4″ or 5″ of sawdust on top of the object or objects and place the next assortment of dry clay objects on top of this layer. Fill the places in and around these with sawdust, add a further 4″ or 5″ layer of sawdust, and so on until the whole can is filled with alternating layers of sawdust and clay formed objects. The top layer of sawdust, at least 4″ deep, should be level with the rim of the can.

273

Light the sawdust from the top with newspaper tapers. When the top layer of sawdust smolders evenly, replace the lid of the can and let the fire work all the way down through the sawdust, coal, and clay product filled can. This should take twenty-four hours or more. If sudden winds increase the burning rate, use moist clay to close some of the holes punched into the garbage can.

The garbage can kiln should of course be placed out of doors on soil or concrete, well away from buildings, dried leaves, and other flammable materials. Peat can be used for fuel instead of sawdust.

After the fire has burned out in the can, let the earthenware cool until it can be handled. Then remove the fired objects and let them cool completely before further handling. They may be slightly sooty. Some of the soot will wash off and the rest will have partially glazed the clay. Such fired articles will have not only utility but also a beauty of their own.

Glaze firing is impractical in such a kiln, first because there is no way to protect the wet, glaze covered surfaces from sawdust and soot; and second because there is not enough heat generated (the heat is not even enough for successful glazing).

274. Firing and Glazing in an Electric Kiln

A bisque (a first glazed or unglazed) firing in an electric kiln requires considerable knowledge and experience. Variations in required times and temperatures for different clays and glazes, and the amount of equipment required, make discussion of these techniques inappropriate here. The bibliography at the end of this book and manufacturers' manuals for the equipment provide the necessary information for young people who are sufficiently interested to pursue this aspect of the craft.

Glazing should never be done by children. Commercial glazes contain concentrations of lead and other toxic chemicals. More experienced young people can use brine or borax, which, like some other harmless substances, give bisque or glaze fired earthenware interesting and durable glazes.[71]

275. The Potter's Wheel

Available models include wheels that, like a lazy Susan, are turned by one hand while the other forms the clay. Such wheels are too hard to use for children or young people. Old-time potter's wheels at which the potter sits, kicking a flywheel with his foot that turns an upper plate on which he wedges and forms the clay, are still available. Treadle and electric motor operated wheels are most commonly used today. The treadle model is the most economic and useful for children and young people.

The clay is first wedged (see 255 and 270) on the wheel by being worked up and down repeatedly between both hands, from a lump placed in the center of the wheel into a tall, slender column, and down again (see diag. 275.a). It is then ready to be formed. The thumb and fingers of one hand press into the edge of the clay while the wheel turns, to form the side wall of the vessel, and the palm of the other hand keeps the overall shape trim and round (see diag. 275.b). The clay should be

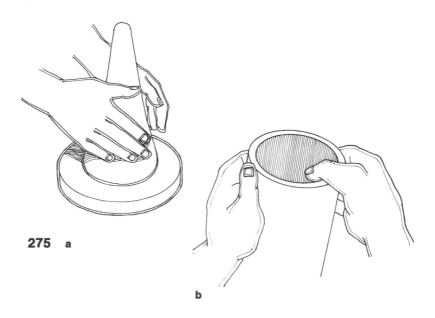

275 a

b

moistened periodically and the sidewalls kept at a uniform thickness. If an attempt does not turn out as expected, the clay can always be worked down to a lump, wedged again, and worked up for another try.

Allow the young craftsman to experiment with forms that grow spontaneously on the potter's wheel and that flow from his own hands. Eventually he can design shapes on paper, make templates (see 263 and 68), and use them to form preplanned pottery. The pottery can be incised, engraved (see 268), decorated with beads, coil, and strips (see 258) or with slip (see 272). When completed, it should be air dried for a week or more, whether or not it is to be fired.

276. Making Handles for Pottery

Draw out a lump of wedged clay in your hand (see diag. 276.a), break off a portion at the narrow end, and form or squeeze it into a handle shape. Or a rim can be turned on a potter's wheel, cut in half or quartered, removed from the base, and attached to the pottery with slip (see diag. 276.b). Strips of clay cut from slabs can also be formed as handles (see 258.c). All handles must be attached to the vessel with slip. Handles should be covered with cloth during part of the air drying time so they will dry last.

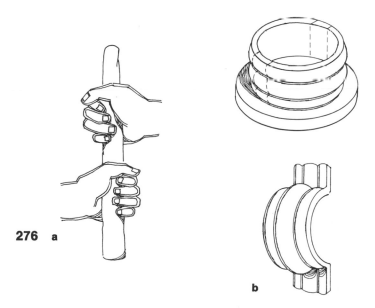

276 a

b

D. SCULPTING, CARVING, AND MOLDING

277. Sculpting with Clay

The techniques and tools described in 251 through 260 and 264 through 272 apply. Sculpture can be coil or slab built (see 264 and 266) or hollowed (see 265) after it has been worked into the desired shape. Use fingers and clay working tools to add and shape the clay. When hollowing the sculpture be sure to leave sufficient wall thickness so that the clay does not collapse under its own weight. Larger sculptures should be draped over armatures (see 51–54 and 146). Hollow clay shapes, whether hollowed or worked over an armature, dry more quickly and evenly and are less likely to develop cracks and flaws than solid ones.

After having dried completely in the air, clay sculptures can be fired if a large enough kiln is available (see 273 and 274), or they can be cast in plaster of Paris and other materials (see 282–288).

When sculpting in clay requires more than one session, it is necessary to cover the unfinished work with a damp cloth and to moisten it periodically to keep the clay pliant and workable.

Textures can be worked into sculptures as detailed in 260 through 262

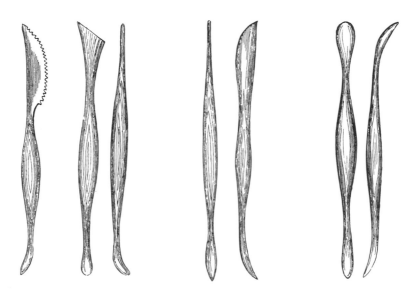

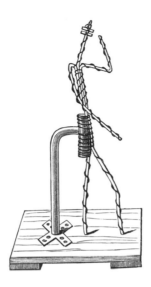

and 268. Keep in mind that the natural texture of clay that has been worked by hand can be most effective, varied, and interesting.

278. Soap and Wax Carving

Tools and materials
> Dull small, long-handled knife
> Pointed etching and engraving tools (see 313)
> Small files (see 152) and rasps
> Bar of soap; beeswax; dental molding or casting wax; or paraffin
> 6″ × 6″ × ¾″ wooden work base
> Candle in holder (optional)
> Forged steel modeling tools

Soap, wax, and paraffin are easily carved with blunt tools. They lend themselves to being worked by children in the young age groups. Show the child how to carve and remove slivers, incise and engrave lines and shapes, smooth or create sharp edges, and form the material to create desired shapes.

When the young craftsman has practiced basic carving skills and when he can be trusted to be careful, light a candle and show him how to warm his tools for carving, cutting, whittling, and shaving the material. Beeswax can be formed in hand; candle wax or paraffin can be melted in a double boiler. Fill a large cooking pot about halfway with water. Break up candles or paraffin slabs into a second, smaller pot and place it inside the larger, water filled pot. Bring the water to a boil until the wax or paraffin liquefies. When it has cooled so that it is warm to the touch, let the child scoop it out and form it in his hand. He can carve and engrave on the wax or paraffin and give it detail and texture with cold or warmed tools.

279. Etching in Plaster

Tools and materials
Dull small, long-handled knife
Pointed etching and engraving tools (see 313)
Forged steel modeling tools
Plaster bat (see 271)

Mix and prepare the plaster slabs or bat as in 271. Once set, it can be engraved and incised like air dried clay (see 268) and painted (see 241).

280. Carving in Brick or Stone

Brick, soapstone, limestone, soft sandstone, and alabaster lend themselves to carving and chiseling by young people, who should wear goggles while working these materials since small, flying stone chips can injure eyes.

Tools and materials
Cold chisel
Stonecutter's chisel
Claw chisel
Stonecutter's gouge
Hammerhead dual-purpose tool
Wooden mallet
Rasps, files, emery paper
Hand drill and masonry drill bits
Goggles

Chips should be removed with small, shallow cuts of chisels and gouges (see 131) held at acute angles and tapped lightly with the mallet. As in all cutting and gouging (see 86, 87, 134, and 305), fingers and hands must be kept behind cutting edges and the tools worked in a direction away from the craftsman. Stone that is to be worked should be sufficiently large so that it does not "walk away" from the tool and mallet blows; or it must be secured with clamps or placed on a wooden board to which strips of wood have been nailed or screwed as a working surface. To drill or carve a smaller stone, clamp it to the work surface with a C-clamp (see 112). Place a pad made of folded rags between the stone and the jaws of the clamp and table, to avoid marring surfaces.

Once the young craftsman gets the feel of the stone and its grain he can learn to judge how large a stone chip can be removed at one time without carving away more than he wishes. First projects should center mostly on giving the stone texture—smoothing it or altering contours slightly. It can be finished with rasps, files, and emery paper or polished with wax and oil.

281. Carving in Wood

(See 131, 134, and 135.)

282. Making an Open Plaster Mold

Children and young people should be discouraged from filling prepared and manufactured molds with clay or modeling compounds and dough (see I.a–h and VI.A.a). Found materials (see XIV) in which papier maché, clay, modeling compounds, or plaster are cast for creative purposes, and molds made by the child from models he or she has sculpted or formed, are something else entirely. There are two good reasons for making and using such molds: to cast an object made of clay and to reproduce it in more durable material, and to make multiple duplicates of the child's creation. For example, he or she may wish to duplicate a modeled or incised plaque to make a necklace of identical modules. Be sure to read 285 before starting the mold if the object is to be duplicated and cast in plaster.

An open mold is sufficient for any small clay object that has a flat base or back. The following steps are required to make such an open mold out of plaster of Paris for duplicating and casting models in clay.

Make sure that no undercuts exist on the original clay model. They would prevent the separation of the mold from the model once the plaster has set (see diag. 282).

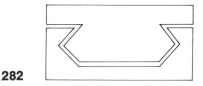

282

Place the air dried clay model, right side up, into a cardboard or wooden box about 1″ wider than the model on all four sides and 1″ higher than the object itself. Mix enough plaster to fill the whole box. Follow the directions and proportions given in 271 for mixing plaster of Paris. As soon as it is mixed, pour the plaster slowly all around and over the object inside the box until the box is completely filled with plaster. Tap the box with a finger all around to allow any air bubbles trapped in the plaster to rise to the surface. If necessary, level the top of the plaster with a piece of lath (see 283).

The plaster will set and harden in fifteen to thirty minutes. Remove the plaster cast and clay model from the box. Tap the cast to release the clay model. If it does not come free easily, attach a small piece of fresh clay to the bottom of the model and pull it gently away from the mold. The mold should now consist of a nearly perfect, reverse replica of the original. Use plaster modeling tools (see 279) to correct or smooth irregularities in the mold and to clean out any clay that may adhere. See 284 for directions on how to make clay duplicates from such a mold.

283. Two-Piece Plaster Mold

A solid, three-dimensional clay model or object that includes undercut detail and shapes must be cast in a mold of two or more pieces. The more convolute the shapes of the model, the larger the number of pieces into which the mold must be divided so that it can be separated from the model and the mold from the eventual casting. (See 285 if the model is to be reproduced in plaster rather than in clay.)

Place the clay model on a flat piece of wood or cardboard that is about 1″ wider on all four sides than the model. Use a sharp-pointed tool, like the point of dividers, to mark a line and incise it in the clay model around at its widest part. Make sure no undercut portion appears on either half of the model. Then wedge clay of a different color than that used for building the model or, if the model is air dried, use the same wet clay. Roll ½″- to 1″-thick coil strips and keep them moist under a damp cloth. Press these coils against the base of the model and, using the technique described in 263 and 264, build the coils up to but not beyond the line incised all around the clay model. Add to and extend the clay base to about 1″ away from the model and flatten the top of the base so that it extends evenly from the incised line in the model to the edge of the coil built clay wall (see diag. 283.a).

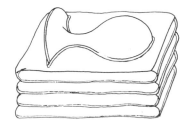

283 a

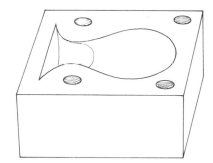

b

Build a closely fitting cardboard or wooden box that encloses the model on the bottom and four surrounding sides. The side walls should be at least 2″ higher than the model. If the box is made out of cardboard, seal all edges with friction or masking tape.

Now mix the plaster in the proportions and manner described in 271. Pour the plaster into the box as soon as it is properly mixed and cover the model with at least 1″ of plaster. Tap the sides of the box to release air bubbles. Let the plaster set for fifteen to thirty minutes. Remove the box and gently dismantle the wet coil strip wall built around the base of the model up to the parting line. Be sure to leave the model embedded in the plaster.

Use a melon scoop or a small spoon to dig three or four "keys" into the top exposed surface of the plaster mold's side walls (see diag. 283.b). These will be registration marks for the second half of the mold, permitting it to be fitted to the first precisely for later casting.

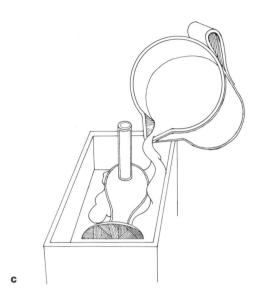

c

Place the plaster embedded model back into the wood or cardboard box, clay model side facing up. Coat the top of the side walls of the bottom half of the plaster cast and the "keys" with soft soap, grease, olive oil, or Vaseline.

Using fresh, wedged clay, roll a 1"-thick coil or cylinder and attach it, with slip, upright, to the topmost projection of the exposed clay model (see diag. 283.c). After the mold has been made this will be the pouring hole for eventual casting of duplicate models.

Mix and pour plaster over the model and into the box as before, covering the top of the model with about 1" of plaster. After the plaster has set, remove the box from the plaster and open the mold at the parting line. It should open easily if it was properly greased. Remove the original clay model from the mold halves and clean out the pouring hole cast in the top half of the mold. Correct and clean imperfections in the mold with plaster of Paris modeling tools. The mold is now ready for casting duplicates of the original.

284. Casting in Clay from a Plaster Mold

a. *Open mold casting in clay* *(for mold preparation see 282)*

Tools and materials
Slip (see 256), mixed to the consistency of molasses
Clay modeling tools (see 264 and 277)
Spatula or lath, longer than the open mold is wide

Pour slip into the open mold until it is filled completely and the clay bellies up slightly. Tap the outside of the mold gently to remove air bubbles. Scrape off excess slip with the spatula or lath and level the top of the mold. After an hour or two the clay will have dried enough so that it can be separated from the mold. Tap the plaster mold to release the casting. If it does not come free, press a wad of fresh clay to the casting and pull. It should then come loose from the mold without difficulty, unless there are undercuts in the mold. The mold can be used for casting additional duplicates after it has been cleaned. Any small irregularities in the casting can be corrected with modeling tools and slip. The casting can then be air dried and eventually fired, if a kiln is available.

b. *Two-piece mold casting in clay* *(for mold preparation see 283)*

Tools and materials
Same as 284a
Metal or plastic funnel

Tie the two mold halves together with string, making sure not to cross the pouring hole opening. Insert the funnel into the pouring hole and pour slip until it fills the hole (see diag. 284). Tap the mold to eliminate air bubbles. Add more slip if required, using enough to fill the pouring hole. Then scrape excess slip out of the pouring hole, using a clay modeling tool. After an hour or two, open the mold and remove the molded

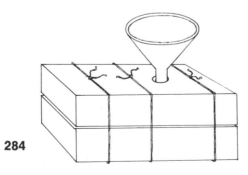

284

object as in 284.a. Clean the mold and correct imperfections in the casting with slip and modeling tools. The mold can then be used for repeated casting.

c. *More-than-two-piece mold casting in clay*

(See 285.)

285. Casting in Plaster

The molds required for open casting in plaster of two or more pieces are the same as those described for clay in 282 and 283, with the following differences.

The whole inside of the plaster mold and parting edges must be coated with an even, thin layer of Vaseline, olive oil, grease, or soft soap before pouring the plaster into the mold. When using a mold for two or more pieces and before tying the various mold sections together, ready for pouring plaster, line all parting edges of the mold, including the keys, with strips of light metal foil (call shims), so that the foil extends ½″ beyond the outside of the mold (see diag. 285). Mix and pour plaster into the open mold or through a funnel and pouring hole as in 284.

An alternate plaster casting method, used by sculptors, produces a multiple-piece mold that is, however, used only for a single casting. Cover the original model with soft soap and then with ¼″ of plaster mixed with blue ink, after the parting lines for the mold portions are marked with shims stuck in the clay. Cover the blue plaster with a second ¾″ layer of white plaster and, after the plaster has set, separate the mold segments along the parting lines. When the hollow, greased mold is reassembled

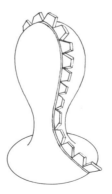

285

and tied, plaster is poured into it through the pouring hole and, after it has set, the plaster mold is chipped away. The blue plaster coating warns the sculptor that he is approaching the surface of the casting and he works more cautiously until the grease coated blue mold surface is removed from the plaster cast.

286. Lost Wax Casting

This is an ancient method of casting. Delicate and detailed wax sculptures containing undercuts can be cast in plaster from a one-piece plaster mold. Only a single casting can be made from each mold.

Tools and materials
    Beeswax or paraffin, and modeling tools (see 278)
    Plaster of Paris (see 271)

Make the original model out of beeswax or paraffin. Embed the whole model in a thin coating of blue stained plaster (see 285) and then in a thicker coating of white plaster, leaving a pouring hole (see 283) and two or three other small holes to admit air to the inside of the mold (see diag. 286).

When the plaster has set, place the mold on a grill inside an oven, the pouring hole facing straight down between the bars of the grill, beneath which a container has been placed. Heat the oven sufficiently to melt the wax. After it has run out of the mold, let the mold cool completely. Fill the mold with vegetable oil and then empty it out, leaving a thin film of oil on the inside surfaces of the mold. Then fill the mold with plaster of Paris through a funnel placed over the pouring hole. When the plaster has set, chip away the mold as described in 285, as well as the excess plaster at pouring and air holes.

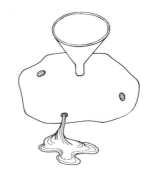

286

287. Making and Casting from a Rubber Mold

Tools and materials
Rubber molding compound (available from art supply stores)
Flocking (available from art supply stores)
Plaster of Paris, and plaster modeling tools (see 279)
Cardboard or wooden casting box (see 282 and 283)

The clay model is prepared as for an open or two-piece (or more) plaster cast (see 282 and 283). Brush a thin coating of rubber molding compound over the model and beyond it, about 1″ all around. Observe the curing time on the package label of the rubber compound. After the first coat has cured, apply a second and let it cure, and then a third. Then mix rubber compound with flocking in proportions recommended on the package. Apply this coating to the rubber covered model in successive layers, each after the last has cured, until the mold half or section is at least ⅛″ thick. Embed each mold section in 1″ of plaster of Paris (see diag. 287) before removing it from the model.

287

If a mold for two or more pieces is required, be sure to mark keys and to line all parting lines with shims (see 285) and coat them with soft soap, Vaseline, or grease, while forming portions of the mold and casting from it in the casting box. The inside of the mold does not need greasing for casting in clay or plaster. The advantage of the rubber mold is that, if properly made and used, it can include some undercuts and still be stripped from model and casting if the outer plaster casing is removed.

288. Other Mold Making and Casting Materials

A greased plaster of Paris or rubber mold can be used for casting hollow papier maché shapes (see 49) or ones of wood dough or modeling dough. Coat an open mold or mold parts with about ⅛″- to ¼″-thick maché mash or modeling dough. Let it air dry in the mold.

Synthetic and plastic mold making and casting materials, including and especially epoxy, are toxic and carcinogenic. Do not allow children and young people to use these materials.

E. MOSAICS

Tile and mosaic making are closely related. The ancient Babylonians, Egyptians, Greeks, and Romans developed this into a fine art. Early craftsmen cut slabs of clay into small tiles and dried, painted, and glazed them for assembly into decorative wall designs and murals. True mosaics were made by cutting and breaking up colored glass into fragments and composing complex designs and pictures with these pieces embedded in chalk mortar.

Glass mosaic tiles are available commercially. Plastic mosaic modules are packaged as toys and activity sets for children. But for the reasons stated in I.a through h and VI.A.a it is preferable if children and young people make their own materials whenever possible instead of working with prefabricated parts. Very young children can make paper mosaic modules (see 29); older ones can make them out of cloth snippets, leather (see 178), clay, and plaster of Paris. Found materials (see XIV), including pebbles and seeds, can also be used.

289. Clay and Plaster Mosaic Tiles

A ⅛" to ¼" clay slab (see 266) or plaster bat (see 271) can be incised with a dull knife and divided into small mosaic modules. Do not cut all the way through the slab or bat. Geometric and nongeometric shapes can be cut and, after the clay or plaster has dried, broken apart and sorted by shape and size (see diag. 289.a). Shaped metal strips (see

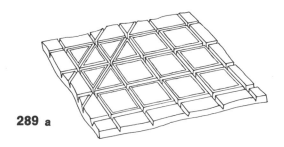

289 a

158), metal tubes, and pipes can also be used to embed shapes in plaster or clay. Or a bottle or rolling pin can be covered with strips of cardboard, wire, or string, outlining a latticework of shapes (see diag. 289.b). This can be rolled over the wet clay slab or plaster bat to incise shapes.

After the clay has dried or the plaster has set, either can be painted (see 226 and 237–241). If water base paints are used, the colors can be made more or less waterproof if the painted tiles are covered with several successive coatings of clear varnish or shellac (see 227), transparent glue (see 16), water glass (see 42), or acrylic medium (see 26 and 237), after the paints have dried.

Mosaic tiles can be set into chalk mortar, a sand and paste mixture, plaster of Paris, or cement. Children in the younger age groups will find it more convenient to work inside a cardboard box lid or wood tray whose sides are no higher than the tiles are thick. Show the child how to cover a small area with mortar or adhesive, set the tiles, and when the coated area is filled prepare the next section until the whole tray is covered with mosaic tiles.

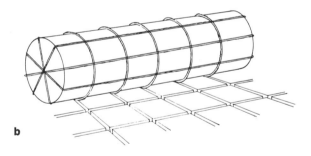

b

VIII

Printing

Let the children make their own equipment as far as they can.—Jean Jacques Rousseau

A. BACKGROUND

If writing gave permanence to the word and allowed the events of history to become known to scholars of future generations, printing brought information within reach of all. The printed picture and word have special value in this age, Marshall McLuhan notwithstanding. In reading a book or looking at reproductions of pictures the reader is able to stop, reflect, and digest what he sees at his own pace. He can reexamine what he read earlier and refresh his memory as quickly and often as he chooses. Film and TV in their present form, except for microfilm, cannot be used in this manner. Sequences are not readily played back, slowed down, or available for instant comparison on TV, for example. Despite their great impact and creative potential, film and TV must be viewed and used in the framework of an entirely different value system from that of print, despite attempts to make them interchangeable or to have the former take the place of the latter. Audiovisual media

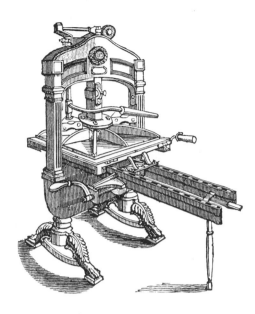

invite a different kind of participation from that of print (see IX) if they are to be thought provoking and educative.

Printing as a craft can be enormously satisfying, especially for young people. It enables them to leave their mark, to experiment with combinations of forms, shapes, textures, colors, and type that they can create, design, and duplicate. Even pre-schoolers can achieve interesting and satisfying results with a wide range of simple printing materials.

Printing was first practiced in China, about 800 A.D.—six hundred years after paper was invented there (see II.A). Paper making and printing have always depended on one another. No other surface lends itself so readily to quantity duplication of stone, wood, clay, metal, and other carvings. The earliest Chinese prints were made from jade and clay seals that were inked and stamped on paper. This inspired the carving of pictures and Chinese characters in stone in reverse for reproduction by rubbings (see VIII.D). Between 841 and 846 A.D. the great "stone classics" were printed in China by carving and inking stones and rubbing on paper laid over them. Twenty-two years afterward, the first book was printed from wood blocks, and this technique for reproducing pictures and text has since developed into a fine art in China.

The ancient Egyptians drew pictures and kept records on the leaves of the papyrus plant. But paper—laid fibers, as the Chinese knew paper and as we know it today—was not invented in Egypt until about the same time wood blocks were first printed in China. The art of paper making was carried from the other side of the Mediterranean to Europe, but printing from wood blocks was not practiced in Europe until the time of the Crusades. Printing from movable type, known to the Chinese for over six centuries, was independently invented by Johann Gutenberg in the fifteenth century in the German city of Mainz, just fifty years before Columbus first landed on the American continent.

From Gutenberg's time to the late eighteenth century, letterpress printing remained nearly unchanged. Once paper was manufactured by machine in large quantities, faster and more efficient letterpress printing methods followed. Two other printing techniques, etching and intaglio, both of which require engraving on copper, became increasingly mechanized. Lithography, invented by accident in 1796, is a printing method based on the principle that oil and water don't mix. Aloys Senefelder discovered, after writing a laundry list on a grease coated stone, that its mirror image was transferred to paper inadvertently placed on top of the stone. This printing method did not compete effectively

with letterpress and intaglio until photographic transfer of screened pic-'
tures and type to metal became possible. The invention of the linotype
machine permitted rapid type setting and casting. Electrotyping, a
method of duplicating printing plates for letterpress, and other innovations turned printing from a craft into an industry. More recently, photo-
type setting, electronic color separation, and computer controlled processes have automated and brought about a further technological
revolution in printing.

These crafts, in their present-day techno-industrial forms, are far removed from the experience of children. There is just no way children
can be actively involved in modern printing processes. Instead, they
must practice earlier, labor intensive methods in order to understand and
use these media creatively. These techniques, though unprofitable to industry, are still required for really fine work. Today they are practiced
only by artists and rare craftsmen and craftswomen. The demand for the
required tools has shrunk to the point where European wood engraving
tools, for example, have become virtually unobtainable. The few remaining craftsmen who make them by hand, and their craft, are threatened with extinction.

B. FIRST PRINTS

290. Blotting Paper Monoprints

Tools and materials
> Poster paints; brushes; drawing paper (see 206)
> Sheets of blotting paper

Suggest to the child that he paint a design on the drawing paper, using
brushes and very moist poster paints. Place a sheet of blotting paper
over the painting before it has a chance to dry. Rub the blotting paper
without shifting it. The painting will transfer to the blotting paper. Place
the original and the blotted monoprint next to one another. Point out that
the monoprint is a mirror image of the original. Let the child look at the
monoprint in a mirror if one is handy. He'll discover that the design appears there as in the original. This recognition is important for future
print making, in which the design cut into the block must be a mirror
image of the expected print. Similarly, type cast for printing—or lettering cut into a linoleum block—must be reversed, and becomes readable
only if looked at in a mirror or after it has been printed.

291. Carbon Paper Duplicating

Tools and materials
    Bond writing or typing paper
    Carbon paper
    Pencil or ballpoint pen

Slip one sheet of carbon paper between two sheets of bond writing or typing paper and suggest that the child draw on the top sheet with a pencil or ballpoint pen. By interleaving five or six sheets of writing paper with carbon paper, he can make several copies at a time. Point out that direct "duplicating" is not the same as printing, in which the original is always reversed.

292. Kneaded Eraser Prints

Tools and materials
    Two or more kneaded erasers (available in art supply stores)
    Black stamp pad
    Newsprint or newspaper

Kneaded erasers can be made malleable by being kneaded in your hand. They can be formed into various shapes—like clay—by rolling, pressing, or cutting them with a knife. Let the child prepare several such kneaded eraser shapes, press each onto the inked stamp pad, and print them like a rubber stamp. Rubber stamp ink pads can be restored when the ink dries out or is depleted, with bottled ink that can be bought in any stationery store. Homemade stamp pads can be improvised by placing a piece of felt in a coffee can lid, and coating it liberally with bottled stamp pad ink or vegetable dye.

Because the ink is difficult to clean off the kneaded eraser, it is best to supply only one color. Cover the table surface with plenty of newsprint or newspaper and provide rags on which the child can wipe his or her hands.

293. Potato and Other Vegetable Prints

Tools and materials
    Stamp pads impregnated with stamp pad ink or vegetable dyes, or with linoleum block water base or oil base ink; or muffin tin filled with very thick poster colors; brush (see 206)
    Dull knife blade
    Newsprint pad or newspaper
    Potatoes; carrots; cabbage stalks; white radishes; turnips; onions; okra; corn cobs; any other close-fibered vegetable or stalks

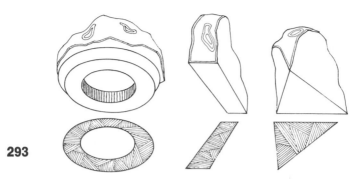

293

Any of the vegetables, if cut in half, into sections or into different shapes, and inked or coated with paint, will print. Do not encourage the child to carve a design into the top of a halved potato. It is easier and better to carve the whole potato half into whatever printing shape has been chosen (see diag. 293).

It is best to make different shapes for each color or to duplicate the same shape if the child wishes to print each in several colors. The ink is difficult to wipe off vegetable stamps, and if the child presses one that still contains one color into other colors, all will soon turn muddy. The poster colors can be painted onto the stamping surface with a brush. (For details on how to make stamp pads or replenish them with stamp pad ink, see 292.)

294. Printing with a Brayer

Tools and materials
    Brayer (see below)
    Sheet of $1/16''$ or $1/8''$ plate glass, Plexiglas, or plastic to roll out ink
    Water base or oil base linoleum printing inks in red, yellow, blue, black, and
        white (and turpentine if oil base inks are used)
    Spatula or palette knife
    Newsprint or newspaper
    Spoon
    Clothesline and clothespins

Cover the table with plenty of sheets of newsprint or newspaper, which make the best printing surface. Dress the child in old clothes or in an apron or smock and have him roll up his sleeves.

A brayer is an ink roller attached to a handle. Inexpensive brayers are made of hard rubber. Professional brayers, made of soft rubber, are much more expensive. A hard rubber brayer is good enough for beginners. Be sure to keep the brayer clean and hung on a nail when it is not in use. Caked printing inks ruin a brayer. Also, if left sitting on its rubber surface, the brayer will flatten and become useless.

A brayer can be used in two ways: to coat a printing block or surface with ink; and to roll over the paper that is placed on top of an inked printing block to make an impression. However, the curved surface of a soup spoon usually obtains a better printing impression than a brayer. A brayer can also be used for rubbings (see 316).

Water base linoleum printing ink, while not as brilliant as oil base ink, is the preferred medium for beginners. Besides, all washing up after printing can be done with water. Oil base inks require turpentine as a solvent and cleaner.

Squeeze about 2″ of ink out of the tube onto the plastic sheet. Use a flexible knife—a spatula or palette knife—to spread the ink ribbon. Then roll the brayer over the ink, moving it back and forth until it covers a portion of the plastic or glass surface with a smooth, tacky film. If ripples and waves appear on the ink surface, it has not been spread sufficiently or it may be too thin. Let the ink dry in the air for ten to fifteen minutes and roll it out again. When the brayer is well covered with ink, roll it over the printing block. If the block has not been printed before, several coats may be needed before it is cured and the ink has penetrated the pores of the material. Move the brayer over the block from several directions. Once cured, a couple of passes with the well-inked brayer over the block, each at right angles to the other, should suffice to ink the surface for a good impression.

Once the block is inked, gently drop a sheet of newsprint on top of it. Do not move the paper once it is in contact with the block or it will smear. Rub the curved side of a spoon all over the paper (see diag. 294) to get a good impression. The first few prints may be unsatisfactory. But these proofs let you know how much pressure to apply; whether the ink is too wet, too dry, or just right; and whether the block needs heavier or lighter inking or deeper cutting in places.

Hang finished prints from a clothesline strung across the room, securing them with clothespins. Do not remove and stack them until the printed surfaces are completely dry and no longer tacky.

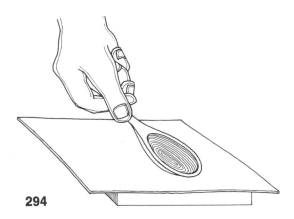

294

These basic printing techniques apply to all media but engraving (see 313 and 314) and stencil printing (see VIII.E), when no printing press is available. Small proof presses can occasionally be bought inexpensively from printers who are anxious to get rid of obsolete equipment. Hand proof presses still require the printing blocks to be inked with a brayer and, save for operating the press, the basic techniques remain the same.

295. Found Material Prints

Tools and materials
  Same as 294

Any material with a deep and well-defined grain or texture can be used as a printing surface. The following is a partial listing of ''found'' and improvised printing surfaces. (See also XIV.)

Coarse linen or canvas cloth	Embossed wallpaper
Cardboard shapes	Bottlecaps
Plant leaves, whole or with the flesh stripped	Bulrushes and moss
from the skeleton	Pebbles
Bottle corks or shapes cut out of flat	Sponge
cork sheets	Coins
Crumpled tissue paper	Bark
Straw matting	Egg carton tray
Raffia or string pasted to cardboard	Woodgrain and lumber scraps

Ink and print any of these onto newsprint or other absorbent paper surfaces, using the techniques described in 294.

For best results with whole plant leaves, coat one side with a thin layer of white paste (see 14–18). When it has dried, paint poster color on the paste covered surface or ink it with a brayer and print as in 294. Several such paste covered leaves or any of the other materials suggested above, each inked with a different color or tint, can be overprinted to form interesting designs and patterns.

C. ADVANCED PRINTING WITH AND WITHOUT A PRESS

296. Modular Shape Printing

Tools and materials
Same as 293 and 294
Modular wood, cardboard, linoleum, or rubber shapes

Sanded woodblock shapes, small pieces of linoleum glued to wood, dowel ends, rubber scraps, and even the edges of thick cardboard strips attached to dowels or stamp handles can be printed next to and overlapping each other in one or more colors. If transparent inks are used, a third color will appear wherever two or more colors are "trapped" by overprinting. I designed a modular printing set in 1956, the Picture Printer, that has been copied all over the world. But anyone can make printing modules him- or herself. The shapes, if they cannot be held comfortably in the hand, can be glued to a wooden board or to cardboard, provided all are the same height. Others can be attached to molding or stamp handles (see diag. 296) and printed like rubber stamps. Make sure the stamp handle closely fits the shape to be printed so that the edges of the wooden base do not print accidentally along with the design (see diag. 296).

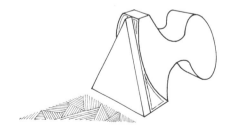

296

297. Glass Monoprints

Tools and materials
Large pane of glass or Plexiglas
Poster colors (see 206), glass paints (see 220), or printing inks (see 294); long-handled student grade bristle brush (see 206)
Blotting or drawing paper; or newsprint

Paint the design on the glass or Plexiglas. The paint or ink should be thinned so that it does not dry out while being applied to the glass. Then place a sheet of blotting or drawing paper on the paint covered glass while the paint is still wet. Press on the paper heavily or lightly to obtain different effects. Then pick up one edge of the paper, peel it back quickly, and let it dry flat on a sheet of blotting paper.

Monoprints, so called because only one print can be pulled from each painting, can be made with other materials as well (see 290). Combinations of media—oil base and water base paints and inks—make a variety of interesting effects.

298. Hectograph Duplicating

Tools and materials
Hectograph gel set (available in stationery stores)
Typewriter paper
Carbon paper (see 291)
Ballpoint pen; typewriter
Sponge

Let the child write, draw, or type, or any combination of these, on the top sheet of two typewriter paper pages between which a sheet of carbon paper has been placed. Press the carbon copy on the gel inside the hectograph box. The letters and drawings will transfer to the gel in mirror image. Then press a clean sheet of typewriter paper on the gel; the images and copy will transfer onto the paper, reading the right way. Up to twenty-five or thirty such prints can be made from one gel negative. Wipe each sheet of paper with the sponge immediately after the impression has been made.

299. Printing from Type

Unfortunately, in most rubber type toy printing sets the type is too small for a child to handle. Larger type can be found and bought, sometimes quite inexpensively. Discarded and imperfect wooden type fonts can be obtained from display houses, typographers, and antique shops. Small-job printers who do not have their own linotype machine are sometimes willing to sell old metal type fonts that are incomplete. Even if a whole font (a complete assortment of all the letters of the alphabet) is not available, large type faces can be useful in the hands of young people. Large letters can be printed individually, like modular stamps (see 296), and become part of a design. Or they can be combined with others of the same or a different size, tied with twine, and locked into a chase with small blocks or quoins (metal wedges) to be printed with or without a press (see 294). A chase (the metal tray in which compositors place type after it has been set), furniture (wood blocks used to fill a chase so that the type is wedged in place), and quoins can often be bought from secondhand printing supply shops or small printers.

300. Cardboard Printing

Tools and materials
Same as 294
Sheets of ⅛″ or thicker cardboard (e.g., the backing of drawing paper pads)
Sharp knife (see 86, 87, and 135)

Cardboard consists of pressed layers of paper. It is relatively easy to cut away several layers with a sharp knife to create relief designs that can be printed when inked like wood or linoleum cuts (see 306, 307, and 309). Lines, textures, and patterns can be cut, engraved, and punched into cardboard and the cut-out portions peeled away. Individual cut-out cardboard shapes can also be glued to a cardboard sheet and printed (see 296). Ink and print cardboard as in 294.

301. Ink Engraving

Tools and materials
Same as 294
Sheet of heavy cardboard
Drawing paper or newsprint
Stylus or used-up ballpoint pen

Use the brayer to coat the cardboard with a thick layer of ink. Cover the cardboard with a sheet of drawing paper or newsprint and draw onto it with the stylus or ballpoint pen. Be careful not to lean on the paper, or to press a hand or finger on it. When the drawing is done, lift the paper off the ink covered cardboard. The lines and textures engraved on the paper with the stylus will be printed on the side of the paper that rested on the ink.

302. Cylinder Printing

Tools and materials
Same as 294
Large bottle; paper tube; or rolling pin
Heavy construction paper
Scissors (see 36 and 37)
Paste (see 10–26)

Cut paper strips and shapes with scissors, and paste them on the thick portion of a bottle, or on a paper tube or rolling pin. The paper must all be of the same thickness and none of the shapes can overlap or cross. Ink the glass or Plexiglas surface as in 294. Roll the bottle, tube, or rolling pin over the inked area, inking the raised paper surfaces pasted to it. Then roll the inked cylinder on a sheet of newsprint or other absorbent paper. The raised and inked paper design pasted to the bottle will print. With careful marking on the end of the bottle or tube where the print ends, either can be reinked and a continuous repeat pattern printed (see 311).

Similar prints can be made with twine, string, or thread pasted to the tube or bottle surface, provided material of the same thickness is used in each case and none of it crosses or overlaps.

303. Carved Clay and Plaster Cylinder Printing

Tools and materials
Same as 260, 266, 268, 271, 279, and 294
Cardboard tubes

Incise, engrave, or press textures and shapes in wet clay or plaster draped around a 2″ to 3″-diameter cardboard tube. Or solid cylinders of

303

clay or plaster can be formed inside such a tube and etched on, after they have dried and been withdrawn from the cylinder mold. Cover the inside of the cardboard tube with soft soap, Vaseline, or vegetable oil to facilitate release of the clay or plaster cylinder once it has set.

Any of these can be inked and printed as described in 302. If two closely fitting, telescoped cardboard tubes are available, use the smaller one to roll and print from the larger one draped with engraved clay or plaster (see diag. 303).

304. Carved Clay and Plaster Slab Printing

Tools and materials
Same as 303 (except for cardboard tubes)

Incise, engrave, or press textures in slabs of wet clay or plaster as in 303, or engrave on dried slabs of either. In preparing the slabs be sure that the surfaces are as level as possible. Carved wet clay or plaster must be allowed to dry. Then use either as a printing plate. Ink with a brayer (see 294), place paper over the inked surfaces, and make impressions with a spoon or a clean brayer.

305. Linoleum Block Cutting

Tools and materials
Unmounted battleship-gray linoleum
Black India ink (see 228); or felt markers (see 197)
Inexpensive No. 4 or 5 watercolor brush
Set of linoleum cutting tools
Oilstone

Unmounted linoleum is easier for young people to control while cutting. Suggest that the young craftsman design directly on linoleum with brush and India ink or black felt marker. Explain that everything not painted black will have to be cut away and that the black-painted portions are the ones that will print.

The linoleum should be fresh, soft, and not brittle. Properly instructed, children as young as age five can design and cut linoleum blocks successfully. Use an oilstone to keep the cutting tools sharp at all times. The sharper they are, the less the likelihood that a blade will skip out of a cut and injure the user. Instruct the child that the hand holding down the linoleum must be behind the tool at all times (see diag. 131.a). The cut should be made in a direction away from the hand holding the material. If these rules are meticulously observed, it is impossible for a child to hurt him- or herself. If a young person cannot be depended on to observe these cautions, he or she is too immature to work with linoleum.

Provide the child with scraps of linoleum on which to try the different cutting blades and to discover the possible variety of effects. Small cuts, dots, and fine lines spaced closely or farther apart create tones and textures. The depth of the cut should be no deeper than half the thickness of the linoleum; it should never be so deep that the fabric backing shows through. To assure a large edition of prints and that the block won't crumble, bevel each cut and never undercut the linoleum (see diag. 305). Point out that if the child decides to cut letters of the alphabet or sign his name, the letters must be drawn and cut in reverse or they won't read when printed (see 290).

305

The block is ready for printing only after all uninked areas have been cut away. Wash the block in mild soap and warm water to remove ink and grease and then let it dry thoroughly on a flat surface.

306. Linoleum Block Printing in One Color

Tools and materials
Same as 294
Newsprint; Japanese rice paper; or tissue paper

Ink and print the block as described in 294. Be sure to cure the linoleum with repeated inking. Drop the newsprint or rice paper gently on the block. Don't move the paper once it is placed or it will smear. The first few impressions, whether printed with a brayer or spoon or on a press, will probably be poor. Compare each proof with the next. They will show where additional cutting, greater or less pressure, or more or less ink may be needed to make the best possible print.

If the block is printed on a press, the block may need "make-ready." This consists of raising portions of the block to get a better impression and greater pressure in some places. Paste a thin piece of paper or tape under the portions of the block where the print is gray or fuzzy compared with the rest. Make-ready requires experimentation until all parts of the block print evenly.

After printing, wash the block with solvent (turpentine, if oil base inks were used; water, if water base inks were used) and then in mild soap and warm water. Clean ink off brayer and glass or Plexiglas plate and hang up brayer and prints (see 294). If quite a lot of ink is left on the glass plate, the ink can be scraped off with a spatula and wrapped in saran wrap for future use.

A properly cared-for block is good for many editions and prints.

307. Linoleum Block Printing in More than One Color

Tools and materials
Same as 305 and 306
Sheets or roll of wax paper

A two-color print—red and black, for example—requires that two blocks be designed, cut, and printed, one for each color (see 317). Design and print the black plate as in 306. Pull several good proofs. Then wash, dry, and apply a heavy coating of orange ink to the same block and print it on a sheet of wax paper. Place the printed wax paper sheet upside down on a second, uncut linoleum block the same size as the first. Rub the back of the wax paper to transfer the design to the second linoleum block. Peel off the wax paper. Let the ink dry thoroughly on the second block if the impression is a good one. If the print is poor, wash the ink off the block and try again, as before.

This transfer of the design on the first block to the second is essential so that the second color cut can be registered more or less exactly with the first. Precise registration is difficult without a printing press, but you can come close. Once the orange ink is dry on the second, uncut block, paint in whatever areas you have chosen to print in the second (red) color with black ink or felt marker. Be sure to ''trap'' (overlap) color areas that are supposed to meet and have adjoining edges. Paint the black ink about ⅛″ over the orange ink in these places. Then cut away all but the black-painted areas.

Pull a number of proofs of the second block until it is cured. Then ink the block with the chosen second color and lay one of the black proofs on the second block. If both linoleum blocks and the paper are cut to exactly the same size, registration will not be too difficult. Print the second color and check the proof for any additional cutting, inking, or make-ready (see 306) that may be needed. Then print a whole edition of the red, second block.

In printing, the lightest color is always printed first and the black last. After the red edition has been printed and has dried, ink the black block again. Place one of the red prints as squarely as possible on the black block, face down, and print. A fairly high percentage of the prints will be sufficiently well registered to be considered good if reasonable care is exercised in printing.

A third, fourth, or more colors can be cut and printed in the same way. Each requires its own block; transfer of the other colors to wax paper and then to the next block that is to be cut; painting in of the desired color area; cutting; and printing, as before.

Close registration is possible only on a press on which corner stops can be attached so that, once a block is positioned, the paper can be registered (see 309) and laid in exactly the same place for each color. Such paper stops can be taped to a linoleum block cut much larger than the picture that is to be cut and printed, even when no press is available.

Another way to make color prints is to cut and print the black block and hand-stamp it with modular shapes, each inked with different colors (see 296).

308. Preserving Linoleum Blocks

Tools and materials
 Plaster of Paris (see 271)
 Used, cut linoleum blocks

A cut and printed linoleum block that is no longer needed for printing can be filled with plaster of Paris and hung like any picture or print. Mix a small amount of plaster of Paris and fill the cut-away portion of the linoleum up to the level of the uncut surface. Wipe any excess plaster off the surface with a damp cloth and let the plaster set. The white plaster will contrast with the printing surfaces, and the block can then be framed and hung.

309. Woodblock Cutting and Printing

Tools and materials
    Same as 294
    Level, square, sanded pine woodblock
    Set of wood cutting knives and gouges
    X-acto or similar knifeblades (and holders)
    Woodblock cutting bench hook (see diag. 309)

Make sure that the woodblock is seasoned, warpage- and knot-free, level on both sides, and well sanded. Paint or draw the design on the wood with India ink or felt markers as in 305.

Wood cutting knives and gouges are shaped differently from those required for linoleum. They are made of better-grade steel since wood is much more dense than linoleum. Suggest to the young craftsman that he experiment with his tools and work them on scrap lumber to discover what effects are possible with each. The cautions and suggestions for the care of tools in 305 apply. Working on the bench hook (see diag. 309) makes wood cutting easier and safer.

Since wood grain runs in one direction, gouging—cutting away portions of the wood—must be done with the grain. Place the woodblock on the bench hook so that the grain is parallel to the sides. The end of the bench hook provides a solid stop for the wood as the surface is gouged. Cutting across the grain of the wood can only be done with a fine, sharp knife blade, or the wood will splinter and fray. The knife or gouge cuts should be shallow in small areas or when cutting lines, and each beveled to avoid undercutting (see 305). In gouging away larger areas and espe-

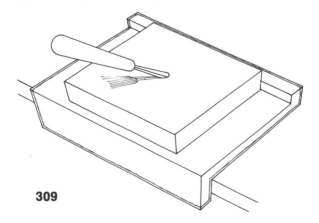

309

cially around the outside of the block, the level of the cut-away wood must be considerably lower than the printing surface—one third to one half the thickness of the woodblock—so that it is not inadvertently inked and printed later. Textures can be achieved through experimentation and by combining a woodblock print with impressions made with textured materials (see 295).

It is safer to gouge away small slivers than to try to remove large areas at a single stroke. Too deep a bite with knife or gouge may cause cracks to appear that spread to areas to be printed.

The block is ready for inking and printing when the whole design has been cut. Wood, because of its porousness, requires more curing with ink than linoleum. Ink and print as in 294, 306, and 307. Newsprint and tissue paper are good surfaces for first proofs. Japanese rice paper, available in different shades, weights, and textures from art supply stores, is best for final prints.

Blocks for two or more colors can be made in exactly the same way as described for linoleum in 307. (See also 317.) Each color requires its own, separate block to be cut and printed in succession. For best registration of successive colors, when printing without a press, make sure that blocks and paper are exactly the same size. When printing on a press or with blocks larger than the size required for the design, use paper stops (see 307) and the registration technique detailed below.

Make each block about 1″ larger on all four sides than the size required for the design. Carve a cross or circle into each corner of the block, outside the area used for the picture or design. Transfer and print the design onto the second and third color blocks as in 307, including the register marks. Cut these as printed on successive blocks and print so that each set of register marks fits directly on top of the others. After the print has dried, excess paper and the register marks can be trimmed off or covered over with a picture frame mat.

310. Wood Engraving

In wood engraving, as distinct from wood cutting, only the end grain of wood is used. Boxwood and various fruit woods are generally employed, due to the fineness and closeness of their end grain. Since the trunks of these trees are small and few portions are entirely knot- and fault-free, wood engraving blocks are pieced together and jointed from several smaller squares and rectangles of perfect wood. End-grain wood engraving blocks are difficult to make and are therefore very expensive. The tools, knives, gouges, and liners are much finer and more delicate than those used for wood cutting. More detail and subtle shadings can be cut into the wood. The tools can cut in every direction. For these reasons wood engraving is not a suitable craft for young people, except for those who have enjoyed a great deal of experience in cutting and printing linoleum and woodblocks.

311. Repeat Pattern Making and Printing

Tools and materials
Same as 292–96, 299–310

Kneaded eraser, potato, vegetable, found materials, cardboard, clay slab, plaster and cylinders, as well as linoleum and woodblocks, can be designed to repeat themselves in all directions. Repeat patterns can be used for fabric and decorative paper printing. The simpler the design, the easier it is to repeat it so that the top and each side of one print fit other sides of the same design, when printed adjacent to each other. Cylinder printing assures a continuous repeat design in one direction, though the ends of the cylinder must be designed carefully so that prints match edge to edge.

312. Fabric Printing

Tools and materials
Same as 311
Rawhide mallet
White or plain colored cotton or silk

Because of the size of the material required even for a scarf, fabric is usually printed with repeat patterns (see 311). All the detailed techniques apply. Oil base printing inks or fabric colors, available from art and craft supply stores, are used to print on fabrics that, when thoroughly dried after printing, are to be washable.

Cover a large table with thick layers of newspaper. Keep the unprinted fabric rolled up at one end. Unroll enough of the fabric to cover the table and tape it to the table edges so that it is slightly stretched and wrinkle free. Place the inked block, face down, on the fabric, starting at one corner of the cut end. Beat the block with the mallet for a good impression. Re-ink the block and make a second impression next to the first one, and so on until the whole fabric surface, taped to the table, is printed.

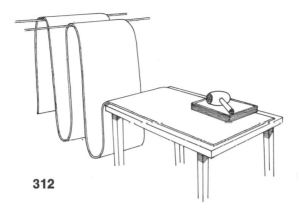

312

Stretch several lengths of twine across the room beyond the far end of the table and drape the printed fabric over it (see diag. 312). Tape the next length of fabric to the table and continue printing as before. Cease printing when you run out of drying space. After the printed fabric has dried it can be rolled up and the printing process continued as before.

313. Engraving, Dry Point, and Intaglio

Copperplate engraving and intaglio require acid and other chemical baths. Dry point is an etching process on acetate that does not require chemicals. All must be printed under considerable pressure on special presses. These requirements make such processes unsuitable and usually impractical for children in younger age groups.

314. Lithography

See VIII.A for a brief description of the process and its history. Lithography requires specially prepared plates and special printing equipment. If a small multilith press is available, young people can draw on and print from lithographic paper and grained aluminum plates. Lithographic crayon and tusche are the required drawing materials. However, the plates are not generally available since most modern lithography is printed from photosensitive plates to which art is transferred photographically. It is not possible to draw on them directly, except to make minor corrections.

D. RUBBINGS

Historically, as pointed out in VIII.A, rubbings from stone preceded the invention of printing. Finding surfaces from which interesting rubbings can be made is a worthwhile quest. It can help make children and young people aware of their surroundings. The following are common surfaces that lend themselves to rubbings, in addition to those listed in 295:

> Pebbled and cut glass
> Plastic or wire mesh
> Vegetable grater
> Brick and cement blocks
> Weathered wooden boards
> Metal manhole covers
> Tombstones
> Stone, metal, or plastic plaques and reliefs

The two techniques described below, one for younger children, the other for more mature young people, allow them to lift designs off incised, engraved, or embossed, yet reasonably flat surfaces. Curved objects require that the paper be taped all round and the textured surface rubbed off, as detailed in 315.

315. Pencil and Graphite Stick Rubbings

Tools and materials
> No. 6B pencil or graphite stick
> Soft, lightweight paper: tissue paper; rice paper; or thin drawing paper
> Drafting tape

Tape paper on top of the object to be rubbed. Use the flat side of the pencil or graphite stick to rub gently over the paper surface. The raised portions of the design to which the paper is taped will soon emerge. Rub more pencil or graphite over the paper until the rubbing is as dark as desired. Don't press on pencil or graphite stick while rubbing. Pressure will force the paper into the recessed portions of the object that is being rubbed, producing a muddy print that lacks detail.

316. Ink and Brayer Rubbings

Tools and materials
> Same as 294
> Drafting tape

Ink the object to be rubbed with the brayer, gently lay the paper on the inked surface, and tape it. Print with spoon or clean brayer as in 294.

Valuable objects, wood, clay, or stone carvings should never be inked directly since it may not be possible to clean them perfectly. To rub them, use the technique described in 315.

E. STENCIL PRINTING

Don't give a child prepared stencils with which to trace or color. Stencil printing has value only if the child makes his or her own stencils. Coloring or printing through prepared stencils may seem like an amusing pastime but it undermines a child's creative drive (see I.A.a–g and VI.A.a).

317. Scissors-Cut Stencil Printing

Tools and materials
   Brown wrapping paper; waxpaper; frisket paper; or wrapping paper soaked in
      vegetable oil
   Scissors (see 37)
   Masking or drafting tape
   Drawing or construction paper (for printing)
   Poster colors (see 206)
   Large, stiff stipple brush

Paper folding and cutting techniques (see 30–41) can be applied to stencil cutting with scissors. Interior cuts can be made by folding the paper (see 38). Using these techniques, very young children can create interesting and unique stencils that they can print in one or more colors.

After the child has cut the design of the stencil from wrapping paper or the like, tape one edge to the drawing or construction paper on which it is to be printed. Mix the poster colors to a stiff paste. Provide only one color of the child's choice as a start. Others can be added later. Then show him or her how to dip the tip of the stipple brush into the color, deep enough to cover only the end of the bristles. Apply the paint around the edges of the cut-out portions of the stencil with a rapid up and down motion of the brush. The brush will require frequent dipping in the paint. After the edges have been given a coat of color, work the brush toward the center of each opening in the stencil, until all are colored. There is no need to cover the whole paper with a thick layer of paint. A stippled, light coating will give the print texture.

Do not remove the stencil from the paper until the paint has dried com-

pletely. Then unfasten the tape and lift off the stencil, and the design will be revealed underneath. If the paint crawls under the stencil edges it means the paint mixture was too watery. Two (or more) color stencils can be designed in the same way as multicolor linoleum or wood blocks.

Various color effects and designs can be created by printing the same stencil a second time, turned to a different position on the paper after the first printing, and using a different color for a subsequent impression. Different stencils can be printed in sequence, one after the other, each in different colors or tones, but only when the preceding coat of paint has dried. Care must be exercised when stenciling one poster color over another. Do not press hard on the stipple brush or the preceding layer of paint may be moistened and dissolved.

Repeat-patterns on paper and fabric (see 311 and 312) can be printed with stencils. Once each impression has dried, move the stencil to the next position and print.

318. Knife-Cut Stencils

Tools and materials
　　Same as 317
　　Stencil cutting or silk-screen film cutting blades and holders (see 86, 87, and 135)
　　Stencil paper (see 317)

Different stencil papers serve different purposes. Frisket paper and some plastic films have an adhesive backing. Don't peel the protective paper away until the stencil has been cut. The stencil will adhere to whatever surface it is pressed on, preventing crawl of the paint under the edges of the stencil. This is why oiled or wax paper is used for stencils printed with water base paints. The wax or oiled edges resist the paints.

All stencil papers can be cut with a sharp knife blade. A surgeon's scalpel, an X-acto blade, a silk-screen film cutter's knife, or any other sharp, thin, pointed blade in a long holder will do. Swivel holders enable the craftsman to cut intricate shapes and curves. A beam compass and double-bladed knives permit circles, panels, and parallel lines to be cut. These specialized tools are not required by the beginning young craftsman, yet he should know that they exist.

For spontaneous stencil cutting, tape the stencil paper or film to a heavy sheet of cardboard. Or a drawing can be designed and placed under or traced onto the stencil paper. Then, holding the knife blade handle like a pencil, trace the drawing on the stencil paper or film with continuous strokes of the knife, as if drawing. Cut sufficiently deep to penetrate the paper or film surface, but no deeper. Cut straight lines along a T-square, but do not use wooden or plastic rulers or triangles for this purpose. Make sure that fingers holding the material are behind and away from the stroke of the knife.

319. Spatter Printing

Tools and materials
    Same as 317 and 318
    Toothbrush or insect spray gun (see also 100 and 216)

Once the cut stencil is taped to the paper, the print can be made by spattering paint onto it from a toothbrush rather than stippling it (see 100 and 216). Or an insect spray gun can be loaded with paint or ink and

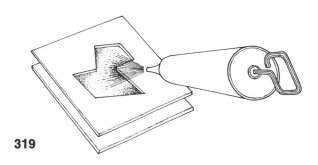

319

sprayed onto the stencil covered paper (see diag. 319). Color and tonal mixtures and gradations will appear where successive stencils overlap in multicolor spatter printing.

320. Silk-Screen Cutting and Printing in One Color

Silk-screen printing, used commercially and for serigraph reproduction, is a highly refined form of stencil printing. It was used in China, Japan, and Egypt centuries ago, albeit in a different form than we know it today. It became practical, with the invention of stencil film in 1929, for display, wallpaper, and fabric printing; printing on glass; and as a fine art medium for original work and for short-run reproductions.

Tools and materials

    Silk-screen frame (see below for construction details)
    Silk
    Staple gun
    Silk-screen stencil paper and film; cutting tools
    Canvas pliers (available at art supply stores)
    Wooden base board for screen
    Two hinges
    Silk-screen printing inks and solvent
    Squeegee (as wide as the silk-screen frame)
    Spatula or palette knife
    Clothesline and clothespins
    Rags

Construct the printing frame out of 1″ × 2″ lumber. A 12″ × 14″ frame is a useful size for a beginner. Joint, glue, and screw corners firmly together (see III). Attach a small length of 1″ × 2″ lumber to one side of the frame so that it can be braced open when required.

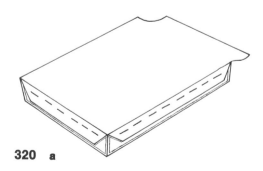

320   a

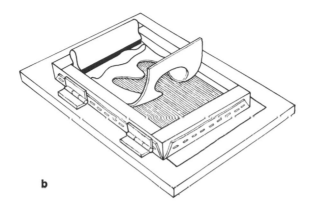

b

Place a sheet of silk, 2″ larger on each side than the frame, directly under it. Use the staple gun to tack one silk edge to one side of the frame as shown (see diag. 320.a), starting with one of the longer sides and making sure that the silk is not wrinkled. Then, using the canvas pliers, stretch and staple the silk on the opposite side of the frame. Keep the silk taut and wrinkle-free. Now stretch and staple the remaining two cdgcs, one at a time, to the short sides of the frame. The silk cover should be drum-tight but not distorted. Attach the two hinges as shown (see diag. 320.b) and screw them to a wooden base board of ¾″ plywood that is 4″ to 6″ larger than the frame on all four sides. The silk side of the frame should be in contact with the top surface of the base board.

The stencil can be cut out of ordinary stencil paper or special stencil film, whichever is available. Cut the sheet a shade smaller than the outside dimensions of the printing frame. Place the whole stencil sheet under the frame to make sure that it fits before cutting it. Cut the stencil with a knife as described in 318. Do not lift the cut portions away from the stencil.

When the screen has been cut, place it under the printing frame. Pour a small amount of the ink to be used into one end of the frame and work it back and forth across the whole screen with the squeegee. The ink will make the stencil adhere to the silk-screen. Open the screen and peel away all cut portions from the stencil. Now the screen is ready to print.

Place a sheet of printing paper between the silk-screen frame and the wooden base board. Close the frame. Pour ink into one end of the frame. Then, using the squeegee, move the ink across the whole screen in one stroke with a good deal of pressure. Make only one pass with the squeegee across the frame for each print. Lift the screen and remove the printed sheet. Hang each print on a clothesline to dry (see 294).

After each color or edition has been printed, wash the screen with ink solvent. The ink adhered stencil will then come off the screen. Clean and store it for future use. Make sure that all ink has been washed out of the silk mesh after every color edition.

As an alternate method for preparing a silk-screen, designs can be painted directly onto the screen with lacquer, shellac, or glue, to mask out those areas that are not to print. Only unpainted portions of the screen will allow the ink to be squeezed through the mesh with the squeegee. The drawback of this method is that the silk can be used for only one color edition, and it must then be cut off the frame and a new silk surface stapled to it for future work.

Small areas, errors, or faults in knife cut-stencils can be painted in and corrected with lacquer, shellac, or glue, which can be dissolved after the stencil is removed.

321. Silk-Screen Printing in More than One Color

Multicolored prints can be made, using the same frame and silk. Cut one stencil for each color (see 317) and adhere and print each in succession as detailed in 307. Accidental and spontaneous as well as planned multicolored prints can be made. The same techniques for separating and registering colors apply to silk-screen as to linoleum and woodcut prints, except that it is easier to get close registration (see 307 and 309). Cut all paper exactly the same size and mark the positions on the base board where paper corners must be placed.

Silk-screen stencils can be made photographically. It is a simple process, but a darkroom, photosensitive film, developer, hypo, trays for each chemical (slightly larger than the stencil size), and a large sink with running water are required. For additional details see bibliography and 336.

IX

Audiovisual Media Craft

Choosing is creating.—*Friedrich Wilhelm Nietzsche*

A. BACKGROUND

TV sets, still and motion picture cameras and projectors, TV and sound tape equipment are now found in nearly every school and in most homes. Yet few young people know how to use any of these media creatively. Nineteenth century craft and activity books for children invariably explained how to make a pinhole camera, blueprints of leaves and flowers, and flip book and zoetrope animations. Recently developed photographic and sound recording processes and techniques offer even more stimulating challenges to young people who know how to use them. Creative work in these media involves inexpensive materials and equipment that is readily available.

". . . Even in the making of the most mechanically contrived image, something more than machines and chemicals are involved. The eye (or ear), which means taste. The interest in the subject and an insight into the moment when it—or it or he or she—is ready. An understanding of just what esthetic values can be further brought in the manipulation of the instrument and the material." [89] Creative work with audiovisual media, instead of their purely passive use, sharpens a child's critical judgment.

One of the by-products of such experiences is that they "provide children with critical skills for becoming active, intelligent, appreciative and selective consumers of the moving image." [90] With the proliferation of audiovisual media beamed at children at home, in the classroom, and in motion picture theaters, and the amount of time today's child spends just watching and listening to them, he or she had best learn to become selective and critical or he or she will be swamped by them. Active involvement in these techniques allows children to become participants where now they are too often spectators.

With few exceptions audiovisual media are used in schools for, rather than by children. Few adults seem to know that this equipment and these experiences can be turned to creative use by children. This chapter details how media can be used in a variety of ways and on many levels as means of expression. Children need little equipment and much stimulation if they are to use them inventively. They need guided experiences that allow them to acquire background and skills; that lead them toward a craft approach in using the materials and making discriminating choices of what they wish to state and how to state it. Used for these purposes rather than as instant magic, the media can be excellent learning tools. The child, who is impatient by nature, receives the rewarding results of his or her creations almost at once. But do not allow this instant quality of the materials to be the sole source of satisfaction. Let young people stretch their attention span by becoming progressively more deeply involved in the creative aspects of the craft. They'll then be able to devote increasingly longer periods, exploring the audiovisual media as a means for realizing self-generated goals. The rewards, as in all learning, become greater the longer they are delayed in time and as more time and effort are expended.

Few of today's children realize that most of these processes are of recent vintage. It is virtually impossible for a modern child to comprehend that his parents or grandparents knew a time without TV, for example. And with rapid technological change, new processes descend on us before we have explored, used, understood, or formed any opinion about the potential of those we already possess. For example holography—three-dimensional laser photography—is already a practical reality, within reach of anyone. [84] It is therefore important for today's children and

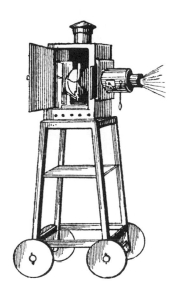

young people to have some idea of the history of audiovisual media and to be in practical, active touch with them, rather than on a ''believe-it-or-not'' basis.

A related series of inventions made still and motion pictures, black and white and color photography, sound recording, and TV possible. During the last century most of these processes were unknown. Yet photography is based on principles well-known in previous centuries, involving optics, perspective, and portrait projection machines invented by and for artists. The principle of the camera's diaphragm shutter was discovered by Daniello Barbara in 1558, who intended to aid painters in achieving greater realism. The camera obscura and camera lucida, widely used for projecting, enlarging, and reducing figures and scenes optically, furthered the art that eventually led to photography. On the purely entertainment side, dimensional peepshows, perspective and shadow theaters, and later slide projection machines, some of which incorporated movement, led eighteenth and early-nineteenth century inventors closer to realizing the possibility of recording, printing, and projecting still and motion pictures.

The first ''fixed'' photograph was produced by Nicephone Niepce in France in 1825. By 1839 William Henry Fox Talbot in England and

Louis Daguerre in France were granted patents for photographic processes. Talbot's invention involved a negative from which any number of positives could be printed. Daguerre's wet-plate process produced a single positive from which no further copies could be made. Shortly after, Sir William Herschel, a famous British scientist with a keen interest in photography, suggested that "hypo" would fix a photographic image printed on sensitized material so that it would not fade in a short time.

By 1851 Frederick Scott Archer had introduced his wet-collodion process, by which he created fine grain glass negatives. This method was used by Fenton to photograph the Crimean war of 1854–5 and Mathew Brady to record the American civil war during the years 1861–5. By 1869 two experimenters, Charles Coos and Ducos du Hauron, produced the first color photograph taken by artificial light, and in 1891 Gabriel Lipman managed this feat by sunlight. In 1871 an amateur photographer, Dr. Richard L. Maddox, invented the dry-gelatin film emulsion that made George Eastman's celluloid roll film and the soon popular, mass-produced Kodak camera possible.

The idea of motion picture film was based on experiments like Faraday's wheel that turned into popular nineteenth century toys—the thaumatrope, phenakistoscope, zoetrope, flicker books, and others, many of which are described and can be made according to instructions furnished in this chapter. These and concurrent advances in still photography inspired Muybridge to experiment with "chronophotography"—the study of human and animal movement recorded on a series of cameras set up and triggered in sequence. Thomas Edison contributed his Kinetoscope in 1893, which made possible the first live motion picture film produced by the Lumière brothers in Paris in 1895.

The first fully animated cartoon was created by James Stewart Blackton, a New York newspaper cartoonist. He had been sent to interview Thomas Edison and this led to their joint production of "Humorous Phases of Funny Faces" in 1906. The animation required 3,000 separate drawings, a number dwarfed since by the feature length cartoons of Walt Disney. By 1907 Emil Cohl produced a series of animated cartoons in Paris, shown at the Folies-Bergère to great acclaim. Winsor McCay's animations in the U.S. in 1909 inspired and led to Fleischer's Popeye, Paul Terry's Terry Toons, and Disney's Mickey Mouse.

TV transmission, developed in the 1920s, did not become a practical reality until shortly before World War II. A multitude of earlier inventions, Thomas Edison's telegraph and phonograph, Alexander Graham Bell's telephone, and more recent ones including the coaxial cable, radar, sonar, magnetic wire recording, and the transistor, provided the technology that has made mass-produced TV sets, videotape, and sound tape recorders possible.

Photography, still in its infancy during the latter half of the nineteenth century and the beginning of this one, was used primarily to portray people and places, and to imitate painting. The unique, creative properties of film were not realized until the 1920s, when the possibilities of still and motion picture film were explored by artists like Man Ray, Moholy-Nagy, the Bauhaus group, and the early Russian filmmakers. The propaganda demands of World War II and the popularity of picture magazines before the advent of TV caused the flourishing of documentary still photography and the picture story, now largely a thing of the past. The Polaroid camera and Land's new color process, among other instant picture taking features of today's still and motion picture equipment, enable anyone to snap a picture or to immortalize baby's first steps.

The instant quality of many of these processes and of much of the most recent equipment can be misleading. "Click" goes the shutter, "whirr" goes the movie camera or tape recorder, and images and sounds are recorded without effort or thought. Ease of operation tends to foster the delusion that the mere possession of the equipment and its casual use enable anyone to be creative. It's not so. According to records kept by processors of amateur film, the repertoire of what is photographed is extremely limited and deadly dull. And most tape recorders are used primarily for business, professional, and surveillance purposes and to lift radio and TV shows or records. This chapter is intended to help young people make better use of the technologies, to be creative producers rather than passive consumers.

B. PHOTOGRAPHY WITHOUT A CAMERA

A camera is not needed to take pictures. A variety of photographic papers and easily available and quite harmless chemicals exist that make many photographic experiences possible in early years at little expense. The processes are simple; the greatest emphasis can be placed on originality and invention, looking for and discovering materials and subjects for image making, and arranging them in new and surprising ways. Once the initial technique of picture taking and print making are mastered, suggest to the child that he or she experiment with exposures of negatives and prints and discover variations on conventional techniques.

Double, triple, over- and underexposures, variations in the relationship between time of exposure and depth of field or focus, and light and shade are controllable factors that provide latitude in expression. Not all attempts will be successful. But there's a benefit to a child's learning to cope with failure and improving with the next trial. Photographic materials are especially useful in this respect. The time between repeated trials is short and failure soon turns to success if the child perseveres.

322. Lenses, Prisms, and Kaleidoscopes

Plastic and glass lenses and mirrors that enlarge, reduce, and invert images; prisms that break up light; and a kaleidoscope that creates optical repeat pattern illusions in motion can be stimulating and diverting toys for children. They also teach. A hair or a leaf seen through a magnifying lens opens up a new world to which the child might otherwise remain blind. The changing patterns of form, color, texture, and light, created by paper clips, glass fragments, snippets of paper, or grains of sand seen through a kaleidoscope, awaken the child to patterns, motion, and visual surprise. It's no coincidence that David Brewster, the inventor of the kaleidoscope, should also have given birth to the stereoscope in 1844, by which two pictures of the same scene, each viewed from a slightly different angle through a stereopticon, create a three-dimensional illusion. The stereoscope became a favorite Victorian amusement for children and adults. And it is still a useful device to help children discover the startling world of optics. All these are essential preparations for an interest in and an understanding of what we know today as "the media"—photography, film, animation, sound and videotape, and holography.

323. Shadow Pictures

Tools and materials
> Cut paper shapes
> Darkened room and a single, strong light source: lamp, candle, or flashlight

Shadows thrown on the wall in the shape of faces, animals, and other figures made entirely with the fingers of two hands have long amused small children. The wiggling ears of the shadow rabbit were children's movies and TV, long before the invention of the latter. Shapes cut from black paper can add to the illusion of moving shadow pictures (see diag. 323). Appreciating and eventually imitating the creation of shadow and

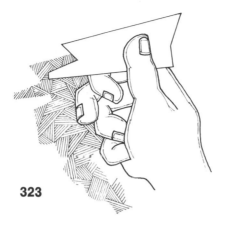

323

silhouette shapes and how they can be combined and projected helps children learn to see and compose images. These are essential disciplines in photography and especially in making photograms (see 327 and 328).

324. Photocollage

Tools and materials
> Black and white and color photographs cut from magazines and travel folders
> Construction paper
> Scissors (see 37)
> Paste (see 9–26)

Encourage the child to cut out photographs and parts of photographs and paste them next to, over, and partially under each other on construction paper to make decorative pictures or to tell a story. A photograph of a standing man can be pasted upside down so that he stands on his head. Funny, expressive, and dramatic combinations of existing photographs are possible, limited only by the available material, the child's insight, and his or her ability to pretend and imagine.

325. Dyeline Prints

Tools and materials
> Package of Dyeline paper and solution (available in photographic supply shops)
> Soft ¾″ to 1″ brush
> Newspaper or large sheet of cardboard
> Sheet of Plexiglas or plate glass
> Found materials (see XIV) that have well-defined silhouettes; leaves, ferns, pebbles, tools, paper clips, cut paper shapes, etc.

Demonstrate how to take one sheet of Dyeline paper at a time out of the package, place it, yellow side up, on the newspaper or cardboard, arrange the chosen silhouette material on the paper, and cover it with glass or Plexiglas. Expose the paper under strong artificial light or sunlight. Read the directions on the package relating exposure time to strength of light source. After exposure, remove the Plexiglas and the objects placed on the paper and brush Dyeline solution evenly over the paper until the exposed portions turn white and the silhouettes of the objects placed on the paper turn black. Double- and triple-exposures are possible with practice.

326. Blueprints

Tools and materials
> Blueprint paper
> Dilute peroxide
> Sheet of plate glass or Plexiglas
> Large sheet of heavy cardboard
> Two enamel, rubber, or plastic trays, larger than the cut sheets of blueprint paper to be used
> Two sheets of heavy blotting paper; or clothesline and clothespins (to dry prints)
> Pitcher of clear, cold water
> Found materials (see XIV); choose those that have well-defined silhouettes, as in 325

Design and arrange the found materials on the blueprint paper sandwiched between cardboard and glass plate as in 325. Follow directions on the paper package label for light source and exposure time. Wait until the exposed paper turns light blue. Then remove objects and glass plate and soak the paper in the tray filled with dilute peroxide solution until the unexposed portions turn brilliant white and the exposed portions of the paper turn dark blue. Wash in the second tray filled with clear water and hang the print on the clothesline or place it between two sheets of blotting paper to dry. Double-exposures are not possible.

327. Direct Photograms

Tools and materials
> Package of No. 2 photographic contact paper
> Paper developer (either powder or in solution)
> Hypo
> Fresh water
> Three enamel, rubber, or plastic trays, each larger than the photographic paper size
> Red darkroom safety light
> 100-watt Light bulb and shade

Two-socket overhead light fixture with separate switch for each socket
Large sheet of heavy cardboard
Sheet of plate glass or Plexiglas
Rubber or plastic apron (to protect against chemicals)
Rags
Found materials (see XIV); choose those that have well-defined silhouettes, as in 325

The technique is the same as in 325; here, however, a wide range of gray tones, as well as sharp black and whites, and multiple-exposures are possible. Start by letting the child print silhouettes of his or her own hands.

It is important that the child learn to remove the photographic paper from the package one sheet at a time only, when the red safety light is switched on and the 100-watt bulb is switched off, using the two-socket fixture. Make sure he closes the paper package carefully so that the paper is not light struck later. Place the paper, emulsion (shiny) side up, on the cardboard and arrange found materials on it. Cover both with plexiglas. Mix all chemicals in advance, each in its own tray, according to the instructions given on the package labels.

Arrange the package of photographic paper to the right of the actual exposure surface and the three trays to the left—developer tray first, hypo tray next, and clear water tray last, in that order. The cardboard and glass exposure surface should be directly under the light source. Switch on the 100-watt light bulb only during the exposure period. Keep the red safety light switched on during development and fixing of the print.

Teach the child to count: "One thousand and one, one thousand and two . . ." for controlled timing of each exposure. On completion of the exposure time, switch off the white light and switch on the red safety light. Remove the glass covering and objects from the paper and dip the paper face down in the developer. Agitate the print, grasping it by one corner and moving it rapidly back and forth. Keep the paper fully immersed in developer. Turn it over for inspection once in a while. When the image comes up, leave the paper face side up in the developer until it reaches the desired intensity of tone. Then let developer run off the paper as it is lifted out of the tray and immerse the print in the hypo tray to fix the image. Follow the timing directions on the paper and hypo package labels. Agitate as before. On completion of the fixative bath, let the hypo run off the paper and immerse the print in clear water. The longer the print washes in clear water the less it is likely to stain in time.

Dry the print between sheets of blotting paper. Weight the blotting paper to keep the print from curling.

The developer is good for many prints as long as the image comes up on the exposed paper with sufficient intensity of tone. However, each print will need longer time in the developer, which weakens with use. Change the hypo after each dozen or so prints and the water after each three or four.

After several prints have been made, suggest that the child try to make a double exposure. Arrange the objects on the paper as before, but expose them for only half the previous exposure time. Then rearrange the objects on the paper for a second exposure a little shorter than the first. When developed, fixed, and washed, the print, if properly exposed, will contain overlapping images in tones of gray as well as in black and white. Encourage the child to play with double-, triple-, and multi-exposures of silhouettes for different designs, effects, and gradations of tones.

328. Scratched Acetate Photograms

Tools and materials
    Acetate or plastic sheets of film
    Black acetate ink and solvent
    Inexpensive No. 4 or No. 5 sable brush
    Drawing pen and holder
    Etching point
    Same as 327

Suggest that the child scratch designs and textures on the acetate sheets with the etching point. He can also draw and paint on the film with ink, pen, and brush. Remind him that only those areas will print that are left more or less transparent and not covered with ink. Let the child print the acetate sheet under Plexiglas in direct contact with the photographic paper, develop and fix the image, wash the print, and dry it as in 327.

One acetate design can be rotated for double- and triple-exposures, provided the time is reduced proportionately for each exposure on the same sheet of paper.

Note: Be sure to wash the brush used for drawing and painting on the film in solvent immediately after use, since the ink is corrosive.

329. Slide Making

Tools and materials
2¼" × 2¼" slide projector
2¼" × 2¼" slide binders (available in photographic supply shops)
Clear acetate or plastic film cut to 2¼" × 2¼" size
Black and white (and colored) acetate inks and solvent
Inexpensive No. 4 or No. 5 brush
Drawing pens and holder
Transparent, colored, pressure adhesive acetate

Let the child draw and paint on the clear acetate or design with snippets of pressure adhesive, transparent colored acetate, or a combination of both. Each completed 2¼" × 2¼" slide can be inserted in a slide binder and projected. A light show can be given with a series of these prepared slides.

330. Photograms Projected from an Enlarger

Tools and materials
Same as 327 and 329
Photographic enlarger with 2¼" × 2¼" film carrier

Suggest that the child make black and white slides on acetate, combining the techniques described in 328 and 329. The scratched and painted 2¼" × 2¼" transparencies can be placed into the film holder of the enlarger and projected onto photographic paper placed on an easel or under a cardboard mat to hold it down. Printing and development remain the same as in 327.

The photographic enlarger head can be moved closer to and farther away from the paper and then focused so that different portions of the acetate design are magnified or reduced when printed. Double-, triple-, and multi-exposures are possible with the same or a succession of different transparencies, if the exposure time is adjusted. As with any photographic printing on the enlarger, exposure times may require experimentation and several trial prints before the right exposure for a particular transparency or negative is discovered.

C. CAMERA CRAFT

In the previous section the child was given exposure to basic photographic processes. In making photograms he or she learns the relationship between negative and positive image making. The child becomes involved in printing and development, in preparing handmade negatives and processing them. All that remains to be learned is the optical photo-negative making and developing process, for which a camera is essential. It is important that the child play with these materials as much as with his perceptions. This is why a pinhole camera is a useful first camera.

331. The Pinhole Camera

The first camera—before the invention of photosensitive materials—the camera obscura, was used by artists to project and reduce real-life scenes on a screen for copying. The pinhole camera is its direct discendant. As shown, it projects the image onto photosensitive film or paper to produce a negative which, after it has been developed, can be printed like the photograms in 327–330.

How to build a pinhole camera:

Tools and materials
    Same as 327
    Mat black railroad board; or shirt board 2½" square
    Aluminum foil, sheet of
    No. 10 sewing needle
    Black construction paper
    Sharp knife blade
    Triangle and T-square
    Black poster paint, or blackboard paint and solvent (to paint cardboard if no
        black railroad board is available)
    Small, inexpensive paint brush
    4" × 5" film or photographic paper (see below for details)

Read 63, 64, 70, 72, and 75 for details on how to design, cut, score, and build the 4½" × 5½" × 5" box shown in diag. 331.a. Cut out the square in the front of the box for the "lens." Cut out two pieces of railroad board or shirt board and a piece of foil, 2½" × 2½" square. Sandwich the foil between the boards and tape the edges, after marking diagonals on one of the boards to find the center (see diag. 331.b). Push the needle through the center point, but no deeper than about halfway from the point to the shank (see diag. 331.c). Center the foil on the inside of the lens opening and tape it down firmly. Now fold the box along the scored lines and lock or paste all tabs except those on the back of the box. Tape all exterior edges, except those on the back of the box, with black tape. Paint the inside and outside of the box black (unless black railroad board was used). Finally, tape a sheet of black construction paper over the lens, as shown (see diag. 331.d), so that it can be lifted up for exposure, but stays folded down between exposures.

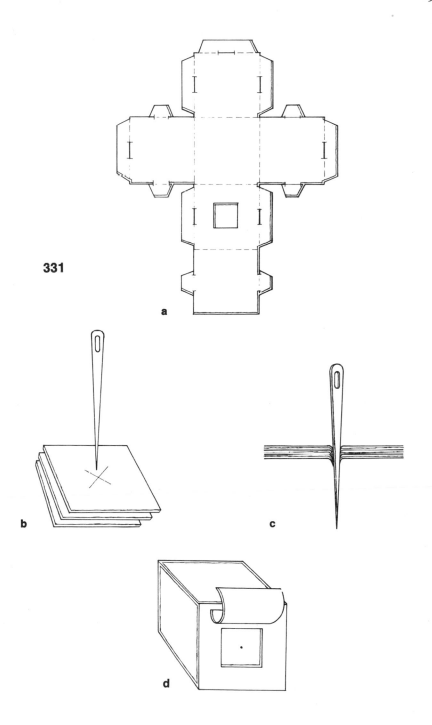

331

a

b

c

d

For paper negatives: Use Kodabromide paper F, No. 1 or No. 2, or a similar substitute available in 4" × 5" size. Tape the paper, emulsion (shiny) side facing the lens opening to the inside back flap of the camera in a dark room, using only the red safety light as illumination. Close the back flap and, if necessary, tape the edges. Make sure that the camera lens flap is tightly closed and take the camera into sunlight for exposure.

For film negatives: Use Kodak Royal Pan Film 4141, extra thick base, or its equivalent in 4" × 5" sheet size. Or a roll of 120 or 620 Kodak Tri-X Pan Film or its equivalent can be cut, in a dark room, into 3"-long strips and taped on the back flap of the camera—one at a time, as above.

To expose the film: Place the camera on a firm base with the sunlight behind it. The required exposure is too long for hand holding. It's a good idea to tape the camera to the surface on which it rests. To expose the film, raise the lens cover for the following exposure times:

Kodabromide Paper F.1 or F.2	bright sun: 2 mins.;	cloudy bright: 8 mins.
Tri-X or Royal Pan Film	bright sun: 1–2 secs.;	cloudy bright: 4–8 secs.

Film processing: Use Kodak Tri-chem pack and follow the instructions on the package, or whichever chemicals are recommended for any other film that is used.

Printing the negative: Follow the directions given in 327, except that the paper negative is placed emulsion (shiny) side up on the bottom and the photographic paper on which it is to be printed, emulsion side down on top of it. Hold the sheets together in close contact with the Plexiglas plate. Experiment with exposures, starting with fifteen seconds. For film negatives, place the photographic paper on the bottom, emulsion side up and the film negative directly on top of it. Start with a ten-second exposure. Develop the print as directed in 327.

Obviously a pinhole camera is a crude instrument; yet remarkably good photographs can be taken with it. Double-exposures can be made, although this requires a good deal of experimentation with exposure times, negative development, and printing. The benefit of the camera lies precisely in that. The young photographer learns by trial and error and gets the feel of the material far better than with an instant camera.

332. The Polaroid Camera

A child should not be given a Polaroid camera until he understands some of the principles of picture taking, negative development, and printing described earlier in the chapter. These are not only essential disciplines, but creative prerequisites. The controls that the photographer can exercise over what he shoots are largely eliminated by instant picture taking. The Polaroid camera, while a useful instrument, does away with many of these controls.

Because of this, it is especially important that the child select his image with great care. Then the advantage of the Polaroid camera in providing an immediate result can be useful, especially for children and young people for whom it is impossible to provide a properly darkened room and the equipment necessary for elementary film processing and printing.

333. The Low-Cost Camera

Any number of very low-cost cameras are available, which are excellent for children and young people. It is much wiser to economize on equipment and be lavish with film than vice versa. Tripods, exposure meters, flash and strobe units, fancy camera bags, and the host of gadgets that are the supposed essentials of photography just get in the way of learning how to use camera and film. Today's high-speed films make flash equipment virtually unnecessary, and the rest is useful only to the most advanced amateur or professional and for special purposes.

334. Hints on Picture Taking

Photography is a creative medium only if the child is highly selective about what he or she shoots, chooses the portion of subject or scene that is most significant, and the precise moment of the peak of the action. If the young photographer fails in these respects, he or she is simply performing a mechanical act at random.

Every camera provides controls on how the picture is to be recorded. Not all offer the same number of controls: the most inexpensive models exclude some. But all incorporate a mechanism for viewing a selected image. So get the child used to looking through the viewfinder, scanning the scene, object, or person, and deciding which segment is most significant and representative of the whole. Suggest that he move closer or farther away, to shoot from a selected angle at eye level, from above or below, and at different exposures. Suggest to the child that he photograph the puddle instead of the whole street, the leaf instead of the forest.

Most cameras include two lens controls: the "f" stop and the shutter speed control. The "f" stop determines how large a shutter opening is to be used; and the shutter speed control determines how long the shutter remains open when the picture is taken. Before placing film in the camera, open the back of the camera and let the child look through the lens at all the "f" stops. He'll be able to see how the shutter opening is enlarged or reduced with each change of "f" stop.

Explain that as the shutter opening is reduced, the overall sharpness of the picture, from background to foreground, increases. When the shutter opening is enlarged the foreground remains sharp, but the background becomes increasingly fuzzy. The photographer can control emphasis by using the different "f" stops. For example, by stopping down the shutter opening as far as it will go, given the proper lighting conditions, the overall effect will be that of a picture postcard in which everything is sharp and there is little distinction between foreground and background. But this is not how the human eye sees; it focuses on what is most important at the moment and blurs the rest. To photograph a closeup, the shutter should be open as wide as possible. The foreground should be in sharp focus if the camera is properly focused. The background will be blurred, as it is in real life when you look close at something.

The "f" stops must also be related to shutter speed. The speed with which the shutter opens and closes determines how much light strikes the film. This is why fast shutter speed settings are used on sunny days, but slower speeds are required on cloudy days or indoors. The illumination determines which "f" stop can be used, since it increases or reduces the amount of light that enters the camera.

Suggest to the child that he follow the "f" stop and shutter speed directions printed on the instruction sheet inside each film package for different lighting conditions, for his or her first exposures of the film. Then, for the next shot, reduce the shutter speed by one setting and increase the "f" stop by one setting. Keep changing the exposures for the same photograph for several successive shots, take notes, and compare the results when the roll of film has been developed and printed. This is how a young photographer learns to control his medium.

Film speed (the light sensitivity of the emulsion on the film) is another control factor. Today's fast films make flash and strobe units unnecessary for all except extremely bad lighting conditions and special or professional camera work. Also, by mixing controlled amounts of borax with developer, fast film speeds can be increased even more and film exposed under extremely poor lighting conditions can produce interesting, readable pictures. Finally, by careful printing and paper development, portions of a negative can be "held back" and others emphasized.

The beginning photographer must learn how to hold a camera. If he wiggles even slightly at the moment of exposure, the picture will be blurred. A tripod is unnecessary for all exposures of a half second or less. Let the child press the camera against his chest while his finger is on the trigger. Then, just before he presses the trigger, let him hold his breath until the picture is taken. This assures relative immobility.

Professional photographers usually pride themselves on being able to compose a picture in the camera so that it can be printed as taken. But a negative can be cropped (only a portion selected) for printing. The ability to select, compose, and photograph exactly what is wanted with the camera, rather than in the enlarger, is the essence of the photographer's art.

335. Film Development

Tools and materials
    Development tank for the film size used
    Film developer and hypo
    Shortstop
    Red safety light
    Sink and running water
    Sponge tipped squeegee tweezers
    Thermometer
    Funnel
    Clothesline and clothespins
    Weighted clips

Follow the directions in the film package about which developer to use. Follow the directions provided with developer and hypo for mixing the chemicals, and for the temperatures at which they should be used. Unroll the film in total darkness or by red safety light and strip away the paper backing. Thread the film on the wire holder of the development tank, then replace and close it again. If the development tank includes a light trap, the rest of the work can be done in daylight.

Pour the developer into the tank through the funnel. Cover the tank opening and let the film develop for the time stated on the chemical package. Shake the tank periodically during the development time. At its end, pour the developer into a brown bottle and store it in the dark for future use. Keep in mind that film developer, like paper developer (see 327), weakens with use and that future development with the same batch of chemicals will require more time. Pour shortstop and hypo into the tank for the required amounts of time. Shortstop halts development; hypo fixes the image on the film. These chemicals can also be re-used two or three times if they are stored where it is cool and dark. After the hypo has been emptied from the tank, let clear water run into it and, after an initial rinse, open the tank and stand it under a running tap for twenty minutes.

When the film is thoroughly rinsed, remove the wire holder from the tank and, grasping the clear leader of the film, unwind it. Run the sponge tipped squeegee the length of the film from top to bottom to remove excess moisture. Do not repeat this operation or it may streak the film. Hang the film by its clear leader from two clothespins attached to the line. Attach a weighted clip to the bottom edge of the film and make sure that it does not touch any surface or object while drying. Leave it hanging undisturbed until completely dry. While removing weighted clip and clothespins, and whenever inspecting film, hold the negative by the edges and never touch the surfaces of the negatives. Fingerprints tend to become embedded in the emulsion and they show up in the finished prints.

Drying time can be speeded by hanging the film over a fan-driven electric heater. If the heat is too great or the heater too close to the film the emulsion may run and ruin the whole stip of negatives.

336. Contact Printing

Tools and materials
Same as 327

8″ × 10″ Photographic contact printing paper
Loupe or magnifying glass
Scaleograph
Red grease pencil

Professional photographers always contact-print all negatives before deciding which deserve enlargement. Whether you send exposed film to a commercial processor to be developed, or whether you develop it yourself, it pays to contact-print film before ordering or making enlargements.

Never cut the roll of film into individual negatives. Cut it into strips of a length that enables them to fit, lengthwise, on a sheet of 8″ × 10″ paper.

Contact-print the negative strips as in 328. After the contact sheet is dry, examine each print with a magnifying glass or loupe and check off the ones that are worth enlarging. Each picture can be cropped (a selected portion marked) with a scaleograph (see diag. 336), available from photographic supply shops. Mark the cropped area with a red grease pencil. This will help decide which portion of each negative should be enlarged.

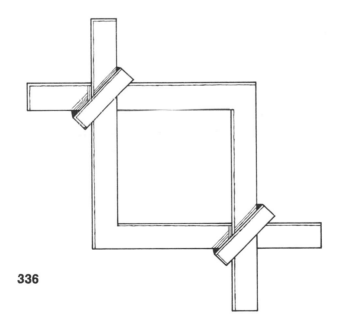

336

337. Enlarging

Tools and materials
Same as 327
Photographic enlarger with interchangeable film carriage for different film sizes

Photographic enlargers are expensive. Unless one is owned or a dark room equipped with an enlarger is available, the chosen negatives must be sent to a processing laboratory for enlargement. One can be found through the yellow pages of the telephone directory. Provide the processor with a marked and cropped contact sheet (see 336) and the desired enlargement size.

If an enlarger is available, place the selected negative in the carrier, leaving the rest of the filmstrip protruding on either side. Switch off the regular white light and switch on the red safety light. Place an ordinary piece of paper, the same size as the photographic paper to be used for the print, on the easel under the enlarger. Move the enlarger head up or down and focus until the portion or the whole of the negative that is to be enlarged is in sharp focus and fills the paper area. Then place one sheet of photographic paper (see 327) on the easel, emulsion (shiny) side up, and print as in 327. Different print densities, gradations of tone, and other effects can be created when printing with an enlarger. Several prints may be required before the best combination of exposure and development time is discovered for a given negative.

338. Color Photography

Tools and materials
Any camera
Color film (check size, number of exposures, film speed; whether indoor or outdoor film; and whether color prints or transparencies are furnished on development)

Color film cannot be developed in a makeshift or home dark room. Virtually all color film needs to be sent to commercial processors for development. When buying color film ascertain whether the processed film is returned as transparencies (slides) or as color negatives and prints. The color fidelity of transparencies is always better than that of negatives and prints, if the exposure was correct, but they require a projector for viewing. Color prints can be made from transparencies, but good type C or dye transfer prints are prohibitively expensive. They are used only for commercial reproductions.

Any camera can accommodate color film, but note that the exposure times required for color film are very different than those for black and white. Be guided by the exposure directions provided for different lighting conditions in the directions packaged with the film. For best results bracket the exposures by shooting at one more "f" stop and one shorter exposure, and then at one less "f" stop and one longer exposure, for each scene, in addition to the combination suggested in the instructions.

The best outdoor results in color photography are obtained in the early morning or late afternoon, or at any time on slightly overcast, dull, or foggy days: in other words, not in brilliant sunshine. Photographs taken under bright, ideal black and white conditions tend to be too highly colored and to look artificial even when exposures are perfect. For good indoor color, strobe or flash bulbs "bounced" off the ceiling or wall are required, unless high-speed film and very long exposures with a camera set on a tripod are used. Once the basic techniques are mastered, suggest to the young photographer that he try unorthodox effects— shooting into the sun at very fast exposures, or extremely long exposures at night.

D. ANIMATION AND MOVIE MAKING

In a parallel to still photography, a child doesn't need a movie camera to make movies. It is much more interesting for him if he starts making movies without a camera and without film, using only materials at hand. The object should not be to urge young people to become "filmmakers" or to lay the foundation for a career in TV. The recommended experiences will give young people keener insights into media that affect their daily lives and outlook. In the following movie making projects and animations, the use of tape recorders (see IX.E) is implicit to add dimension to the art, wherever possible.

339. Thaumatrope

Tools and materials
> 4″ to 6″ white construction paper discs
> Large sewing needle or hole punch (see 5)
> Thread or twine
> Wax crayons (see 194); or cut-out photographs, colored paper (see 347), and
>   paste (see 12–26)

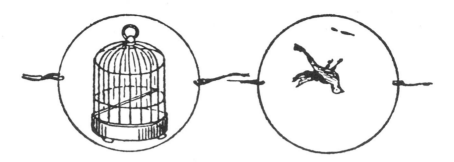

The thaumatrope was probably the first movie invention. Punch two holes on opposite sides of each disc and thread a loop of thread or twine through each set of holes. Draw or paste two related but different pictures, or paste two such photographs, on each side of the disc. For example, place a bird on one side and a bird cage on the other. Now wind up the string by holding each loop in two fingers of each hand and swing the disc in an arc in one direction until it is thoroughly twisted. Then pull at each end in an opposite direction, relaxing the pull as the string unwinds and the disc begins to twirl. The bird will appear to be inside the cage. If the string is pulled and relaxed alternately, the illusion will continue indefinitely. Primitive as this toy may be, it illustrates the stroboscopic effect on which all motion picture production is based.

340. Phenakistoscope

Tools and materials

    Sheets of 8″ × 10″ or larger white construction paper
    One or more sheets of shirt board
    Black poster paint and brush (see 206); or 8″ × 10″ or larger black construction
       paper and paste (see 12–26)
    Scissors and sharp knife blades and holder (see 86 and 87)
    Coat hanger and pliers (see 149–152)
    Crayons; or poster colors; or colored paper and paste
    Burnisher
    Paper clips
    Large mirror
    Heavy cardboard work surface

This is how individual pictures, drawn in sequence, were first animated. Invented in 1832 by J. A. F. Plateau, a Belgian, the phenakistoscope was a popular toy that can be made by anyone. It was also the forerunner of the zoetrope (see 341) and of flip book animations (see 342).

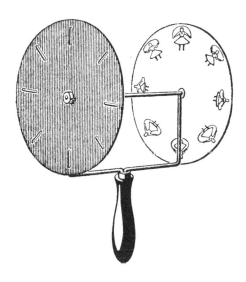

Draw the largest circle possible on one of the sheets of white construction paper, checking that another circle of the same diameter can be drawn onto the shirt board. Cut out the paper circle and fold it in half; quarter it; then fold in half again. Make sharp creases at all the folds with a burnisher. Now make the scissors cuts as shown (see diag. 340.a), and unfold the circle (see diag. 340.b). Use the circle as a template to trace and cut other identical, slotted paper discs of the same size, without folding them first. Use the template also to trace and cut a cardboard disc and slots out of shirt board. Punch a hole in the center of the cardboard and paper discs, large enough so that coat hanger wire will fit through it. Paint one side of the shirt board disc black.

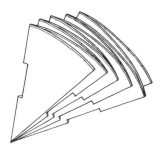

340 a   b

c

Cut off about 8″ of doubled wire at one bent side of the coat hanger and twist one end as shown. Bend and insert the other end of the wire in the center hole of the cardboard disc (see diag. 340.c).

To make the animation, draw a simple sequence of pictures on each of the eight spaces between the slots cut into one of the paper discs. For example, a two-color cross, turned clockwise one-eighth in each space, will seem to be turning when viewed in the phenakistoscope. The same principle can be applied to a clown turning a somersault and to more complex animations (see XIII). Clip the paper disc on which the pictures are drawn to the unpainted side of the slotted cardboard disc so that the slots in the paper line up with those cut into the disc (see diag. 340.c). Hold the assembled phenakistoscope to a mirror, the black side of the disc facing the eye of the viewer. Look in the mirror through one of the slots and spin the disc on its wire holder. The crossed animation, described above, will appear to be spinning around and around.

Any succession of movements drawn or pasted onto the disc, and momentarily blanked out by the black paper between the slots, creates the illusion of motion. The human brain imagines the intervening movements that aren't there.

The child can draw animations or design them with colored paper on both sides of each white construction paper disc. His movies, real or abstract, will be limited only by his imagination. The illustrations are examples of some of the early animations made for the phenakistoscope.

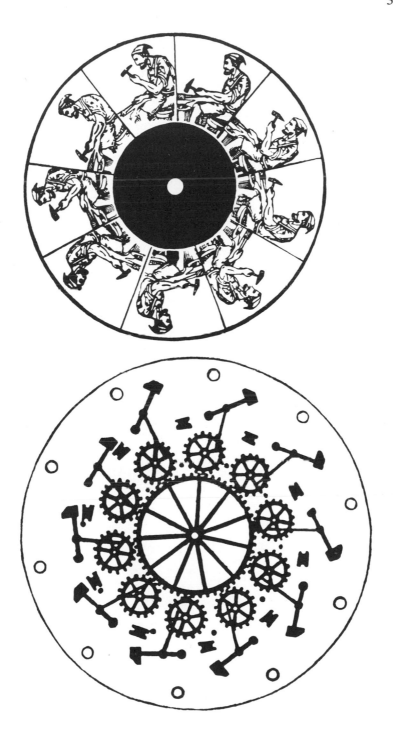

341. Zoetrope

Tools and materials

> 10″-diameter × 2″-high round cheese box or cookie tin; or cardboard constructed turntable (see diag. 341.c)
>
> Four or more 14″ × 5¼″ strips of white construction paper; or paper pasted together to this length and width
>
> One 14″ × 5¼″ strip of black construction paper; or black paper pasted to this length and width
>
> Burnisher
>
> Compass; ruler; right-angle triangle; HB pencil
>
> Scissors; sharp knife blades and holder (see 86 and 87)
>
> Masking tape; paper clips
>
> Crayons; poster paint and brush (see 206); colored paper and paste (see 12–26)
>
> ½″ Dowel (6″ long); roofing nail, or large thumb tack
>
> Hammer
>
> Two 1″-diameter washers with a ⅛″ hole in each
>
> Blackboard paint and brush; paint solvent
>
> Heavy cardboard work surface

The nineteenth century's zoetrope came complete with printed animations. In the nineteen-fifties I designed a similar toy that enabled children to make their own animations—the Movie Maker. The following are plans for a movie maker that enables children to create drawn, painted, and pasted animations.

If no cookie tin or cheese box of the right diamter is available, construct the zoetrope turntable as shown in the exploded view and diagrams (see diag. 341.c; and 85–87 and 74 for construction suggestions). Punch a hole in the center of the cheese box, cookie tin, or constructed turntable with the hammer and nail. Add the handle as shown and brush two coats of blackboard paint on the outside of the turntable.

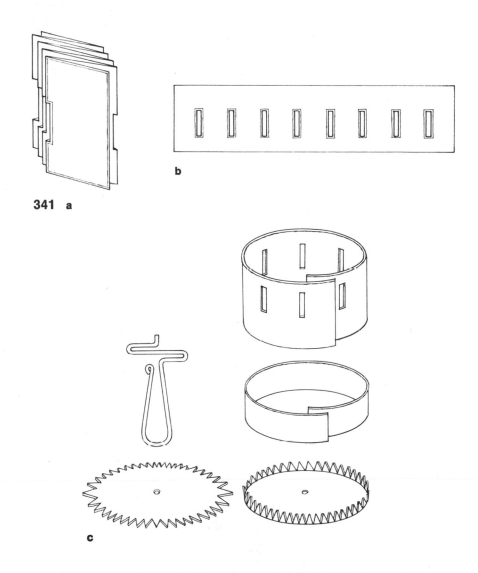

341 a

b

c

Fold one of the 14″ × 5¼″ white paper strips in half; halve twice more. Crease the folds sharply with the burnisher and cut slots on both sides of the folded sheet as shown (see diag. 341a). When unfolded, use this sheet as the template (see diag. 341.d; and 68, 340) for the other black and white paper strips. Mark the slots on them and cut them out with a sharp knife blade. Place the paper on a thick sheet of cardboard for cutting so that the table top is not damaged. Paste the black slotted paper strip to the inside rim of the turntable (see diag. 341.c).

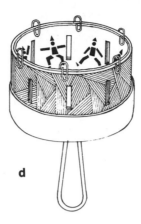

d

After the slots have been cut, draw animations between the slots of the white construction paper strips (see 340 and animation illustrations). On completion of each sequence, insert the white strip in the turntable, lining up slots cut into the black and white papers. Attach the white paper strip to the black with paper clips all round (see diag. 341.d). Spin the turntable while looking through one of the slots. The pictures will appear to move.

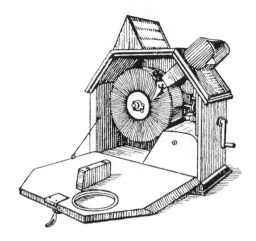

342. Flip Book Animation

Tools and materials

Several paper signatures, 8–16 pages each, folded and gathered as in 103. Use bond or lightweight drawing paper. Each page need be no larger than 2″ × 3″

Hole punch; paper fasteners

Wax crayons (see 194)

Draw a picture on each page of the gathered signatures in a sequence, starting with the first page. Use the same animation techniques described and pictured in 340 and 341. When all the pictures have been drawn and the flip book is filled, run the edges of the pages through the fingers of the other hand. The images drawn on the pages will appear to be in motion.

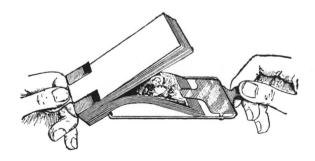

343. Story Board Collage

Tools and materials

Story board pad (available from art supply stores)
Old magazines; travel folders; picture postcards; photographs; colored paper
Scissors; paste (see 37 and 12–26)

Before animated—and many live—films are made, a story board is prepared that shows the main sequences to be shot. Each picture on the story board indicates a highlight of the action and describes in the small panel below it how one scene leads into the next. Action is achieved in motion picture making not only by the movement of the characters or objects, but also by camera movement—across the screen (panning), coming closer and pulling back from the scene (dollying in or out), shooting close-ups, medium, and long shots, and choosing camera angles. Abrupt changes from scene to scene (cuts) or slow dissolves (fade in or out) are indicated on the audio panels of the story board, along with dialogue and sound effects.

Making a story board is not only a useful and necessary preparation for filmmaking but fun in its own right. A child can prepare a make-believe movie on a story board pad, using photographs clipped and cut out from magazines and other sources, and combine them with cut paper shapes and other found material (see 324).

If no story board pad is available, a child can make his or her own. Divide a large sheet of drawing paper into panels as shown (see diag. 343) and number them in sequence.

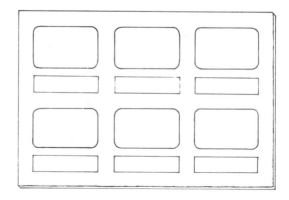

343

344. Drawing a Story Board

Tools and materials
    Same as 343
    Wax crayons; lecturer's chalks (see 194 and 195)

Suggest to the child that, in drawing a story board (see 343), he should keep the drawing in each panel very simple and concentrate on dramatic action rather than on detail.

345. Scripting a Story Board

At ages at which children can write short stories, writing a shooting script is an interesting variation as well as a useful preparation for film-making. Let the child tell his story, sequence by sequence (see 343 and 344), suggesting what he wants shown in successive scenes. He should also indicate focus (long shot, medium shot, or close-up), camera movement (dolly in, dolly out, pan to the left, or pan to the right; see 343), and camera angle (at eye level, or seen from above or below). Suggest that the young film writer think of and describe sound effects and dialogue to accompany each scene (see IX.E). Such a shooting script can be incorporated in a story board and written on the small audio panel under the video panel (see 344).

346. Photographing a Story Board

When the young photographer has mastered some of the elements of still camera work (see 331–338), story board making, and script writing, he can photograph a story board in individual still pictures, each representative of a particular sequence, based on a script (see 343–345). He will need some guidance in basing his script and subject on material he can find in his own environment or neighborhood, using his friends as a cast. Emphasize that he should follow his own directions for close-ups, medium, and long shots, and camera angles. When developed and printed, the photographs can be pasted in position on the story board pad or sheet (see 343) to describe the film in still sequences.

347. Cut-Out Paper Animation

Tools and materials
    Colored paper
    Scissors
    Paste (see 12–26)

347

Thaumatropes (see 339), phenakistoscopes (see 340), zoetropes (see 341), flip book animations (see 342), and story boards (see 343–346) can be made with cut-out paper shapes and figures. One of the advantages of cut-out paper shape animations is that many copies of the same shape can be cut simultaneously by accordion folding the paper (see diag. 347), making the work less laborious. For example, the same torso, legs, and arms can be cut in multiples with the scissors, then jointed and pasted down in different positions on each frame or space (see diag. 62.a).

348. Drawing and Scratching on Film

Tools and materials
    8 mm. or 16 mm. movie projector
    720 Frames of clear 8 mm. or 16 mm. film leader
    Acetate inks in different colors; solvent
    No. 3 student grade watercolor brush; drawing pen nibs and holder
    Needle point, or tipped etching tool

Movie film runs through camera and projector at the rate of twenty-four frames per second; 720 frames of clear leader will produce a thirty-second film, which is about as much as a young filmmaker can handle without becoming tangled up. If prestriped, single-sprocketed clear leader can be obtained, the filmmaker, in addition to drawing his animation on film, can scratch sound onto the sound track (see 356).

A continuous animation on film can be created by drawing, painting, and scratching on film. When run through a projector, the image will appear to be in motion. Suggest to the young filmmaker that he let the

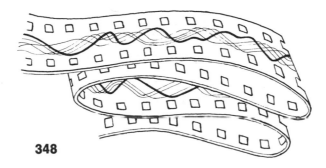

348

design flow together and dissolve over the whole length of the film, rather than drawing on individual frames (see diag. 348). See 328 for additional information about drawing and painting on film and acetate.

349. Jointed Flat Puppet Animation

Tools and materials
    Still camera (see 333)
    Jointed paper puppet (see 62)
    Tripod; or enlarger; or homemade camera stand (see below)
    Two 100-watt photographic floodlights
    Large sheet of white no-seam paper
    Masking tape

Limit the animation to thirty-six frames (three rolls of twelve-exposure film). Suggest that the first ''movie'' be confined to animating a single jointed figure against a white or one-color background. Other figures and backgrounds can be introduced for subsequent films. Let the young filmmaker discover how much motion can be created by moving the limbs of the figure and the figure across the frame and by dollying in and out (see 353).

If neither enlarger nor tripod is available for mounting the camera, build the braced stand shown (see diag. 349), marking matching lines 1″ apart on each of the uprights. Tape the camera firmly to the cross beam with surgical tape. Be sure not to tape down the shutter or to cover the lens, viewfinder, or film transport. Attach the cross beam that holds the camera to the two uprights with C clamps so that it can be moved up and down, or with pegs as shown.

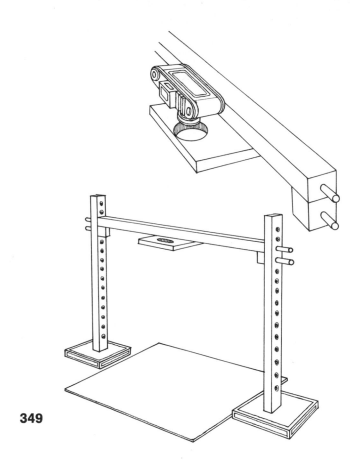

349

The white no-seam paper must be large enough to cover the whole field of vision when the camera is raised as far as the stand or tripod allows. At that point the viewfinder of the camera must be reachable by the young photographer to focus and check each exposure. Mark the position of the camera on the cross beam before removing it to change film.

Place the jointed puppet on the no-seam paper and compose it for the first photograph. Turn on the floodlights, focus the lens, and set the exposure according to the instructions furnished with the film. Rotate or move the figure or its limbs in arcs no greater than 45° or 1″ for each exposure. Reload the film when necessary, after all thirty-six frames are shot. Develop and contact-print the film and bind the contact prints into a flip book sequence (see 342).

Any number of animations can be created in this manner. The child can introduce backgrounds that, when moved, add to the animation of the figures. Suggest that abstract shapes, human figures, animals, flowers, and objects be animated, some moving in opposite directions. If the animation is shot with a 35 mm. camera, several rolls of film can be spliced together and run through a 35 mm. projector if one is available.

350. Animation with a Movie Camera

Tools and materials
    Same as 349 (but no still camera)
    8 mm. or 16 mm. movie camera that allows single frame exposure
    8 mm. or 16 mm. movie projector
    Splicing and titling kits (see 353)

The principles of animation and the procedure are the same whether a still or movie camera is used (see 349), except that the finished animation can be run through a movie projector. Iconographic animations (see 351), cel animations (see 352), or jointed puppet animations are possible with such a camera. Limit the young movie maker to 720 frames of animation (30 seconds) at the start. Otherwise he or she will become discouraged.

351. Iconographic Animation

Tools and materials
    Same as 349 and 350

One or more drawings, prints, or paintings can be used, singly or in combination, for a form of animation by isolating, photographing, and editing details and arranging them in sequence. Stop-frame animation, required for iconographic films, assures smooth movement and transition from one scene or detail to the next. Sequences must be edited and spliced so that, in combination, they tell the story (see 353). Dissolves and cuts can heighten the dramatic effect.

Aside from providing insights into the problems of selection and camera movement, many details of animation and filmmaking are illuminated for the young filmmaker while working on an iconographic movie. If no single-frame movie camera is available, a flip book animation can be made of short sequences (see 342 and 349), each frame copied from the original with a still camera or by photostat enlargements obtainable from photocopying sources.

352. Cel Animation

Tools and materials

    Paper and acetate cels (available from art supply stores in 8½″ × 11″ or 10½″ × 12½″ sizes)

    Cel-vinyl cartoon colors (available from art supply stores); or poster colors for paper cels (see 206)

    No. 4, No. 6, and No. 8 student sable brushes

    Drawing pens and holder

Professional animations seen on movie and TV screens consist of thousands of individual drawings, each of which represents one small movement, and each drawn onto a separate cel. Each cel or group of cels is photographed individually in turn with a single-frame movie camera mounted to an animation stand. Such an animation stand allows the camera to dolly in closer and farther away and the cel to be moved, a fraction of an inch at a time if need be, in any direction.

Cel animation is laborious. It is not recommended except for young people who have considerable experience in the animation and photographic techniques described earlier in this chapter. For those who are interested in making a short animation, the following suggestions suffice for a start.

Keep in mind that film runs through the projector at twenty-four frames per second. Each frame represents a slight movement of one kind or another. Cel animation therefore requires a well-thought-out story board that makes the most out of a minimum number of cels through imaginative editing, cutting back and forth, and repeated use of the same cels. The camera can be mounted on an improvised animation stand similar to any of those suggested in 349–351.

Once the story board has been planned, draw each key situation on a cel with a brush and cel-vinyl colors and work out the required movements, one cel per movement and frame, each laid over the last. Moving backgrounds can heighten the illusion of motion of the figures. Each successive cel requires careful registration, both on the drawing board and on the animation stand. The holes punched into the top edge of the cels allow for such registration. Sink two dowels into a ½″ plywood board, placed so that the cels can be attached to them, one over the other (see diag. 352). Obviously cel animation requires a great deal of improvisation and experimentation, limited only by the available equipment and how cleverly it is adapted and its limitations taken advantage of.

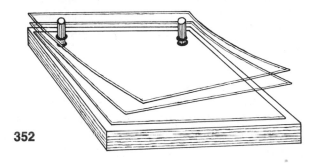

352

When the cels have been drawn and painted, each must be photographed, the film processed, edited, spliced, and titled. Sound can be added, either on film or played, synchronized to the film, on a tape recorder. Professional animation is made after the sound track has been recorded. But this procedure requires skills and equipment that are beyond the reach of young animators.

353. Inexpensive Movie Making

The cost of filmmaking can be considerably reduced if proper advantage is taken of the medium. Most home movies are shot in the hope that something dramatic will chance to happen while the film is running through the camera. The object of the filmmaker should be never to shoot unless something is happening, or to film a scene so that only the camera creates movement. Experience in animation techniques is a useful preparation for any kind of motion picture camera work. The same principles suggested for still photography apply (see 334 and 338).

Suggest to the young filmmaker that he shoot first without film. Let him compose and plan each sequence in his viewfinder, decide from which angle to shoot, how to move the camera, and when to pan or dolly in and out. He thus learns to capture the essence and spirit of motion or to contribute motion to whatever scene he views. Dolly shots with a zoom lens are easy. Shooting without film gets the young filmmaker used to anticipating action and to looking for it. It allows him to move, plan, and foresee possibilities that are his personal contribution. He won't be restricted to recording whatever flows past his lens.

Once the technicalities of focusing and exposure are under control and the camera is loaded with film, suggest that the young filmmaker use it with discretion. Each sequence should require decision and commitment. Once committed, he should be willing to shoot about fifty percent more film than is needed. This will give him ample footage for editing, dissolves, and splices.

Good movies are made in the editing. In addition to a movie camera, film, and projector, the young filmmaker needs a film splicing outfit and a titling kit. The instructions needed are included in each. A stopwatch is also a useful investment. Let him run off the processed film in the projector, timing sequences and taking notes. Then he can rearrange the footage, cutting back and forth and, when desirable, repeating some portions in order to tell and dramatize whatever was filmed. Movie making requires a point of view along with basic skills and equipment: it then becomes a story telling medium and a means of expression rather than an exercise in pushing buttons (see IX.E for sound and sound effects production).

354. Videotape

Currently available videotape recorders are so expensive as to be out of reach of most families and many schools. Of those available, most do not lend themselves to the editing and splicing that, as discussed in 353, is perhaps the most crucial process in filmmaking. In the not too distant future, succeeding generations of videotape recorders may become more economical; resolution and picture quality of the tape may improve; and videotape recorders may replace the motion picture camera in some respects. When this takes place, all the techniques detailed for filmmaking will apply to videotape production.

Videotape offers several advantages to the young filmmaker. Like sound tape, it can be wiped clean and reused. Disregarding the fact that the picture quality of magnetic video-tape may not be as good as that of film, it may turn out to be much less expensive than photosensitive film in the long run.

E. SOUND CRAFT AND TAPE RECORDING

Like the still and motion picture camera, the tape recorder has not yet risen to the level of a creative tool in the hands of most young people who own one. Tape recorders are used largely as duplicating machines; but a cassette tape recorder, or preferably two of the same model, can be used by young people for craft purposes. Children, once they master the knack of pushing the right buttons, can find this a fascinating way of learning and expressing themselves.

Discovering, making, and arranging sounds can be highly creative experiences, which call imagination and selective judgment into play, heightening the capacity to listen, to distinguish the meaning of sounds, and to use them inventively. Try turning off the sound on your TV set, letting children and young people in the family guess what sounds go with the pictures unfolding before them, or make up the dialogue.

The skills required for operating a cassette tape recorder are slight. All that needs to be learned is the buttons to push for record, playback, fast forward and reverse winding of the tape, how to insert and remove the cassette and how to clean the sound head. Transferring sound from one recorder to another is only slightly more complicated.

355. Sound Instruments

One of the problems that stands in the way of a creative use of sound is that this subject is studied only in elementary science classes. Classroom experiments with sound usually don't concern themselves with meaning and sequence. The human voice is a remarkable solo instrument, able to imitate a wide range of sounds and effects. Encourage the child to mimic animal noises, the sounds of cars, sirens, bells, trains, airplanes, and boat whistles, water rushing in torrents or rain drops splattering. Found materials can aid in such sound production: sticks rubbed or

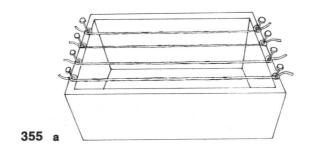

355 a

struck on wood; a fingernail scratched over fabric, glass, or eggshell; a dowel or metal spoon struck or rubbed over a cooking pot lid. These are common experiences that enable a child to experiment with sounds.

Homemade musical instruments can be constructed that introduce the child to rhythm and interval. Rubber bands stretched across a cigar box (see diag. 355.a), or a series of water glasses, each filled to a different level (see diag. 355.b) and struck with a dowel, can produce musical sounds and be recorded on tape. As the child plays back sounds he has created, he'll get ideas for producing others.

b

356. Scratching Sound on Film

Tools and materials

720 Frames of prestriped, single-sprocketed clear leader (8 mm. or 16 mm.)
8 mm. or 16 mm. sound film projector
Needle point, or tipped etching tool

Given the basic understanding that sound is recorded on magnetic tape in wave form, a child can make a spontaneous sound track on film. Scratch on the opaque colored band on the unperforated edge of the film with the needle or etching tool. By varying the configuration of the

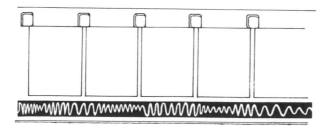

356

scratches (see diag. 356), a variety of high, low, screeching, and bleeping sounds can be created that are made audible when the film is run through the projector. If such a sound track is to accompany a directly drawn animation on film (see 348), it is important to keep in mind that the sound head in the projector "reads" the sound track twenty-six frames beyond the picture it matches. In other words, the picture projected on frame No. 1 is accompanied by the sound on the track next to frame No. 26.

357. Finding Sounds

Encourage the child to take his tape recorder with him wherever he goes—to the zoo, airport, circus, or fun fair, and on any excursion to places where unusual or interesting sounds are likely to be found. At home he or she can record the meowing of the cat, the barking of the dog, the ring of the telephone, or the kettle boiling on the stove. These found sounds, recorded on tape, can be built into a library of natural sound effects (see 358) that the child can use in his or her play and in making animations or movies.

Demonstrate how the meaning of sounds changes when they are rearranged in different sequences:

Cat's meow	Cat's meow	Footsteps	Footsteps	Door slam	Door slam
Footsteps	Door slam	Cat's meow	Door slam	Footsteps	Cat's meow
Door slam	Footsteps	Door slam	Cat's meow	Cat's meow	Footsteps

These, or any other three sounds, can be arranged in six different ways, each sequence conveying a different set of events and meanings.

358. Making Sound Effects

Professional movie makers and TV producers do not rely exclusively on natural sounds recorded on location. At times artificially produced sounds are more convincing. For example, thunder is produced by shaking a large metal sheet; rain, with metal foil or by pouring dried lentils or peas on a wood or metal tray. The galloping hoofs of horses can be replicated by striking two blocks of wood together or in a sand filled box. The air rushing out of a toy balloon, when amplified, suggests a storm at sea. Inventing sound effects and recording them on a tape recorder is a useful experience. These effects can be edited into story telling tapes (see 359) or used for animation and filmmaking.

359. Story Telling on Tape

Suggest to children and young people that they tell or read stories into the tape recorder, producing and using sound effects (see 355–358) at appropriate moments to dramatize the story. When the tape is played back, let the child listen to his diction and make suggestions for future improvement, slower speech or reading, greater separation of words, better pacing and pronunciation.

360. Tape Editing and Splicing

Casette tape is more difficult to splice and edit than reel-to-reel tape. However, splicing kits for both tape recorder models are available. They include detailed instructions.

Editing can also be done by recording directly from one cassette tape recorder into another. Plug a double-ended lead from the monitor outlet of one into the microphone outlet of the other. Set the volume control on the second recorder to medium and that of the first one to zero for best results. If a microphone is used to edit and rerecord from one tape recorder to the other, a great deal of background noise and the hum of the recorder's meter are picked up.

X

Reed and Fiber Craft

If between the ages of five and fifteen, we could give all our children
a training of the senses through the constructive shaping of materials—if we could accustom their hands and eyes, indeed all their
instruments of sensation, to a creative communion with sounds and
colors, textures and consistencies, a communion with nature in all its
substantial variety, then we need not fear the fate of those children
in a wholly mechanized world.—*Bernard Shaw*

A. BACKGROUND

Despite the absence of absolute proof, it must be assumed that braiding
and wicker work were among the earliest crafts, predating pottery and
metal working. Pottery (see VII) had its beginning as mud and wattle
pressed against the walls of wicker baskets to make them more efficient.
There is proof that early potters used wicker basket molds around which
to form their earthenware. Ancient shards and pots, unearthed from
tombs and the sites of prehistoric settlements, have wicker patterns
pressed into them. Some of these are the result of such molding. In later
ones the texture became a traditional decoration that stemmed from the

earlier molding practices. Even the conventional shapes of prehistoric and early historic pottery are derived from basket weaving rather than from spontaneously evolved clay forms.

The first likely products of weaving—wind breaks, fences, and palisades—were probably inspired by man's awakening to a consciousness of animal behavior—nest building and spider web and cocoon spinning. This probably led to imitation and the eventual discovery of original weaves and patterns. These skills were inevitably applied to various purposes and products—hair ornamentation, baskets, fish traps (still used in Malta), coracles (wattle daubed wicker boats used until recently in Arab countries and Great Britain), ritual offering vessels, chests, huts, and even chariot carriage and wagon bodies. Between the period of the rude beginnings of this craft and its eventual, partial replacement by work in other materials, twisting, spinning, weaving, and knotting vegetable fibers became possible as man's ability to make tools—bone awls, threaders, and needles—developed.

Many examples of woven baskets, and of course cloth, are pictured in Assyrian and Babylonian murals, sculptures, and reliefs, and in later Egyptian and Greek friezes and vase decorations. Archaeologists have found relics of ancient baskets, their weaves still intact, that are more than 3,000 years old. The common use of wicker baskets in early times is reflected in the story of the infant Moses, left in a basket on the shore of the Nile. Among the Incas of Peru, North American and East Indians, as in Sino-Japanese, Mediterranean, and northern European cultures, basket making and its products were considered holy and associated with religious sacrificial rites. During the time of the Roman occupation, Britain's Druids are reported to have woven huge replicas of the human figure, each several stories high and filled with votive offerings. These wicker monuments were burned to the ground during annual religious ceremonies. The bearskin "busbies" of Britain's Royal Guards are lined with wicker even today, but the origin of that tradition is obscure. Hawaiian and Pacific islanders still weave straw and wicker hats, but in former times made armor and helmets out of woven palm fronds.

Many problems had to be overcome before thinner, softer, and more fleecy fibers than straw, twigs, and leaf fronds could be woven. A way had to be found to lengthen and strengthen the fibers. Flax, jute, sheep's wool, cotton, and, in China, the excretion of the silk worm needed to be twisted into continuous strands to provide fibers for weaves that eventually replaced animal skins as man's clothing. By the time of the flowering of the Incan and Egyptian empires, weaving had become so refined that the closeness and delicacy of the cloth has been seldom matched since.

Primitive weaving was very slow. The warp threads (the vertical strands; see 375) had to be lifted one by one so that the weft (the hori-

zontal strands; see 375) could be passed over and under them alternately to form the weave. This hand method is still practiced among some American Indian tribes and in remote parts of India and Mexico. Improving the loom became something of a preoccupation of craftsmen throughout the world. The invention of heddles by an unknown genius of the distant past allowed each set of warp strands to be lifted alternately as a group, as shown above; and the shuttle, which holds the weft strand, as shown below, to be thrown rapidly. It is essential to understand these simple principles of weaving, the proper terms, and the basic mechanism so that they become second nature to the young craftsman. The need to speed up the weaving process made invention and improvement of equipment a matter of concern, second only to agriculture, to those who first experimented with mechanics and water power. The cotton gin, the mechanical spinning frame, and the power loom are milestones of what we now call the Industrial Revolution of the late eighteenth century. Unfortunately, this mechanization also undermined the consumer's reverence for the product and the laborer's reverence for his work. The latter declined to machine minding.

The chronology of this chapter, as in the rest of this book, follows that of the historic development of skills. It embodies a logic that underlies

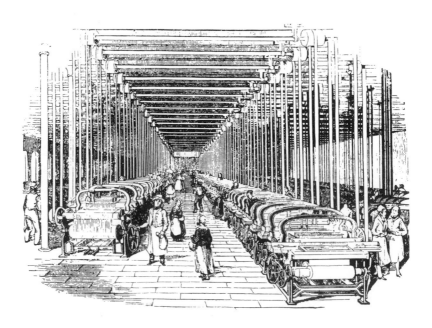

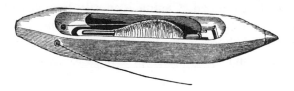

the progression of discovery and invention from the primitive to the complex, as from the infantile to the mature. But there the similarity ends. The child is not condemned to an environment that is so hostile and difficult that he need confine himself to production as did most of his forebears. Instead, as hands and fingers become more nimble, he can draw on the accumulated experience of preceding generations, learning some of the traditional forms, converting them, and inventing others according to his conceptions and insights.

One of the problems concerning these crafts is that until some of the basic braids, weaves, and knots are mastered, it is impossible to be inventive. Aside from these a child should be left free to be inventive. Discourage children and young people from copying patterns. Encourage them to invent their own designs even if they re-invent many that were traditional in the past. Conventional weaves can be readily deduced from the basic ones. Should any child or young person need to know these for practical reasons, he or she can find the particulars in the existing literature.[105] What is far more important and what is of primary concern is that the child learn to create and recognize patterns as a result

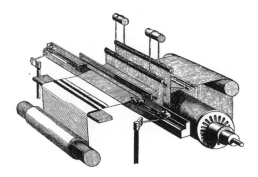

of his experience inspired by this and the following chapter. For these reasons some of the less creative aspects of the craft, like caning, have been deliberately excluded. Caning is mostly limited to particular patterns by utility and necessity rather than convention. The emphasis here as elsewhere in this book is on developmental learning so that the child can comprehend and apply basic principles to creative and expressive ends.

B. WINDING AND STRINGING

361. Unraveling

Tools and materials
> Old wool sweater or other garment
> Cardboard shuttle (see diag. 361.a)

Unraveling a discarded garment and winding the wool into a ball or on a shuttle can be an interesting activity for nursery and kindergarten age children. The garment should be made of thick, coarse fiber, preferably wool. The turned-over warp strands (see X.A), or bound-off knitting (see 384), should be cut through with scissors at the hem so that the child can separate the weft easily (see diag. 361.b). Caution him not to unravel more wool than what he can wind on the shuttle at one time. The wool thus unraveled can be used in many of the projects described above and below. (See also II.C, 27, 28, 96, 97, 111, 179, 218, 235, 260, 295, and 350.)

Young children generally learn best by knocking things down, taking them apart, or undoing them before they can learn to fit them together

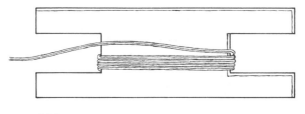

361 a

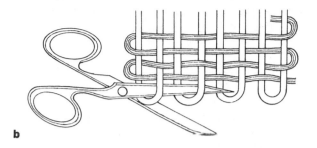

b

and to construct.[3] This same principle applies to fiber craft. A child who has separated braids and weaves, and who has some of the differences between them pointed out to him, will understand that such differences exist and how they can be recognized, analyzed, and invented. The over-and-under principle of plaiting and weaving becomes obvious, but first it must be experienced in a tangible manner. The child's attention must be directed to it so that he does not unravel mechanically. Praise him or her for being neat and winding the wool tightly on the shuttle.

362. Cord Construction

Tools and materials

    Open cardboard box; cardboard or wooden frame
    Hole punch (see 178 for round drive punch and mallet), or hand drill and bit (see 116)
    Ball of twine, yarn, or wool

Punch holes in the sides and bottom of the cardboard box or construct an open framework of any desired shape and drill holes into all frame members (see diag. 362.a). The constructions shown are representative

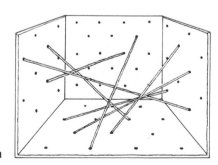

362 a

examples only. Any number of differently shaped ones can be given to or made by the child, each usable for inventing many different string designs and patterns. The idea is not to thread the twine through every hole but to choose those that, when threaded, make the design interesting.

Start the child by cutting off a foot or two of twine, knotting one end, and threading the other through any one of the holes in the frame or box. Pull the whole length of the twine through the hole and then choose another hole on any opposite side through which to thread it. Pull the twine tight and continue weaving across the box or frame from hole to hole. Whenever the length is used up, knot more twine to its end until the design is finished. Different-colored yarn can be knotted together for multicolored effects.

More experienced young people can combine warp (vertical) designs with weft (horizontal) designs, weaving over and/or under to create almost any configuration that grows spontaneously out of the work. Caution the child not to pull too hard on the weft strands, or he may distort the cardboard box sides or frame. If the frame is very solidly constructed, it is possible to distort the warp design deliberately by tightening up on the weft strands (see diag. 362.b).

The same box or frame can be used repeatedly for different designs, after unraveling.

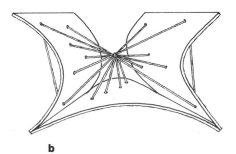

b

363. Stringing

Tools and materials
    Threader (see 4) or large needle (see 180, 186, and 386)
    Macaroni shapes, fresh beans, peas, dried berries, seashells (with holes drilled in
       them; see 116); and beads (see 44 and 258)

Stringing some of the shapes and objects suggested above and of cut paper shapes (see II.C) can be very satisfying to young children. It helps develop coordination. Professional bead work is usually done on a loom, but free-hand bead stringing, using basic forms (see 379) is a prerequisite. The bead stringing method shown, and variations such as combination with braided, knotted, or macramé patterns (see 367–370), as well as alternating bead sequences, can lead to interesting, spontaneous design forms.

364. Pasting

Tools and materials
    String, twine, wool, thread, and fibers
    Paste (see 9–26)
    Sheet of heavy cardboard or construction paper

String, twine, wool, thread, and fibers can be dipped in paste and used as collage materials (see 27); or the cardboard can be given a thick coating of white or acrylic paste and strands laid into it in patterns and combinations of the child's choice. (See also 28, 96, 111, 177, 235, and 260.)

365. Mesh Weaving

Tools and materials
    Large screen plastic mesh, 4" × 4" or larger
    String, twine, wool, raffia, or straw threader (see 4)

This is a very simple form of embroidery. Show the child how he can insert the threader or fiber anywhere between the mesh, pull it almost all the way through, and thread it over, under, and across portions as he chooses. Don't insist on or explain formal embroidery stitches. Allow the child to find his own way. He'll get great satisfaction out of seeing patterns emerge from his spontaneous stitching. As in all other early arts and crafts, the required insights and the skills to develop symmetrical or asymmetrical patterns can only come after the materials have been played with and explored. (See also 380–382.)

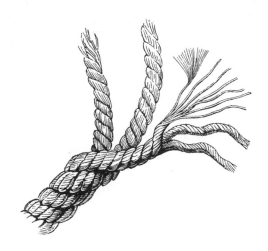

C. TWISTING, BRAIDING, AND KNOTTING

Knots are part of not only the weaver's craft, but the sailor's. There are more than 150 different ways of knotting and splicing twine and rope, but only a small number of them are of practical value to the young craftsman. The first ropes were probably made of twisted vines, thong, or animal gut. The knot was an inevitable invention born of the need to keep long hair from interfering with full movement, to secure bundles, and to tie off ends of coarse braids and wicker weaves. Peruvian Incan and Egyptian ropes, about 3,000 years old, have been discovered in ancient tombs. The Incas knotted rope to make a kind of abacus. The Greek Gordius supposedly tied a knot 3,000 years before Christ whose ends were so cleverly concealed that no one could discover how to untie it. Legend had it that whoever untied the Gordian knot was to rule the entire Asian continent. According to myth, Alexander the Great severed it with a stroke of his sword and fulfilled the prophecy.

Folklore and superstition surround the knot all over the world. The knot has been a part of rituals from tying the umbilicus of the new born to the marriage ceremony. In some cultures, like the Lapps of northern Scandinavia and the natives of Borneo, pregnant women are forbidden to wear any knotted garment or ornament for fear this might hinder a safe delivery.

A child can be shown how to make his own rope. Take a bundle of single or twisted fibers—twine, string, or thread—and gather it even at one end. Tape the end securely with friction or masking tape and secure in a vise or C clamp (see 112 and 113). The whole bundle of fibers should be about ¼" thick. Cut the other end even and insert it in the chuck of an ordinary hand drill. Turn the drill and a rope will begin to form (see diag. X.C). It's a good idea to moisten the fibers before twisting and then dry them while still held under tension by vise and drill. Bind the end near the drill chuck with tape before unfastening the rope from the chuck. This, in principle, is how the old rope walks operated in which manila rope was made for the sailing ships of the past.

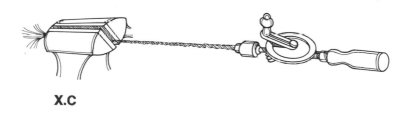

X.C

When a child has learned how to tie his shoe laces, he is ready for some of the projects described below. Each braid and knot, by itself and in combination with bead work and weaving patterns, can produce individual and inventive results. As with all other craft, don't try to teach too much too soon. Let the child himself explore the possibilities of each new form he masters or tool he acquires. He'll then be able to use both imaginatively and add them to other skills he discovers.

366. Cat's Cradle

It is appropriate to mention this Eskimo and Oriental game here—since any knotting can ruin the design. Cat's cradle is played with a loop of string of which the ends are tied together and stretched between the outstretched palms of two hands (see diag. 366). One or more fingers of each hand pick up the loop behind the opposite palm; this forms all sorts of string patterns. Cat's cradle is not only an amusing pastime: it develops finger dexterity and an understanding of some of the properties of fibers. It's too large a subject to describe in detail—the interested reader is referred to the standard work on the subject.[101] But even without de-

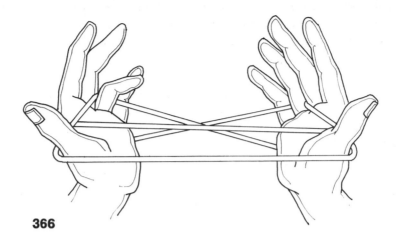

366

tailed instructions, a child can weave intricate designs of his or her own invention in endless variation, using the basic principle of cat's cradle shown in the diagrams.

367. Braiding

Tools and materials
> Cane; rushes; corn husks; grasses; reeds; raffia; rattan; hemp; palm leaf; split palmette; willow twigs; wheat, rye, or oat straw; fern stems; honeysuckle vine; wool yarn; twine or string (see 8, and below)
> Scissors

Each fiber used in braiding, as in basketry, caning, and weaving, requires special preparation. The following describes the methods appropriate for each material:

Straw (*wheat, rye, or oat*): Gather at harvest time. Cut off sheaf with scissors. Select only those straws of which the thin (top) end can be inserted easily into the thicker tubular bottom end to make longer straws if required. Soak straw in water overnight before plaiting or weaving.

Corn husks: Gather green or dry. Remove outer husk and use only the softer, inner husks. Dry indoors in the shade and tear each husk into narrow strips. Dampen in water for a few minutes before use.

Grasses (*sedge or slough grass is best*): Gather during summer and fall. Cut near ground with scissors. Cut off tips and remove outer covering.

Dry indoors in the shade. Use dry, but dampen slightly after braiding or weaving and then press between blotting paper and cardboard on which weights are placed evenly.

Cattails and rushes: Gather before the end of summer. Clip off tips and dry indoors in the shade. Rushes can be used whole, or split down the middle followed by scraping off the sticky pitch on the inside surface with a knife. Soak in cold water for fifteen minutes before use and keep wrapped in a damp towel until used.

Palmetto, palm leaf, yucca: Use the full-grown, outer leaf. Allow it to cure on the tree, or cut green, and dry indoors in the shade. If allowed to cure on the tree, cut when the frond turns yellow and then let dry completely indoors. Palmetto, the fan leafed palm, can also be used. Cut the leaf next to the bud leaf once it has grown 2″ to 3″ above the enveloping boot of the tree. Cutting this leaf does not injure the tree. Cut the frond as close as possible to the trunk. Store indoors, each frond separated from the others. To prepare for braiding or weaving, fold each frond outward over its stem and cut away the leafy part. This can be done with scissors along both sides of the stem or with a pin stuck in a board (see diag. 367.a). Each frond half can then be cut down to the required width, using a scissors or needle as before. Keep waste cutoffs for other braiding and weaving. Soak the cut fronds for fifteen minutes before use. Soaked palm leaf should be used within two days or else it will ferment. Dry out unused portions and resoak before use, as before.

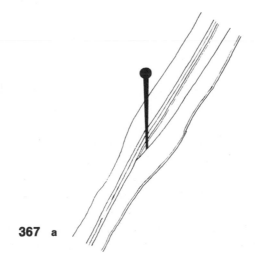

367 a

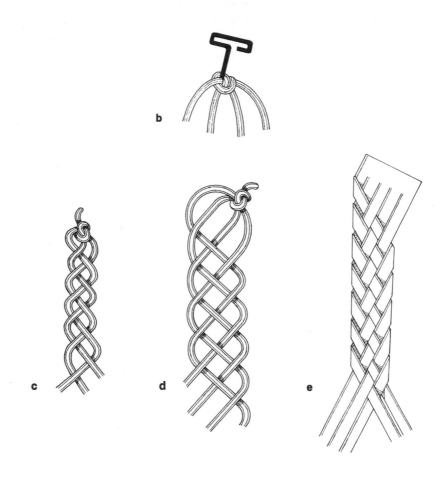

Rattan: Dip, but do not soak, in water before use.

See 8 (paper strips) for elementary flat braids for wider fibers like palm leaf or corn husks used flat. For other braids see diags. 367.c, d, and e. The various braids are shown in ascending order of difficulty, each involving more strands. Whenever an even number of strands is braided (four, six, and so on), fold the fibers so that each end is a different length and additional strands can be added at different places. Cross two or more of the folded fibers at the creases and secure the folded end to a board with a T pin (see diag. 367.b). Except for hollow grasses and straws, which can be fitted end to end, overlap the next strand by about 2″ when an addition is required. Braid the strand into the work rather than knotting it.

Braiding is an essential skill for macramé, bead work, and basketry and for making many useful and decorative objects (see XIII). When a sufficient number of lengths or a long length of fiber has been braided, the fibers can be coiled and formed into flat or hollow shapes, or coiled around different forms, such as bottles, boxes, balloons, and slab built or other pottery (see 266). Such coiled shapes can be either tied or sewn together (see diag. 383.f).

368. Knotting

Tools and materials
   Twine or string

The ten most basic knots and how to splice rope are shown below (see diags. 368.a–l). One or a combination of several can be used in macramé (see 370), weaving (see X.D), bead work (see 379), braiding (see 367), and netting (see 369).

368

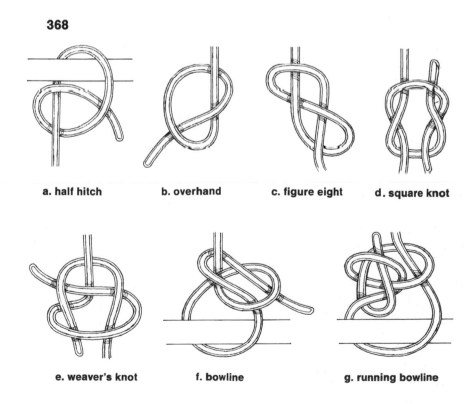

| a. half hitch | b. overhand | c. figure eight | d. square knot |

| e. weaver's knot | f. bowline | g. running bowline |

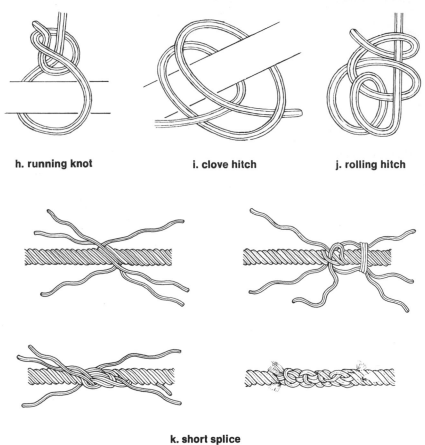

h. running knot   **i. clove hitch**   **j. rolling hitch**

k. short splice

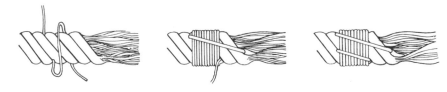

l. palm and needle whipping

369. Netting

Tools and materials
>Shuttle or needle (see diags. 369.a and 375.b)
>Mesh stick, made of wood or heavy cardboard, about 10″ × 1″ (see diags. 369.b–f)
>Twine or rope

Net making is useful for practical and decorative purposes. It can be combined with needlework, beading, and macramé.

Net making requires a stirrup—a loop of twine—attached to a second, larger loop secured to a window catch, door handle, or cup hook. (See diag. 369.b). The stirrup is eventually withdrawn entirely from the netting, but only after the whole net has been knotted. The first row of loops is knotted over the mesh stick and on the stirrup (see diags.

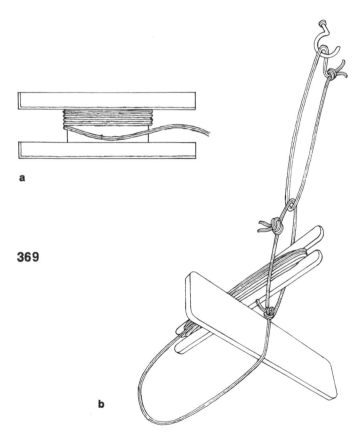

a

369

b

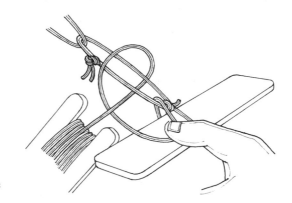

c

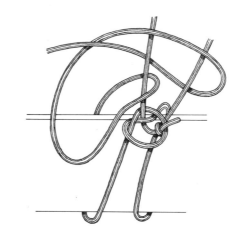

d

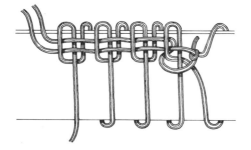

e

369.b–e). Be sure to knot each loop firmly on the mesh stick to keep the work uniform. After the first few knots, netting becomes very easy. The knots in these diagrams are opened up for easier viewing. In the actual knotting it is essential that each knot be drawn as tight as possible before making the next. It is useful to keep a thumb on the loop that hangs loose over the mesh stick (diag. 369.c) and to withdraw the thumb just before tightening the knot.

The number of knots tied to the stirrup and the number of loops knotted to the mesh stick in the first row decide how wide the net will be. For beginners a first row of nine loops is sufficient. When the first row is completed, slide the nine loops off the mesh stick, turn them over, and begin knotting over the mesh stick as before (see diag. 369.f). Continue knotting, row after row, sliding each completed set of loops off the mesh stick, turning over the net, and continuing as before, until the net reaches the desired length. Then cut the stirrup free and pull it carefully out of the first row of loops. It may be necessary to tighten some of the knots of the first row as the stirrup is withdrawn. Diag. 369.g shows the result.

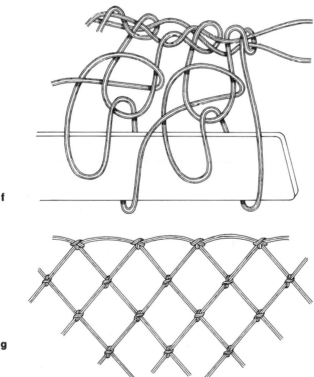

f

g

370. Macramé

Tools and materials
Twine or jute
Knotting board (see below)
T pins
Scissors
Embroidery needles (see 382); crochet hook (see 383); or leather lacing needle
    (see 179)
Beads or metal rings

Macramé consists of tightly knotted patterns made of twine or jute. The objects made may be utilitarian or purely decorative—wall hangings, mats, jewelry, and belts and other wearing apparel (see XIII).

The steps in preparing the material are uniform, no matter what will be made or which knots or supplementary materials will be used. Customarily two basic knots are used, the square knot and the half hitch (see 368, and diagrams below). However, these, singly or in combination with each other as well as with those described in 368, can be used to achieve an infinite variety of designs and effects.

A knotting board is essential to hold the material while the knots are being made. A piece of 8″ × 12″ wallboard or Styrofoam is sufficient. Knot and pin a "holding cord" to the board. The holding cord should be pinned about one-third of the way from the top edge of the knotting board so that, held in one's lap and leaned against a table edge, the work can be done in comfort.

Cut off lengths of twine, each about eight times as long as the estimated length of the finished product, and double each in half. Attach each doubled length of cord to the holding cord, using a double reverse half hitch knot (see diag. 370.a). (The width of the finished work depends on the number of double strands knotted to the holding cord.) Begin knotting, using one or another of the standard macramé knots shown below (see diags. 370.b–d); but bear in mind that any others can be improvised or combined with those shown (see 368).

It is important to keep the holding cord taut and to add T pins to secure finished portions of the work as close as can be to the cord ends not yet knotted. The finished work should be securely pinned to the holding board. If the work becomes uncomfortable because it is too close to the bottom of the board, unpin the knotted, finished portions and the holding cord, and move both farther toward the top edge of the board.

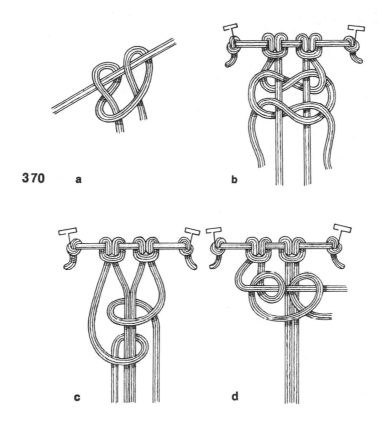

370   a   b

c   d

Beads, rings, and other ornamental findings can be knotted into the work or to its ends or edges as it progresses, depending on the craftsman's purpose.

For children in younger age groups or less experienced young craftsmen, the lengths of twine and the number of strands should be kept to a minimum. Two or three doubled lengths of twine, each a foot or so long, tied to the holding cord, suffice for a start. Emphasis should be on spontaneity rather than on formal repeat patterns: no preprinted pattern should be followed. Examples of more complex forms of macramé can be found in the literature.[106,107]

It's a good idea for young children or beginners to wind the ends of each twin strand on a mesh stick (see 369). The lengths of twine won't become tangled and can be more easily handled. As many mesh sticks as needed can be made out of cardboard.

D. WEAVING

The weaving process is the same whether spun or natural fibers are used. It doesn't matter whether a wicker basket, table mat, rug, belt, or cloth is woven: the same principles apply, so weaving as a whole, not by product or material, is discussed below. Once a child has mastered the basic skills, he or she can apply them to any material or purpose. The reader is urged to read X.A and to explain the basic warp and weft principle to the child before introducing him or her to these crafts.

371. Interweaving

Tools and materials

Paper or leather strips (see 7, 8, 42–47, 179, 180; and diagrams below); or fibers (see 367); or twine, wool yarn, or thread

Sheet of heavy cardboard

Heddle sticks (see 375)

Scissors

Masking tape

A sheet of paper or split leather, cut into strips but not all the way through, and taped by the uncut edge to the cardboard (see diag. 371.a), becomes the warp. An identical sheet or strip, cut but not fully separated into strips and laid alongside the warp at right angles, becomes the weft. The weave can be angled (see diag. 371.b).

Fibers and yarn can be used similarly, the top ends of the warp and the ends on one side of the weft being taped together, after the fibers are laid down side by side (see diag. 371.c).

The advantage of this type of interweaving is that it bridges the gap in skills between braiding and weaving. Warp and weft strands are easily arranged and kept in order. If the number of warp and weft strands is kept to seven or nine each, any pre-school nursery or kindergarten child can learn to weave in this manner.

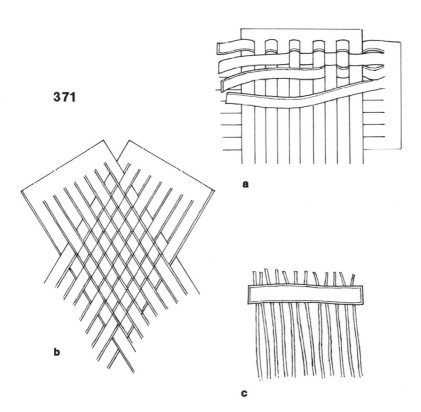

371

a

b

c

372. Paper Weaving

See II.G.

373. Wicker Work and Basketry

(See also 367.)

A comparison of the various weaves used in fabrics and in wicker work shows that there is very little difference in the working methods required for weaving natural fibers like rushes, reeds, and palm fronds, and spun fibers like wool, cotton, and silk. Broad-leaf fibers can be slotted, bent, or crossed to form variations in the warp, or the weft can be twisted (see diags. 373.a–e). Except for these differences, the same basic working methods apply to natural and spun fibers.

373

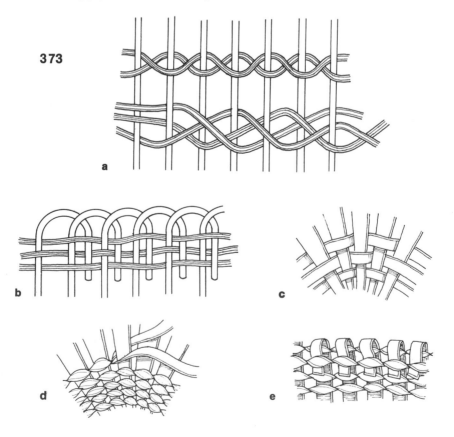

374. Stick Loom

Tools and materials
Wool yarns; thread; or fibers (see 371 and 373)
Two dowels
Heddle sticks (see 375)
Mesh stick or shuttle (see 369)
Scissors

American and East Indians have used stick looms from time immemorial. Tie an odd number of warp strands, each about ¼" equidistant from the next, to one dowel. Tie the other end of each warp strand to the other dowel in the same manner, so that the dowels are parallel when hung (see diag. 374). Suspend a dowel overhead or from a nail in the wall. Insert the heddle sticks as in 375. If yarn or thread is to be used as the weft, wind it on a mesh stick or shuttle (see 369) and begin the weave from the top, working down. Use the heddle stick to force the last woven weft strand close to the already woven fabric. No shuttle is needed for natural fibers and grasses.

If a shuttle is used, pass it alternately from left to right and from right to left. Do not distort the weave by pulling the warp strands together. When the warp is filled and the weave is completed, withdraw the dowels and heddle stick, tie the end of the weft to the last warp strand, and tie adjacent warp strands to each other, using any knot that serves the purpose (see 368) or seems decorative.

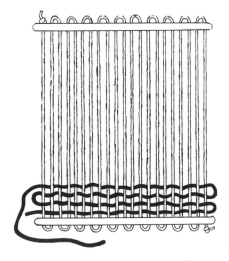

374

When fibers, grasses, or wicker are woven in this manner, the warp and weft strand ends are either turned over (see diag. 373.b and e) and secured in the weave, or they are sewn together (see 367, 382, and 389).

375. Frame Loom

Tools and materials
Wood or cardboard frame (see diag. 375.a)
Wool yarn, string, or fibers (see 371 and 373)
Heddle stick (see diag. 375.b and c)
Mesh stick or threader (for wool yarn, twine, or thread; see 369)
Scissors

Though a frame loom is customarily used only for heavy rug weaving, it is especially useful to young people for all kinds of weaving that are adapted especially for the purpose. The wood or cardboard frame can be any size. Drill holes in the top and bottom of the frame, ¼" or less apart. Leave enough room at the sides (see diag. 375.a) so that the yarn or fiber can be woven. String the warp and tie it top and bottom. Insert the heddle stick (see diag. 379.b). Turn the heddle stick to lift alternate sets of warp threads. Toward the end of the weave it will have to be withdrawn and the remainder woven without it. Then start the weft with a mesh stick or theader.

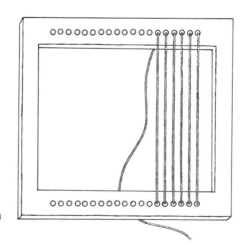

375   a

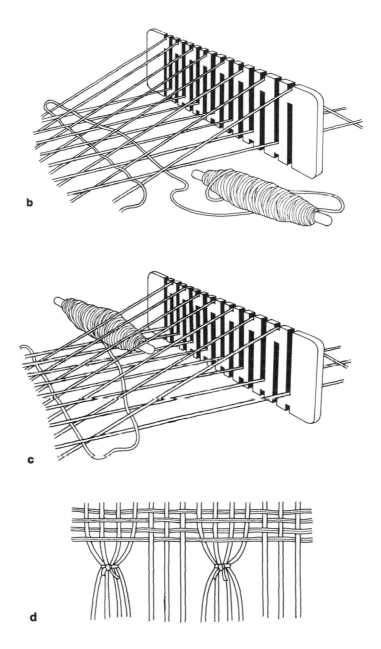

b

c

d

Once the weaving principle is understood, a great variety of patterns, designs, and color combinations can be woven. Weave without the heddle stick. Bind any section of alternate warp strands with a loosely tied piece of yarn or twine of the color to be used (see diag. 375.d). Then

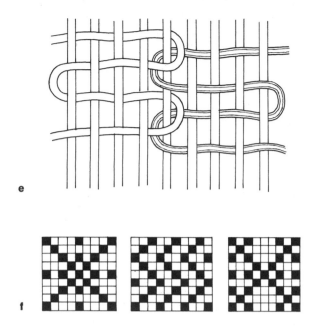

e

f

weave that portion of the warp only to the desired depth before changing
the color or pattern of the weft. Portions of the warp adjacent to what is
tied off must be woven so that they overlap as shown (see diag. 375.e).
Diagonal or more complex weaves require either careful planning on
graph paper in advance or tying off warp strands for the first pass of the
shuttle and carefully counting the required additional warp strands for
every subsequent pass (see diag. 375.f).

376. Paper, Cardboard, and Wood Form Looms

Tools and materials
　　Wool yarn, string, or fibers (see 371 and 373)
　　Heddle sticks
　　Paper or cardboard shapes (see 73–82, and II.J); or wooden base (see below)
　　Mesh stick or shuttle (for wool yarn, twine, or thread only; see 369)
　　Scissors
　　Sharp knife blade
　　Ruler

The simplest kind of cardboard loom consists of a flat square or rectangular piece of heavy cardboard in which notches have been cut, top and
bottom, at about ¼″ distances (see diag. 376.a). Wind and secure each

warp strand under opposite, matching notches and weave as before (see 373 and 374), either with or without heddle sticks (see 375) or mesh stick or shuttle (see 369). When the weave is completed, remove it from the cardboard and tie each warp and weft strand to the next to make a fringe or, if wicker is used, tuck warp and weft ends under the first and second row of the weave (see 373). Fiber weaves can also be hemmed or sewn at the edges (see 367, 382, and 389).

A round piece of cardboard can be similarly notched around its edge and the warp threads secured and strung as described above. Start the weft at the center, weaving around and around, over and under, working toward the outer edge (see diag. 376.b). Flat natural fibers (see 367) do not require such a template for round, flat, or hollow woven shapes. They can be notched and crossed (see diag. 376.c–e) and, if required, the

376

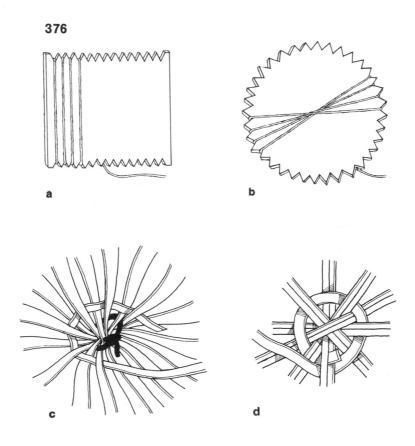

a

b

c

d

ends can be turned up to form the warp (see diag. 376.f). Permanent wooden bases with holes drilled around their edges are also used for wicker work trays and baskets. Pass the fibers under the wooden base and up through opposite holes to form the warp (see diag. 376.g).

Open dimensional shapes made of paper and cardboard, tubes, boxes, tin cans, and bottles (see 73–82, II.J, and IV.E) can be used as templates for wicker and fabric weaving. Cut notches, drill holes, or secure the warp thread with tape on two opposite top edges of the shape (see diag 376.h). Attach the weft strands to one of the remaining sides. Turn the shape over, its open side facing the table. Now stretch the weft strands across the side to the edge of which they are attached and weave them over and under the previously strung warp strands on the bottom surface only. As each weft strand completes its weave, tie it to the top edge of the opposite side of the shape (see diag. 376.i). Turn the shape right side up when the bottom has been fully woven. Using a new thread or fiber, tie one end to the very edge of the bottom weave at one

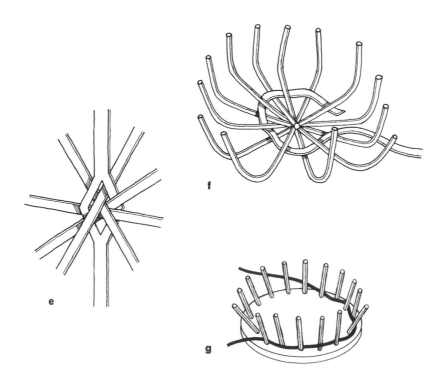

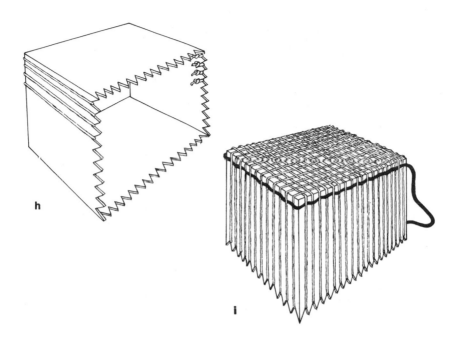

h

i

corner, and start weaving all round the four sides (see diag. 376.i). This method can be adapted to any shape. When the whole weave is completed, the template can be withdrawn if desired, after the ends of the fibers are released from the notches. They can be tied together, hemmed, or sewn so that they do not unravel (see 367, 374, 382, and 389).

377. Weaves

Tools and materials
Same as 371–376

Whole volumes are dedicated to the wicker and fabric weaves that have been invented through the ages.[104,105] So far as children and young people are concerned, the emphasis should be on experimentation, improvisation, and invention, once the basic processes are understood. The warp can consist of multicolored strands or strands strung in a sequence of colors or a variety of fibers. The weft need not be woven over and under each warp strand. Two or more warp strands can be woven in regular or irregular patterns. Different-colored yarns or fibers can be interwoven in regular or irregular sequences (see 374). Or different-colored weft strands can be joined end to end for random patterns.

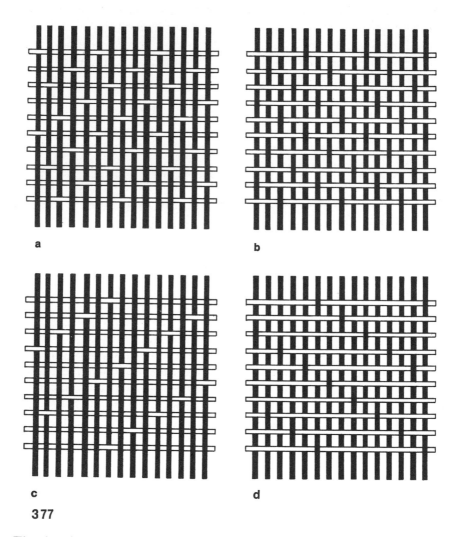

a

b

c

d

377

The drawings (see diag. 377.a–d) show some of the conventional weave patterns. These are not to be copied; instead they can suggest how weaves, braids, knots, and skills can be combined, enabling a child to improvise his or her own fabric or wicker patterns.

378. Weaving on a Loom

Conventional handicraft looms are available in many sizes and styles. Before one is given to a child, the young weaver should be familiar with the processes and techniques of weaving without a regular loom, described above, or else he or she may be overwhelmed by the seeming complexity of the equipment. Weaving on a proper loom is quite simple and embodies all the principles detailed for weaving without one. Each model is usually accompanied by instruction literature on how to set it up, how to string warp and heddles, and how to operate them and the shuttle. A two-way loom suffices for a beginner; he may graduate to a four-way loom if his interest is maintained.

It is relatively valueless to introduce a child to a regular loom until he can assemble it and set it up. Without this experience and the insights it provides into the possible variety of designs and weaves, weaving may be reduced to the tedious labor of passing the shuttle back and forth.

379. Bead Weaving and Stringing

Tools and materials
Beads (see 44, II.H, and 258)
String and twine; or threader (see 4)

Pre-schoolers enjoy stringing beads, macaroni, and drinking straw ends. (See also 4.) This develops finger dexterity and the discovery of patterns. More advanced bead work is usually done on a loom,[108] but for most purposes the two bead stringing methods shown here suffice (see diag. 379). In combination, or combined with braids, knotting, and macramé (see 367, 368, and 370), they permit invention of an infinite variety of bead stringing designs.

379

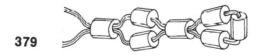

E. NEEDLE WORK

380. Hook Stitching

Tools and materials
Plastic mesh
Punch needle (see diag. 380.a)
Colored wool yarn

Choose the wool after purchasing the mesh. It is important that the yarn be heavy enough so that it cannot slip out of the mesh easily, once

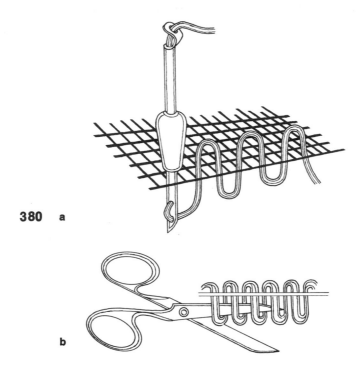

380 a

b

stitched to it. This method of stitching, also possible with a simple threader attached to the yarn end (see 365), can be used to design and make varicolored pile fabrics.

Thread the punch needle for the child or attach the threader (see 4, or diag. 380). Show him or her how to pass the yarn through the mesh, the slotted side of the punch needle facing as shown, leaving as long a yarn loop on the underside of the mesh as the desired length of pile. Show how to feed yarn through the needle and hold the loop on the underside to assure that successive loops are more or less the same length. Different-colored yarns, threaded into the punch needle and sewn into the mesh at various intervals, can allow the young craftsman to create colorful designs.

After the mesh is covered with stitching, turn it over and cut through the top of the yarn loops as shown (see diag. 380.b). For permanence, cut a sheet of lightweight cardboard, burlap, or linen that matches the size of the stitched mesh exactly, cover it with a coating of fabric glue, and paste it to the underside of the mesh before cutting the loops.

381. Knotted Hook Stitching

Tools and materials
Latch hook (see diag. 381.a)
Coarse plastic mesh
Colored wool yarn

This technique also produces a pile (see 380). Make a loop of yarn and slide the latch hook over it (see diag. 381.a). Pull the hook down over the loop but leave it large enough so that more yarn can be fed through the loop later. Bring the hook holding the yarn loop down through one of the mesh openings, feeding the loop into the next adjacent mesh opening (see diag. 381.b). Pull the free double strand of yarn through the yarn loop to form a double half-hitch (see 368, and diag. 381.c). Cut the doubled yarn ends evenly to form the pile. If a number of different color yarns are used, designs and pictures can be woven in this manner.

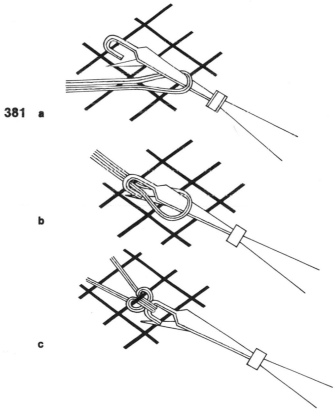

381 a

b

c

382. Embroidery

Tools and materials
Tapestry or lacing needle (see 179)
Coarse woven linen or burlap
Yarn or heavy colored thread
Embroidery frame; or heavy cardboard frame

Embroidery is closer to sewing than to weaving. It is related to both and serves as a good first introduction to basic stitches which, singly or in combination, allow the child to be inventive and yet complete simple projects without losing interest. Keep first projects small and allow the child to explore the possibilities of each stitch shown him by using it in

382

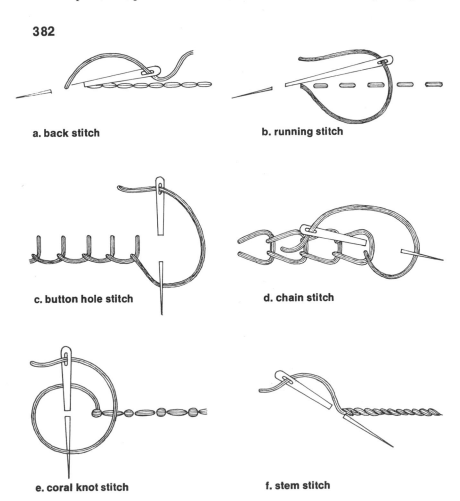

a. back stitch

b. running stitch

c. button hole stitch

d. chain stitch

e. coral knot stitch

f. stem stitch

spontaneous sewing. Stretch, tack, or staple the linen or burlap to an embroidery frame, available in notions and sewing shops, or a simple frame made of heavy cardboard. The basic embroidery stitches are shown below (see diags. 382.a–k and 389). Many of these stitches can be "whipped" and bound with a thread of another color.

Fine embroidery is usually done on densely woven fabrics; the coarser weaves allow the child to make evenly spaced stitches, using a tapestry or lacing needle without being confused. He can count intervening mesh spaces if he wishes. In couching, two or more threads are laid parallel on the fabric and then sewn on the material, using any of the basic stitches.

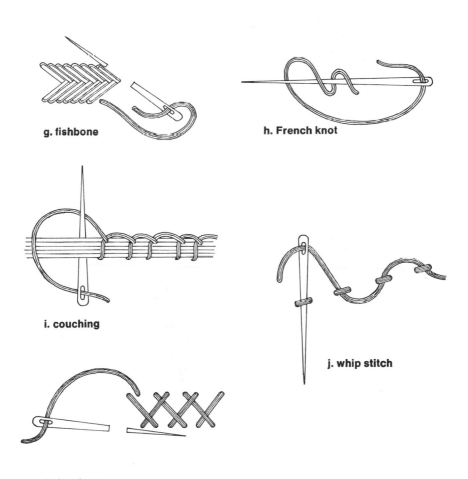

g. fishbone

h. French knot

i. couching

j. whip stitch

k. herringbone

383. Crochet

Tools and materials
    Crochet hook
    Colored wool yarn
    Wool box (see diag. 383.a)

The ball of wool should be kept in a cardboard wool box in which a hole has been punched and the end pulled through (see diag. 383.a), so it cannot unravel accidentally. The basic stitch is the chain stitch, started

383

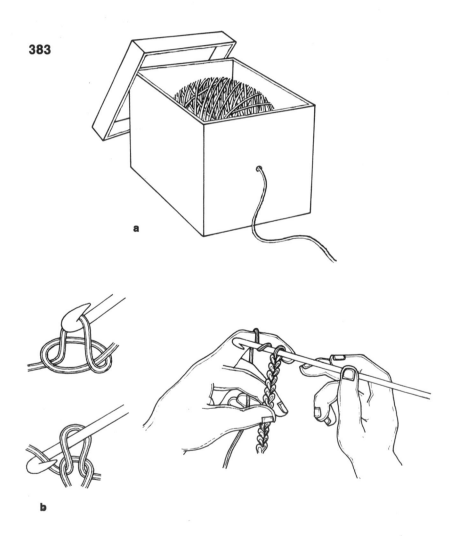

a

b

with an ordinary slip knot and the loop pulled through and repeated (see diag. 383.b). The stitch is identical to the chain stitch used for embroidery (see 382), except that here it is hooked rather than sewn (see diag. 383.c). Crochet can be done with fingers only.

The completed crochet chain can be coiled in a variety of designs, round, square, or hollow shaped (see diag. 383.d). At more advanced stages it can be crocheted together (see diag. 383.e). Interweave or tie

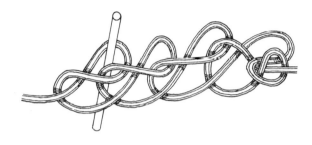

c

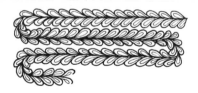

d

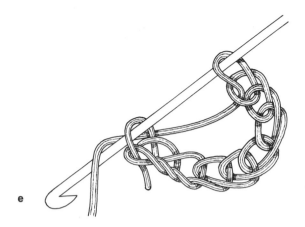

e

the loose end of a crocheted chain or design to the last loop that has been hooked.

The crochet chain is really the base material. The child can use it to improvise, often in combination with other knots and stitches (see 368, 382, and 389).

384. Knitting

Tools and materials
  Two knitting needles
  Colored wool yarn (wound in a ball and kept in a wool box; see diag. 383.a)

Basic knitting includes four operations: casting on; knitting; purling; and binding off. Purling can be left out of the instructions at first, but the other three are essential.

Casting on: It is easiest for a child to learn to cast on using only one knitting needle. Tie the yarn end to the needle with a slip knot. Then twist the yarn into a loop (see diag. 384.a) and slip the loop loosely on the needle. Repeat the slipping on of loops until you attain the width required for the fabric to be knitted (see diag. 384.b). Do not pull the loops tight or they will be difficult to knit, especially by beginners.

Knit stitch: Pass the point of the second knitting needle through the underside of the first loop strung on the first needle (see diag. 384.c). The second needle ends up on top of the first. Loop the excess yarn over the

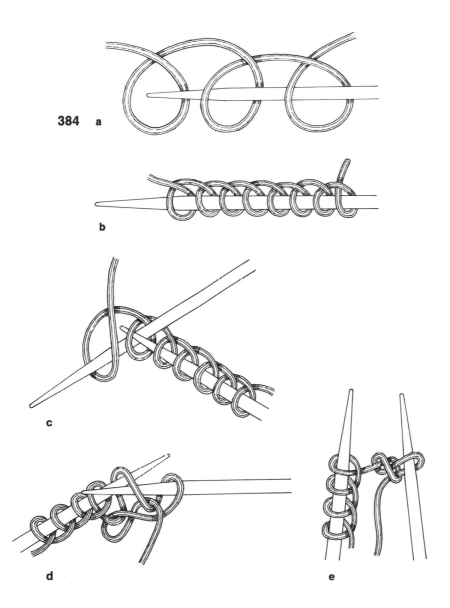

384 a

b

c

d

e

point of the second needle, back to front, as shown. Next, push the point of the second needle down close to the first, and lift the inner loop now formed on the first needle onto the second needle (see diag. 384.d and e). Repeat the series of operations until all loops have been lifted off the first needle and knitted on the second. Reverse the position of the needles in your hand and continue to knit as before.

Purl stitch: Cast the yarn on the first needle. Pick up the first loop on the first needle with the point of the second as before, except that it is knitted from back to front so that the second needle ends on top of the first (see diag. 384.f). Loop extra yarn around the second needle, front to back and around between both needles (see diag. 384.g). Pick up the innermost loop on the first needle with the second, passing the point of the second up from below and lifting it off entirely (see diag. 384.h). Continue to purl, reversing needles after each row has been knitted.

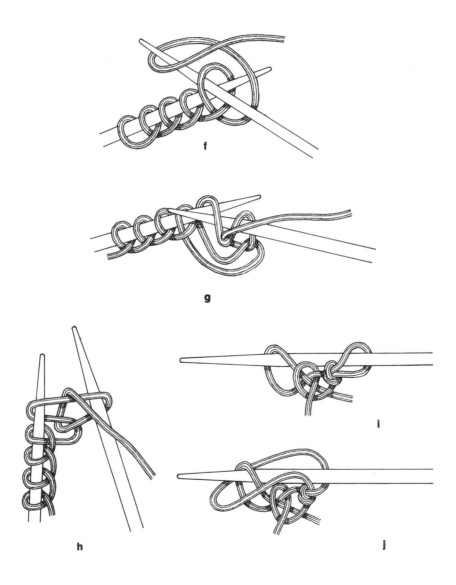

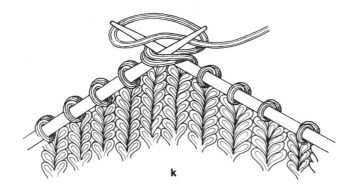

k

Binding off: When the fabric has reached the required length, it must be bound off so that the yarn does not unravel. Knit two loops from the first onto the second needle, using the knit stitch (see diag. 384.i). Slip the first loop over the second and off the needle (see diag. 384.j). Then knit another and slip the second loop remaining on the needle over the last and off the needle as before. Continue to the end of the row and tie off the remaining wool end to the last loop.

These techniques allow only square or rectangular shapes to be knitted. To vary shapes from the rectangular, a regular progression of a number of stitches must be added or reduced in successive rows.

To decrease stitches: Knit two successive loops together at one time for each of the number of stitches by which a row is to be reduced (see diag. 384.k).

To increase stitches: Pick up one loop from the row just knitted and knit it into the next row for each of the number of stitches by which that row is to be increased.

Other methods for increasing and decreasing rows exist, but these are the simplest.

Different-colored yarns used in various portions of a knit design allow the young craftsman to develop multicolored patterns, cutting off the yarn used up to a point and tying on another of a different color.

Fabric Craft

The lif so short, the craft so long to lerne.—*Geoffrey Chaucer*

A. BACKGROUND

Most instructions for young people on how to work with cloth concentrate on teaching the skills required for following patterns. This may solve economic problems for future housewives but, as pointed out in the introduction (see I), that is not and should not be the sole object of education. The prevalent view has made necessity the mother of copying, rather than of invention as it once was. It is also unfortunate that education in working with cloth is directed almost exclusively to girls. In our time this is as absurd as restricting work with more solid materials to boys. Despite the fact that sewing in the home has been a traditionally female craft, cloth, no less than paper, wood, or metal, can inspire both sexes to do creative, decorative, and useful work.

This chapter, like most of the others in this book, is not exhaustive. It concentrates on the development of a point of view and the beginning skills that can lead to more mature craftsmanship. The parentage of all craft is physical and esthetic necessity. In a child who is cared for as a matter of right, physical necessity consists of the exercise of his or her developing functions. Esthetic necessity gives this development purpose. The child's development follows that of the historic development of the various crafts themselves. The invention of weaving in prehistoric time supplanted the exclusive use of animal skins for apparel. The techniques for joining, fastening, and binding cloth were primarily inherited from work with leather. The earliest clothing was mostly bound at the edges, laced, and then draped, rather than sewn. Only the need to decorate, to make plain cloth more beautiful, inspired embroidery and stitching that ultimately led to more complex sewing. This in turn made it possible for woven cloth to be cut up in fitted patches which could be reassembled and sewn to follow the contour of the human figure and furniture. Inevitably this led to a need for a large variety of fine needles and other sewing implements and eventually to the sewing machine.

Sewing, other than hemming, was not widely practiced in Europe until after the Crusades. But the needle workers of the Orient and the ladies and their servants in European castles wove, embroidered, and stitched decorative cloth for religious and regal ceremonies. Stitching and cloth working skills served primarily to adorn royalty and nobility, as status symbols of wealth and power, and to enrich ritual. The techniques developed as playful and luxurious art forms before they were applied to everyday life.

The sewing machine, which became popular just after the middle of the nineteenth century, caused a revolution in the handling of cloth. It is inappropriate to mourn its advent as an example of mindless mechanization. The invention of the sewing machine made it possible for many of the world's population, who had heretofore lived in rags, to be adequately clothed and protected against the elements. Despite this considerable benefit, and due to miseducation and misapplication, the loss of creative skills in sewing crafts has been great since the advent of the sewing machine. Without hand skills and finger dexterity the proper and creative use of the machine cannot be learned or appreciated. The craftsman can no longer decide which operation is best done by machine or by hand. Eventually he becomes totally dependent on the machine.

Advanced sewing requires patterns. The number of cloth shapes and their relative complexity make it impossible to leave sewing a modern garment entirely to spontaneous creativity or to chance. But it is a far cry from making such a pattern to merely following prefabricated patterns. To make a properly fitted garment from a preprinted pattern requires changes and adaptations that can only be made successfully by

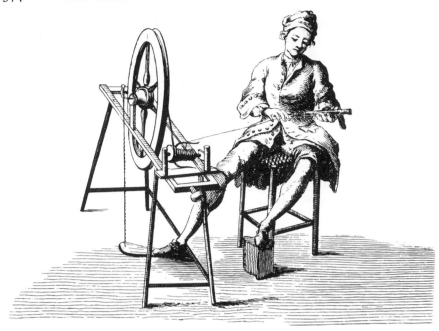

those who have the ability to develop their own designs. Successful sewing of a garment depends on paper cutting, template making, and designing skills (see II and XII), not on just following an existing pattern. Without experience in inventing patterns, following printed patterns can be frustrating—and it results in ill-fitting garments.

To become familiar with the characteristics of cloth the child must first learn to explore and use the different kinds that are commonly available—wool, linen, cotton, velvet, silk, and felt—as he would on being introduced to any other craft. He'll discover, for example, that fibers in all fabrics (except felt) unravel at the edges unless they are bound or hemmed. Hole punching, lacing, and binding, in cloth or in paper, give the child experience in joining one piece of material to the next. He needs exercise working in the flat as well as in working dimensionally in the round. He must start with relatively coarse thong or yarn until he can graduate to finer thread. These, like all other handicrafts, are developmental processes that reach perfection only through exercise. Without it they are imperfectly formed and the coordination and esthetic potential that are the birthright of every child are stunted.

Sewing in the abstract, save for the making of collages, appliqués, and quilts, has little appeal to young people. And so even relatively early sewing projects demand that the child be inspired with some sense of purpose within which he can find an outlet for his expression. One of the most potentially inventive of such purposes is costume making, sewing, or constructing garments and accessories out of paper and cloth for make-believe play,[114] by taping, pasting, stapling, or sewing together scraps of material. It is useful to keep a box full of colored cloth and paper remnants, ribbon and twine, discarded clothing, jewelry, and sewing findings to choose from.

B. CUTTING AND PASTING

Many of the skills required for working with cloth are identical to those used with paper (see II), leather (see V.B), and fibers (see X.E). It helps to be thoroughly familiar with the skills described in the chapters and sections cited before proceeding below.

385. Fabric Pasting

Tools and materials
    Heavy cardboard or shirt board
    Fabric and felt scraps
    Scissors
    Glue or paste (see 9–18 and 26)

When buying glue or paste, check the label to discover whether it is suitable for fabric. Fabric adhesive should retain some elasticity after it has dried completely. Rubber cement is not recommended.

Show the young child how to bend over, hem, and glue fabric edges (other than felt) to avoid unraveling. All the suggestions made for gluing paper apply (see II.D, 16, 27–29, 96, 111, and 177). (See also 227.)

386. Hole Punching and Lacing

Tools and materials
    Same as 4–8, 178, and 179
    Fabric scraps

The same skills, tools, and materials apply to cloth as to paper and leather. Lacing through holes punched into the fabric and binding it along the edges give the child a first insight into sewing cloth.

387. Snap Fastening

Tools and materials
    Same as 185
    Fabric scraps

Snap fasteners are easily attached to fabric by children old enough to punch holes and handle a hammer. They can insert the male and female parts of each fastener into holes punched into different or the same pieces of fabric and then secure them with the die (see 185). An adult can do this for younger children. Playing with snap fasteners, as with buttons and buttonholes, helps a child learn to dress himself or herself.

C. SEWING

388. Cutting Fabric

Tools and materials
    Scissors or pinking shears
    Fabric

Cutting shapes out of fabric with scissors or pinking shears requires prior experience with paper. Start the child with relatively small cloth scraps. Show him that it is best to pin or tape smooth and wrinkle-free fabric to a large sheet of cardboard by one edge before trying to cut it. Hold the bottom edge firmly in hand while cutting. Rather than snipping with the point of the scissors, the child should try to cut fabric from the bottom of the cutting edges, where the scissors blades are joined.

389. Basic Stitches

Tools and materials
    Fabric scraps
    Large sewing needle
    Coarse thread
    Thimble
    Pincushion

Show the child how to moisten and twist the end of the thread before trying to thread the sewing needle. Children who suffer vision or coordination defects should have this done for them. See 382 for basic stitches, which apply to sewing as to embroidery. The first to be taught should be the running stitch, the easiest one to learn. The stitches shown in the diagram can also be useful.

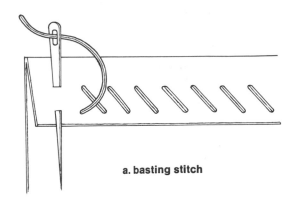

389

a. basting stitch

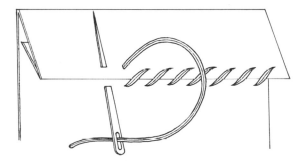

b. hemming stitch

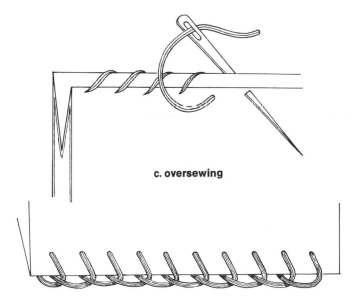

c. oversewing

d. blanket stitch

390. Appliqué and Quilting

Tools and materials
Same as 382, 388, and 389
Backing fabric (linen, burlap, or cotton)

Appliqué is essentially cloth collage, except that cut cloth shapes are sewn, rather than pasted, to a background. A running or back stitch (scc 382) is easiest for beginners, but more complex and decorative stitches can be used by experienced young craftsmen. Assure that the child hems each piece of fabric before sewing it on the backing, so that the appliquéd shapes do not unravel at the edges. (See also 385.) Children in the youngest age groups should use felt shapes, or they can hem other fabric with tape.

An appliqué shape can be partially sewn onto the backing, stuffed with cotton wool, or kapok, and then fully sewn to form patchwork quilting. Both appliqués and patchwork quilts can be designed spontaneously as the work progresses, or the cut shapes can be laid out in advance and pinned to the backing cloth with straight pins, sewn in position, stuffed if quilted, and then finished, using any of the simple or more decorative stitches described in 382 and 389.

391. Gathering and Pleating

Tools and materials
Same as 386, 388, and 389
Adhesive binding, or perforated gathering tape

It is easiest for beginners if they apply prepunched or perforated binding or gathering tape to one edge of the fabric. By lacing through precut holes children can form natural pleats. Or a child can punch holes into one edge of the fabric (see 386) after taping it with adhesive binding, or perforated gathering tape, and then lace and gather it. Prepunched pleating tapes are available at sewing and notions stores and departments. The pleats can be left loosely gathered or the child can sew them partially or fully, depending on the intended design or purpose (see diag. 389.c). The three basic forms, knife, box, and reverse pleats, can be gathered this way (see diags. 391.a–c and diag. 31).

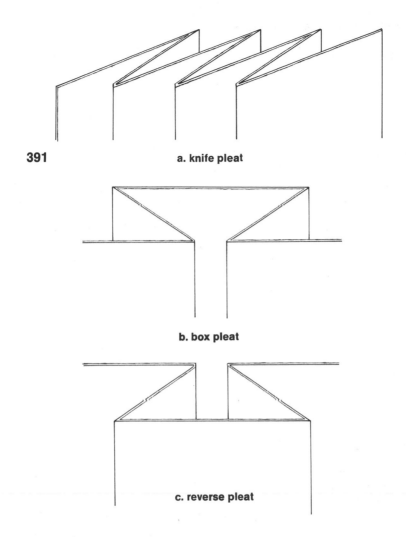

391

a. knife pleat

b. box pleat

c. reverse pleat

D. PATTERN MAKING

392. Paper Templates

Tools and materials
Same as 66–69, 73–82, and XIII

Fabric that is to fit a three-dimensional shape requires a pattern. The shape around which the fabric is to be draped—a clothespin doll, cushion, or human figure—must be selected in advance and paper shapes cut to determine size and where the seams will fall. The paper pattern should be cut and assembled like the paper mock-up described in 67, and pieces added, snipped off, or folded until they fit the shape to be covered with cloth. When completed, separate the mock-up so that it lies flat on the table. The flattened portions must later be cut out of cloth, hemmed, fitted, and then sewn together.

Make sure the young craftsman adds widths of fabric on both edges of any portion that is to be sewn together with other portions, and along hems. Variations in fullness or shape of the finished garment may require tapering of edges, gathering, or pleating (see 391). Armholes, for example, need special shaping so that sleeves, when sewn to them, don't bunch under the arms. Give the child opportunities to examine and if possible take apart discarded clothing or furniture covering along the seams, so that he can discover how to design templates for cloth.

The paper mock-up, when cut apart and flattened, becomes the template or pattern for the fabric. Such a pattern can consist of a single, flattened sheet which, when transferred to cloth, requires only folding over at seams and hems and sewing together, or of several individual shapes, each of which is hemmed separately and then sewn to the main body of the work.

393. Transfer from Paper to Cloth

Tools and materials
>   Paper template or pattern (see 392)
>   Straight pins
>   Pincushion
>   Tailor's chalk
>   Cloth

Flatten the cloth on a table top and pin the paper pattern shapes to it. Make sure that sufficient space is left between the shapes for seams to be added where needed. Trace the edge of the paper pattern on the cloth with tailor's chalk, adding a second parallel line where an additional width for seams and hems is required (see diag. 393). Keep the paper pattern pinned to the cloth until after it has been cut. Pleats can be indicated on the paper pattern and then transferred to the cloth. Cover the back of the paper pattern with a solid layer of chalk, repin it to the cloth, and trace the pleat lines marked on the pattern with a ballpoint pen. They'll transfer to the cloth. Pin the portions of traced pleats with

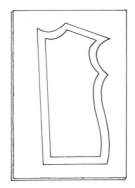

393

straight pins wherever they are to be sewn, after cutting the cloth, so that they can be found and sewn later even if some of the chalk has rubbed off.

394. Sewing from a Pattern

Tools and materials
Same as 388 and 389

After the cloth has been cut and the paper pattern unpinned from it, chalk the lines previously marked again to be sure they will remain visible. Then sew along all marked seams, hems, and pleats. Remind the child that all seams and hems must be sewn on the reverse side of the fabric and the final product turned inside out after it has been completed, so that the ragged cloth edges of seams and hems are hidden.

E. DECORATING CLOTH

395. Painting on Fabric

Tools and materials
Textile paints and solvent
Fabric
Muffin tin for mixing colors
Sable brushes
Cardboard mat, embroidery frame, or canvas stretcher
Newspaper covered worktable

Textile paints are colorfast, and fabrics painted or stenciled with them can be laundered. Pin or tape the fabric that is to be painted to the mat, frame, or stretcher so that all surfaces to be decorated are stretched on top over the opening. Make sure the fabric surface is wrinkle-free and reasonably taut. It must not touch any other surface while being painted or before it has dried completely. Caution the child not to overload the brush or fabric with paint. A certain amount of crawl or bleeding of colors beyond the width of the brushstroke can be expected at times. Section VI.A and 210–212 apply to fabric painting, as to any other surface.

396. Stenciling and Printing on Fabric

Tools and materials
Textile paints (for stenciling); textile printing inks

See 292–296 for found materials printing; 311 and 312 for general printing instructions; 302–304 for cylinder, clay, and plaster block making and printing; 305–307 for linoleum block making and printing; 317 and 318 for stencil making and printing; 320 and 321 for silk-screen making and printing. All these processes apply to printing on fabric.

When silk-screening fabrics, the material must be securely taped or tacked to the table surface, as in linoleum or wood block printing. It is usually easier to move a small silk screen and reposition the printing frame for successive repeat pattern printing than to release, move, and refasten the fabric for each impression.

397. Dyeing

Commercial fabric dyes like those used for leather are highly toxic. They must be kept out of reach of small children, and even more mature ones should not be allowed to use them. However, young people can learn to make and use relatively nontoxic vegetable dyes. But note that even the most harmless dyes, due to their high concentration, can be ir- ritating to the skin of some young people.

Before fabric can be dyed it must be treated with a mordant so that it is colorfast when dyed. The cautions about dyes apply to mordants too. Young people should wear rubber or plastic gloves while dyeing cloth, work in well-ventilated areas, and avoid inhaling the fumes from the boiling mordant and dye baths.

To prepare cloth for dyeing, the following are needed.

Tools and materials
Copper or enamel kettles, large enough so that the fabric to be dyed can be completely immersed and stirred in mordant and dye bath without spilling

Mordant (see below)
Dye (see below)
Long-handled wooden spoon

Preparing wool for dyeing: Wash the fabric thoroughly in warm water, soap, or detergent. Fill a kettle with the required amount of water (see caution above) and bring to a boil. Add 1 oz. of alum and ¼ oz. of tartar for each gallon of water. Immerse the fabric in the mixture and boil slowly for one hour. Stir the fabric with a wooden spoon to assure even saturation. Let the mixture and fabric cool until it can be handled safely, and then rinse the fabric thoroughly in cool water. Squeeze out excess moisture without twisting the wool and let dry overnight on a clothesline. Whether or not it is completely dry, the fabric will be ready for its dye bath next day.

Preparing cotton, linen, or rayon fabrics for dyeing: Wash the fabric as above and boil the water. Add 1 oz. of alum and ¼ oz. of ordinary baking soda for every gallon of water and proceed as with wool fabrics.

Preparing the dye bath: The following dyes can be made by boiling various plants, roots, nuts, and berries until the solution reaches the desired color intensity. Gather plants while they are young—roots in the fall; leaves as soon as they are full grown; and berries, seeds, and nuts when they have ripened.

Vegetable Matter	*Color*
Goldenrod (chop the whole plant into small segments and boil)	Yellow
Pear or peach tree leaves	Pale yellow
Black walnut husks and shells	Yellow-brown
Sumac leaves (ground to a powder)	Yellow-brown
Sumac roots	Yellow
Sumac berries	Purple
Sunflower seeds and larkspur flowers	Blue
Beets	Violet
Dandelion roots	Dark pink

You can mix and dilute these to obtain other colors and shadings—blue and yellow make green, for example. Add the concentrated dye to a kettle of gently boiling water. Be sure not to fill the kettle more than enough to soak and cover the fabric (see caution above). Keep the kettle boiling gently while the cloth is immersed and keep stirring with a wooden spoon until the fabric is dyed a color of the desired intensity. Then remove with the spoon, rinse in clear running water, squeeze out the excess moisture gently, and hang with clothespins from a line so that the cloth does not come into contact with itself or any other surface until it is completely dry.

398. Tie-Dyeing

Tools and materials
 Fabric
 Mordant (see 397)
 Dyes (see 397)
 Thread or twine
 Steam iron and ironing board

Tie-dyeing is an ancient craft still practiced throughout the Far East, in Africa, and in South America. Cloth is crumpled and tied into a ball, twisted into a spiral and tied, or folded and tied, or sewn temporarily so that, when immersed in a dye bath, the color penetrates the fabric in certain places only. It is dyed according to the degree of penetration of

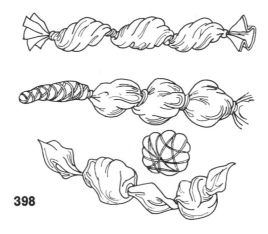

398

the color into the folds and creases of the wadded together, tied, or sewn fabric.

The illustrations show some of the methods of crumpling, twisting, folding, tieing, and sewing cloth for immersion in a dye bath (see diag. 398). The fabric must first be thoroughly washed and immersed in mordant and ironed, before it is prepared for the dye bath (see 397).

399. Batik

Tools and materials
　　Same as 230 and 231
　　Dyes (see 397)
　　Fabric

Read 229–231 for a basic description of the batik process. Prepare the material as for dyeing (see 397). Stretch the dried fabric over a mat or frame (see 395). Using a Tjanting needle (see also 231) or a paint brush, draw or paint the design on the fabric with melted wax. When the wax has cooled and dried, immerse the fabric in the dye bath (see 397). If the fabric is removed from the frame and crumpled before immersion, the wax may crackle and produce interesting textures as the dye seeps into the fissures. Rinse and dry the dyed cloth as before (see 397).

Iron off the wax as described in 231. Multicolor effects are possible by repeatedly painting the cloth with wax after ironing off the last layer, and dipping it into successive and different-colored dye baths.

XII

Planning and Design

It is, indeed, possible and even usual, for men to sink into machines themselves, so that even hand work has all the characteristics of mechanization.—*John Ruskin*

A. BACKGROUND

Emphasis in the preceding chapters is on spontaneity because this aspect of art and craft education is least stressed and often ignored in the majority of books on these subjects and by many teachers. Spontaneity is a developmental and creative necessity at early as much as at mature stages. After a few initial years of spontaneous exploration children begin to look ahead as they play with materials. They awaken to the fact that they can make, form, draw, or re-create experiences. The child may not have this objective in mind as he sets to work. Instead, while handling tools and materials in an experimental way, he may suddenly get a desire or a flash of insight that spurs him to represent or form a particular object. A shape he creates accidentally inspires recognition and a need to develop it further so that it becomes recognizable to others.

It requires great sensitivity to children in general and especially to a particular child to recognize and work with his or her vision and inspiration. It is not enough to leave the child undisturbed. He may really need help. The decision to leave well enough alone or to intervene is subtle and sometimes difficult to make, especially with very young children.

Older children are likely to make a decision before they start to work and then try to represent it. The child now needs a working method that allows him to reach his self-originated goal by the most productive, though not necessarily the shortest, route. The objective is not the most efficient form of production. The experiential, learning, and formative processes are far more important to the child. The child can then be made aware of the possibility of planning, of making rough mock-ups, templates, and models out of paper that allow him to work out problems in advance. He can't be expected to foresee all the things you can. But he still has to discover by experiment and through spontaneous play. He'll learn as much from his mistakes as from his successes. He'll begin to anticipate, plan to avoid or overcome some of the more obvious difficulties of design and creation.

Do-it-yourself, preplanned, and fabricated assembly kits help young people avoid the design problem, but they also keep the child from making the mistakes he must make in order to learn. They deny him experience and the development of foresight. The result of any art or craft activity will suffer if it is the product of a purely mechanistic approach.

To do something by design means to execute it deliberately and on purpose. Design can teach the child how to plan in two or three dimensions

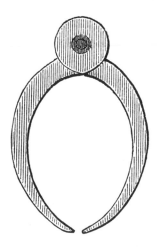

with expendable materials before he works with more permanent and durable ones, and before making the final commitment implicit in every creative act. But design does not preclude spontaneity in planning and execution. There must be room for inspiration, adaptation, and change during every stage of execution, in planning and in working out a rough model as in final design. Opportunities must exist for the happy accident as for an error that, in the fixing, requires a change in design. This should be as true of one-of-a-kind production as of the young craftsman's duplication of his original creation. No two need be alike. Each is uniquely valuable if it displays variations from the original.

None of the following design suggestions should be imposed on a child. They are not preconditions to working in the arts and crafts. They are supplementary; they should not be taught until spontaneous methods of creation have been exhausted or unless the child is aided by them in the development of his or her own imaginative conceptions. Needless to say, the planning suggestions offered refer to working out the young craftsman's own ideas. Even where they can be applied to copying the work of others or to following prepared plans, such work should be discouraged. (See also II.I and J, III.A.c and D, 153, 181, 204, and XI.D.)

B. DRAFTING

Almost all measurements of related parts of a construction, where this is called for, can be made with paper, compass or dividers, straightedge, and pencil. No other mathematics or instruments are required. Even a compass can be improvised (see 124), as can right-angle and other triangles (see 407) and protractor templates (see 407), using only the methods detailed below. Virtually any geometric shape can be designed with their aid.

Angles must be designed and plotted with some precision for well-fitting joints in paper and cardboard construction (see II), carpentry (see III), metal work (see IV), leather (see V), and even work with fabric (see XI). Measurements must be halved with precision and geometric shapes designed for certain work that, in the absence of a full assortment of drafting tools and sophisticated mathematical skills, can be frustrating to the more experienced young craftsman. The following techniques, though far from exhaustive, will give young people enough insights so that they can improvise and discover how to make precise measurements with a minimum of tools.

400. Free-Hand Sketches and Mock-Ups

Tools and materials
  Paper and pencil
  Scissors
  Paste and drafting tape

(See also 67.) Rough sketches of what is to be made or built out of more durable materials are useful when the construction is relatively complex and embodies details or parts that can't be fully imagined before the work is started, or improvised once it has begun. Paper mock-ups can reveal flaws in conception and inspire essential changes. They can be flattened for estimates of the required raw material. If the ultimate material cannot be folded, the mock-up must be cut into suitable components, each part representing a piece of material, eventually to be assembled and jointed. Allowances must be made for the thickness of the final material so that parts can be glued, stapled, nailed, screwed, bolted, soldered, or sewn together. The flattened mock-up or templates may need portions added to edges at which finished material parts are to be joined before they can be used as templates. Or if geometric precision is required, as in the fitting together of the sides, top, and bottom of an ordinary wooden box, the mock-up may need redrawing so that the angles of joints and thickness of the material can be accurately incorporated in templates or plans before transfer of the design to the final material.

The following sections are not intended as a prerequisite to the exercise of craft, or as lessons in mechanical drawing, except to the extent that they enable young people to realize their own imaginative conceptions at appropriate stages of development.

401. Transfer of Plans and Mock-Ups

Tools and materials
  Graphite stick or 6B pencil
  Tracing or layout paper
  HB or harder pencil or ballpoint pen
  Tape

See 291 for transfer of drawings with carbon paper and 393 for transfer of patterns to fabric. For transferring large drawings to materials other than fabric, blacken the back of the original plan or drawing with a graphite stick or a 6B or softer lead pencil. Tape the drawing to the material, blackened side down, and trace the lines of the plan with the HB pencil or ballpoint pen. Do not lift the design until it has been completely traced.

402. Scaling

Tools and materials
Graph paper
HB pencil
T-square, right-angle triangle, and ruler

An original sketch, drawing, or plan can be enlarged or reduced in proportion with a pantograph (see diag. 402), which can be homemade or bought in an art supply store. In the absence of a pantograph, enlargements and reductions can be made with graph paper.

Draw a grid of equal-size squares over the original plan. Choose a size for the squares that can be conveniently increased or decreased in the desired proportion. For example, for a two-thirds reduction in size draw ¾″ squares; the desired reduction can then be made on graph paper containing ¼″ squares. Use the graph paper to copy the original drawing, square by square, duplicating what is found in each square as exactly as possible either reduced or enlarged, as required.

403. Halving

Tools and materials
- Bond paper
- Compass
- Ruler or straightedge
- HB pencil

An ordinary piece of paper, its edge marked with the precise width, length, or thickness to be halved, can be used by folding the edge so that the two pencil marks overlap precisely (see 31). Make a sharp crease at the fold. When unfolded, the crease shows the position of the center, halving the dimension between the two marks with sufficient precision for most craft purposes.

For more exact halving of a measurement, draw a pencil line with a ruler on a piece of paper and mark off the precise length to be halved. Set the compass to the exact distance between the marks and draw large arcs from the marks, large enough so that each intersects with the other above and below the line. Join the two points where the arcs intersect. This vertical line will bisect the original line precisely (see diag. 403). Incidentally, the angles between the horizontal and vertical line will be perfect right angles that can be used as templates for constructions. The original line or distance can be subdivided into quarters, eighths, and smaller proportionate measurements by halving the compass opening

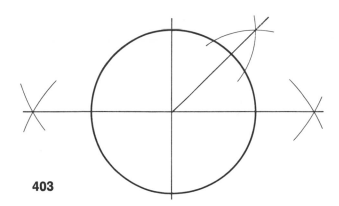

403

repeatedly, and drawing arcs and joining the points where they intersect above and below the line.

404. Finding the Center of a Circle

Tools and materials
    Same as 403

In building with found or scrap materials like dowel ends or tin can lids, it is often necessary to find the center of a circle, either to drill a hole or to divide the circle into segments. The following method, while not exact, suffices for most craft purposes.

With a pencil, trace the circular shape on paper as accurately and as close to the material's circumference as possible. Insert the compass point anywhere on the circumference of the circle and open the compass jaws so that the compass lead just touches the opposite side of the circle when an arc is drawn. Set the compass point at more or less the exact place where the arc and the circle's circumference meet. Draw a second arc of the same diameter as the first. Draw a line joining the two points where both arcs intersect outside the circle. Then draw a line joining the two small holes into which the compass point was set on the circumference of the circle. The point at which these two straight lines intersect (see diag. 403) is the approximate center of the circle. Cut out the circle and glue or paste it to the shape from which it was taken. Be sure the paper disc fits evenly all around. Mark the center with a nail or hammer or, if the material is soft, with a pin or compass point. Depending on the care taken in these various steps, the center will be accurately enough placed for most young people's craft purposes.

405. Finding the Center of a Triangle

Tools and materials
    Same as 403

If any two angles of a triangle are bisected and the line halving each is extended through the center of the triangle, the point at which the lines intersect is the true center. (For the sake of accuracy it's a good idea to bisect all three angles.)

Place the compass point on one of the vertices of the triangle. Draw an arc that intersects the two sides forming that angle. Keep the same compass setting and draw an arc from each of the points at which the

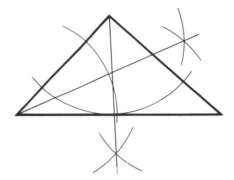

405

first arc intersects the two lines (see diag. 405). Draw a line from the vertex of the triangle to the point where the last two arcs intersect. This line bisects the vertex angle. Repeat at the other two vertices of the triangle. The point where the three lines intersect is the center of the triangle.

406. Finding the Center of a Square or Rectangle

Tools and materials
   Same as 403

Draw the two diagonals (see diag. 406). The point at which they intersect is the center. The diagonals create four triangles within the figure. Using the method given in 405, the square or rectangle can be further subdivided into quarters, eighths, and smaller equal sections.

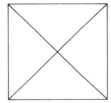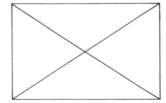

406

407. Dividing a Circle

Tools and materials
Same as 403

A circle can be divided into halves, quarters, eighths; or thirds, sixths, twelfths; and smaller equal sections, with considerable accuracy, using only the compass and ruler (or straightedge). This is a useful technique for designing and constructing triangles (see diag. 407.d), squares (see diag. 407.a), hexagons (see diag. 407.b), and other many-sided geometric figures, and for gear trains and other mechanisms that require precision.

Draw a circle with the compass. Use the ruler to draw a line through the center of the circle to form the diameter (see diag. 407.a). Set the compass points as wide as the diameter and draw two arcs, each from the points at which the diameter intersects the circumference. Connect the two points at which these two arcs intersect outside the circle (see diag. 407.a). Now reduce the setting of the compass points to the length of the radius (half the diameter). Insert the compass point at the same two points as before and draw two arcs, each intersecting the circumfer-

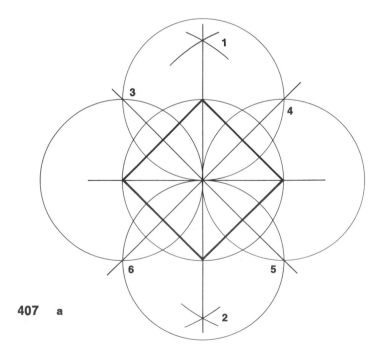

407   a

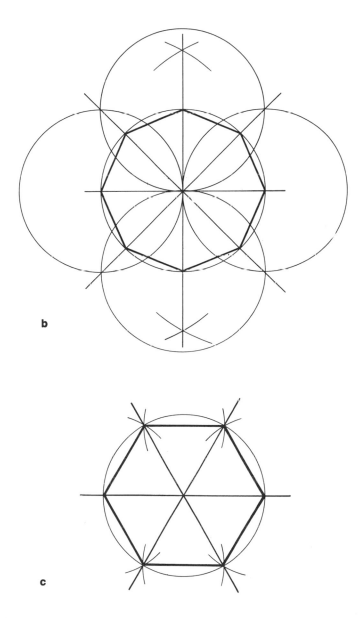

b

c

ence at two points. Connect the points at which the arcs intersect outside the circle with diagonals and the circle is divided into quarters (see diag. 407.a). By connecting the six sets of arcs as shown (see diag. 407.a) the circle will be divided into eighths (see diag. 407.b). Four sets divide the circle into thirds (see diag. 407.c), and so on. By connecting two sets of

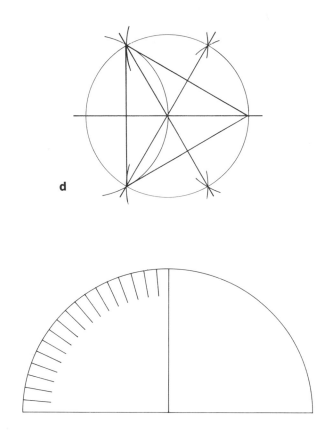

d

e

arcs with one of the points at which the diameter meets the circumference, a perfect equilateral triangle (see diag. 407.d) can be made. Accurate templates can be made of these figures, as can a protractor (see diag. 407.e) that enables young craftsmen and designers to mark off required angles without reconstructing geometric figures each time they are needed.

408. Measuring the Circumference of a Circle or Tube

Tools and materials
    Ruler
    Twine or string

In the absence of calipers or a caliper rule, or lacking basic mathematical skills and formulas, the young designer can measure the circumference of any circle, tube, or sphere by laying string or twine round the circumference and marking it where the ends meet. Place the length alongside a ruler and measure the distance.

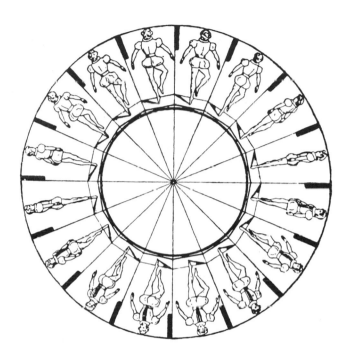

XIII

Applications

Art as a virtue, the practical intelligence is the wellmaking of what is needed. . . .—*Eric Gill*

"What shall I make? draw? sculpt? weave? photograph?" These questions are reasonable when asked by a child old enough to be aware that he or she can create things that are beautiful and useful. They do not necessarily imply that the child has no ideas of his or her own. Instead, the child may want to know what is most useful, needed, wanted, or appreciated. Ideally a child should work on projects he has thought of himself and that he considers worthwhile and interesting for their own sake. But sometimes a hint is appreciated if only to give the child's own inventiveness direction. Such a hint must be broad enough to invite creation and to allow the child to produce something that is uniquely his or her own.

The following idea file is intended to serve these purposes. It lists general subject categories, each of which demands invention and design. In keeping with the approach favored elsewhere in this book, the young craftsman should be encouraged to create his own ideas, forms, shapes, proportions, and construction methods and to carry them out according to his own conceptions and plans.

Example: Each major heading in the table (A. Decorations and Parties, etc.) is followed by a number of ideas for applying the skills, materials, and tools described in the chapters above. Idea B.10, under Tableware, is a breadboard. Looking across the breadboard line, you can see entries in the columns for Chapter III, Carpentry, and Chapter VII, Plastic Arts and Crafts. These numbers refer to projects in the text. For page numbers corresponding to the project numbers, see the table of contents. The cited sections describe methods, materials, and required tools for making a breadboard at different skill levels, with many variations. The design of the breadboard—round, square, rectangular; with indentations to facilitate bread slicing; not to mention other innovations—should be left to the young craftsman or -woman.

There is no reason why a child should not be able to invent an entirely new kind of breadboard, wastebasket, lampshade, or puppet. There is every reason why he should want to and be able to improve the world around him esthetically and practically, based on his own experience and imagination. He looks at life with a fresh point of view. He can come up with surprising and ingenious results, given the chance and encouragement, and these, rather than imitation of manufactured goods, should be the object of his exercise of skills.

Some entries are cross-referenced to avoid duplication. For example, B.12 (Tableware: Candy dish) refers to B.11 (Butter dish), both requiring identical tool, material, and craft selection.

An audiovisual-idea file at the end of this chapter serves as a general art and craft stimulator for still photography, movie animation, and filmmaking and sound production.

Specifically excluded are ideas of what to draw, paint, and sculpt, for reasons detailed elsewhere (see I.a, e, f, and g; and VI.A.a). The "idea file" is arranged so that once a child has settled on a category or has been led to adapt it, he can discover some of the prime materials (and crafts, etc.) in which it might be executed. A butter dish can be made of paper, wood, metal, leather, clay, or fiber, or from two or more of these materials.

Project Ideas	Paper and Foil Craft (II)	Carpentry (III)	Wire and Metal Craft (IV)
A. Decorations and Parties			
1. Birthday	3;27–29;31–41;42–47;77		142–144
2. Christmas (See A.1)			
3. Easter (See A.1)			
4. Fancy dress	9–28;34;36–39;48–59;60–82		
5. Greeting cards	9–29;35–41;98–101		
6. Halloween	9–29;36–39;48–59;77;78;98		
7. Masks	9–27;35–39;48–59;98		
8. May baskets	9–27;30–34;35–39;42–47;48–59;60–82		149–152
B. Tableware			
9. Bread basket		112–141	149–152
10. Breadboard		109–111;120–130;136–141	
11. Butter dish		109–112;118–130;136–141;III.H	
12. Candy dish (See B.11)			
13. Cereal bowl			
14. Cheese board (See B.10)			
15. Coasters	9–27;29;35–39;45–47;99–102	114–115	156
16. Cookie jar (See B.11)			
17. Cup and saucer (See B.13)			
18. Drinking mug (See B.13)			
19. Fruit basket (See B.9)			
20. Fruit bowl (See B.11)			
21. Hors d'oeuvres tray (See B.11)			
22. Jelly and marmalade dish (See B.13)			
23. Juice, water, and wine jug (See B.13)			
24. Napkins	9–27;30–33		

Leather Craft (V)	Drawing and Painting (VI)	Plastic Arts and Crafts (VII)	Printing (VIII)	Audiovisual Media Craft (IX)	Reed and Fiber Craft (X)	Fabric Craft (XI)
	202;207; 225		293;295; 296;317	327;358– 360	362–364; 372	385
176–182; 188–190	206;237; 245;246		293;295; 296;312; 317			385–399
	194–201; 206–218; 229–231		290–314	324–338; 358–360		
	194–225; 237;247; 248	263–265	290–314; 317	324–338; 358–360		385–399
	194–201; 205–219; 237					
179–186	194–200; 206–219; 229–231;237	262–266	290–301		371–379	
179–193	243–245	262–266; 272–276			371–379	
		266;272–276; 289				
		262–266; 272–276				
		262–266; 272–276				
176–180; 189–193	197;206– 217;243– 248	251–266	317–321		367–384	388–390
			293–296; 300;305– 308;317		374–378; 382	388–390

Project Ideas	Paper and Foil Craft (II)	Carpentry (III)	Wire and Metal Craft (IV)
B. Tableware (*cont.*)			
25. Plate (See B.11)			
26. Platter (See B.11)			
27. Punch bowl (See B.13)			
28. Salad bowl (See B.11)			
29. Salad dish (See B.11)			
30. Salad fork and spoon		129–141	152;155; 156;157; 162
31. Salt and pepper shakers		131–141	153–162
32. Sugar bowl and creamer (See B.13)			
33. Tablecloth	27;35–39; 99–102		
34. Tablemats	7;8;27;30–33; 35–39;45–47; 83–89;99–102	114;115	153–162
35. Tea or coffee pot (See B.13)			
36. Wine bottle rack		112–129; 136–141	149–152
37. Wine cooler			153–163; 166–170
C. Household Accessories			
38. Ashtray (See B.37)			
39. Bed cover			
40. Bed tray (See B.36)			
41. Bulletin board	83–89;93–95	112–129; 136–141	
42. Candelabra		112–141	145–170; 174–175
43. Candlesticks (See C.42)			
44. Candy box	48–59;83–97; 99–102	107–129; 133–141	153–157
45. Cigarette box (See C.44)			
46. Coat rack		107–131; 135–141	147–152; 164–168
47. Curtains			
48. Cushion			
49. Dog or cat basket		107–130; 135–141	

Leather Craft (V)	Drawing and Painting (VI)	Plastic Arts and Crafts (VII)	Printing (VIII)	Audiovisual Media Craft (IX)	Reed and Fiber Craft (X)	Fabric Craft (XI)
		258;262;266; 273;274;276				
		251;252;262– 266;273;275				
			293;296; 300;302– 312;317		369–378; 382–383	385;388– 391;395– 399
176–193	194;197–200; 206–218;231; 243–246	251;252;266; 273;274	293;295; 296;300; 301;304		364;365; 367–378; 382–384	385;386; 388–390; 395–399
		260;263;265; 266;273;274; 275				
	246		302–312; 317–321		369; 375–384	388–391; 395–399
	243					
		251–266; 272–274				
181–193	206–218; 232–245	251–266; 272–276; 282–285;289	317–319		371–379	385
	243;244	266;267;272; 273;276;281				
					368–370; 374–379	385–391
180–193					370;371; 374–379	385–399
					373	

Project Ideas	Paper and Foil Craft (II)	Carpentry (III)	Wire and Metal Craft (IV)
C. Household Accessories (*cont.*)			
50. Door mat			
51. Foot stool		107–131; 134–141	
52. Hat rack (See C.46)			
53. Lamp base (See C.46)			
54. Lampshade	10–18;26–31; 34–41;45–47; 60–82;98–102		145–147; 149–152; 166–168
55. Mobile	4–41;60–82; 98	106–111	142;143; 149–152; 168
56. Penny bank	83–97	107–128	
57. Pet feeder		107–129; 136–141	142–147; 149–161; 166–170
58. Picture frame	83–97	107–128; 134; 136–141	153–162; 169
59. Pillow cover (See C.48)			
60. Planter (See C.57)			
61. Punch bowl		134–141; III.H	
62. Record cabinet or rack	83–97	107–131; 135–141	149–152; 166–168
63. Room divider	83–97	107–131; 135–141	
64. Sampler	9–29;98		
65. Scatter rug (See C.50)			
66. Shoe rack		107–131; 135–141	
67. Shoeshine box (See C.66)			
68. Tape cassette rack (See C.62)			
69. Tea cart (See C.66)			
70. Tool box (See C.66)			
71. Tool rack (See C.66)			
72. Tool tray (See C.66)			
73. Tray (See B.10)			
74. Umbrella stand (See C.49)			
75. Vase (See B.13)			
76. Wall hanging	4–102	104–111	142–161

Project Ideas	Paper and Foil Craft (II)	Carpentry (III)	Wire and Metal Craft (IV)
C. Household Accessories (*cont.*)			
77. Wind chime	4–7;9–28; 30–46;48–59; 60–82		142–159; 165;166; 173
78. Window box		107–131; 136–141	153–159; 164–166
D. Jewelry and Personal Accessories			
79. Beads	4;44		
80. Bracelet	4–8;48–59;91; 92	111;114;116; 136–141	142–173
81. Brooch		111;114–116; 136–141	142–145; 149–173
82. Chain	4–8;36–39;57		173–175
83. Comb		114;116; 136–141	153–163; 174;175
84. Cufflinks (See D.81)			
85. Earrings	5–7;27–29; 35–39;44; 48–82;96–98	114–116; 136–141	142;143; 149–175
86. Hair ornament (See D.85)			
87. Jewelry box		107–128; 133–141	153–175
88. Necklace (See D.85)			
89. Pendant (See D.85)			
90. Ring			142;149– 175
91. Tie clip (See D.81)			
92. Watch chain			173–175
93. Watch fob			149–175
E. Kitchen Accessories			
94. Breadbox (See C.46)			
95. Coffee, tea, sugar, flour, and cereal containers (See C.46)			
96. Cookie cutters			153–159; 164;166; 169
97. Cup rack		107–128; 136–141	145–152; 155;166; 168
98. Dish rack (See E.97)			

Leather Craft (V)	Drawing and Painting (VI)	Plastic Arts and Crafts (VII)	Printing (VIII)	Audiovisual Media Craft (IX)	Reed and Fiber Craft (X)	Fabric Craft (XI)
		251–259; 273;274				
		253–266; 269–274			373	
		258;273;274			363;368–370;379	
176–180; 185; 188–193	197;237;238; 243–245	251–266; 272–274			363;367–379	385
176–180; 188–193	197;243–245	251–263; 266–274;279; 281–289			367–370; 373;379; 383	
	197;237;244					
	243;244	266;272–274; 281				
176–180; 188–193	197;237;238; 243–245	251–266;272–274;281–288			367–370; 379;383	
181–193	197;237; 243–245	262–268;272–274;200–209			370;373	
	244	263–266;272–274;281–288			367–370; 379;383	
180	244;245				367–370; 379;383	
176–180; 188–193	244;245	251–266; 272–274;279; 281–288			367–370; 379;383	
	243;244		317;318		373	

Project Ideas	Paper and Foil Craft (II)	Carpentry (III)	Wire and Metal Craft (IV)
E. Kitchen Accessories (*cont.*)			
99. Dishtowel holder (See E.97)			
100. Glassware rack (See E.97)			
101. Hot mat		107–128; 136–141	153–163; 174;175
102. Knife holder		107–131; 136–141	
103. Paper towel holder (See E.97)			
104. Potholder			
105. Salad drainer			153–162
106. Shopping bag			
107. Shopping basket (See E.106)			
108. Spice shelf (See C.78)			
109. Vegetable bin or basket (See C.78)			
F. Miscellaneous Articles			
110. Camera bag			
111. Camera case (See F.110)			
112. Tape recorder case (See F.110)			
G. Outdoor Accessories			
113. Beach bag			
114. Butterfly net			
115. Dog kennel (See C.66)			
116. Fish net (See G.114)			
117. Flower pots			
118. Hammock			
119. Outdoor games		107–131; 136–141	149–161; 164–173
120. Picnic basket (See G.113)			
121. Playground equipment (See G.119)			
122. Sandbox (See C.66)			
123. Seedling box (See C.66)			
124. Sundial		107–141	149–172
H. Sewing and Laundry Accessories			
125. Clothespin bag			
126. Knitting basket	55;83–95; 99–102;104	107–128; 136–141	
127. Laundry bag (See H.125)			

409

Leather Craft (V)	Drawing and Painting (VI)	Plastic Arts and Crafts (VII)	Printing (VIII)	Audiovisual Media Craft (IX)	Reed and Fiber Craft (X)	Fabric Craft (XI)
176–193	243–245	263;266;273; 274	317;318		370;373; 383;384	385;390
	243	265;266; 272–274				
					370;373; 383;384	385–390; 395–399
		265;266;273; 274;276			373	
176–193	245				367–370; 373–378; 380–384	385–394; 395–399
179–193	245					
179–193					373	
					368–370	
		251–266; 272–274			373	
					369	
	243;244				368	
		251–274				
179–193					368–370; 373–379; 382–384	385–391
179–193	237;243–245				370–384	385–399

Project Ideas	Paper and Foil Craft (II)	Carpentry (III)	Wire and Metal Craft (IV)
H. Sewing and Laundry Accessories (*cont.*)			
128. Laundry basket (See H.126)			
129. Pincushion			
130. Sewing box (See H.126)			
131. Sewing thread spool rack (See C.66)			
I. Stationery Accessories			
132. Book cover	9–26;35–39; 99–104		
133. Bookends (See C.66)			
134. Bookmark (See A.5 and H.129)			
135. Book rack or magazine rack (See C.66)			
136. Book shelf (See C.66)			
137. Briefcase (See F.110)			
138. Desk blotter	9–26;83–88; 103;104		
139. Desk calendar	9–26;83–88; 103;104	107–110; 114;118–120; 136–141	
140. File box		107–128; 136–141	
141. Knife or scissors sheath			
142. Letter file	83–95;99– 102;104	107–129; 136–141	149–162; 164–170
143. Letter opener		109;114;115; 120;136–141	153–163
144. Letter tray (See I.142)			
145. Pen and pencil tray	83–95;99– 102;104	107–129; 136–141	149–170
146. Pen holder		107–129; 136–141	149–170
147. Photo album	99–104	107–129; 136–141	
148. Photo frame (See C.58)			
149. Portfolio (See I.147)			
150. Scrapbook (See I.147)			
151. Stationery rack (See I.142)			
152. Telephone note pad (See I.139)			
153. Wall calendar (See I.139)			
154. Wastebasket (See C.49)			
155. Writing pad (See I.147)			
J. Toys—Baby			
156. Mobile (See C.55)			
157. Noisemakers		107–120;134; 136–141	

Leather Craft (V)	Drawing and Painting (VI)	Plastic Arts and Crafts (VII)	Printing (VIII)	Audiovisual Media Craft (IX)	Reed and Fiber Craft (X)	Fabric Craft (XI)
176–180; 188–193					374–378; 380–384	385–389
176–183; 188–193	237;245		290–311; 317–321	324–328; 331–337	370–378	385
176–193	237;243	266;273;274	317;318			
	243	266;273;274; 289	317;318		373	
177–193	245					
176–193	237;238; 243;244	266;273;274	317;318		373	
181–193	243–245	266;273;274; 280;281				
181–193	237;238; 243–245	266;273;274	317;318		373	
181–193	237;238; 244;245	266;273;274				
176–193	206;237; 243;246		293–312; 317;318	324–328; 331–337		
		263–265; 272–274			373	

Project Ideas	Paper and Foil Craft (II)	Carpentry (III)	Wire and Metal Craft (IV)
J. Toys—Baby (*cont.*)			
158. Stuffed toys and animals			
K. Toys—Building			
159. Blocks	60–82	112–121; 136–141	
160. Nesting blocks (See K.159)			
161. Panoramas	9–27;31;36– 40;60–66;98		
162. Peg and hole jointed blocks		112–126; 136–141	
163. Play houses and stores	35–41;48–59; 60–98	107–128	
164. Play town (See K.163)			
L. Toys—Dolls			
165. Doll accessories (See D.)			
166. Doll cradle	9–28;30;31; 36–39;48–97	107–128; 136–141	
167. Doll dresses	9–27;30–39; 60–82		
168. Doll heads (See N.180)			
169. Dollhouse (See K.163)			
170. Dollhouse furniture (See B.;C.;E.;K.163)			
171. Doll playground equipment	48–97	107–128; 136–141	142–152
172. Rag doll			
M. Toys—Musical			
173. Bell set			153–162; 166;173; 174;175
174. Drum	9–28;36–39; 60–97	107–116; 136–141	153–162; 174;175
175. Flute and whistle		134;135	
176. Tambourine		107–116; 136–141	153–162; 174;175
177. Xylophone (See M.176)			
N. Toys—Theatrical			
178. Finger puppets	9–28;32;36– 39;48–50; 60–80	114;134; 135–141	
179. Flat, jointed puppets	9–28;36–39; 60–62	114;116; 135–141	153–165; 174;175
180. Hand puppets		134–141	
181. Marionettes (See N.180)			

Leather Craft (V)	Drawing and Painting (VI)	Plastic Arts and Crafts (VII)	Printing (VIII)	Audiovisual Media Craft (IX)	Reed and Fiber Craft (X)	Fabric Craft (XI)
					367–370; 373;384	385–399
179–184	206;237;243; 245;246		317;318		373;384	385–399
	237;238;243		317			
	237;238;243	251–266; 272–274;281	317			
	197;246				382–384	385–399
	237;238;243; 244	251–266; 272–274;281				
					384	385–399
	237;238; 243;244		317;318			
		251–262;273; 274;277;281				385–391; 395;396
176;178; 186	206;237;238; 243–245	266;273;274		349		385–387; 395;396
		251–262;273; 274;277;278; 281				385–394; 395;396

Project Ideas	Paper and Foil Craft (II)	Carpentry (III)	Wire and Metal Craft (IV)
N. Toys—Theatrical (*cont.*)			
182. Shadow puppets	9–28;36–39; 41;60–82	114;116; 136–141	153–165; 174;175
183. Shadow puppet theater	9–28;36–40; 60–97	107–129; 136–141	
184. Toy theater and scenery (See N.183)			
O. Toys—Wheel			
185. Bus	9–28;48–59; 60–97	107–128; 136–141	149–172; 174;175
186. Car (See O.185)			
187. Crane (See O.185)			
188. Earth moving equipment (See O.185)			
189. Pull toys (See O.185)			
190. Push toys (See O.185)			
191. Riding toys		107–131; 136–141	149–172; 174;175
192. Train (See O.185)			
193. Truck (See O.185)			
194. Wagon (See O.191)			
P. Toys—Miscellaneous			
195. Airplane (See O.185)			
196. Ball	1;9–28;60–73; 78		
197. Beanbag			
198. Board and table games (See G.119)			
199. Boat (See O.185)			
200. Castle (See K.163)			
201. Costumes	9–27;30;31; 35–39;48–59; 60–96		
202. Glider (See O.185)			
203. Hobby horse		107–120; 136–141	
204. Jigsaw puzzle	84–87	114;115	
205. Jumping jack	4–7;36–39; 83–96	114–116	149–161; 164;165; 169
206. Kite	9–39;60–68	107–110;114	
207. Noah's ark (See O.185)			
208. Play house (See N.183)			

Project Ideas	Paper and Foil Craft (II)	Carpentry (III)	Wire and Metal Craft (IV)
P. Toys—Miscellaneous (*cont.*)			
209. Play people	4–7;9–28; 36–39;48–59; 62;83–97	114;115	149–159; 164–166
210. Sandbox (See C.66)			
211. Sand bucket		107–120; 136–141	
212. Sand rake		110;120–124; 126;136–141	152–162; 164–169
213. Shovel (See P.212)			
214. Sled		107–131; 136–141	152–162; 164
215. Toy animals	4–7;9–27; 30–33;36–39; 48–59;60–98	114;116; 136–141	142–162; 164–169
216. Waterwheel		110;114;116	149–162; 164–169
217. Windmill	48–97	110;114;116; 136–141	149–162; 164–169
Q. Wearing Apparel and Accessories			
218. Apron			
219. Belt		114;116; 136–141	142–163; 164–169; 174;175
220. Belt buckle		114–116; 136–141	144–147; 149–163; 164–169
221. Bib			
222. Billfold			
223. Bonnet			
224. Cap (See Q.223)			
225. Cravat			
226. Ear muffs		110;114;116	145;149–152
227. Eyeglass case		112–124;131; 133–141	153–162; 165–169; 174;175
228. Fan	30;31;36–39; 63;66;83–89; 99–102	109–116;120; 136–141	145–152
229. Gloves			

Project Ideas	Paper and Foil Craft (II)	Carpentry (III)	Wire and Metal Craft (IV)
Q. Wearing Apparel and Accessories (*cont.*)			
230. Hairnet			
231. Hat	9–27;32; 36–39		
232. Head band (See Q.231)			
233. Mittens (See Q.229)			
234. Muff (See Q.229)			
235. Muffler			
236. Pocketbook (See Q.222)			
237. Sandals		109–116;131; 134–141	
238. Scarf (See Q.235)			
239. Shawl (See Q.235)			
240. Socks (See Q.229)			
241. Tie (See Q.235)			
242. Tie rack (See C.46)			
243. Veil			
244. Wallet (See Q.222)			

Leather Craft (V)	Drawing and Painting (VI)	Plastic Arts and Crafts (VII)	Printing (VIII)	Audiovisual Media Craft (IX)	Reed and Fiber Craft (X)	Fabric Craft (XI)
					368–370	
176–193					367–379; 382–384	385–399
	246		293;295; 296;305– 309;312		370; 374–378; 382–384	385–399
176–193	243;245					
					368–370	

AUDIOVISUAL MEDIA IDEA FILE

This list suggests ideas for still photography, animation, and film and sound recording sequences (see IX), which also lend themselves to scripting and planning story boards (see 343–346). The list is neither definitive nor complete. It should be used only as a point of departure for consideration of ideas that can be developed through audiovisual media.

Still photography, motion picture, and sound recording ideas:

Adventure	Ice cream man	Rain
Airport	Merry-go-round	Sad
Animal shelter	Moving day	Shopping
Baking	My day	Street
Candy store	Neighbors	Surprise
Carnival	Party	Town
Circus	Pets	Traffic
Construction	Playground	Trip
Family	Policeman	Work
Happy	Railroad station	Zoo

Flipbook and animation ideas:

Acrobats	Leapfrog	Splash
Balls	Nursery rhymes	Swing
Clowns	Round and round	Trapeze
Growing things	Seesaw	Tricks and magic
Joke	Somersault	Up and down

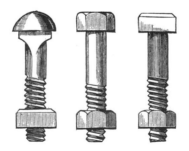

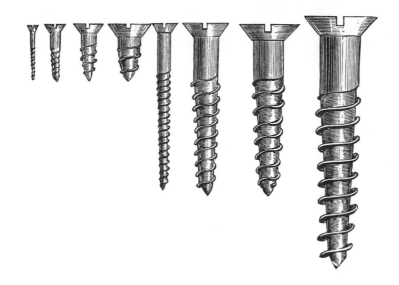

XIV
Found Materials

Man is a tool-making animal.—*Benjamin Franklin*

The table of found materials shows how they can be obtained free or inexpensively at home or from neighborhood stores. Broken and discarded objects are excellent raw material for young people's art and craft activities. An old cookie or food tin, empty bottle, discarded cooking pot, pan, or kettle, or clock broken beyond repair (with its mainspring removed)—contain sufficient parts intact to be salvaged and used in crafts. The remnants in the sewing basket, old clothes, sheets, pillowcases, shoes, or purses contain usable portions of sound material that can be converted by deft hands. Packaging materials, cellophane package windows, plastic box covers, cartons, and the Styrofoam padding in which appliances are cushioned on their way from factory to store are base materials that can often be had for the asking from neighborhood stores. A moth damaged sweater, unfit for wear but free of insect eggs, can be unraveled and the wool used for weaving and knitting. The act of unraveling provides the young child with insights into the weaving and knitting processes.

We have lived through several wasteful, heedless decades. Raw and processed materials we considered expendable are likely to become

Found Materials	Sources	Projects in Which They Can Be Used
Acetate, cellophane, and transparent film	Home; grocery; drugstore packaging and wrapping	5–7;9;16;27;28;36–37;40;41;63;68;70–82;84–87;177;214;215;220; 222;247–250;293;297;313;317–319;328–330;348;352;392
Bark	Countryside; park	V.A;27;28;109–111;114;116;177;214;215;243;260;295;315
Beans, peas, and seeds	Home; grocery	11–18;26–28;56;96;97;111;289;363;379
Bones	Home; butcher	114;116;120;134;137;206;222;295
Bottles (washed, nontoxic; glass and plastic)	Home; drugstore; soda fountain	16;19–28;42;43;51;54;57–59;220;222;237;247;266–268;297;302; 312;396
Bottle caps	Home; drugstore; soda fountain	27–28;56;161;172;185;189;222;244;260;261;289;295;379
Bottle corks	Home; restaurant; bar; chemical supply house	27;28;56;97;134;138;177;222;243;281;295;296;311;363;379; 396;404
Bricks (old)	House wrecker's junkyard	222;261;268;273;280;304;315;316
Buttons	Home; sewing and notions shop or department	4;8;9;26–28;56;96;97;111;177;186;260;295;363;379;385;386
Cardboard (shirt board and backing of writing and drawing tablets)	Home	4–7;9–29;51;53;60–97;98;104;111;114–116;177;194;195;197;200; 206;210–213;218;229–231;240;289;292–295;300;302;318;331; 376;392
Cardboard boxes	Home; shoe store; candy store; chain store; photographic shop and lab; stationery store; drugstore	5;9–29;42;43;51;53;83–97;177;194;206;210–218;222;266;282– 285;289;362;364;376
Cardboard tubes	Home; fabric and wallpaper store	42–43;51;53;74;92;96;97;111;114;116;181;206;222;237;266;300; 302;322;355;376;404
Cheese boxes	Home; dairy; specialty food store	9–29;42;43;51;57;83–97;109–111;114;116;177;197;206;210–212; 222;266;355;362;375;376
Cigar boxes	Home; cigar and candy store	51;54;106;110;111;114;116;121;122;136–141;206;222;237;238; 266;282;362;363;375;376

Clay	Bank of stream, river, or swamp; art supply store	51;251–289;303;304;311
Cloth remnants	Home; sewing or notions store or department	4;5;8;27;28;96;97;104;111;237;246;260;312;320;321;343;361;380–382;385–399
Clothespins	Home; grocery or chain store	28;42;43;51;54;109–111;112–114;116;134;137–140;142;243;295;385
Coathanger wire	Home; cleaner	51;54;146;149–152;163;171;172;174;175;295;373
Cork (sample sheets)	Home decorator and floor covering shop	4–7;9–29;175;197;237;238;295;296;300;376
Corrugated board and cartons	Home; grocery; furniture and appliance store; mover	9–29;51;53;54;73–98;111;114;121;142;178;194;197;206;210–212;218;222;229;230;237;238;240;242;266;282–285;295;300;375;376
Crates	Mover; storage warehouse	51;54;106–116;120–141;222;237;238;243;260;266;270;271;281;285;289;295;296;303;304;309;311;312;320;321;362;363;374–376
Crockery (broken)	Home; restaurant	253;269;289
Driftwood	Ocean beach	105–114;116–120;129;131–141;146;197;206;214;215;222;237;238;243;260;281;295
Drinking straws	Home; grocery	4;7;9–18;27–29;37;44;56;96;97;111;177;214;215;237;260;295;327;343;373;376
Egg cartons	Home; restaurant; dairy	9–18;27;28;48–59;194;197;206;210–212;237;362;363
Eggshells	Home; restaurant	27–29;56;197;222;229–231;237;260;289
Eroded glass	Ocean beach	16;27;28;56;96;97;111;171;172;175;177;247;260;289;322
Fabric samples and scraps	Home; sewing and notions store or department	4–18;26–29;37;45–47;56;96;97;111;177;179;180;246;260;295;320;321;343;361;382;385–399
Feathers	Poultry farm; pigeon fancier	9–18 27;28;56;96;97;111;214;215;237;260;295;325–327;343;364
Felt remnants	Home; fabric shop or department	4–18 26–29;37;96;97;111;177–180;183–186;191;197;295;343;371;385–391;396

Found Materials	Sources	Projects in Which They Can Be Used
Ferns	Countryside	9–18;26–28;96;97;214;215;260;295;316;325–327
Film canisters (empty)	Movie film processing lab	29;42;43;54;144;153–172;174;175;244;266;341;355;358;362;363;376
Fish bones	Fish store; restaurant	9–18;26–28;96;97;111;197;206;222;237;260;295;315;316;325–327
Floral wire	Florist	51;54;145;146;149–151;173;372;373
Floor covering samples	Floor covering shop	(See Linoleum samples; Rug samples; Vinyl tile samples)
Flour	Home; grocery	9–15;17;18;27;28;252
Flowers	Countryside; garden	215;295;325–327;350;367
Foil	Home; grocery	5–7;9–29;30–39;41–47;56;60–82;84;96–98;111;143;153;154;157–160;171;174;175;177;189–191;197;208;223;237;244;317;358;371–373;385
Hardware	Home; junkyard; hardware store	27;28;96;97;111;155;169–175;177;222;244;327 (see also Metal scrap)
Ice cream sticks	Home; soda fountain	28;29;42;43;51;54;95–97;106;107;109–112;116;137;138;142;197;206;207;222;237;243;260;295;327;349;373 (see also Lumber scraps)
Jewelry findings	Home; notions store or department; jewelry supply shop	28;29;56;96;97;111;144;164–175;177;185;327;363;364;367–370;379;385
Leather findings	Home; shoemaker; tannery	18–28;56;74–82;97;111;175–193;197;222;245;367;373;375;385
Leaves	Countryside; garden	16–18;26–28;214–216;222;260;290;295;315;325–327;330
Linoleum samples	Floor covering store	85–88;114;296;305–308
Lumber scraps	Lumber and demolition junkyard; carpenter	106–141;146;158;184;197;206;210–212;222;237;238;243;260;266;270;281–285;289;295;296;309;311;312;355;358;362;363;373–376 (see also Bark; Cheese boxes; Crates; Driftwood; Ice Cream Sticks)

Machine, instrument, and old clock parts	Home; junkyard; surplus shop	9–18;26–28;56;111;147;152–175;177;191;244;260;295;325–327;350 (see also Metal scrap)
Metal scrap	Home; junkyard	(See Film canisters; Hardware; Machine, instrument, and old clock parts; Tin and coffee cans)
Milk carton	Home	9–28;39;42;43;111;194;229–231;318;355;358;376
Mirror (broken)	Home	(Wrap inside heavy cloth bundle; then break up with mallet; smooth edges with emery paper)—16;26–28;96;97;111;175;177;260;358
Newspaper	Home	9–29;30–34;36–39;41–59;111;194;197–202;206;210–212;215–218;221–223;225;292–296
Nutshells	Home	9–18;26–28;96;97;109–111;116;206;237;238;243;260;295
Oilcloth remnants	Home; hardware store; notions shop	4–8;19–28;39;41–47;96;97;208;215;237
Old clothes	Home	I,j;III.a;IV.b;260;311;312;361;382;385–399
Paper bags	Home; grocery	5–7;9–28;194;195;197;206;210–212;216;218;222;237;292–296;317
Paperclips and fasteners	Home; stationery store	26;28;30–33;38;39;41;47;56;60;61;67;73–82;98;149–152;168;169;171;172;174–176;222;233;260;295;322;325–327;385;391
Paper cups	Home; grocery	5–7;9–28;36;37;39;42;43;61;111;197;222;229–231;260;296;376;385
Paper doilies	Home; stationery store; grocery	9–28;36–38;98;111;206;215;222;237;295;315;317;325–327;330
Paper plates	Home; stationery store; grocery	5–30;36–39;52;61;97;111;194–197;200;203;204;206;210–214;217–219;222;229–231;242;271;279;317;362–364;376;385
Paper scraps	Home; printer	4–29;30–39;41–47;60–82;98–103;111;194–201;203;204;206;210–219;229–231;237;239;291–297;299;301;315–319;323–327;343;347;349;471;372;385;392;400;401
Pebbles	Ocean beach; countryside	27;28;96;97;111;177;194;197;206;222;237;260;280;289;295;327

Found Materials	Sources	Projects in Which They Can Be Used
Photograpns of distant places and people	Travel agency; air or shipping line	7;9–29;36–39;41;56;96–98;111;222;324;343
Pine cones	Forest	9–28;96;97;111;206;222;237;243;260;295;327;355;358
Pipe cleaners	Home; cigar and candy store	9–18;26–28;54;56;96;97;142;149–151;206;222;237;295;327
Plastic bags (small)	Home; grocery	11–18;49;136;209;252
Plastic foil	Stationery store	4–7;9–29;30–39;41–47;60–82;98;111;177;197;249;250;317;325–327;358;372;385 (see also Foil)
Plastic mesh and netting	Gardening, seed, and hardware store; sewing and notions store or department	7;9–28;45;56;96;97;142;249;250;260;296;315–317;325–327;363–365;372;377;380;381;385
Plastic squeeze bottles (empty)	Home; drugstore	26–28;42;43;54;96;97;237;250;266
Pocketbook or purse (discarded)	Home	9–28;96;97;111;176–187;189–192;245
Reeds and grasses	Countryside	9–28;45–47;56;96;97;111;218;222;260;293;295;325–327;367;372–378
Ribbon remnants	Home; sewing and notions store or department	8–28;42–47;56;96;97;111;191;246;295;325–327;372–378;385;386;391
Rope and twine	Home; stationery store; mover; storage warehouse	4–8;9–28;52–54;56;96;97;111;191;218;222;235;260;290;295;303;304;325–327;361–379;383;384 (see also Yarn and wool scrap)
Rubber bands	Home; stationery store	9–28;31;42–44;52;96;97;222;295;322;325–327;355;358
Rubber scrap	Home; plumber; surgical supply store	19–28;96;97;295;296
Rug samples	Floor covering store	9–28;96;97;111;222;260;295;385 (see also Floor covering samples)
Sand	Ocean beach; sand and gravel pit	56;111;242;260;327
Seashells	Ocean beach	9–29;206;222;237;260;289;379
Shirt board	Home; laundry	(See Cardboard)

scarce and expensive again. After an interlude of cheap food, fuel, wood, paper, fibers, and metal, materials we discarded cavalierly merely because of artificially created obsolescence will once again be husbanded and used until they are literally useless. Learning to recognize, collect, treasure and above all use scrap and found materials in craft may be essential education for a future in which our children are likely to have to preserve, rather than consume, the world's goods.

Aside from ecological and economic considerations, found materials acquaint children and young people with a variety of textures and qualities, each of which renders a different effect and requires different approaches, working methods, and tools. Young craftsmen become conscious of what they tend to take for granted or overlook as consumers. These are excellent reasons why young people should be encouraged to collect and use found materials in their arts and crafts.

Bibliography and Notes

References cited in the text are identified here by number. Books, catalogues, and information sources relating to subjects discussed in each chapter that are of special interest to parents and teachers are identified in this bibliography with one or more squares that precede the number. Those that are valuable in all respects are marked ■■■. Others that should be read for technical information only, in which creative directions are inaccurate or misleading, that offer plans to follow, copy, or trace, or that are badly illustrated, are marked ■■. These sources are listed only for areas in which no better ones are currently available. Catalogues and information sources dealing with supplies, materials, and tools are marked ■. A very few of the listings are annotated where required.

The starred books can form an essential library nucleus for any elementary or junior high school or teacher's college that offers art and craft courses. Parents should buy or borrow those relating to particular arts and crafts in which their children are interested and engaged.

None of the listed suppliers' catalogues or those books that are squared and part of a series are to be construed as an endorsement of any product or of other volumes not specifically mentioned. In all instances where distributor or trade names are given, they are listed as representative sources or sample materials related to the text. Alternative sources and materials exist or may become available in the future that may or may not be as good, better, or less expensive.

In addition to the references cited in the bibliography, the following periodicals are useful resources for craft, tool, material, and education information in the arts and crafts:

Big Rock Candy Mountain, 1115 Merrill St., Menlo Park, Cal. 94025 (publ. quarterly).

Craft Horizon, American Crafts Council, 44 West 53 St., New York, N.Y. 10019 (publ. quarterly).

Directory of Craft Courses, American Crafts Council, 44 West 53 St., New York, N.Y. 10019 (publ. annually; lists universities, colleges, junior colleges, private workshops, museum schools, and art centers that offer craft courses throughout the U.S.).

Fox Fire, Southern Highlands Literary Fund, Rabun Gap, Ga. 30568 (publ. quarterly).

The Whole Word Catalogue, Teachers and Writers Collaborative, % P.S.3, 40 Hudson St., New York, N.Y. 10014 (publ. quarterly).

Introduction

1. Cohen, Dorothy, H., "Children of Technology: Images or The Real Thing." In *Childhood Education,* J. of The Association for Childhood Education International, Washington, D.C., 48:6:3.72, 298–300.
2. Swift, Jeremy, *The Other Eden,* London: Dent, 1974.

Chapter I: Approaches and Attitudes

3. Arnold, Arnold, *Teaching Your Child to Learn from Birth to School Age,* Englewood Cliffs, N.J.: Prentice-Hall, 1971.
4. ———, *The World Book of Children's Games,* New York: Thomas Y. Crowell, 1972.
5. Arnold, Francis, personal communication.
6. Berne, Eric, *Games People Play,* New York: Grove Press, 1964.
7. Callois, Roger, *Man, Play and Games,* Glencoe, Ill.: The Free Press, 1961.
8. Commoner, Barry, *The Closing Circle,* New York: Alfred A. Knopf, 1971.

■■■ 9. D'Amico, Victor; Wilson, Francis; and Maser, Moreen, *Art for the Family,* New York: Museum of Modern Art, 1954.

■■■ 10. ———, and Buchman, Arlette, *Assemblage,* New York: Museum of Modern Art, 1972.

■■■ 11. ———, *Experiments in Creative Art Teaching,* New York: Doubleday, 1960.

12. De Bono, Edward, *The Dog Exercising Machine,* London: Jonathan Cape, 1970.

13. Gofman, John W.; Gravel, Mike; and Clark, Wilson, *The Case for a Nuclear Moratorium,* Washington, D.C.: Environmental Action Foundation, 1972.

■■■ 14. Groch, Judith, *The Right to Create,* Boston: Little Brown & Co., 1969.

15. Huizinga, Johan, *Homo Ludens,* Boston: Beacon Press, 1955.

16. Just, Ward, *Military Men,* New York: Avon Books, 1970.

■■■ 17. Lowenfeld, Viktor, *Creativity and Mental Growth,* New York: Macmillan, 1957.

■■■ 18. ———, *Your Child and His Art,* New York: Macmillan, 1954.

19. Marland, Sydney P., *Annual Report of the U.S. Commissioner of Education,* Fiscal year 1971, submitted to Congress March 31, 1972, Washington, D.C.: DHEW, OE 72-105; USGPO HE 5.211:10032-72.

20. Mead, Margaret, "Creativity in Cross-Cultural Perspective." In *Creativity and Its Cultivation,* ed. by Harold H. Anderson, New York: Harper & Bros., 1959, pp. 220–235.

21. Montessori, Maria, *The Discovery of the Child,* New York: Ballantine Books, 1972.

22. National Education Association, *Today's Education,* Washington, D.C.: 61:7:72, 8. Quote from the Report of the National Assessment of Educational Progress: "Most American young children and young adults can read, *at least in everyday* situations. . . . For example, 65 percent of nine-year-olds and 95 percent of thirteen-year-olds surveyed *could read labels on merchandise. . . .* About 35 percent of the seventeen-year-olds *were unable to write a title which reflected the main idea in a story they had read.*" (Italics added.)

■■■ 23. Pluckrose, Henry, quoted in *The Fourth R: A Commentary on Youth, Education, and the Arts,* by Joseph Featherstone, New York: Associated Council of the Arts, 1972.

24. Plowden Report, The, *Children and Their Primary Schools,* Central Advisory Council for Education, London: Her Majesty's Stationery Office, 1967, Vol. II, pp. 676–685.

25. Read, Herbert, *Art and Industry: The Principles of Industrial Design,* London: Faber & Faber, 1934.

26. Skinner, B. F., *Beyond Freedom and Dignity*, New York: Alfred A. Knopf, 1971.
27. Spitler, Judy Ann, "Changing View of Play in the Education of Young Children," New York: Teachers College, Columbia University, 1971 (Ph.D. thesis, unpublished).
28. Watkins, Ray, *William Morris as Designer*, New York: Reinhold Publishing Corp., 1967.

Chapter II. Paper and Foil Craft

■■■29. Cf. 10, 11.
■30. Association for Childhood Education International, *Equipment and Supplies Catalogue*, 3615 Wisconsin Avenue, N.W., Washington, D.C. 20016.
■31. Brown, Arthur, & Co., *General Catalog of Artists' Materials*, 2 West 46 St., New York, N.Y. 10036.
■32. Flax, Sam, Inc., *Art and Craft Materials Catalogue*, 25 East 28 St., New York, N.Y. 10016.
■■■33. Hartung, Rolf, *Creative Corrugated Paper Craft*, London: B. T. Batsford Ltd., 1966.
■■■34. Lidstone, John, *Building with Cardboard*, New York: Van Nostrand Reinhold Co., 1968.
■■35. Murray, William D., and Rigney, Francis, *Paper Folding for Beginners*, New York: Dover Publications, 1960.
■■■36. Roettger, Ernst, *Creative Paper Craft*, London: B. T. Batsford Ltd., 1961.
■■37. Sakade, Florence, *Origami*, 3 vols., Rutland, Vt.: Charles Tuttle & Co., 1957, 1958, 1959.
■■38. Seidelman, James E., and Mintoyne, Grace, *Creating with Papier-Maché*, ills. by Christine Randall, New York: Crowell-Collier Press, 1971.
■■■39. Sharkey, Anthony, and Naiman, Adeline, *Cardboard Carpentry*, Newton, Mass.: Educational Development Center Inc., 1968.
■40. Workshop for Learning Things Inc., *Our Catalogue*, 5 Bridge St., Watertown, Mass. 02172.
■41. X-Acto Inc., *Catalog*, 48-41 Van Dam St., Long Island City, N.Y. 11101.

Chapter III. Carpentry

42. Cf. ■30, ■31, ■32, ■■■34, ■■■39, ■40, ■41.
■■■43. Roettger, Ernst, *Creative Wood Craft*, London: B. T. Batsford Ltd., 1961.

■■■44. Rogers, Edward, and Sutcliffe, Thomas, *Introducing Constructional Art,* New York: Watson Guptil, 1970.

■■45. Sloane, Eric, *A Museum of Early American Tools,* New York: Funk & Wagnalls, 1965.

■■46. ———, *A Reverence for Wood,* New York: Funk & Wagnalls, 1965.

■47. Stanley Tools, A Division of Stanley Works, *Broad Line Catalogue,* New Britain, Conn. 06050.

■■48. ———, *How to Work with Tools and Wood,* ed. by Robert Campbell and N. H. Mager, New York: Pocket Books, 1972.

■49. ———, *Tool Guide,* New Britain, Conn. 06050.

Chapter IV. Wire and Metal Craft

50. Cf. ■30, ■31, ■32, ■40, ■41, ■47.

■■51. Dank, Michael Carlton, *Scrap Craft,* New York: Dover Publications, 1969.

■■52. Gentille, Thomas, *Step-by-Step Jewelry,* New York: Golden Press, 1968.

■■53. Stribling, Mary Lou, *Art from Found Materials, Discarded and Natural,* New York: Crown Publishers, Inc., 1970.

Chapter V. Leather Craft

54. Cf. ■30, ■31, ■32, ■41.

■■55. Cherry, Raymond, *General Leathercraft,* Bloomington, Ill.: McKnight & McKnight Publishing Co., 1955.

■■56. Di Valentin, Maria M., *Getting Started in Leathercraft,* New York: Collier Books, 1972.

Chapter VI. Drawing and Painting

57. Cf. ■■■7, ■■■9, ■■■10, ■■■11, ■■■12, ■■■17, ■■■18, ■30, ■31, ■32, ■40.

■■■58. Association for Childhood Education International, *The Coloring Books Craze,* 3615 Wisconsin Avenue, N.W., Washington, D.C. 20016.

59. Buros, Oscar K., *The Sixth Mental Measurement Yearbook,* Highland Park, N.J.: Griphon Press, 1965.

■■60. Lidstone, John, *Self Expression in Classroom Art,* photographs by Roger Kerkham, Worcester, Mass.: Davis Publications Inc., 1967.

61. Mumford, Lewis, *The Urban Prospect,* New York: Harcourt, Brace & World, 1968.

62. Read, Herbert, *Education Through Art,* London: Faber & Faber, 1958.

63. ———, *The Grass Roots of Art: Problems of Contemporary Art,* No. 2, New York: Wittenborn & Co., 1947.

64. Ruskin, John, *Elements of Drawing.*

■■■65. Sproul, Adelaide, *Teaching Art Sources and Resources,* photographs by John Urban, New York: Van Nostrand Reinhold Co., 1971.

66. Walter, W. Grey, *The Living Brain,* New York: W. W. Norton & Company, Inc., 1953.

■■■67. Wyman, Jenifer D., and Gordon, Stephen F., *A Primer of Perception,* New York: Reinhold Publishing Corp., 1967.

Chapter VII. Plastic Arts and Crafts

68. Cf. 57, ■■■65, ■■■67.

■■■69. Ball, Carlton F., and Lovoos, Janice, *Making Pottery Without a Wheel,* New York: Reinhold Publishing Corp., 1965.

■■■70. Duncan, Julia Hamlin, and D'Amico, Victor, *How to Make Pottery and Ceramics,* New York: Museum of Modern Art, 1947.

■■■71. Green, David, *Experimenting with Pottery,* London: Faber & Faber Ltd., 1971.

■■■72. Hofsted, Jolyon, *Step-by-Step Ceramics,* New York: Golden Press, 1967.

■■■73. Irving, Donald J., *Sculpture, Material and Processes,* New York: Van Nostrand Reinhold Co., 1970.

■■■74. Mavros, Donald O., *Getting Started in Ceramics,* New York: Bruce Publishing Co., 1971.

■■75. Memmott, Harry, *The Art of Making Pottery from Clay to Kiln,* London: Studio Vista, 1971.

■■■76. Roettger, Ernst, *Creative Clay Craft,* London: Batsford Publishing Ltd., 1963.

Chapter VIII. Printing

77. Cf. ■30, ■31, ■32, ■40, ■41.

■■78. Biegeleisen, J. I., *The Complete Book of Silk Screen Printing Production,* New York: Dover Publications, Inc., 1963.

■■■79. Schachner, Erwin, *Step-by-Step Printmaking,* New York: Golden Press, 1970.

■■■80. Erickson, Janet A. D., and Sproul, Adelaide, *Print Making Without a Press,* New York: Reinhold Publishing Corp., 1966.

Chapter IX. Audiovisual Media Craft

■■■81. Association for Childhood Education International, *Children Are Centers for Understanding Media,,* 3615 Wisconsin Avenue, N.W., Washington, D.C. 20016 (includes excellent bibliography of books and films dealing with teaching young children how to use audiovisual media creatively).

■82. Book sources and catalogues of books about audiovisual media and film making:
Cinemabilia Inc., 10 West 13 St., New York, N.Y. 10011.
Filmstaks, Suite 400, 888 Seventh Ave., New York, N.Y. 10019.

■■■83. Bryne, Daniel J., *Grafilm,* New York: Van Nostrand Reinhold Co., 1970.

■■84. Eastman Kodak Company, *Index to Kodak Information,* Rochester, N.Y. 14650 (lists large inventory of booklets on many different aspects of still photography, including how to make a pinhole camera).

■85. Edmund Scientific Company, *Catalogue,* 555 Edscorp Building, Barrington, N.J. 08007 (scientific materials and instruments, including mirrors for making kaleidoscopes, lenses, prisms, holograms, and "Kalvar" film for making instant positive transparencies and slides from ordinary photographic negatives).

■■86. Feininger, Andreas, *The Complete Photographer,* London: Thames and Hudson, 1966.

87. Films about movie making and animation:
Basic Film Terms (15 minutes); available for rental from University of Michigan, Audio-Visual Communication Center, 416 4th St., Ann Arbor, Mich. 48103; for sale from Pyramid Films, Box 1048, Santa Monica, Cal. 90406.
Frame by Frame (15 minutes); available for rental and/or sale (see preceding entry).
Synchronomy, by Norman McLaren, drawings direct on film; available for rental from University of California, Extension Media Center, Berkeley, Cal. 94720; for sale from Learning Corporation of America, 711 Fifth Ave., New York, N.Y. 10022.

■88. Hudson Photographic Industries Inc., Educational Products Division, *Catalogue,* Irvington-on-Hudson, N.Y. 10533. (Materials include "U Film," a double-sprocketed 35 mm. clear leader on which designs and animations can be drawn directly with ordinary drawing and painting materials. Customarily used for filmstrips, it can also be adapted to short stop-frame animations, directly drawn on film.)

89. Lecuyer, Raymond, *Histoire de la photographie,* Paris: Baschet et Cie, 1945.

90. Mumford, Lewis, *Art and Technics,* New York: Columbia University Press, 1952.

91. Newhall, Beaumont, *The History of Photography from 1839 to the Present Day,* New York: Museum of Modern Art, 1970.

■92. Super 8 Filmmaker, *Quarterly* (periodical with information on how to use the 8 mm. stop-frame movie camera for live and animated film making), 342 Madison Ave., New York, N.Y. 10017.

■■■93. Thomas, D. B., *Camera: Photographs and Accessories,* a Science Museum Illustrated Booklet, London: Her Majesty's Stationery Office, 1966.

■■■94. ———, *The First Negatives,* a Science Museum Monograph, London: Her Majesty's Stationery Office, 1964.

■■95. Trojanski, John, and Rockwood, Louis, *Making It Move,* Pelaum-Standard, 38 West 5 St., Dayton, Ohio 45402.

■■■96. Workshop for Learning Things, *Camera Cookbook,* 5 Bridge St., Watertown, Mass. 02172.

■■■97. ———, *It's So Simple: Click and Print,* 5 Bridge St., Watertown, Mass. 02172.

■98. Cf. 40.

Chapter X. Reed and Fiber Craft

99. Cf. ■30.

■■100. Dryad Handicrafts Leaflets:
    No. 12, *Handles for Baskets*
    No. 16, *Cane and Rush Seating*
    No. 43, *Stool Seating*
    No. 83, *Spinning Wool*
    No. 85, *Rug Weaving*
    No. 89, *Weaving on Four-Way Table Looms*
    No. 90, *Dryad Foot Power Looms*
    No. 91, *Hand Weaving on Two-Way Looms*
    No. 92, *Netting*
    No. 100, *Card Loom Weaving*
    No. 111, *Tablet Weaving*
    No. 112, *Rush Baskets and Mats*
    No. 127, *Cord Knotting*
      Dryad Handicrafts, Northgates, Leicester, England.

101. Furness, J. C. *String Figures and How to Make Them,* New York: Dover Publications, Inc., 1962.

■■■102. Hartung, Rolf, *Color and Texture in Creative Textile Craft,* London: B. T. Batsford Ltd., 1965.

■■■103. ———, *Creative Textile Craft,* London: B. T. Batsford Ltd., 1964.

■■ 104. Navajo School of Indian Basketry, *Indian Basket Weaving,* New York: Dover Publications, Inc., 1971.

■■■ 105. Oelsner, G. H., *A Handbook of Weaves,* New York: Dover Publications, Inc., 1952. (Note: This reprint of the 1875 classic is of value only to the most advanced young weaver working with a loom.)

■■ 106. Phillips, Mary Walker, *Step-by-Step Macramé,* New York: Golden Press, 1970.

■■ 107. Torbet, Laura, *Macramé You Can Wear,* New York: Ballantine Books, 1972.

■■ 108. White, Mary, *How to Do Bead Work,* New York: Dover Publications, Inc., 1972.

■■ 109. Znamierowski, Nell, *Step-by-Step Weaving,* New York: Golden Press, 1967.

Chapter XI. Fabric Craft

110. Cf. ■31.

■■■ 111. Adrosko, Rita J., *Natural Dyes and Home Dyeing,* New York: Dover Publications, Inc., 1971.

■■ 112. Butterick Fashion Marketing Co., *Ready, Set, Sew,* New York: 1971.

■■ 113. Deyrup, Astrith, *Getting Started in Batik,* New York: Bruce Publishing Co., 1971.

■■■ 114. Haley, Gail E., *Costumes for Play and Playing,* London: Methuen, 1976.

■■ 115. Maile, Anne, *Tie and Dye: As a Present Day Craft,* New York: Ballantine Books, 1963.

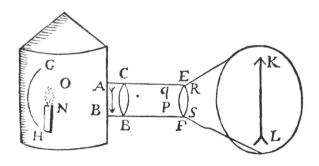